LILLIE LANGTRY

Laura Beatty worked in the art world in London and New York. She is married with three children and now lives in Buckinghamshire. *Lillie Langtry* is her first book.

WITHDRAWN

To C.E.L.K.

WITHDRAWN

Laura Beatty

LILLIE LANGTRY
Manners, Masks and Morals

V

VINTAGE

Published by Vintage 2000

2 4 6 8 10 9 7 5 3 1

Copyright © Laura Beatty 1999

The right of Laura Beatty to be identified as the author of
this work has been asserted by her in accordance with
the Copyright, Designs and Patents Act, 1988

This book is sold subject to the condition that it shall not
by way of trade or otherwise, be lent, resold, hired out,
or otherwise circulated without the publisher's prior
consent in any form of binding or cover other than that
in which it is published and without a similar condition
including this condition being imposed on the subsequent purchaser

First published in Great Britain by
Chatto & Windus in 1999

Vintage
Random House, 20 Vauxhall Bridge Road,
London SW1V 2SA

Random House Australia (Pty) Limited
20 Alfred Street, Milsons Point, Sydney
New South Wales 2061, Australia

Random House New Zealand Limited
18 Poland Road, Glenfield,
Auckland 10, New Zealand

Random House (Pty) Limited
Endulini, 5A Jubilee Road, Parktown 2193,
South Africa

The Random House Group Limited Reg. No. 954009
www.randomhouse.co.uk

A CIP catalogue record for this book
is available from the British Library

ISBN 0 09 928785 4

Papers used by Random House are natural, recyclable
products made from wood grown in sustainable forests.
The manufacturing processes conform to the environ-
mental regulations of the country of origin

Typeset by Deltatype Ltd, Birkenhead, Merseyside
Printed and bound in Great Britain by
Cox & Wyman Ltd, Reading, Berkshire

Contents

List of Illustrations

The author and publishers have made every effort to trace the owners of copyright. They much regret if any inadvertent mistakes or omissions have been made. These can be rectified in future editions.

We may have lost courteous manners, gentle voices and upright figures, but we have gained in luxury and freedom. The emancipation of women has saved thousands from the life of hopeless apathy which the girl of the last century had to live, tied to her parents by a foolish convention until all vestige of youth and good looks had vanished. Everything she wanted to do was vetoed as being 'fast' or 'peculiar', and it took a very strong character to strike out and make a fight for liberty.

Augusta Fane

. . . . it takes an exceptional woman, one gifted with an overwhelmingly strong personality, irresistible charm and astonishing brains, to 'get away' with complete originality and informality of conduct in this world. Unless you are, in effect, a sort of superwoman, you had much better stay inside the safe, though boring, boundaries of social behaviour defined by the English county families.

Claude Beddington

AN INTRODUCTION

Chapter I

Brief Lives

This is the story of a woman who sold her human nature for a legend.

It tells of a girl who looked enough like a goddess to want to be one; a girl who was born more human than most, but who found herself so susceptible to the adulation she inspired that she would go to any lengths to preserve it. London called her Venus Annodomini, and that was what she wanted to stay. Nothing was too great a sacrifice: not family, nor reputation, nor friendship, nor love. Whatever held her back or did not fit she shrugged aside. The needs and the affections, that so inconveniently accompany and define humanity, she trimmed away, burnt like offerings in the blaze of her ambition. For she was brave and not afraid of difficulty.

To be a goddess of beauty and love she would endure all hardships and endure them alone – or so she thought. But once she was set on her course of myth-making she found there was no going back. In her adopted role, she was wondered at, criticized, judged and ridiculed. Nor could she drop the mask, even for a moment, to disabuse her critics. When people were jealous or sniping there was no solace, no chance to climb down from her pedestal to explain her position, no possibility of companionship or of sympathy. She had sold her humanity and she had paid the price.

Familiar though the concept is, wholesale self-invention is rare; its demands terrible. Stepping so lightly into her role, she did not see the trap that closed about her; did not guess the toll of the discipline that her fiction would demand for its maintenance. She forgot in her haste – if she ever knew – that goddesses are inscrutable and therefore misunderstood, that they are set apart from mankind and are therefore lonely. Too late she found that the centre of her invention was ever the old self which suffered the inevitable hurt, in silence and in isolation.

Not every beautiful girl feels it incumbent upon her to become a goddess. Why Lillie Langtry did was a mixture of bad luck and bad timing. There were several factors. The first was the nature of Society when Lillie made her first appearance in its midst in 1877. The second was Oscar Wilde, who saw an opportunity in her deification and grabbed it. And the third, of course, was Lillie herself, and the way that she was at the outset. Without the first two Lillie would not have thought of making a reputation out of her looks alone. She was, in those days, not vain enough. When London first knelt at her feet, she was genuinely astounded.

It is a strange city that is so happy to be fooled. What was it like this London in which Lillie found herself, and which she grew half to love and half to despise? Since the accession of Queen Victoria things had begun to change. Railways were being built, making the capital more widely accessible. There was more and cleaner popular entertainment. There were exhibitions for rich and poor alike and the first organised sports. The franchise had been widened, with the passing of the Second Parliamentary Reform Act in 1867. The Cabinet had absorbed its first radical working-man*, and Disraeli, who was Jewish, was poised again for premiership. There was money and position to be made. So, there was a rising middle class, but however powerful the new men were they were not acceptable at Court. London was still led, and, to a degree, the country still governed, by Society, and Society was closed. Trade, actors, Jews, the professional middle classes, all were debarred. Only the aristocracy was allowed, and yet even that suffered, in its way. Its old freedoms had no place under the sombre cloud of Prince Albert's influence. He and the Queen had set a tone of sobriety and mutual affection that the fast set, with one foot still in the Regency, found hard to accept. Adultery, bawdy conversation, immodesty of dress or behaviour were all out, and piety of all kinds was in. Among the Prince Consort's more arcane rules for conduct were the avoidance of the 'foolish vanity of dandyism' and a decorous horror of the practical joke.

Then, in 1863, with Albert dead, and the Queen sunk in mourning, the Prince of Wales took a beautiful foreign wife and set up a court at Marlborough House. He was young, dissolute and full of charm, and suddenly it was not enough just to be virtuous and well-born. The Prince's restlessness, held so long under the yoke of his father's taboos, was infectious. With the first touch of this freshening breeze Society

*John Bright was the son of a Rochdale mill-worker.

awoke, and found itself in an agony of boredom. Concessions were made. The Rothschilds, Sir Blundell Maple, the Sassoons, Sir Thomas Lipton and Colonel Astor were taken, like a tonic, and there followed a decade and a half of vain and frantic pleasure. But pleasure was not the answer. Sated, but never diverted for long, Society searched for something out of the ordinary; something that would lift it from its torpor and yet still be allowed, something that would fit within the rigid conventions and yet somehow refresh, revitalize, transcend.

When Lillie was 'discovered', Society's surprise and its adulation knew no bounds. Socially, aesthetically, carnally, she answered all its prayers. Certainly, she was beautiful. She was also poetically impoverished. Most potent of all, she was a stranger. To a world whose houses, parents, horses and possessions were all numbered and ticketed, mystery was an intoxicating commodity. And London drank deep. For four years it gave itself up to a frenzy of devotion. Commoners, painters, aristocrats, aesthetes, all trampled each other in the scramble for the shrine, and among them happened to be Oscar Wilde.

Wilde worshipped with his eyes open and he was quick to see Lillie's potential. He drank in her unearthly beauty that was so conveniently in the Ancient Greek mould. He knew the boredom of Society, its longing for the mystery that its conventions forbade. And he saw that the suddenness of her arrival on the London scene had about it more than a touch of the godsend. There she was, as goddesses always are, with no identifiable background, without the inconvenience of parents, just in time, and quite out of the blue. But, if Society had spotted that she was a goddess, *he* could tell it which one. Mrs Langtry, he announced, 'arose from Jersey like Venus from the foam'.

In fact there was a good deal of wryness mixed with the extravagance of Wilde's claims for Lillie. In a different way, though he was only 23, he too had subjugated London. He was known to have confided in the wife of Julian Hawthorne, who confided in *Harper's Bazaar*, 'I should never have believed, had I not experienced it, how easy it is to become the most prominent figure in Society.' He knew how far Lillie had come and he probably knew too how far she had to fall.

When they became friends, in 1879, Lillie was embarking on her third season. For two years she had enjoyed an unprecedented popularity. But her star was already, though imperceptibly, on the wane. True, she was still the centre of attention, but she was hopelessly entangled both emotionally and financially. The sands were running out and she knew it. So she looked for someone who could shore up her position, for a promise that she would never be demoted – and the same luck that had brought her to London at just the right moment now introduced her to Oscar Wilde.

Wilde, too, was treading the path from obscurity to stardom. It was he who showed Lillie how to manage and maintain her profile, he who fanned the flame when it wavered. Wilde helped her to create a persona for herself and he stripped away the last vestiges of her fear of notoriety. Most important of all, while he taught Lillie, he also taught Society at large. He showed it how to treat its divinities. His version of aesthetics – just popular enough for the uninitiated to know what they were missing, and to desire it – created the language by which Lillie was to be worshipped. Rose petals were to be strewn in her path by poets in buckskins, a single amaryllis carried to her door, armfuls of water lilies thrown into her carriage by dripping marquesses in evening dress. Meanwhile he, the acknowledged high-priest of beauty, would shout her credentials from the rooftops. He lay on her doorstep all night when composing her poem. He spent his money on flowers, which he carried in state, on foot, across London. He told the world that she was the mind of Phidias incarnate, and soon, when a lecture was given in the British Museum, it was necessary to have Lillie sitting in profile on the dais. Whatever Lillie actually was or had been was irrelevant. Wilde swathed her in his vision. By the end of the year Lillie did nothing without consulting him first – not even dress herself for a dance. He, of course, revelled in his influence, enjoying the decadent conflation of slave and master, so evident in his camp complaint to the painter Graham Robertson:

> The Lily is so tiresome . . . She *won't* do what I tell her . . . I assure her that she owes it to herself and to us to drive daily through the Park dressed entirely in black in a black victoria drawn by black horses and with 'Venus Annodomini' emblazoned on her black bonnet in dull sapphires. But she won't.

Whether or not she always obliged him, Wilde's myth of Lillie was potent. The world believed it and Lillie herself, though too sensible to believe, saw its value. After two years as Society's darling Lillie found she could not go back. She needed the adulation and the flattery. She needed the luxuries that the Court circle took so easily for granted. She was used to idleness and pleasure and vapid exchange, and she had forgotten that there was ever anything else. Venus Annodomini was born, but her birth, though it had been so easy and so unconscious, had stifled the old self from which she had sprung. For Lillie, unlike real goddesses, did have a background.

Lillie was born on the island of Jersey, in October 1853, during an autumn of freak storms. She was christened Emilie Charlotte Le Breton, but called 'Lillie' from childhood, and she was the last but one in a family of six boys. Home life, on which the foundations of all character are laid, was for her particularly happy and affectionate. The Le Bretons were close and self-sufficient. She had a liberal and educated father, and a mother who, we are told, was adoring, though semi-invisible. Liberality and invisibility resulted in a childhood that for Victorian times was remarkably free from parental control. Running with the boys in all their games, their escapades a constant test, Lillie strove to match them in endurance, in independence and in daring. Pleading weakness was never an option, and she would not be left behind. The effort of living up to her brothers left an abiding legacy. For the rest of her life she kept up, whatever the conditions and whatever the cost to herself or to others.

The idyll of her childhood was sacred to Lillie but it was soon over. By the time she was twenty-six, five of the Le Breton boys had died. An influence that had been, as that of siblings always is, unconscious and mercurial was at once embalmed, and her childhood enshrined with their memory. Even in the disaffected twentieth century the dead are perfect. How much more so must they have been in an age when death was fashionable. After the Prince Consort's death, Queen Victoria, with a little help from Dickens, had endowed her nation with a whole aesthetics of mourning and enshrining. There were hierarchies of death in which the mother, the innocent and the serviceman came out on top. Four of the Le Breton boys had died heroes' deaths in foreign countries. They were preserved for ever in their promise, perpetually free from the wrack of failure or disillusion. This, when Lillie looked back from the emotional shipwrecks that constituted her adult life, gave her childhood a double potency. These memories belonged not just to another country but to other, and lost, lives.

We are now culturally in revolt against sentimentality and the soldier's sacrifice, but it is clear that Lillie did not have to be particularly sentimental to regard her childish happiness as talismanic. In fact she warred all her life with sentiment. Her catchphrase 'Don't let us fuss, please', delivered in 'a soft, plaintive voice', was a danger signal, not just to those around her, but also to herself. If she was to survive the slings and arrows – and she was a survivor – she must stifle her own Victorian tendencies. But memory is the most intractable of opponents and the brothers' influence lived on. In all the adult world Lillie either could not, or would not, find anyone as big as her brothers had been.

This, then, is the case from the outside, and it resulted, between the years 1879 and 1882, in a form of nervous crisis. No one could have protected Lillie against her collapse but Wilde could and did teach her the rudiments of self-invention. When Lillie rose, like a phoenix, from the ashes of her failure, it was in Wilde's plumage.

This time Lillie made sure that she was invulnerable. She discarded her old, softer self, and all dependence on others. She pieced together all that she had learnt since her arrival in London, and she forged herself a new identity. Hardier than her mentor, she was quick to learn his lessons. Though it was at first unwelcome, she got used to the blaze of publicity that illuminated her every move. If the public saw her in a certain way she played on it, blinding them with the mirror-dazzle of the star they had imagined. She learnt that she could hide her real self behind it like an eclipse. She learnt to talk to her public while withholding what was private or precious. She learnt that charm equals power and she denied no one. She welcomed into home and hotel room the fox-faced newspapermen. She gave them champagne and cigars and her marvellous smile. She coaxed them, confided in them, and still sent them away at the end with nothing. Wilde had taught her all too well.

When Wilde's star burnt out, Lillie's genius, which was that of survival, blazed on. But survival in the public eye is a question of manipulation, and what had started as a means of defending her own privacy soon seduced her and became fascinating in its own right. Controlling the public's perceptions became her obsession, the perpetuation and perfection of Wilde's myth her driving concern.

By the time she came to compose her memoirs she had learnt that everything could be rewritten. Whatever had been sad, unworthy or unscrupulous was transformed at the touch of a pen. She could produce something that was elegant, and gracious and consistent, and the world would believe her. The myth became at once her carapace and her monument. Under it she buried every trace of character, origin, attachment or trauma that did not fit. Her errors were erased, her demons of conscience silenced. In her determination she left us an upended Dorian Gray, the breathing woman stamped out by a painted picture.

There were only a few who saw something different. When she died, among the many obituaries written of her was one by an MP called

O'Connor, which is worth quoting at length, if only because it is alone in attempting to penetrate Lillie's version of herself.

> If poets read into her face visions of a soul that was in the skies, the material for these impressions was in their imagination and not in either the face or the soul of Mrs Langtry. If time and some hard experiences gave an impression of calculation to the face, it was certainly not its original suggestion when I saw her. I should say that she looked simple, frank, even business-like . . . just the kind of woman who would give birth to a family of robust, courageous, eager young Britons, who would either make fortunes in the city or be pioneers of new worlds.

It is a common-sense account that has the ring of truth to it. Lillie did not have an artistic or even a particularly sensitive temperament. Like her brothers she was robust in attitude, impatient of small dignity and enjoyed the ridiculous. Perhaps, too, she would have been the mother of Empire builders had she not arrived in London when she did. She was dazzled both by the attention she was given and by the grace and breeding of its donors, but she was quick to see through it. She saw, but still she could not resist.

What is interesting about a life is the choices it makes, or has forced upon it, the combination and conflict of individual character with the constrictions of social conditions. Whatever Lillie was, and whatever she became, was informed by three things. The first was a lunatic public following. The second, a childhood memory of happiness, which was geographically and temporally out of reach. And the last, her own ambitions which Wilde allowed her to realize but which warred with her sacred past. The choices she made as a result of these forces have been castigated by posterity. It is assumed that she was the person she pretended to be – cold, amoral, opportunistic. In truth, she dealt with her demons with gusto and originality. Her place in Society was bought, not with her body, but with the long hours and extreme pressures of life on the stage. She flouted petty conventions. She suffered loneliness, hurt and disillusionment. She knew that she had sold her soul, but she never complained, never blamed anyone else, never repined.

The road from innate character to invented self is not simple. In the case of Lillie Langtry there were many stops along the way. She was several different people before she found the one that she could sustain. The result is not a life so much as a series of lives, tried for a while and then put off, like a hat – each one distinct from the next, their demarcations highlighted by the wilful severing of previous ties or by dramatic emotional and psychological upheaval. As a whole it falls naturally into four periods. The first is her childhood on Jersey, the second her London seasons and her years of collapse. The third is her successful stage career, her racing career and the building of her fortune. The fourth is old age, vaudeville, her exile and her final, crushing, loneliness. The first is the life Lillie threw away, not because she disliked it, but because she was practical and it was over. The second is the life she dreamed of, tasted and found rank; the third the life she chose and lived successfully until age caught up with her; and the fourth is the end that she thought she could avoid, the reassertion of her humanity, in which ugliness and unhappiness and vulnerability stifled the goddess and left her empty.

Lillie's legend has been considered before, but always from its outward trappings, from the scandal and the luxury and the gossip that surrounded her. If we are to understand why she needed a myth, to look clearly at the different lives she tried and see why each was cast aside, if we are to find the woman she was, and the woman she became, and the woman who, in the end, survived, we must lift the masks that Oscar Wilde taught her to wear. We must be able to see the difference between the mask and its wearer, and understand the relationship between the two. We must assess the costs of successful self-invention, and notice their effect. To that end, this book will be the life of her mind and the story of its choices, not the historical account of her actions and activities. For the mind keeps separate time from the body. Three years of happiness can seem three days; a month of sadness an eternity. To follow her mind through its mazes of determination we must travel at its pace. We must exchange the measured chronological procession of events for the imbalance of her four lives – a leisurely childhood; a momentary glitter of social activity; a limbo of choice; and then a lifetime of consolidation, of carrying out a decision and living with its penalties.

Motivation is the key to character, and Lillie's reasons, for doing the things she did, range through panic and muddle to greed and plain wrong-thinking. She was after all seduced, and it will not be possible to exonerate her from the ultimate charges of corruption and betrayal of self. Her life is, in the richest sense, a sort of rake's progress. But it was a strange and deluded path she chose, and she was hounded all along it by the furies of her conscience, which took a deal of strangling. The genius is the only type of human whose agenda is pure enough for his motives to be incontrovertible. Lillie was not a genius. She was an ordinary woman subjected to extraordinary conditions of public acclaim and attention. In defence of what I am about to write I would argue that the electric equilibrium of an ordinary person is something that the biographer, with his crude and inappropriate armoury of definition, is particularly unsuited to prise apart. It will be enough if, in these pages, Lillie breathes again, to be reappraised by a generation gentler than her own.

A word about sources.

Although there is no shortage of letters from the last, public part of her life, from the late 1880s on, these are mostly administrative. They concern plays she is about to perform, costumes, tour arrangements, the general management of her affairs; or they are letters to playwrights about work she has commissioned. They are gracious, professional and manipulative. They give us few insights into what was going on, if anything, behind the masks.

For the early years, the sources are scarce. There are her memoirs, which are interesting for what they obscure and distort, the few letters she did not destroy, and the few clues that are let slip by friends in their own letters or recollections. But Lillie was a master at covering her tracks. Like all of her generation who availed themselves of the *fin de siècle* loosening of morals, she was fanatically discreet. Important people like the Prince of Wales and the Marquess of Hartington had private secretaries who were responsible for their good character. Lord Esher, whose fingers were constantly occupied in the pies of others, made a positive bonfire of Society's intrigues; every personal letter or diary entry that was compromising was destroyed. Lillie did not have the services of an Esher, so she did it for herself. She made sure, having rebuilt herself, that there would be no weaknesses, nothing by which her careful invention might be unravelled.

However, two rich sources did escape loss or destruction. These are Lillie's love letters to Arthur Jones, kept in the green case she bought for him, hidden in an attic in Jersey, and her revealing correspondence with her older confidant, Lord Wharncliffe.

LILLIE 1853–1877

Chapter II

Family and Childhood

By the time Lillie came to write her memoirs, in the 1920s, she had learnt the lessons of notoriety. The long years of mauling by socialites, pressmen and reviewers had made her wary. Generous with her time and attention, she was constantly in the newspapers, her slightest movement lit by a blaze of publicity. Even so, she had many secrets. She had found she could stand in the glare of the limelight and still shield what was private, behind her in the dark. As it was in life, so it was in her writing. In her memoirs, lovers, family, hurt and disappointment, anything that had been precious or painful, are either dressed in sunny platitudes or simply left out. But, between the lines, had she known it, she left the negative of her real self. Her careful obfuscations are an index of those things she held dear enough to protect, chief among which is her family.

Lillie's father, William Corbet Le Breton, was the Dean of Jersey. Though he was a Jerseyman himself, he had been educated in England, first at Winchester, which was then a week away by boat, and, after Winchester, at Oxford, where he had gone as a scholar to Pembroke and finished as a fellow of Exeter. The queens of the Edwardian stage, among whom Lillie was later to count herself, always had fathers who were the handsomest men in the world and Lillie is no exception. The Dean was vigorous and six foot tall. His bearing was said to be majestic. He had a luxuriant head of hair, though by the time Lillie was able to remember him it was prematurely white. His complexion was ruddy, and his calf shapely. His eyes, as Lillie recalled, were blue and 'looked one through and through' (a trick he had developed for the most beautiful members of his congregation, and passed on to his daughter). Striding about his island parish in ecclesiastical gaiters and glowing health, he must have cut a picturesque figure. More importantly for his family, he was kind. Lillie quoted with evident pride that 'he was widely adored for his geniality and charm of disposition'. Certainly at Oxford he had been popular, his worst recorded excesses being a propensity for uncontrollable laughter. His friend Pyecroft remembered him, in his book *Oxford Memories*, as 'a man with the least possible command of countenance, so keen was his sense of the ridiculous'. His family hoped he might become an academic but he grew out of Oxford, and matured, after ordination, into 'an eloquent preacher, a good speaker, and with a marked talent for recitations'. Lillie always maintained that he would have made a fine actor. His susceptibility to the ridiculous never left him. Genetically tenacious, it resurfaced in his children, all seven of whom were spirited arch-debunkers.

After Oxford, William went to St Olave's in Southwark as curate. It was an unfashionable and impoverished parish. The devastation of railway construction had left hundreds of families crammed into rickety tenements. Unambitious and unworldly, William drew no social distinctions. He had no horror of the slums among which he found himself. Harnessing his energies to a youthful idealism, he worked and preached and visited, doing what little he could to relieve his parishioners in their foetid and grinding poverty. He grew happy and radical. Watching his progress from Oxford and Jersey, the old Le Bretons began to be uneasy. Though shorn of much of their former glory, they still considered themselves one of the senior families of Jersey. An eccentric or iconoclastic descendant would not enhance their standing.

In fact it was snobbish of the Le Bretons to be so jealous of what little position they held on the island. They were never particularly distinguished. In the dim and distant past they had been seigneurs of Noirmont, one of the prettier Jersey manors, but one or two profligates had disposed of the fortune and left their descendants to depend on the Church. After that, there were bishops and judges, with one crazy aberration. This was Raoul, the Channel Island Pirate, Lillie's favourite, who took it into his head to capture Paris for himself. With five hundred retainers, he fought his way up the Seine to the gates of the city, where, unsurprisingly, the Parisians were prepared for his arrival and sent him home again. Soon after his defeat he hung up his cutlass and retired to respectability. Vaunting ambition aside, he was chiefly remembered on the island for a splendid service of communion-plate, probably stolen, which he gave to St Brelade's church in atonement. Closer in time, and of more consequence to William, was Thomas Le Breton, a distinguished scholar and fellow of Pembroke, who was bailiff of Jersey. He was William's great-uncle. Based in Oxford he was naturally in an ideal position to oversee his nephew's university career and was no doubt pleased with his ability. It was he who in the 1840s was keeping such a stern eye on the future Dean, grooming him, no doubt, for some august island position. But William resisted grooming. Later, when he compounded his faults by deciding to marry a portionless English girl, the family's unease turned into outright disapproval. William was admonished by his elders and when he failed to respond, they boycotted his wedding.

Emilie Martin, William's choice, lived with her widowed mother in Chelsea, in what the Le Bretons saw as inconveniently straitened circumstances. William, however, was not looking at her purse so much as her face. A match for her dashing young curate, she was 'petite and lovely, with blue eyes, a perfect skin and complexion, regular features, curling auburn hair and the most fascinating smile'. Charles Kingsley, who lived next door, brought her poetry and remembered her as 'the most bewitchingly beautiful creature' he had ever seen. Both the Kingsley boys were very taken with her and there was much coming and going between the Martins' small cottage and the Kingsleys at the rectory. Charles's younger brother Henry even nursed hopes of marriage. But it was William Le Breton who, in 1842, led Emilie down the aisle of St Luke's in Chelsea. In due course the couple went back to Southwark, settled down and, within a year, their first son, Francis, was born. At about this time the position of Dean of Jersey fell vacant and William was offered the post. From his teeming London parish it must have seemed something of a sinecure and, on his father's advice, he turned it down. A radical Dean would not have been smiled on in Jersey and old Le Breton must have hoped that time and the pressures of fatherhood would bring his son round. So William pleaded youth and stayed in Southwark. His father was right. Four boys down the line, William was beginning to look for somewhere better than the smoke-bound city to bring up his boisterous children. The family welcomed the prodigal back into the fold. The parish of St Saviours was found for him and this time he accepted.

In 1859 Francis, William, Trevor and Maurice Le Breton were bundled up, with their few possessions, and Lillie's parents returned to Jersey. Here, in the rambling deanery, they were comfortable; but for Emilie, used to London, island life proved provincial and inhibiting. Their position meant they were expected to take part in the rather constricted social circuit of the Jersey élite. On Emilie, who missed the conversation and, no doubt, the attentions, of people like the Kingsleys, it quickly palled. Her parish duties were probably rather more genteel than they had been in London but they would not at any rate have been pressing. The main change to her life would have been in her surroundings, and the leisure to enjoy them. She could ride out about the island and, like Voltaire, she could, and did, cultivate her garden. This had always been an interest. Now it became both a passion and an escape. She was losing, it seemed, not just her former involvement in her husband's affairs but sadly also his attention. This was largely because there was little of substance for the Dean to do. The agricultural labourers and peasants, to whom he might naturally have devoted his energies, though poor, were less clamorous and less questioning than their London counterparts. Time hung heavier and heavier on his hands until, in the end, this new-found ease took its toll. William tried to combat his growing restlessness by devoting himself to his books. He sat in his new study and took to learning reams of poetry. Each day he set himself lengthy targets, both English and Latin verses. To no one's surprise, poetry did little to soak up the tide of his energies. Then came the arrival of their fifth son, Clement, in 1851, and poor Emilie's charms were finally mired in motherhood. She grew dumpy and abstracted. She lost the glow that had captivated the Kingsleys, and William, casting around for occupation, compounded her aesthetic collapse by a growing compulsion for philandering. The Jersey ladies were particularly susceptible, it seems, to zeal and a stockinged leg.

There is no shortage of accounts, some more slapstick than others, of the Dean's amorous escapades. Most of them are probably false, and all are exaggerated. On one occasion, no doubt a typical Sunday, emerging from church with a beauty on each arm, he was ambushed as he reached the lych-gate. The beauties' husbands, who had presumably skipped the service in the interests of vengeance, leapt out on him, tossing their cuckold's horns and brandishing walking sticks. The Dean, unruffled through long custom, sidestepped the blows to leave Colonel Knatchbull and Admiral de Saumarez belabouring each other, too blinded by jealousy to recognize their mistake. It is a good story. What it does reveal is that the Dean was interesting enough to be talked about. There is about most of the Le Breton family, and Lillie in particular, the feeling that to the islanders they were in some sense different and larger than life. They were, as a breed, intolerant of the island's proprieties and quick to ridicule self-importance or affectation. In return, the islanders surrounded them with an aura of technicolour apocrypha. They saw the Dean as someone who strode about in gaiters, fathering illegitimate children, and preaching vehement and disturbing sermons. They felt challenged when he imperilled his dignity by giving local crones a lift up St Saviour's hill in his carriage. Unable to see his vitality in the round, informing as it did his intellect, his liberality, his impatience of pointless decorum and his appetites, they saw only a lustful and incomprehensible eccentric. Lillie, who had her father's energy, suffered much the same fate. Later, when she was famous, they were greedy to claim her for their own but in her youth they clicked their tongues. Like her father she was first misunderstood and then mythologized, marked out as something between a witch and a hoyden. The boys were dreaded for the wildness of their escapades, for the range and daring of their practical jokes. Worst of all, the tragic death, in 1876, of Reggie, the youngest and most uncompromising of the Le Bretons, was muddied by whispers of instability and incest.

The only person who escaped the rumour-mongers was the true foreigner among them, Lillie's mother. But then Emilie was elusive. Even in her daughter's memoirs she is a shadowy figure. Perhaps, being a stranger to the island, she lacked her family's recklessness of its customs and opinions. Certainly she took a back seat, not just in the parish and the island's social round, but in her home too. She did not appear to share the family's resilient high spirits, and by the time Lillie was fourteen she had almost stopped going out at all. Perhaps there were too many piercingly blue-eyed children among her husband's congregation. She took to her bed. The mentions of her in Lillie's accounts of her childhood are few and it is almost impossible to salvage Kingsley's sprightly angel from the matronly photographs that have survived. Emilie looks timid and solid, her small eyes sunk in a dough of resignation. So we must imagine her in Lillie's early childhood tending her gardens with Hawk, her greyhound, and Jacko, a pet seagull, for company. She rode and walked about the island often in those days, and when Jacko mauled a family of tame partridges she had fire enough to reprove him with her riding whip. By 1873 two of her children, Francis and Trevor, had died in the services overseas. Trevor, a lieutenant, was killed aged twenty-five in Toronto. Francis died in Calcutta. Mrs Le Breton's grief for her sons was profound but it was no more than a catalyst to the damage already done by life on Jersey. Somehow she lost her spirit. She retired and the burgeoning Lillie took her place.

It was the Dean who appears to have had most influence over his children as they grew up, despite his policy of minimal intervention. Emilie was not as energetic as her husband either cerebrally or physically.

She was in awe of him and remained loyal to him to her death but it seems that, when Lillie was in her twenties, her parents finally drifted apart. As a result Emilie grew closer to Lillie. Lonely and impressionable, she seems to have been uncritical of her daughter's escapades. Most important of all, for someone as obsessively private as Lillie, Emilie was almost always in her confidence, and when her daughter's horizons proved wider than the island could compass Emilie was the first to understand.

The Le Breton children had no complaints about their island home. Lillie always wrote of it with pride and nostalgia. In her autobiography she is unashamedly gushing.

> Jersey enjoys the benefits of the Gulf Stream, and therefore the climate is so mild that ixias, camellias, palms, and geraniums flourish in the open air throughout the winter. The sky is intensely blue and the sea more violet than the Mediterranean. Indeed with its indented shores fashioned by nature into numberless small and beautiful bays with their stretches of golden sand, its country lanes with their high hedges topped by green aisles of arching trees, its apple orchards, its soft-eyed cattle browsing knee-deep in cool valleys through which brooklets of clear water wander, and the comely milkmaids in native costume, the little isle is certainly most attractive.

In all this Eden the children were allowed to run wild, and they were soon notoriously ungovernable. No one interfered with their games or curtailed their liberties. The Dean was both absent-minded and unorthodox as a father. He punished only their wildest excesses, and then only when the crime was brought forcibly to his attention. Lillie tells many stories of pranks against their mystified and long-suffering neighbours, stories which are not in themselves interesting or unusual, but which are an indication of the Dean's relaxed attitude to animal spirits. On one occasion, as Lillie recalls, the children took as their target a retired tradesman called Wilkins,

> Having relieved him of his door-knocker one evening, we tied a long, strong cord to his bell, making the other end fast to a stone which we threw over a wall opposite, with the result that everyone who passed by, either afoot or on horseback, struck the cord, causing the old man's bell to ring furiously. At each fresh clanging, Wilkins emerged with the promptitude of a cuckoo clock striking the hour, and hurled the most violent language at the innocent wayfarers. Finally our audible chuckles behind the wall

located the real culprits, and Wilkins preceded us to the deanery, where, after an interview with my father, fitting chastisement was inflicted on us.

Wilkins exacted his retribution, but it left little mark on its victims. Certainly the Le Breton children grew up in ignorance of those Victorian childhood companions, Guilt and Shame. To the Dean, ebullience and practical jokes were the natural and desirable by-products of healthy youth. So, Lillie and her brothers swam, fished and rode their ponies across the sands. Clearly their Jersey was a paradise but behind the purple of Lillie's recollections lies the truth that the island came to represent a haven of innocence, whether real or imagined, from which at times she felt herself barred and to which, instinctively, she turned when in desperation.

The deanery, where the Le Breton family grew up, was a long, low, serviceable-looking house, built of local granite around three sides of a courtyard. A hotchpotch of additions, it was originally built in 1100, the date being cut into one of the coping-stones. The house itself took up two sides of the courtyard. The third side was made up of a collection of outhouses originally used for cider making, still equipped with a huge stone wheel for pressing the apples, and a variety of stone troughs and vats. In the middle of the courtyard stood a dovecote. Beyond was a large walled garden in which Mrs Le Breton would increasingly lose herself. 'She had', according to Lillie, 'a passion for flowers and unusual taste in grouping them.' Flowers, too, covered the outside of the house, 'climbing roses – red, white, pink, blush and . . . the single damask. Underlying these were cherry and pear trees of great age, the blossoms of which in spring time mingled with the roses in delicious disorder.' Around the window of Lillie's own room there was 'an immense white jessamine', and 'a vigorous climbing deep-red rose'. Inside, the house was dark. Lillie remembers it having two entrances, one plain one which led to her father's study and their schoolroom, and the other, which was her mother's, covered by a glass portico that was filled with flowers. The children lived in one wing attended by a soapy nurse, Madame Bisson, in a purple-ribboned mob cap. The rest of the building contained her father's study, kitchens, her mother's room and a new and airy drawing-room and dining-room added by the Dean. These last looked out across the sloping lawn at the back of the house and on over the counterpane of the Jersey 'cotils'. Upstairs the house was higgledy-piggledy, 'a labyrinth of small, low rooms, with deep window-seats and many-paned case-ments', reached and divided by separate twisting stairways.

The children kept rabbits, guinea pigs, canaries, ferrets and several breeds of chicken. The soapy nurse turned out to be the mother of a smuggler, which was neither unusual nor surprising in a sea-faring community. Bloodshed and contraband were the stock in trade of her bedtime stories, and Lillie spent sleepless, nervous nights. Madame Bisson's father had witnessed a French invasion and any unusual noise brought the children 'bolt upright' in their beds with terror. By day Lillie was at the mercy of her brothers and nervousness was out of the question. She was daring and extremely self-willed but she was not naturally tough. She had to steel herself to their exploits – or be excluded. She recalled,

> my brothers lost no opportunity during my earliest youth of impressing on me what a miserable handicap it was to be a girl, a silly creature, given to weeping on the slightest provocation, easily scared and full of qualms. So I was quick to perceive that, in order not to be left out in the cold, I must steady my nerves, control my tears, and look at things from a boy's point of view.

This, as it turned out, was the best possible training for her later life. So she learnt not to cry, to ride bareback, swim, fish, sail, steal doorknockers, and patrol the churchyard on stilts with a sheet over her head. She never lost either her flair or her relish for the practical joke, the crueller the better. Only occasionally, when the boys planned something particularly outrageous, was Lillie barred on grounds of gender. Their worst escapade took place at night and Lillie was left in bed; their target a statue in the middle of St Heliers nicknamed 'George Rex'. By Lillie's account, it stood 'unmolested' for many years until her brothers 'conceived the appalling idea of tarring and feathering this royal and stony individual'. Significantly, Lillie remembered the anger, not of her father, but of the islanders. 'I shall never forget,' she vowed, 'the tremendous and wrathful outburst which ensued when the townspeople discovered the outrage.' So the Dean's children became a byword for destruction, irreverence and havoc. Whenever there was mischief discovered, the Le Bretons got what Lillie, with schoolboy slang, referred to as 'the name without the game'.

Even the Dean could not avoid the question of education. For the boys this meant the local public school, Victoria College, to which they went by day. Lillie, on the other hand, never went to school at all. Girls were not supposed to know too much. Clare Sheppard, born half a century later to the rigorous Balfours, gives a dry account of the required gloss that she so bitterly resented as a child.

When I was young the only thing aimed at in the bringing up of girls was 'tone' . . . A girl was expected to speak French really well, and one or two other languages tolerably (but not more than two). She should be able to play the piano – perhaps a second instrument could be allowed – and know how to sing in parts and at sight.

A wide but unthorough reading of the English classics was to be encouraged and learning poetry by heart. A few landmarks in history had to be grasped, but the rest was deliberately planned as a light skim on the surface, except for embroidery, gardening and horses, on which subjects a thorough knowledge was allowed.

Not surprisingly, the Dean could see no point in sending Lillie away to acquire nothing but the arts of needlework and deportment which were chiefly what the island had to offer a girl. She was taught at home, first by a French governess, who quickly admitted defeat, and then by a series of local masters in French, German, music and drawing. In the evenings, when the boys came home, a tutor from the college coached them in Latin, Greek and mathematics. Lillie was made to attend. What she absorbed in these lessons, though academically insignificant, was enough to breed intellectual independence and habits of mind that were, for her day, more masculine than feminine. By her own account, not always the most reliable, she read constantly, 'longer sometimes than my parents thought good for me'. Years later in the 1890s when Edward Michael was her manager, he marvelled at the range of her reading and information. He remembers her as 'remarkably well-read', his account continuing,

it was always with me a matter of surprise that she found time for her reading, for I have never known any topic – and I use the world 'any' deliberately – literature, science, arts, or any other subject, which she was unable to discuss with specialists.

Lillie's most frequent and adored companion was Reggie, the youngest of the Le Breton boys, born after her in 1855. When they were respectively eight and ten they made a carriage out of an old 'rumble' they found in the coach house. The carpenter fitted it up for them and the lawn-mowing donkey was put into the shafts. In addition they hired a farm-hand's little boy at a penny a week. Nearly smothered in one of her soldier brother's scarlet coats and an old ecclesiastical hat of the Dean's, he sat in front and was groom. Round and round St Heliers in great pomp they drove, much to the amusement of the locals. But the donkey was only the beginning. Once a year there was a race meeting on Gorey

Common to which the whole of Jersey went. The Le Bretons crammed themselves and a vast picnic into the family barouche and set off for the day. Ladies were not allowed to leave their conveyances and were not expected to watch the races. They were simply there to eat. When the last race was over they returned home, gorged and branded by the blazing summer sun, to a week of smarting and bathing in buttermilk. This ordeal failed to leave its mark on anything more than Lillie's complexion and she and Reggie were enthralled by the whole racing scene. They determined to try their own luck. At the Jersey cattle market they found a 'weedy English mare', which they bought for thirty shillings, splitting the cost between them. She was called Flirt. Reggie brought her home in secret and kept her in a disused outhouse. Here they fed her from the family stable bin, blistered her suffering legs, and nursed her back to health. They took turns to ride, Lillie hacking her about the roads 'to divert suspicion', while Reggie put in the serious training along the island's cliffs. They won, the first time they entered her, with Reggie himself in the saddle. The Dean, who was, by his daughter's account, 'rather unobservant', knew nothing of the escapade until he read of the win in the local paper. Others took a dimmer view. Sir John Le Couteur, a local dignitary, noted in his diary for 1866 that 'pretty Lillie' had had a bad riding accident. 'Called to hear how the Dean's daughter was,' the entry goes, followed by the abrupt observation, 'Imprudent to allow a girl of thirteen to ride a racer with a snaffle.'

How, and when, did Lillie grow up? Stepping into her mother's shoes must have forced the issue, but emerging from childhood with so many boys watching her would have been awkward whenever it happened. Never having been to school, Lillie had few girlfriends to help her with the transition and, like a boy whose voice is breaking, she swung from bursts of boyish exuberance to the grave state of a lady. She became intimate with some of the previously scorned island girls and took to table-turning. This was a tremendous vogue in the latter half of the century, so Lillie's interest was not unusual. However, she became engrossed enough to persuade herself, for a while, that she was a medium. Never one to do things by halves, she records 'one moonlight night' when she and her two associates were dragged 'on a large sofa from one end of the drawing-room to the other, amid a weird rustling like the whirring of huge wings'. Reggie was disgusted.

In fact, Lillie never really shook off the tomboy. All her life she was to be easier with men than with women. Now, with her mother increasingly indisposed, she did her share of visiting the sick and the needy, accompanied the Dean on his visits, taught at the Sunday school and even gave away prizes at the local academy. Once she had established that she was not expected to give up the fishing or the long gallops across the sand, she could enjoy her new position. Indeed she soon found her increased stature suited her and it even went to her head. Always fond of freedom, she decided, though she was only fourteen, that she should be included in the island's social life. This consisted mainly of 'small informal' picnics and dances. Her mother, for whatever reasons, agreed, and Lillie became officially a part of Jersey society. Ungovernable as a child, she saw no reason to change now that she was a lady. To the islanders she must have seemed extraordinary. With her precocity tempered by a streak that was both fierce and farouche, she was a strange combination of recklessness and calculation. The whispers about her grew louder. Simpering island misses, whose supremacy was threatened by this new and headstrong rival, consoled themselves with risqué stories. Lillie was supposed to have stripped and made a dash up the deanery lane in response to a dare. She wore boys' clothes for her morning rides, her Titian hair streaming loose in the wind. Her bewitching beauty, undeniable even at fourteen, they ascribed to nightly face packs of raw mince and rising at dawn to roll naked in the dew of the deanery meadow. Whatever the truth of the stories, Lillie's effect was incontrovertible. Before she was fifteen she had received her first proposal.

Arthur Longley, the soldier son of the Archbishop of Canterbury, was garrisoned on Jersey and must have caught sight of Lillie as she went about the usual round of parish duties and picnics. He was immediately smitten and somehow made himself known to her. How much she encouraged him is not known. Writing of him later she claimed bewilderment at his attentions. Though his proposal was what she described as 'a very serious one' she was insistent that 'he failed to find favour in my eyes'. At any rate Longley remained unaware of her indifference and asked the Dean for her hand. A gentle refusal on the grounds of her minority left him so stricken that he applied for immediate transfer. Evidently he was not prepared to wait for a wife.

Longley was not the only person to spot Lillie's extraordinary charms. Lord Suffield, a member of the Royal Household, spent his summers on Jersey. He met Lillie at one of the inevitable picnics in 1868 or '69 and is supposed to have observed, 'Do you know, Miss Le Breton, that you are very, very beautiful. You ought to have a season in London.' Whether it was this or another unauthorized attachment that galvanized Lillie's mother, Mrs Le Breton rose from her bed and, shaking off her customary apathy, announced her intention of taking her daughter to London. The new swain was a fisherboy and this time the affection was said to be reciprocated. The gossips went to work in earnest and it was rumoured that he was Lillie's natural brother, one of the blue-eyed and imprudent multitude. Clearly something had to be done. A 'season', as Suffield had suggested, would have been too long and expensive, and besides the Le Bretons had very few contacts. Mrs Le Breton compromised, and a visit to London of a couple of weeks was planned. The fisherboy was banned and Lillie whisked off to be fitted for a new dress. Lord Suffield, true to his word, provided them with their one treasured invitation, to a ball at Gloucester Place, and with the dress packed they were ready. Early one morning they crossed from Jersey to England on the steam packet.

No one, it seemed, had considered whether or not Lillie was ready for Society proper. Lord Suffield's remark about the London season had been somewhat disingenuous. Despite the Prince of Wales's influence, Society was still comparatively closed. Although the Dean was a gentleman, he had no house in London and, even if he had, the Le Bretons did not know enough people to be asked to many of the balls or At Homes. (When Lillie did finally get to London as a married woman she was to wait a year before a chance encounter resulted in an invitation.) Lord Suffield, though older, was a friend of the Prince of Wales, and his brother Walter was married to a Rothschild. This made him part of the 'fast set'. Jews and wealthy people in trade were new Society. Officially, they were still frowned upon. It was the Prince, bored with the dim and dutiful old aristocracy, and naturally attracted by the energy and enterprise of self-made men, who broke the taboo. He made many Jews his friends – the Rothschilds, the Cassels, the Hirschs – and demanded Society's acceptance. In fact, Lord Suffield himself, like the rest of his family, did not approve of his brother's marriage (one of his less enlightened remarks being, 'Walter would do anything dirty for a five-pound note.'). The guests at Suffield's ball would have been, at worst, fast and, at best, affectedly cliquey.

Not surprisingly Lillie's visit proved a lesson in humiliation. Mrs Le Breton could not have been expected to know what ladies of fashion were wearing and the dress which had seemed so pretty in Jersey proved hopelessly dowdy. Etiquette, too, was a foreign language. Lillie could not cope with the serried silver flanking her place at the dinner-table, and, when honoured with an invitation to dance, was unable to compass the intricacies of the steps. They left London immediately and with relief.

Lillie, with a fury born of injured pride, engrossed herself in her former bumpkin pursuits. Her brother William, returning home on leave, saw her galloping bareback alone along the shore and took her for a boy.

When the storm of Lillie's indignation abated, she found that mortification had matured into ambition. Now she began a programme of intensive self-education. Later she said that, 'between the ages of sixteen and twenty I learned the magic of words, the beauty and excitement of poetic imagery. I learned there was something in life other than horses, the sea and the long Jersey tides.' Though she does not mention it, sixteen was the age of the disastrous London visit. The reading was her response to failure, and her acknowledgement of the requirements demanded by this first sight of a goal. In her many (much later) accounts of early girlhood, the London visit is completely ignored. There is no record of it at all in her memoirs. There are many events in Lillie's life that in retrospect she glossed over, or simply excised. The excision of her first encounter with London could be, like many of these, simply poetic, made to make her subsequent whirlwind fame more piquant or mysterious. In this instance it seems unlikely. With details of her life that had a deep or lasting impact she is consistently and determinedly obscurantist.

Lillie now saw that the island was too small for her. None of the Le Breton boys ever intended to stay on Jersey. One by one, with the exception of Reggie, they chose careers in the services as the surest means of escape. How natural, then, for Lillie, bred to think like her brothers, to assume that her life would be elsewhere. London was her only sight of the world outside Jersey and, rejection or no, it became her objective.

Not many options were open to Lillie. There were very few escape routes, other than marriage. She could have been a governess or a seamstress, but both of these would have limited her choice of husband. If she wanted notoriety and to support herself, she could become an actress, but actresses were barely acceptable as human beings let alone as wives. This was to change during Lillie's lifetime but she could not have known that, nor at this point was she likely to have been aware of the stage as a possible profession. She had few and unformed interests so was guided instead by ambitions and these, nebulous as they were, were still entirely social. Marriage was what she settled for.

Lillie had a long wait. In 1873, her brother William came home on leave again, this time to be married himself. There were to be great celebrations, not the least of which was a ball given by Mr Edward Langtry at the Jersey yacht club. Langtry was a widower whose sister-in-law, Elizabeth Price, was to be William's bride.

Sometime during the spring Edward Langtry and Lillie Le Breton met. To the islanders, and therefore to Lillie, he looked like a man of the world. He also appeared to be very rich. In fact he was quite the reverse.

At the beginning of the century the Langtrys had been the richest shipowners in Belfast. George Langtry, the grandfather of Edward, had made himself a comfortable fortune from a fleet of trading vessels that shipped linen and other goods to London and Liverpool. In 1809 he bought Fortwilliam House, a new mansion on the edge of Belfast, large and splendid, with sweeping views over Belfast Lough, so he could watch his ships come and go. There were elegant and extensive grounds, woods, lakes and grand new glass-houses. They lived in some style. Langtry's trading ships were all sail-powered but he also had one of the first steam packets, the *Waterloo*. Though privately owned, it was available for journeys to and from England. There was no such thing as a ferry service in those days. Anyone wanting to cross the Irish Sea begged a passage off one of the smacks or trading vessels and made shift amongst the cargo. In 1824 a rival band of merchants spotted the gap in the market and set up the Belfast Steam Packet Company. The Langtrys had been rather slow off the mark. Four years later they set up their own company, along with several others, and there was a scramble for supremacy. Then in 1841 old George Langtry died. His will, a hard-nosed document full of covering clauses that revoked his bequests in the event of any of his children quibbling over their lot, left land all over Antrim and County Down, mills, tenanted farms, cottages, cattle and machinery, besides Fortwilliam, and Belfast-based businesses and money amounting to about £50,000. But there were many legacies. He had four sons and a daughter, and there were annuities for two of his servants, 'my old and faithful nurse Elizabeth Green' and Molly Sewell, so the famous fortune was soon carved up. The business, too, became problematic, after a fare war between the Langtrys and a rival ferry service from Dublin. At one point it was possible to cross first-class, with a berth and dinner, including meat and porter, for only thruppence. Though the Langtrys won in the end it was at a price.

The Langtry boys were not long-lived. Robert, the eldest, and George, the second, both predeceased their father. Edward's father was Richard, the third son, and he too died young, in 1858, after a long illness. He was only forty-eight. He left everything – Fortwilliam, his estates in County Down, his shares in the business, and a fortune of £18,000 – to his wife Elizabeth. But things were not as good as they seemed. In 1859, Charles, the only surviving brother, sold the shipping company to their old rivals, the merchant-owned ferry service, now called the Belfast Steamship Company. In the same year Elizabeth sold the house and moved, with her children, into Belfast. Edward would have been eight at the time, quite old enough to remember the glory of his former life in Fortwilliam House. They kept the lands, farms and mills they owned elsewhere in Antrim and in County Down. These, tenanted out, provided the family with income and were the basis of Edward's fortune. It was not ideal. The Irish, living often, as Trollope had been so shocked to find, in the worst conditions of penury and famine, were dilatory in the payment of rents. By the time Edward came of age the money mostly ran out faster than it came in.

Edward (Ned) was Richard Langtry's only son and had, perhaps unfortunately, been educated as a gentleman. Treasuring the memory of his sumptuous early years, he was petulantly determined on his own importance. But a dwindling fortune based on trade in Belfast cut no ice in England. Besides, he was weak and indolent and, also, surprisingly shy. This last quality at least preserved him from the dangers and temptations of London. Frightened by Society and its expectations, he kept to the provinces. When Lillie met him he was living way beyond his means. Apart from his evident disinclination to work, he had several boats, including the *Gertrude*, a racing yawl, and the *Red Gauntlet*, which were a considerable drain on his intermittent income. Yachting was as good a way of passing the time as any other and, besides, a miniature flotilla of beautiful boats gave him a cachet and a position that he could never have carved out for himself. Through them he could be part of the racing fraternity with only minimal demands being made on his personal graces. They made the splash for him, so to speak, and in Jersey he was well known.

In 1873 Ned was in his thirties. He was newly widowed, his beautiful and submissive wife, Jane, having succumbed to tuberculosis only the year before. The Prices, into whom he had married, would have thought of him as part of the family, but by the standards of the day he was still in mourning. There was no reason for him to be lavish in his celebration of William Le Breton's wedding, unless, that is, he wanted to impress.

The yacht club had been transformed for the evening. Bunting festooned the walls and there was a generous supper. Down the staircase and across the hall the crew of Langtry's yacht were lined out, in pristine white sailor suits. Lillie knew enough of men, and of Ned himself, to know that it was all in her honour. In a dress decorated with real tea roses, dizzy with her own dreams, she danced and she drank champagne. Small wonder if the music, the coloured flags and all the tinsel show made her an easy fool. In her own words, 'It was a far more elaborate and extravagant affair than anything I had hitherto witnessed, and it electrified me . . . it was simply dazzling, an Arabian Nights' Entertainment.' But Lillie was longing to be dazzled. She was twenty. It was four years since she had been to London, and so far no one so promising had appeared on the island.

Ned's ball was followed by a summer of courtship. This took the form of a series of cruises in the *Red Gauntlet*, including one to the French coast and back. Seaborne, Ned was safe. Lillie adored sailing and could busy herself with making a delirious cocktail of confusions. Ned, the yacht and the promise of moneyed ease coalesced into one irresistible attraction. Her father, in a state of negative susceptibility, accompanied her. Whether Mrs Le Breton was again indisposed, or whether she suffered from seasickness, is not known. At any rate she stayed at home. There is no record of what the Dean's feelings had been about the trip to London, but it is certain that Mrs Le Breton, fuelled perhaps by her own disappointments, was more responsive to the allure of the self-styled nobility. Later, she was to condone all kinds of romantic irregularities in her daughter. Very likely, growing apart as they were, the Dean thought his wife silly, and only too capable of over-enjoying the boat trips. So it was that he went as Lillie's chaperone. Though imprudent in his own attachments, he was never so with those of his children. He did not approve of Ned.

Sometime towards the end of the summer, Ned proposed and Lillie accepted him. Her parents attempted to talk her out of the match. The Dean's reason was her inexperience. He wanted her to see more of the world before she married. Her mother 'had set her heart on . . . a London season'. But Lillie was older by several years than the girls who would be coming out for the first time. Besides, a season was, as Lillie knew only too well, never an option. Her determination carried the day. The only person who was never reconciled to Ned was Reggie.

Once the marriage was a certainty, the Dean, in a last bid to open his daughter's eyes, or protect her if she persisted in her blindness, had Langtry's affairs looked into. We may assume that he was not surprised by what he found. He had always disliked Ned for the small man he really was. Later, in her memoirs, Lillie wrote,

When I became engaged to be married to Edward Langtry he was the complacent proprietor of a stud of hunters, a coach and four . . . an Elizabethan house, called Cliffe Lodge, near Southampton, and, besides the schooner-yacht *Red Gauntlet* . . . he had a sixty-ton fishing-cutter, equipped with a plethora of piscatorial apparatus, and a small racer, the *Ildegonda* . . . All these possessions had filled my youthful mind with pleasurable anticipation.

Her account is vastly misleading. Ned did not own Cliffe Lodge, and it was not Elizabethan, nor did he own the *Ildegonda*. His racer was the *Gertrude*. The *Ildegonda* belonged to the Prince of Wales. Quite why she was so inaccurate is unclear. Perhaps she felt in retrospect that she had been cheaply bought.

Lillie's brother Clement, who was newly qualified as a solicitor, helped with the inquiry and a contract was drawn up. An income of three thousand pounds per year was not enough to sustain what amounted to a small fleet. Most of the boats were sold, at the Dean's insistence. He also approached Ned's mother, who agreed to settle a sum on Lillie against Ned's death. What Lillie's own feelings were at the humiliation of her suitor, who knows, but she was not persuaded to give up the match. Had her engagement been the result of calculation, she would surely have capitulated once Ned was exposed. As it was, she endured the delay and wore the diamond engagement ring Ned had given her. At some point she scored her name with it into the glass of her bedroom window. Eventually, they were married in March 1874, in St Saviour's Church. The Dean performed the ceremony, which took place in the early morning with Clement the only one of her brothers to attend. Reggie, who was at home, disapproved so strongly he went riding instead, alone, along his favourite cliffs. With tomboy determination Lillie refused to have a fuss made over a wedding gown and chose to be married in her travelling dress, saying later, 'I hated the idea of a big wedding and the conventional bridal array.' After a quick breakfast the couple set sail on the *Red Gauntlet* for a honeymoon cruise that would take in Ned's family in Ireland.

Many years later she gave a particularly disenchanted account of her engagement to a newspaper: 'One day there came into the harbour a most beautiful yacht. I met the owner and fell in love with the yacht. To become the mistress of the yacht, I married the owner . . .' It makes chilling reading, but in the intervening years Ned had subjected her to violence, bankruptcy and his own alcoholism. Not surprisingly, she had come to loathe him, and the fact that he was still alive when she made the statement must have counted for something. At the height of her career she was given to making cynical statements, but then it was fashionable and amusing to be disenchanted. Viciousness was never a part of her make-up. Here, it is the bitterness of disillusionment, an indication that she felt she had suffered unfairly, rather than a record of her feelings at the time of the engagement. At twenty, though she was ambitious, she was by force of circumstance naïve. In her memoirs she says, 'I thought myself desperately in love with him.' If she did she would not be the first to confuse the suitor with the lifestyle he offered.

It may be that Ned thought they would settle down and live in Ireland, but Lillie was not willing to change one form of provincialism for another. She wanted to live in England and since Ned refused to contemplate London they settled for Southampton.

They rented a large and charmless house, Cliffe Lodge, one of a series of new Palladian villas on the fringes of Southampton. They took it, from the Reverend Horne, who owned it, for five guineas a week. The last tenants had been a retired lieutenant on half pay and his family, who had a staff of two, a parlourmaid and a cook. Lillie took a maid with her from Jersey, an Italian called Dominique, and the Langtrys too would have had a cook. It was not so very different from her parents' lifestyle on Jersey, and fell far short of the luxury she had dreamt up for herself in the days of her courtship. The house's only redeeming feature was an unbroken view over Southampton Water. Perhaps for Ned it was a small reminder of Fortwilliam and his grandfather's fleet of merchant traders. They were not happy for long. Ned was shy and Lillie exacting; so their social life was limited. Lillie is supposed to have reported, later, that they had so little to say to each other that they took to eating even breakfast apart. In her memoirs there is no record of her response to her new surroundings. The only time she refers to Cliffe Lodge, she calls it, rather affectedly, Ned's 'yachting pied à terre'. She adds, 'I need dwell no further on my life at this period. It was uneventful . . .' So much for marriage.

How long it took for the scales to fall is unclear. Lillie did love the racing.

> I entered eagerly with him [Ned] into the sport of yachting, and we lived all that summer on board an 80-ton racing yawl called the *Gertrude*, going from one regatta to another to compete in sailing matches, of which we won several, the most important of these being the International Yacht Race at Havre, which the *Gertrude* carried off in a gale. How I enjoyed the excitement of that race crowding on sail to the verge of danger, with a swirling spray drenching us to the skin.

Inevitably, not all races were either exciting or successful. There were often periods of boredom and inactivity when the couple must have relied on one another for diversion. She continues,

> Occasionally . . . yacht racing could be dull in the extreme. To roll about becalmed for hours, whistling for a breath of wind, was deadly. Once, in a big race up the Thames from the Nore to Erith, we drifted along so sluggishly that I went to bed in disgust, and though we floated past the winning post in the small hours, Mr Langtry refrained, out of consideration of my slumbers, from firing the announcing canon, and discovered to his consternation the next day that he had lost the prize by not doing so.

So she was treated like a princess in her new life. Not many of her future society gallants would have spared a thought for her rest when a prize was in sight.

Eventually the money ran out and the last two yachts had to go. This was a bad moment. Without his boats Ned was very spare. Lillie remained unconvinced by the charms of Southampton society, and discontent set in. Nothing would persuade Ned to take a house in London. At last Lillie's irrepressible spirits sank and she fell ill. Ned was delighted and told his family she was pregnant. The doctor, called in as a formality, took no notice of Ned's bluster and diagnosed typhoid. The disease took hold and Lillie lay alone at the hated Cliffe Lodge, wild with fever. There is no record of her family either being told of her illness or being at her bedside, though typhoid was often fatal. Was Lillie too proud or too ill to tell her parents? Or was Ned so offended by the Le Bretons' resistance to the marriage that his dislike had matured into total alienation? Still the fever mounted. Days of raving gave way to days of convulsions but, miraculously, Lillie survived.

Lying in bed in Southampton recovering slowly, the old desire to go to London, previously the only fixed landmark on Lillie's shifting psychological map, grew until it became paramount. She clung to it as the only thing that would revive her flagging energies, and right the wrongs of her marriage. In her weakened state she confided her disenchantment to the doctor. Moved by the bravery of his patient and, no doubt, bewildered by the violet of her eyes, he agreed that a cure was imperative. He might sensibly have suggested Jersey and a mother's care. Lillie, however, had seen her chance. He prescribed London.

Chapter III

London

In January 1876 Lillie arrived at her Mecca and filled her convalescent lungs with sooty air.

Ned, who still loathed the idea of the city, had capitulated and found them modest lodgings in Eaton Place. Presumably the typhoid had left its mark on him too. It must have crossed his mind that he did not want to watch a second young wife die. Lillie, too, was changed by her illness. The old robustness of attitude had collapsed. She now felt herself to be weak. Though in time she recovered her health and her exuberance, the sense of vulnerability, both physical and mental, remained. And so began a period of intense, and uncharacteristic, dependence on those around her, which was to last for the next five years. She was constantly on the watch for symptoms of cold or exhaustion, and capable of sinking indefinitely into listlessness and low spirits. Her letters home must have struck her parents with their alien petulance. To Ned, she may have seemed not unlike his sickly and submissive first wife, Jane.

Later, Lillie remarked with considerable disingenuousness, 'I have no idea what led us to select the great, smoky, noisy city as a sanatorium, but we arrived at Waterloo Station one murky morning in January . . .' But she did know, and must have banked on a chance meeting with one of their Jersey acquaintances to give her a second bite at the cherry.

Southampton had made her lonely. She was bored by Ned's friends – and also excluded by them. This was something new. Being a wife was different from being the sister of a pack of boys. If she could make a few friends of her own, her position, and the dullness of her husband, would be tolerable. After all, she was the daughter of an educated man, and educated, to a degree, herself. She needed an outlet for her energies, whether physical or intellectual, and, like many people who are exceptionally energetic, she wanted to do or be something without having the faintest idea what that something might be. Ambitious she certainly was, but at this stage her ambitions had no discernible goal, beyond that of widening her immediate horizons.

Waiting for a chance encounter in the London of 1876 was not such a forlorn hope as it might seem today. Society, being still small, met at the same few times a day in the same few places. 'Between the hours of twelve and two,' as Lady Randolph Churchill records, 'the Park was . . . the most frequented place in London, the fashionable world congregating there to ride, drive, or walk.' *Vanity Fair* went one further:

> The Row is pre-eminently and indelibly stamped as the most fashionable ride, walk, and lounge in England, nay in the world . . . Rotten Row in the Season is a microcosm, and the great world goes round and round it.

People went to see and be seen first, and to ride or take a walk second. It was essentially an unstructured social event. Lady Randolph's recollections give a good idea of the performance required by this public taking of exercise.

> Mounted on thoroughbred hacks, the ladies wore close-fitting, braided habits, which showed off their slim figures to advantage. The men, irreproachably attired in frock-coats, pearl-grey trousers, and varnished boots, wore the inevitable tall hat . . . For two hours a smartly-dressed crowd jostled one another, walking slowly up and down on each side of the Row. Well-appointed vehicles of all kinds made the Park look gay, from the four-in-hand coach and pony-carriage to the now obsolete tilbury, with its tiny groom clinging like a limpet behind. In the afternoon the stately barouche made its appearance, with high-stepping horses, bewigged coachmen and powdered footmen in gorgeous livery.

The Park clearly provided not only healthful activity for the convalescent but also the best chance of meeting what few acquaintances the Langtrys could muster. In her memoirs Lillie lists the people they knew: the Suffields, the Rendleshams and Lord Ranelagh, all of whom wintered on Jersey from time to time. In was not an extensive list, as she knew only too well, and its exiguousness allowed her an innocent disclaimer in her autobiography. 'It seemed unlikely that the "long arm of coincidence" would bring us into contact with any of these. Indeed, neither my husband nor I remembered that we had any acquaintances in the vast city.' It was more elegant to believe it was 'the finger of Fate' that 'pointed the way' to the eventual encounter with Lord Ranelagh, rather than two years' conscientious traipsing around fashionable haunts.

*

When the Langtrys first arrived, both of them strangers, they spent the days together, 'as country cousins do – walking in the Park watching for Royalty to pass . . . and in going to museums and picture galleries'. Lillie had a brief resurgence of high spirits. They saw more of one another than they had done since the yachting honeymoon. Indeed the picture of them sightseeing together and then returning to Eaton Place to dine is a touching one. Lillie was newly recovered from a near-fatal illness and Ned was anxious to please. There is no reason to think they were not, temporarily, happy again. However, the novelty of London's delights was soon exhausted. The summer of 1876 passed without their solitude being broken. The season came to an end and London emptied. *Vanity Fair* made its usual jaded report on how dull the world was. Seldom, indeed, it yawned,

> have so many lamentations been heard on every hand of the badness of the London Season; and seldom have they been so well justified . . . Dinners, of course, have been given, for people must dine somehow . . . but balls have been very few and far between, and as compared with their usual unbroken succession, when it is usual for any decent person to race through at least three or four an evening, have lamentably fallen off both in glory and number.

Perhaps the Langtrys were not missing so much after all, but then, fashionable boredom would have been preferable to the desperation that must have mounted in Lillie as they prepared to sit out the winter in Eaton Place. Lillie's letters home reported that it was very cold. She began to spend days in bed taking refuge with the latest novels and periodicals.

Their frozen vigil was interrupted in December, when a telegram brought news of a tragedy at home. Reggie had fallen from his horse while riding on the cliffs.

Desultory with boredom and cold, Lillie delayed. Perhaps she failed to realize how serious his condition was, or perhaps she was still piqued by his refusal to acknowledge her wedding. For she had not seen him since that day. Certainly when she left home as Mrs Langtry she had intended to move on. Marriage meant the end of the old life. Two years' absence had increased the distance. She started for home too late. For three days and three nights Reggie lay in the deanery dying of his injuries and on

17 December he gave up the struggle. He was dead by the time Lillie reached him.

Worsened by guilt, her sorrow at this first precious loss proved deep and difficult to shake off. In her later accounts she expunged her complicated response to the news of his fall. The telegram in her doctored account contained no warning of tragedy, only a *fait accompli*. 'By telegram I heard of my youngest brother's death,' she wrote. 'Crushed by the young mare he was riding, he fought against his injuries for three days, only to succumb at last. And I didn't even know of the accident.'

Even in the affluence and comfort of her sixties the incident haunted her. Reggie was the first of her ghosts of conscience and by the time she brought herself to rush to Jersey remorse and misery had already laid hold of her. Later she recalled, 'The interminable journey to Jersey, during which I lay weeping all night; the agonised grief of my mother when we met – all these things made me feel that life was over.'

On the island they were talking of suicide. Reggie had been found at the foot of the cliffs, having somehow slipped or ridden over.

Ned took Noirmont Manor, above Belcroute Bay, so that Lillie could be near her parents. She was unable to contemplate any kind of return to normal life, and he took advantage of her catatonic state to be out of hated London a while longer. With Reggie gone, it seems, she first began to acknowledge the extent of her mistake over Ned. They stayed on in Jersey through the spring of the following year. Gradually Lillie's fighting spirit returned. She is reported to have gone out sailing with two of Sir Robert Marret's sons in dangerous conditions. Both boys drowned when the cutter tipped over in Belcroute Bay. Lillie swam to shore so she must have been persuaded that life had something to offer after all.

In April 1877 the Langtrys returned to London and took up the old Eaton Place lifestyle. Lillie, resolutely taking her constitutional at the fashionable hour, spotted the Prince of Wales riding in the Park and wrote to her parents, 'He is a very large man, but appeared to ride well for one of his bulk.' She was still in mourning, depressed and disillusioned, and it seems now walked out a great deal alone. The young painter Walford Graham Robertson saw her in the street, and left an unforgettable description of her, as she was in that last twilight before the dawn of her discovery.

> One day I was crossing the road at Hyde Park Corner and idly noted a figure making its way past Apsley House towards the Park.

At the first glance it seemed a very young and slender girl, dowdily dressed in black and wearing a small, close fitting black bonnet: she might have been a milliner's assistant waiting upon a customer for all her gown said to the contrary, or a poorly paid governess hurrying to her pupils. As I drew near the pavement the girl looked up and I all but sat flat down in the road.

For the first and only time in my life I beheld perfect beauty.

The face was that of the lost Venus of Praxiteles, and of all the copies handed down to us must have been incomparably the best, yet Nature had not been satisfied and had thrown in two or three subtle improvements.

The small head was not reared straight on the white column of the throat as a capital crowns a pillar, but drooped slightly forward like a violet or a snowdrop, the perfect nose was made less perfect and a thousand times more beautiful by a slight tilt at the tip. The wonderful face was pale with the glow of absolute health behind the pallor, the eyes grey beneath dark lashes, the hair brown with glints of gold in it; the figure in its poise and motion conveyed an impression of something wild, eternally young, nymph-like . . .

Here the Barnes bus drifted gently into me.

'Where are yer gittin' to?' enquired the driver, but when I looked about me the Venus of Cnidus had vanished.

Graham Robertson's appreciation, though fulsome, is fascinating. It has the powerful authenticity of surprise though the detail of the description is the product of subsequent acquaintance. Better than any of the later tributes it illustrates the thunderbolt quality of Lillie's looks at that time. It is no coincidence that he was an artist for it was to artists that she appealed first. Only a month after this first anonymous encounter, painters would discover her and make her the type of an aesthetic movement. Within the space of a few months she would be indistinguishable from the pale Pre-Raphaelite models, on whom, for Society, she had set the stamp of reality. Lady Wilton, seeing her at Cowes later on in the year, was to remark that she 'was like the women's faces in Leighton's or Burne-Jones' pictures, very pretty . . .' She became a sort of breathing canvas. Though Society would lionize her too, she was the artists' creature and to Lillie's credit she recognized this. In the end it would be with Bohemia, and not the aristocracy, that she would throw in her lot.

With the spring London began to fill up again. It was one day late in April that Lillie persuaded Ned, now an increasingly recalcitrant companion, to accompany her to the Aquarium at Westminster. Only recently opened and still rather short of fish, it was nevertheless a new and popular resort and here, strolling among the crowds, the long wait came to an end. The couple were spotted by Lord Ranelagh, a faintly ridiculous roué, famous for his wasp-waisted coats and jauntily angled top hat. He had property on Jersey and though he had never married had a family of seven children, by the same woman. With him on that April afternoon were two of his daughters, who were known to Lillie. Naturally admiring Lillie, Ranelagh invited them down to Fulham for a few days. Equally naturally, having nothing to do, the Langtrys accepted.

In those days Fulham was not so much a leafy suburb as real country, and 'a convenient drive from town'. Lillie describes Ranelagh's house as 'a delightful creeper covered mansion', with a large kitchen garden which supplied strawberries for the Viscount's Sunday tea parties. Later, a frequent guest, Lillie remembered that, 'everyone enjoyed having tea on the mossy, tree-shaded lawn, sloping down to the Thames, and interesting people were always to be found there'. 'Interesting people' was probably a euphemism. Ranelagh's usual associates were young members of the corps de ballet, two of whom were once spotted three paces behind him at Waterloo Station, walking in step, their thumbs to their noses. What Victorian Society made of his openly acknowledged natural family is hard to imagine, but he was always something of a fringe figure. His guests at Fulham probably constituted the more outré and bohemian end of society, amateur actresses and minor aristocrats, rather than the real nobility.

That day in April would hardly have been the weather for tea on the lawn and, besides, the Season had not yet begun. Its official opening was the first of May. On this first occasion it was probably just a family party. But a stay of a few days was plenty of time for Lillie to take Lord Ranelagh into her confidence, perhaps even enlisting his help. She was always good at getting what she wanted, and what she wanted now was introductions.

The spell in Fulham over, Lillie and Ned returned to Eaton Place and the old routine. Soon afterwards they were surprised by an invitation. It was a card for a Sunday evening At Home, from friends of Lord Ranelagh, the Sebrights. They were unknown to the Langtrys and Lillie describes the arrival of the invitation as 'quite unexpected'. There is a particular tone of arch surprise in her memoirs that is invariably untrustworthy. It is almost certain that Lillie and Lord Ranelagh had agreed between them that he should furnish her with some sort of an entrée into Society. He knew many people; she knew none. She was young and beautiful. She was respectable and she was lonely. There was no reason for him to demur. Stranger than her appeal and his acceptance of it is Lillie's later determination to cover it up. It must have been obvious just in conversation that the Langtrys were living in London without a programme. Perhaps Ranelagh pitied her, lively as she was, trapped in Eaton Place in a rapidly souring marriage. Perhaps he spotted that she was just what Society wanted.

Lady Sebright was known for a lovely speaking voice. An 'enthusiastic' amateur actress who collected writers and artists, she was remembered by her brother-in-law Arthur as having 'no claims to beauty, but in spite of that fact she was one of the most fascinating women in London, extremely clever, and a centre of attraction in society'. Unfortunately, she also had a developed taste for gambling and was later to ruin her husband. Arthur's account continues, 'I well remember the late Lord Ranelagh asking my sister-in-law one night at dinner whether she would send an invitation for a reception that she was about to hold to a friend of his who he said came from Jersey, was very beautiful, and whose name was Mrs Langtry.'

The Sebrights lived at 23 Lowndes Square. 'The evening came,' Lillie begins,

> and we rattled up to Lady Sebright's house . . . in a humble four-wheeler. Being, of course, in deep mourning, I wore a very simple black, square-cut gown (designed by my Jersey modiste), with no jewels – I had none – or ornaments of any kind, and with my hair twisted carelessly on the nape of my neck in a knot, which later became known as the 'Langtry'. Very meekly I glided into the drawing-room, which was filled with a typical London crush, was presented to my hostess, and then retired shyly to a chair in a remote corner, feeling very un-smart and countrified. Fancy my surprise when I immediately became the centre of attraction, and, after a few moments, I found that quite half the people in the room seemed bent on making my acquaintance.

'Quite half the people' included John Everett Millais, Henry Irving, James Abbott McNeill Whistler, and Oscar Wilde's future room-mate, the young artist Frank Miles. Millais took advantage of his Jersey birth and when there was 'a rush of cavaliers' to take Lillie down to supper his easy claims of kinship won the day. 'Fearfully shy', as in truth she was, she must have been grateful to him for his robust jocularity, so like her father and her brothers. She went down to supper on his arm and promised to sit for him before anyone else. Miles, whose brief star was still rising, knew his own position on the list of painters to be low. He did not wait for a sitting but drew a sentimental pencil drawing where he stood, and it was this first image that graced the penny-postcard stands on every street corner before May was out.

It must have been hard, even for Lillie herself, to realize quite what had happened to her in the course of that evening. She and Ned returned home in the hired carriage. Ned's reaction is not recorded but for Lillie it was a sort of dream. 'This wonderful experience', as she calls it, 'was still fresh in my mind the next morning, and I felt nothing could eclipse it.' Normal life was briefly resumed and they went for their usual walk. When they returned in the afternoon it was to a heap of invitations. They were asked to dine, to lunch, to dance. Suddenly the whole of society was At Home to the unknown Langtrys.

In the unaccustomed whirl Lillie and Ned were finally swept apart. 'A complete transformation seemed to have taken place in my life overnight,' she observed, her marriage wrecked on that single possessive pronoun. It was Lillie whom Society wanted, not the Edward Langtrys. To Ned, who remained shy, whose only pleasures were the yachting he could no longer afford and fishing, the change was insupportable. Unable to share his wife's enthusiasm, he was nonetheless forced to accompany her for the sake of decorum, only to find, when he got there, that his dullness left him largely ignored. Lady Wilton, who was to notice Lillie at Cowes in August, concluded her observations on Lillie's beauty with the remark, 'Then we are always afflicted with Mr Langtré, who is nothing, le mari de sa femme.' To Lillie, unaware of Ned's discomfort, or simply not caring, the attention was simply 'quite staggering, and thenceforward', she recalls, 'visitors and invitations continued to pour in daily, until they became a source of grievance to our landlady, who was obliged to engage an extra servant to respond to the battering of powdered footmen on her humble and somewhat flimsy door.' Finding her stroke, she forgot her husband and in the end, inevitably, it was Lillie who swam while Ned sank.

The first engagement after the Sebrights that the Langtrys attended was a dinner given by Lord and Lady Wharncliffe in their elegant house in Curzon Street. Long, low and pedimented, it stood back from the road in its own garden, as Lillie remarked, 'more like a country mansion than a town house'. It was the centre for a group of successful painters and minor writers. Like the Sebrights, the Wharncliffes, though rich, thought of themselves as bohemian, 'lawless people' who did not know the rules of Mayfair or Belgravia. They were above Society, though still a part of it, and there was a great deal of posturing among their clique about simple ways and beauty. Wharncliffe, with whom Lillie was to become intimate, had been among the clamouring cavaliers at Lowndes Square, influenced, no doubt, by the admiration of Millais and Whistler. He was the latest, and least distinguished, scion of a cultivated family descended from Mary Wortley Montague. His father had been an enlightened agriculturist and his grandfather a scholar and politician. Edward Montague, however, had little of his forebears' edge or ability. As it turned out he needed neither since he found coal on their estate at Wortley outside Sheffield. Riches gave him stature and in 1876 he was created an earl. With this twofold boost to his fortunes he began a programme of intensive patronage of the arts. His wife, probably part of the same investment, was the arts and crafts devotee Susan Lascelles, daughter of Lord Harewood, known for her dyed blonde hair and extravagant displays of out-of-season flowers. They had a son who died in infancy, and after that no more children, lavishing affection instead on nephews and nieces. The rest of their energies were devoted to maintaining their position as London's leading salon for painters. (Writers gathered elsewhere, at Mrs Jeune's.) And artists need feeding, spiritually as well as physically. Lillie was invited to dinner, that first time, as bait for the painters. Keeping their coterie happy and inspired was an exacting business, and the Wharncliffes deserve credit for spotting so early on that Lillie would do just that.

The first of the artists to benefit from the Wharncliffes' new acquisition was Sir Edward Poynter. Lord Wharncliffe had commissioned four vast canvases for the hall at Wortley, but Poynter had found himself soon abandoned by the Muse. Lillie, of course, brought her running back, when she agreed to pose as Nausicaa, the central figure for one of the panels, with the golden Lady Wharncliffe, her friend Miss Violet Lindsay and Poynter's wife, performing classical functions in each of the others. Lillie was also to sit for a portrait, painted in the Pre-Raphaelite style, looking dreamy and sensual in a vaguely Shakespearean bodice against a backdrop of velvet and gold brocade.

After Poynter there were many others, ranging indiscriminately from Strudwick to the grand old man of Pre-Raphaelitism, Burne-Jones himself, whose reaction to her was ecstatic. Old and easily tired, Wharncliffe had been afraid that he would find the meeting too taxing, but Burne-Jones, writing to allay his fears, and to thank him for the introduction, had clearly found Lillie a tonic. He wrote,

> I was only refreshed and brightened by the evening and was quite happy – and think it was boundlessly kind of you to arrange things so after my desire. It was the first time I had ever seen the Beauty – and I didn't like to stare too much . . . but I felt quietly happy as one does in the presence of any beautiful thing . . . for many a day I have wanted my work to cheer more than it has done yet . . . she isn't fit for a tragedy and I'm glad of it and hope she will never know what a bad word it is . . . I can't imagine a face more radiant or look more serene – like day itself she is . . . She was thoroughly kind to me and offered to sit to me – Though I have heard and believe, in spite of what she says, that it is a bore to her – of course it is – but for the good of the commonwealth she must suffer. If I could get into my mind the lines of her brow and great long head all I could do afterwards would be bettered.

But patronage alone was not enough for the Wharncliffes. Both of them wanted to have their own place among the artists around them, not just pay the bills. She took up embroidery and produced a profusion of complex Morris-inspired cushions and hangings. He indulged in nebulous literary leanings, which found expression mainly in correspondence with young and affected poetesses. The most constant of these was Violet Fane,* a follower of Swinburne and the Decadents, whom Lillie remembered as writing 'ardent love poems, which in those hypocritical days was considered highly improper'. Violet encouraged Wharncliffe in his own watery poetic endeavours, returning his verses with advice and comment. 'Feeling as you do,' she wrote, 'I cannot but think (and hope) that you are a poet – perhaps unknown to yourself. The feu sacré must be there and only waiting to assert itself, if it has not done so already.' Wharncliffe, who was a sad man, was comforted into taking his sadness for talent. They were 'poor struggling poets' together, and he saw nothing incongruous about sending, in return for her support, hampers of plovers' eggs and strawberries from Wortley. Writing to thank him, with the affectation that was the currency of the whole coterie, she pronounces herself 'quite unused to such good things, as I think I have the nature of a student or the anchorite and that I was intended only to

---

* Violet Fane was the pseudonym of Mary Montgomerie Lamb, married first to Henry Singleton and then, on his death, to the first Lord Currie (then Sir Philip), HM Ambassador first in Constantinople and later at Rome. She began publishing poems and essays, under the name Violet Fane, in the 1870s.

live on roots and nuts in some sort of hole or cave in the rocks'. The cave in the rocks, as it happens, was a large house in Grosvenor Place.

This, then, was the society that first claimed Lillie, serious, slightly alternative, and awash with whimsy. They were the inheritors of the Aesthetic movement and of burgeoning Pre-Raphaelitism, the self-proclaimed devotees of beauty. They were earnest and rather ludicrous, qualities that Lillie had been brought up to scorn. But, over the self-conscious chatter, in justification, towered the giants the coterie had paid for: Millais, Whistler, Burne-Jones, Watts and Poynter, whose genius redeemed the silliness of their followers, and whose burning attention was now focused on Lillie. Small wonder that she was dazzled. To be plucked from the obscurity of Eaton Place and deposited in the pedimented mansion at the Wharncliffes' table was enough, but to be deposited there as the guest of honour, the breathing embodiment of the beauty they were all trying to capture on paper and canvas, was incomprehensible. It is just possible, through the generous condescension of her memoirs, to glimpse in Lillie's recollections of these early encounters the disorientation and the schoolgirl awe of the outsider. She saw, as yet, nothing ridiculous in this couple in their fifties, languishing like disaffected youth and running after the Muses. Lady Wharncliffe was 'brilliantly clever and artistic', 'tall', 'handsome', the 'perfect example of the *grande dame*'. 'I am not sure,' Lillie marvelled, 'whether she was more beautiful that night, sitting at the head of her table, which glowed with golden tulips that matched her golden hair, or as I saw her later at Wortley, near Sheffield, bending her graceful head over her embroidery frame, at which she seemed to work as perpetually as Penelope.'

Lady Wharncliffe was famous for her wit and for the habit of scintillating her guests. Lillie's cloistered, male-dominated background must have been thrown into sharp relief. The Wharncliffes were, after all, the same age as her own parents. Lady Wharncliffe's brilliant pre-eminence among distinguished company made a striking contrast to the bed-bound and beleaguered Mrs Le Breton. Lillie closes her description of the evening with a poignant instance of her hostess's sophistication and her own naïvety. The lovely Lady Wharncliffe was fast, it seems, as well as clever, and Lillie is forced into a rare exclamation. 'But, oh!' she cries, the recollection of it suddenly strangely sharp, 'after that first dinner at Wharncliffe House, she smoked cigarette after cigarette, and my country soul was shocked.'

Less obvious to Lillie than the rakish cigarette smoking, but no less an indication of the Wharncliffes' independence, was the levening of outcasts among their distinguished guests. For Lillie's first night there was Madge Kendall, semi-acceptable on account of her purity and her conventional marriage, but an actress all the same, and Lord Randolph Churchill, Society's newly elected pariah. He was the brilliant but unsavoury second son of the Duke of Marlborough, ostracized by the Prince of Wales for blackmail. Lillie would have read of the scandal in the papers in her year of waiting. It had taken place during the Prince's Indian tour, and centred on the projected elopement of Lord Blandford, Churchill's brother, with Lady Aylesford. Lord Aylesford, popularly known as 'Sporting Joe', was among the Prince's company in India, no doubt greatly contributing to the big game bag. He had responded to the news that his wife was eloping with a decision to sue for divorce. There was not much to choose between divorce and elopement: both would have resulted in public scandal. Hoping to panic the Prince into suppressing the divorce, he took the matter into his own hands. Gathering up a packet of compromising letters that the Prince in former days had written to Lady Aylesford, he set off for Marlborough House, boasting that he had 'the Crown of England in his pocket'. Not unnaturally his attempts, in the absence of her husband, to threaten the Princess enraged the Prince of Wales, and Randolph had to leave the country. He went first to America and then to Ireland, where his father, to get out of the limelight, had taken up the position of Viceroy. Eventually an apology of sorts was made and accepted, but Society never really took him back. Socially, it seems, he was little more refined than he had been in handling the scandal, insisting on one occasion, 'I don't like ladies at all. I like rough women who dance and sing and drink – the rougher the better.' However, in good health at the Wharncliffes', he was not above appreciating the Dean's daughter. To his long-suffering wife Jennie, left behind in Dublin, he wrote, 'I took in to dinner a Mrs Langtry, a most beautiful creature, quite unknown, very poor, and they say has but one black dress.'

Lord Randolph's observations to his wife after dinner at the Wharncliffes' encapsulate Society's response to Lillie in the first days of her success. There was never any shortage of new faces – girls who were fresh from the schoolroom, their hair up for the first time, their reputations ahead of them and their purity advertised in debutante's white. The silent beauty in the corner of the Sebrights' drawing-room was a stranger, and she was dressed in black. Her beauty was one thing, and if it was in the much prized Greek mould then so much the better, but to the jaded and privileged classes her poverty and her mourning dress were what set it alight. Knowing nothing of her, save that she was acceptable, Society was free to indulge its fancy. It could endow her with all the qualities of the classic Victorian heroine – the poignancy of Graham Robertson's milliner's assistant, the orphan or the gentle governess – and its principles would be intact. She could be poor, and beautiful, and unknown, and bereaved, and still be invited to dinner with the Countess of Dudley and the Prince of Wales.

Chapter IV

First Success

Lillie always made her success in Society seem instantaneous. One moment, she was a lonely nobody, and, the next, duchesses were standing on chairs in the Park to get a better look at her.

In fact, little had changed between her first desperate visit to London at sixteen and the Sebrights' reception – except her fellow guests. The people who mobbed her in her demure corner of the Sebrights' salon, with the exception of Henry Irving, were artists and patrons, and it was they who were banging on the flimsy Eaton Place door in the weeks to come. It was the painters who first noticed her, walking, as it seemed to them, straight out of the newest canvases; validating what, till then, had been a theory, only just beginning to be realized in the work of Millais and Burne-Jones. To them she was the incarnation of a new movement. Her appearance underlined and confirmed their thinking, accelerating the transformation of the avant-garde into common-currency.

In the second half of the nineteenth century the English artistic pantechnicon was grinding through the gear shifts of aestheticism and pre-Raphaelitism in the search for a new language. Graham Robertson, who had spotted Lillie first from behind the Barnes bus, was scathing about the absurdity of the fashionable Aesthetic following, and neatly encapsulates the freshness of Lillie's appeal. He roundly blames Oscar Wilde for comparing Ellen Terry to 'some wan lily overdrenched with rain', after which, he asserts,

> all the women at once saw themselves as wan lilies and, well, it is not a style becoming to everybody.
>
> It was very deplorable; for the Aesthetes by their antics killed the thing they proposed to love as dead as a door-nail, and the great Art Revival of the seventies from which so much had been hoped passed away in the eighties amidst peals of mocking laughter . . . Suddenly, as if in reproof of

the artificial and unhealthy type then masquerading as beauty, there glided across the social firmament a vision of that divine loveliness dreamt of by painters and sculptors since Art began.

The vision was of course Lillie in her black dress. In fact Rossetti, Millais and Holman Hunt had been painting in the new natural style for some time, with the emphasis on a rather strained sensuality, inherited in part, across the disciplines, from Swinburne and the Decadents. What Lillie so forcibly embodied was a human cocktail of the Greek type upheld by the Aesthetes with the heavy-lidded intimations of animal appetite that had fired the Pre-Raphaelites. If, as Ruskin suggested, the Pre-Raphaelites were to 'paint from nature only', here at last was something real they could all paint without being false to their creed; and paint her they did.

However, the serious artists took time to produce their paintings. It was not they who were immediately responsible for the spread of Lillie's name. The person who did that was Frank Miles. He was more or less the same age as Lillie, well connected, talented and colour-blind. In the seventies, when Lillie met him, he was enjoying the patronage of the Prince of Wales and his monochrome portraits were all the rage. These, though successful, were no more that pot-boilers. They made him a living, and allowed him to pursue his real interests, among which he counted the management of a pottery in Cardigan, which produced 'artwork pots' for conservatory plants. Sadly, despite his success, he was misunderstood. Posterity, with its selective and lubricious memory, has highlighted his friendship with Wilde, his mental instability and his proclivities, which included an interest in little girls. And in his own day Society did not do much better. Augusta Fane, Lillie's future friend, known for her gentleness and generosity, recalled, 'I have a dim recollection of an unhealthy-looking young man, who drew pencil portraits of fashionable ladies and who ended his career by committing suicide.' Lillie was less unkind. She had a natural affinity with iconoclasts and fringe-figures and Frank was probably her first real friend in London. Her own account of him is particular and protective.

Frank Miles was a gardener first and an artist afterwards, and every time I sat to him there would be some new flower awaiting me. He was the pioneer in the revival of the abandoned herbaceous border and also in bringing flowers within the means of the general public. Through him Oscar Wilde became a flower worshipper and popularised the daffodil and the daisy, but Frank had won reputation as a cultivator and hybridiser of beautiful lilies and narcissi before Oscar ever thought of pinning his love to them.

Miles's interest in horticulture was in fact serious. He was a friend and admirer of the well-known William Robinson, author of *The Wild Garden*, with whom he corresponded. His carefully formulated ideas about the herbaceous border were imaginatively avant-garde. They were adopted by Robinson, who acknowledged Miles's expertise, and quoted them verbatim in a tribute to Miles after his death in a Bristol asylum in 1891. His other pet scheme, perhaps even formulated with Lillie, was to plant in the London parks bulbs that children would be allowed to pick. Later she disowned the project, calling it 'naïve' and impractical, but plants were nevertheless a real shared interest. Lillie was no professional but she had inherited her mother's passion and was later to build gardens on Jersey and in Monaco. She must have enjoyed her sittings.

When Lillie first met Frank, he was artist-in-chief to the periodical *Life*, for which he had been commissioned to run a series of portraits. They were of the best-known Society beauties and, besides appearing in the pages of *Life*, engravings of the portraits would have been available for sale at penny-postcard stands on street corners. This had been the fate of Miles's first sketch of Lillie, and though she was as yet unknown to society it put her immediately in the same bracket as the richest and rarest of its members. The first official portrait Miles did, another rather delicate rendering of Lillie's sleepy features on a background of pencilled lilies, was bought as soon as it was finished by Prince Leopold, who hung it over his bed in Buckingham Palace.

But Miles, though he was a soul-mate of sorts, did not have the monopoly on Lillie. There were other painters who had seen her at the Sebrights' At Home: Millais, Whistler and Leighton, and friends of theirs such as Watts, Walford Graham Robertson, Poynter and Burne-Jones, who had been told of her, or possibly introduced, all of whom would have left cards and invitations in that first week of Lillie's discovery. For many of these Lillie began modelling without delay. Now, when she woke in the morning, it was with a sense of purpose. Her extensive reading of newspapers and journals was no longer simply a way of passing the time and piquing herself with things she was missing. She was preparing herself to be able to converse with this new and educated acquaintance. In the mornings, liberated from an increasingly disgruntled Ned, she would sit for one painter or another and, slowly, in their studios, coming and going from their own sittings or inspecting commissions, she began to meet Society proper. She was the new aesthetic find, and anyone arriving would be introduced and expected to marvel. Chance meetings resulted in formal introductions, and soon it became apparent that it was not only artists who were inspired by the unknown Mrs Langtry. Frances, Countess of Warwick, whose portrait Miles was drawing, remembered making a special visit to the studio with her stepfather, Lord Rosslyn, to 'gaze' on Miles's latest model. She was little more than a child but even she was impressed, writing later,

> In the studio I found the loveliest woman I have ever seen. And how can any words of mine convey that beauty? I may say that she had dewy, violet eyes, a complexion like a peach, and a mass of lovely hair drawn back in a soft knot at the nape of her classic head. But how can words convey the vitality, the glow, the amazing charm that made this fascinating woman the centre of any group she entered? She was in the freshness of her young beauty that day in the studio. She was poor and wore a dowdy black dress, but my stepfather lost his heart to her, and invited her there and then to dine with us next evening at Grafton Street.

It was early days and Lillie was still grateful for any impromptu invitation. Though she was sitting to painters every day, she was spending the evenings quietly with Ned at Eaton Place. They must have been hopelessly out of step. There were no reasons for Ned to enjoy London. The tourist walks, which had palled, were no more, and Lillie was slipping away from him. He was jealous, full of his own unrecognized importance, and cross. Lillie, on the other hand, was full of purpose and excitement. She had friends she could talk to and, at last, a vent for her ambitions. And, of course, she was admired. Probably they quarrelled. Certainly they were not enjoying each other's company any more than they had in Southampton.

The Rosslyns secured their prize. Lillie bullied or cajoled Ned into chaperoning her and the invitation was accepted. They must have heard people talking of Lillie already, or perhaps they too were aware of what a sensation she would create, for they quickly invited a large party to meet her. She came on the appointed day, accompanied, in Frances's words, by 'an uninteresting fat man – Mr Langtry – whose unnecessary presence took nothing from his wife's social triumph'. So the sporting Mr Langtry had got fat in London. Perhaps he had already resorted to his later and fatal ally, the bottle. At any rate it would be hard to find a more brutal assertion of his irrelevance, a state to which Lillie unquestionably contributed, consciously or unconsciously, by her own evident lack of interest. There were plenty of obese and unprepossessing men in the drawing-rooms of London. Had Lillie wished it, Society would have absorbed her husband, as it did so many others.

Lillie's entry at Grafton Street that evening was watched from the stairs by Frances and her little sister Blanche and it was electric. Whether it was dash or ignorance that governed Lillie's sartorial decisions in those days it is hard to tell. Evidently she had not quite shaken off all her brothers' boyish lessons, remarking later that, 'the poverty of my wardrobe was not due to motives of economy, but rather to my dislike of the "fitting" process, and, frankly, also the result of my absolute indifference at the time to elaborate frocks, though my views regarding finery changed completely later on'. Perhaps the humiliation of that first Jersey-made London dress still lingered and she decided not to attempt to conform. From behind the banisters, at the Rosslyns', the girls saw Lillie in the same 'dowdy' black dress she had worn in the studio the day before, 'merely turned back at the throat and trimmed with a little Toby frill of white lace, as some concession to the custom of evening dress'.

The company at Lady Rosslyn's was quick to catch on and Lillie's launch into Society was now underway. Lord Houghton, Swinburne's great patron and a poet himself, became an enthusiastic admirer. The Langtrys were often in demand at his house in Arlington Street where the entertaining was easy and, again, bohemian. Lillie remembered him as the 'most delightful host of his time in all London', observing in the memoirs, 'I was always so pleased when he invited us, and he did very often, to lunch, to dine, and to receptions'. At one such event she met the eccentric American poet Joaquin Miller who presented her with her first poem, a rather banal offering, which he read out before the assembled company.

> If all God's world a garden were,
>   And women were but flowers,
> If men were bees that busied there
>   Through endless summer hours,
> O! I would hum God's garden through
>   For honey till I came to you.

The banality belied his admiration and Miller, with his golden hair so long that it lay in curls on his shoulders, and his unconventional dress, was soon a constant acolyte. One evening, arriving at a concert at Lady Brassey's, Lillie found him waiting for her at the foot of the huge staircase. As she proceeded up it to greet her hostess Miller backed before her, 'scattering rose leaves, which he had concealed in his broad sombrero, upon the white marble steps, and saying with fervour: "Thus be your path in life!"'

As the season progressed and the acts of worship became more numerous and more extravagant, Lillie's fame spread. It was not long before the black dress was in demand at two or three different events each evening, dragging the fat and uninteresting Ned in its wake. They went to balls in all the grandest London houses, to dinners, receptions, At Homes. The Marquess of Hartington, laconic heir to the Duke of Devonshire, and lover of Skittles, the first of the professional courtesans to ride out in Rotten Row, asked them to a political party at Devonshire House. The black dress made its entrance up the enormous marble staircase and 'Harty Tarty' abandoned the visiting dignitaries in its favour. Leaving his position at the head of the receiving line he gave her a personal tour of the house's treasures. Grave and sardonic, with a patrician beard, he showed her room after room of pictures, ending with an indoor courtyard, where Lillie particularly admired the marble pools full of coloured water-lilies. Nothing daunted by his evening dress Hartington plunged in up to the elbow. 'He drenched his clothes,' Lillie recalled, 'pulling them out as an offering, as also the gorgeous liveries of the footmen, into whose arms he flung them and who strewed our brougham with such quantities of the dripping blossoms as to make the latter conveyance rather moister than was convenient.' And this was not a bohemian gathering of artists looking for a new Muse. It was a State Occasion. It must have crossed Lillie's mind that London had gone mad. She was twenty-four and, but yesterday, had been nobody. Now it seemed that even statesmen stopped at nothing to adore her for a moment.

VENUS ANNODOMINI 1877–1880

Chapter v

A Muse in Context

It would be impossible, from the distance of the twentieth century, to overstate the grandeur of the backdrop that Society presented for Lillie in her one black dress. Vita Sackville-West wrote in *The Edwardians* of 'the pageant of the Season, the full exciting existence in London, the crowds, the colour, the hot streets by day, the cool balconies at night, the flowers filling the rooms and the flower-girls with baskets at the street corners, the endless parties with people streaming in and out of doors and up and down stairs; the display, the luxury, the wealth, the elegance . . .' Frances Warwick remembered staying with the Duke and Duchess of Marlborough when it was normal to change four times a day. First, morning dress. At Blenheim, where even breakfast was a ceremony, the ladies wore 'long velvet or silk trains'. Then, walking or riding dress, followed by an elaborate and flowing tea gown, commonly known as a 'teagie', and finally the grandeur of full evening dress. For men, evenings meant medals, gloves and white tie and tails. For women it must often have been an ordeal. Their dresses, from the outside, were bare and fabulous in their extravagance. From the inside, they were a prison of whaleboning and upholstery. *The Edwardians* also contains a long description of a Duchess's evening toilette, attended by her maid, written through the eyes of a little girl.

Her mother was seated, poking at her hair meanwhile with fretful but experienced fingers, while Button knelt before her, carefully drawing the silk stockings on to the feet and smoothing them nicely up the leg. Then her mother would rise, and, standing in her chemise, would allow the maid to fit the long stays of pink coutil, heavily boned, round her hips and slender figure, fastening the busk down the front . . . then the suspenders would be clipped to the stockings; then the lacing would follow, beginning at the waist and travelling gradually up and down, until the necessary proportions had been achieved . . . Then the pads of pink satin would be brought, and fastened into place on the hips and under the arms, still further to accentuate the smallness of the waist. Then the drawers; and then the petticoat would be spread into a ring on the floor, and Lucy would step into it on her high-heeled shoes, allowing Button to draw it up and tie the tapes . . . Button, gathering the lovely mass of taffeta and tulle, held the bodice open while the Duchess flung off her wrap and dived gingerly into the billows of her dress . . . She reached down stiffly for the largest of her rubies, which she tied first against her shoulder, but finally pinned into a knot at her waist. Then she encircled her throat with the high dog-collar of rubies and diamonds, tied with a large bow of white tulle at the back, and slipped an ear-ring into place.

With an ostrich feather fan, gloves and bracelets, the Duchess's toilette would be complete. The whaleboning that, in this passage, sounds so glamorous was often ferociously tight, so that any attempt at movement was accompanied by a terrible creaking of stays. It was one of Lillie's most alluring qualities, when she first appeared on the London scene, that her dress was uncorseted. Margot Asquith, razor-sharp in mind and tongue, observed that 'she held herself erect, refused to tighten her waist, and to see her walk was as if you saw a beautiful hound set upon its feet'. Jewellery, of course, was *de rigueur*, as much of it as could be fitted about the neck and arms and pinned around the waist and bosom. Seated at dinner next to a lady who had come down unadorned, the Prince of Wales had turned to her and asked tetchily, 'If I can take the trouble to dress for the evening why can't you?' And on top of it all there were the headdresses. These were, as Lady Frederick Cavendish observed, 'remarkable', elaborate confections of hair, both real and false, teased and prinked into a 'frizzled mop' and crowned with the obligatory tiara. It was nothing if not a carnival.

The complexity of the dress code was partly the result of the Prince of Wales's influence. He was the acknowledged head of Society and his partiality for elaborate costumes was almost fanatical. On his Indian tour he appalled the intellectual Lieutenant-Governor of Bengal, who saw his obvious abilities diminished by what he termed 'low and childish' tastes. His wife observed that he suffered from

a perfect mania on the subject of dress. Dr Fayrer told me that he was quite sick of perpetually changing his clothes, as fresh orders come nearly every hour about what the suite were to wear and if a button is wrong it is at once noticed and remarked upon. His other tastes are for smoking and eating and drinking.

The Prince, who was not interested in pictures, particularly prized beauty in womankind. Margot Asquith described the seventies and eighties as 'the days of the great beauties', remembering that 'London worshipped beauty like the Greeks'. The most beautiful – Lady Dudley, Lady Dalhousie, the Duchess of Leinster, Lady de Grey, Lady Londonderry, Mrs Cornwallis West – became known as the Professional Beauties. They were the queens of Society and no self-respecting hostess would hold a gathering without them, the term professional meaning nothing more than acknowledged. They were in reality unpaid models for the newly emerging art of photography. They posed in various states of dress and fancy dress, for it was not only the aristocracy that was interested in beauty. The pictures of the 'PB's on sale in the shops and on street corners were bought for a penny by rich and poor alike. 'Photographs of the Princess of Wales . . . Mrs Cornwallis, Mrs Wheeler and Lady Dudley collected great crowds in front of the shop windows.' Changing clothes four times a day was an obvious consequence of an obsession with appearance but it was also a reflection on the nature of Society itself. It punctuated the day and it provided variety in an environment that must, at times, have been fairly stale.

Before putting Lillie back into the picture it is worth taking a look at the structure of the society that the Prince had inherited from his mother. Today, many of us have a picture of late Victorian, early Edwardian society, where the rich were rich, and indolent, and decadent, and the poor were very, very poor. And the picture is a true one in many respects. But to the *grandes dames* themselves looking back on their youth from the 1920s the atmosphere was remarkable for being as rarefied as it was short-lived. Frances Warwick, the little girl watching Lillie's arrival at the Rosslyns', started as a millionairess in her own right, threw week-long parties at her Essex estate, kept a menagerie, had an affair with the Prince of Wales and became one of the prototype champagne socialists. By the time she wrote her memoirs the Society she had grown up in had disappeared enough for her to have to describe it to the reader. She writes,

When I came out social prestige meant something. There was a definite aristocratic society of the landowning families. These families owned then practically the whole of the land of England. It was difficult to enter that society from the outside, and impossible unless Royalty approved. The Prince of Wales was broadish minded and inclined to welcome some of the professional class. A few artists and doctors were accepted. Sometimes a rich manufacturer might be able to poke his nose in but he caught it for his temerity no matter how rich he might be. Political people were included, and any outstanding man or woman, say an explorer or a musician, but brains were rarely appreciated and literary people and intellectuals were not welcome.

Lillie herself, also writing in the 1920s, attributed her success to the smallness of Society and she too felt the need to describe it. She apologizes for 'chronicling the curious whim of the public', explaining that, 'in the vastly enlarged society of today, the excitement caused by my advent could never be repeated'. Her own description of the conditions which created her runs,

> In my day London society was very different to what it is now. Actors and actresses were not then generally received, the Stage being regarded as an undesirable vocation. Rank was more highly considered, and the line more finely drawn between the social grades, the inner circle being, consequently, comparatively small and rigorously exclusive, and people were more hypocritical and narrow minded. America and the Colonies had not the enormous accumulated wealth which they boast at present; South Africa had not yet yielded her crop of millionaires, and the leisured classes which now fluctuate between the mother country and their own land scarcely existed.
>
> Travel was less easy and much less luxurious, and very few Americans were to be found in London.

England was an island and so, in a sense, was its aristocracy. Closed to outsiders, it entertained itself year after year with the same round of pleasures. The same old faces were relieved periodically by the maturing of new ones from a schoolroom in some stately home. For the most jaded and cynical account of its concerns we must turn to *Vanity Fair*, which summed it up as follows:

> London Society has a high and holy mission. That mission is to amuse itself; and the only amusement it has yet discovered, or ever seems likely to discover, is that of meeting itself. To this end all efforts tend, and to effect this purpose various devices have been invented, such as balls, parties and the like, the whole object of which is to bring together people who know each other, in order that they may say, 'How do you do?' as many times as possible within an hour. To this important occupation twelve hours of the day are held sacred. At noon, when the day of Society may be said to begin, then comes the morning walk or ride, followed by

luncheon, a drive, dinner, and the evening parties. In none of these is anything like conversation to be found. It would be considered impertinent and presuming for anybody to make a remark exceeding twenty words in length, or including more than one idea.

For those who were not intellectual, nor philanthropic, nor disciplined, boredom was a real enemy. So more entertainments were constantly devised. There were ever more lavish balls and receptions. Whimsically designed menus and dance cards were written on lily petals and miniature ships' sails. There were more foreign dishes at dinner, grander flower arrangements, more hothouse flowers, more silverware, more exotic clothes, bustles, stays, fabulous jewels. Society became faddish and sensation-hungry. There were crazes for music-hall singers, actors, and freaks. London was never so susceptible nor so greedy. There was Kate Vaughan, dancer at the Gaiety, for whom men took to black kid gloves and women to black silk stockings with gold clocks. There was Mrs Shaw, the American society whistler, who whistled up a storm. There was Joaquin Miller, American poet, who attended balls and dinners in buckskins and a flowing beard. There was Sarah Bernhardt. There was Oscar Wilde. And there was Lillie. Each in turn was swept up by Society, fêted and adored and then cast aside like flotsam in favour of some new attraction. This is Lillie's proper context, this spangled and voracious tide of privilege and hedonism. In its midst, as it rolled through the London season, and on through race meetings, yachting and shooting parties, we must at last set her down – jewel-less, stay-less, her hair unadorned, in her cheap black dress.

Chapter VI

Votaries in Bohemia

The records of Lillie's life at this time are very few, but her duties were simple enough. She had to sit to painters, wear her dress and be seen everywhere. How, and with whom, did she spend her days? By June 1877 it was no longer just the painters who provided her with friendship and occupation. She now had friends in Society too and as her circle of acquaintance widened so did the range of her activities. Her nights belonged to Society but her days, in the Season, were divided. Generally she would have sat for a portrait in the late morning, returned home for lunch, walked out, either shopping or purely for exercise, and then had tea, often back in a studio, this time in a social capacity. At this hour, between four and six or seven, Society and Bohemia* came together. The great ladies were diverted by the informality of the artist's life. There was something frowzy about the dais and its rumpled draperies, full of the recently departed model, who was so often a mistress. The conversation was refreshingly abstract and therefore, in a measure, conscience salving. And the refreshments would have been a titillating view of the *vie Bohème*, the rougher the better. So, studios were natural meeting places, not always the garrets of popular imagination, but great light rooms, often equipped, as du Maurier describes in his novel *Trilby*, with a piano, and plenty of space for entertainment and recreation. 'The studio', his description runs, 'would be thrown open and people would come and go, gossip, look at the pictures, and fence. "French, English, Swiss, German, American, Greek" dropped in, curtains were drawn and shutters opened; the studio was flooded with light – and the afternoon was healthily spent in athletic and gymnastic exercises till dinner time.' In the early days, when her acquaintance was still too small to guarantee callers, Lillie

*The use of the word Bohemia as a blanket term for that eclectic social group which included artists and models, actors, poets, drinkers, political activists and self-publicists, though anachronistic at this date, is the only one that adequately covers all of the above.

passed many afternoons, in one studio or another, just drinking tea and enjoying the jumble of people who dropped in for business or pleasure. Miles's studio, her favoured spot, she describes as being,

> in a curious old-world house looking over the Thames, at the corner of Salisbury Street, Strand, London. It was a very ghostly mansion, with antique staircases, twisting passages, broken down furniture, and dim corners. In the late afternoon interesting people, artistic, social, and literary, of both sexes, found their way to his dusty old studio . . .

She goes on to list the company. Poets came, Rossetti, and the tiresome Violet Fane, foraging for roots and nuts, William Morris, Walter Pater, even Swinburne, who was in his final pre-Dunton blast and must have made rather lurid company. There were 'many purely social lights' such as the Duchess of Beaufort, the Duchess of Westminster, Lord and Lady Dorchester and of course the Rosslyns, all of whom apparently 'thoroughly enjoyed the bohemian atmosphere'. There, too, were Forbes-Robertson, Ellen Terry, Whistler, a sprinkling of Oxford undergraduates, and Oscar Wilde. What this extraordinary company found to talk about is hard to imagine.

At this stage Lillie, though she was flooded with offers of friendship, was not making any conscious choices about whose company she kept. She was going wherever the offers, or her own interests or ambitions, took her, and she was turning down nothing. Because of the size and comprehensiveness of her following, she did not have the time to form real attachments. She was wide-eyed about the kindness of everyone. She was in love with all of her new milieu, star-struck by the beauty, the breeding, the ease and elegance of society's elect. As lovers are, she was blind to all but virtue. She noted their charm and their grace and their 'entire lack of self-assertion'. Writing later about the balls and receptions at which she spent her evenings, she noted, 'While I carried away with me from these functions a general sense of pomp and grandeur, there was a simplicity about the people which one finds only in those born to greatness . . . they were absolutely free from the affectation and "small-ness" which, sooner or later, make their appearance in many who merely buy a position with money.' The aristocracy were not just blue-blooded. They were generous in spirit and natural and eager to welcome her into their hearts. When the star of her popularity guttered and sank, Lillie would sing another song. As her friends melted away she suffered bitter disappointment and disillusion. In too many cases she found that their hearts were not as developed as their pedigrees. And she learnt, most brutal lesson of all, that charm is a habit, not an indication of affection.

With the loss of Lillie's social innocence came the knowledge of who her real friends were, all of whom she met in this first Season, but not all of whom she recognized as such. In Society, they were Gladys Lonsdale, Augusta Fane and Mrs Cornwallis West, the Reuben Sassoons, and the society solicitor George Lewis; in Bohemia, Frank Miles, Millais, Whistler and Oscar Wilde. These last two, though their influence belongs more to Lillie's later years in Society, 1879 onwards, were to have a profound and permanent effect. Her friendship with both men, of the utmost importance in her development, is frustratingly sparse in its documentation. In the case of Whistler, whom Lillie met at the Sebrights' party, there are no accounts of her sitting for a portrait before 1881, after her crisis and departure from London. In fact they must have begun some kind of an acquaintance immediately after they met in May 1877. Lillie was the artistic sensation of the moment and Whistler was an impatient man. It is impossible to imagine him waiting in line behind Millais, Watts, Burne-Jones and Poynter before pursuing Lillie as muse or model or mistress. Besides, he and Frank Miles were already close friends and Miles was making quite a fanfare of Lillie as his Muse. Miles was to claim that he discovered and invented Lillie. He made sure that she was introduced to his Society patrons and he also made sure that she was seen by the painters of his acquaintance, chief among whom he would have counted Whistler. Leslie Ward, the portrait painter and cartoonist for *Spy*, recalled Miles collaring him at a reception in 1877, saying, 'Leslie, I know you like to see lovely faces. I have one of the most wonderful creatures I have ever seen coming to my studio. Come and I'll introduce you.'

Frank Miles was also responsible for introducing Lillie to Oscar Wilde. He and Wilde had met two years earlier through Lord Ronald Gower, second son of the Duke of Sutherland, a sculptor and a homosexual. Miles had visited Wilde subsequently in Ireland and by 1877 they were friends enough for Wilde to stay in Miles's London lodgings for a fortnight or so, after Magdalen had rusticated him for truancy. His offence was an extra-curricular trip to Greece that extended itself into term-time. He was outraged by his punishment, claiming later that he was sent down 'for being the first under-graduate to visit Olympia'. Nevertheless, rustication had its compensations. He was in residence with Miles during that first week in May when Lillie took the Sebrights' drawing-room by storm. Miles would have returned to

Thames House full of her beauty, regaling Wilde, perhaps over a shared late breakfast, with the details of her Phidian perfection and her poverty. Later that evening Wilde excused himself, after an outing with his Oxford friend Bodley, to watch *Our Boys* at the Vaudeville, on the grounds that he was going 'to meet the loveliest woman in Europe'. Wilde, of course, was bowled over, though it would be a year or so before he could begin his worship of Lillie in earnest. He had to return to his problems, academic and financial, but the seeds of an important alliance had been sown. Later, Lillie, Miles, Wilde and Whistler shared an intimacy that Lillie's few notes show her to have treated as golden.

Not all painters had such lively, or socially productive, studios as Miles. Lillie also spent a great deal of time with George Frederick Watts, to whom, of course, she was sitting. He was the grand old man of British painting, known for scooping up Ellen Terry at seventeen to be his child-bride (he was in his forties) and then deserting her because she was too immature. There is, in her memoirs, an amusing account of how he chose to depict Lillie in 'a quaint little poke bonnet from which', she recalls, 'he ruthlessly tore the opulent ostrich feather which I regarded at that time as the glory of my head-gear'. Her sessions with Watts were very unlike those with Miles. Miles was a friend, but Watts a master, and Lillie was grateful to be able to sit at his feet. Her account is affectionate and evocative.

> Watts . . . lived absolutely alone, rather hermit like, in a reposeful, artistic, Queen Anne house off Holland Park . . . One always felt at rest with him. I spent hours and hours posing without experiencing strain or fatigue. For one portrait alone I gave him forty sittings, and it still remains unfinished. It was to be called 'Summer', and represented me full-face, in purple and gold drapery, holding a large basket of roses in my arms, and with a background of bluest sky.
>
> Sometimes scarcely a stroke of work was done in the studio. Watts would ring for tea, ignore the sitting and, instead, entertain me with lengthy dissertations on art. They were really absorbing lectures, and through him I learned in some measure to appreciate the mysteries and splendours of his favourite Italian school. Subsequently, when I visited the famous galleries of Europe, I realized what a debt I owed to him. He had an extremely sympathetic nature, and interested himself in the smallest details of my life; some of my happiest hours were spent in the company of this soft-voiced, gentle-mannered artist, whom I shall always regard as the greatest poetical painter of his time.

It is a glowing and emotional tribute. In part this is because Lillie was a social chameleon. She had great charm, and this charm made her suit herself to the mood or requirements of her companion. The process was effortless because instinctive. Many have accused her of manipulation and of course charm is manipulative, but in these days she did no homework about her acquaintance. She divined the needs of those she met like she breathed. She charmed, and she met the results of her charm with warmth not opportunism. One day while sitting to Watts she happened to notice 'how strikingly his pointed white beard, flowing gown, and black skull-cap, make him resemble the master he worshipped – Titian'. Lillie naturally made the comparison – having probably just discovered, from him, what Titian looked like. 'Nothing', she recalls, 'pleased him so much as to be told of this resemblance. It produced in him the ingenuous pleasure of a child. How simple are the great! And such a charming simplicity!'

Watts's interest in 'the smallest details' of Lillie's life means that she was talking to him about herself and, given her tendency to confide in older men, she more than likely told him of her marriage and its shortcomings. Why she did not talk to her father is unclear. Perhaps she felt he was too far away, or perhaps she was too proud to admit that her family had been right about Ned. Whatever the reason, she continued to find father-figures among those around her, and lean on them for support and guidance.

Another friend, a truer and closer confidant than Watts, was Millais, the first to stake his claim at the Sebrights', and always the favourite. Lillie spent many hours sitting to him or walking out with him in the Park near his house. He was very like Lillie in many ways, natural, vigorous, fond of practical jokes. Lady St Helier, hostess to literary London, gives a charming account in her memoirs.

> He was the most joyous, happy, delightful creature – apparently the
> strongest man in the world – full of 'go' and fun, and had an endless fund
> of conversation of which he never tired, with a delightful way of forcing
> his audience to listen to him by talking very loudly, and striking his hand
> on the table in order to attract their attention.

'Go' is what the Le Bretons had in abundance. Interviewed in later life Millais' grandson, the 'Bubbles' boy, said that all his life Millais disliked 'authority and restriction'. He was expelled from the only school he ever attended, when, on the third day, he bit the master. Lillie's brothers would have approved. Like the Le Breton boys, too, Millais had a refreshingly irreverent attitude towards the great and the good. Lillie recalls one incident when the two of them were walking in Knightsbridge. They came across a mutual acquaintance, Lord Wolseley, who was looking 'rather self-satisfied'. She goes on,

> We stopped to speak to him, and the artist, with a sly glance at me, said, 'We have just been admiring a first-rate portrait of you!' Lord Wolseley, who was very pleased, asked, 'Where?' 'My dear fellow,' replied Millais, 'you will find it on the pavement a little farther on, sandwiched between the Eddystone Lighthouse and a flitch of bacon!'

No wonder she felt so at home with him. Besides, he was also strikingly good-looking. Lady St Helier called him, 'to the last day of his life . . . quite one of the handsomest men of his generation'. Lillie's own account is simply reminiscent of her father.

> He was tall and broad shouldered; his handsome, ruddy, mobile countenance was strong rather than sensitive in character, and his swinging walk suggested the moors and the sportsman. Manly is the only word which will accurately describe the impression he made. Later, when I came to know him better, I discovered that he affected none of the eccentricities of dress or manner usually ascribed to artists, that he was quite sane, and that in his working hours he did not wear a velvet jacket, but a well-worn home-spun coat, which, I am sure, had done yeoman service on his beloved Scotch moors.

So Lillie was walking out with Millais as well as sitting to him. There was clearly no room in her life for Ned, except in the evenings, when his possessiveness still drove him to act as her chaperone. She must, at twenty-four, have had emotional needs that were not answered by a family in the Channel Islands and a husband by whom she was bored. Was she perhaps a little in love with Millais? It would be surprising if she were not. He was, after all, so very like the adored father and brothers she had left behind. At this date, too, she did invest a great deal, sometimes with confusing results, in her relationships with men. She was missing her family. In the case of Millais, he was robust enough to survive her attentions, and would have seen them for what they really were: evidence of loneliness and a warm nature. When Lillie first sat to Millais, in May 1877, he would still have been in his studio in Cromwell Place. Here he painted her as Effie Deans, the first of her portraits to be formally exhibited, shown at the Royal Academy the following year. She continued to sit to him over the next two years and became genuinely fond not just of Millais but also of his Scottish wife, Ruskin's Effie, spurned by him because, when he undressed her, he found she was flesh and not marble.

In the summer of her second season Lillie knew the Millais family well enough to take Ned to stay for a month with them in a rented house in Scotland. This for Lillie was the calm before the storm, since she was, for the first time, emotionally out of her depth in a love affair, and afraid to capsize. Ned, who was losing patience, was appeased by the fishing and the absence of crowds and Lillie won herself a breathing space. Both were naturally more at home in the country. While the men fished, Lillie and Lady Millais walked and picnicked in Birnam Wood. At the end of the day's sport there would be tea on the lawn, at which Lillie remembered,

> Sir John would settle himself in a chair and make sketches of me in every position and on any scrap of paper that was handy, evidently for the pure pleasure of using his pencil, for when the drawings were finished he would carelessly throw them down anywhere, but his wife, shrewd Scotch-woman that she was, went about carefully gathering them up, and saying, 'These will be verra valuable one day.'

It is a warm and energetic account, and the mimicry was very much a trademark. She must have felt freer. But, however hearty Millais was and however free from affectation, his attention to her beauty was still unflagging and exorbitant. She was always a model and a Muse. While painting, he would apply himself for twenty minutes and then stop to smoke and stare for a quarter of an hour before resuming his work. 'He told me,' Lillie recalled, 'that I was the most exasperating subject he had ever painted, that I looked just beautiful for about fifty-five out of sixty minutes, but for five in every hour I was amazing.'

Chapter VII

Idolaters in Society

If she was being grateful and demure in the studios of the masters, Lillie was learning other lessons in society. She had begun, not unnaturally, to acquire admirers. Many were married, some were not. The general rule for the fast set was that a woman was untouchable until she had secured her husband's line with a couple of heirs. After that, no one would raise an eyebrow because the younger children in the nursery had hair or eyes of a different colour. Intriguing was another way of passing the time. Many women had at least one lover and 'a scandal was a romance until it was found out'. Divorce was out of the question and husbands who were jealous or possessive dealt with their discoveries in their own ways. Lord Londonderry, who was shown his wife's adulterous love letters, refused to speak to her for half a century, reiterating his vow on his deathbed, but lived in the same houses, ate at the same table, and stood at her shoulder receiving guests every time they held a reception. His intransigence was exceptional but many people would go to any lengths to prevent a scandal. The servants knew the rules: when the child of a worker on the Duke of Westminster's estate claimed to have seen the Prince of Wales 'lying on top' of Mrs Cornwallis West in the woods, she was beaten by her father and told she would be 'killed if she repeated the story'. If a woman was found out and her husband proved jealous, he could ban her from communicating with her lover and she had to comply. If the couple were wilful, the Prince of Wales could be relied on to reinforce the husband's edict with a royal command. Hearts were often broken. The active Mrs Cornwallis West was in love with the Irish rake Lord Rossmore when they were discovered and banned from meeting. Leonie Jerome, in a letter to her sister, gives a good picture of how things could go wrong for even the most accomplished of flirts. She had seen Mrs Cornwallis West at a hunt ball, arriving late for dinner in travelling clothes, and writes,

She really is lovely. She had on a stamped velvet cloak, the satin part red and the velvet part black, and a black velvet beret – poor thing she looked so ill – but so pretty . . . It seems she came to the ball expressly to see Rossmore – as she had just arrived from Cannes, but Rossmore promised Mr West never to speak to her again et elle a beau faire he won't – so she only stayed one hour and then went back to the lodge . . . But isn't she lovely!

Discretion was the golden rule but a great deal of the pleasure, for those in the know, was vicarious. A couple of years later, her Society lessons truly learnt, Lillie was to write to Lord Wharncliffe, 'And so Lady Walters is with Shouvaloff at Carlsbad! – It must be rather amusing to watch that affair – She is *really* very much in love with him.' A hostess had to be up to the minute with her information, so as to arrange the bedrooms to everyone's convenience. Corridor-creeping was rife, the pack being frequently, and often farcically, shuffled. There are plenty of stories which feature the wrong lovers in the wrong rooms, including one in which Charlie Beresford, the Prince's particular friend, leapt into bed between the Bishop of Leicester and his wife, roaring, 'Cock-a-doodle-doo!' The story was such a good one it was recycled several times with different protagonists. To make sure that everyone was back in his proper place when it mattered, gongs were beaten, once in the evening, to announce the arrival of servants to attend the dressing for dinner, and again in the morning, before the maids set out with tea and hot water for washing.

During the season the favoured time for dalliance was *le cinq-à-sept*, between tea and dressing for dinner. Ladies shopped, made calls and rode out in the morning. In the afternoon they were at home. Gentlemen called in the afternoon, taking their hats and canes into the lady's drawing-room with them and laying them down by their chair. This was meant to give the impression that they would be staying only for a moment. It also saved the husband, should he return from his club or his own assignation early, from any uncomfortable feelings of usurpation. Corsets and stays were changed for loose flowing tea-gowns that looked not unlike sumptuous nightdresses. Finally, the lady would ring for tea and it was then understood that no one would disturb her and her guest until she rang again for it to be taken away.

For lovers who wanted to chance walking out together there were, according to Daisy Warwick, more rules. 'If a society woman met a man – even her own brother – in the park or in a restaurant, when he was accompanied by his mistress or an actress, he would not raise his hat to her. He cut her and she understood.' This was more often for cases where the mistress was a professional, not a member of Society. In general it was thought preferable for a young man to take a lover from his own class rather than an actress or a prostitute. There was always the possibility that he might feel tempted to propose and if his beloved was already married to a fellow peer then so much the better. No one wanted the purity of the great houses diluted with bad blood. These were, after all, the days of the *demi-monde* and the professionals were often much better at looking like ladies than the ladies themselves. The second half of the century, alive to the danger they represented, saw endless complaints in magazines and journals about 'fine young English gentlemen' openly associating with London's harlots. Paul Pry observed in 1857 that 'there can be no disguising the fact that at the West End, at Brompton, at St John's Wood, Foley Place, Portland Road, Regent's Park . . . some of the most magnificent women in London live under the protection of gentlemen'. One gentleman's club made a brave attempt to clear the moral muddle, pinning a notice on the door of the ladies' dining-room which ran: 'Members are requested not to bring their mistresses into the club, unless they happen to be the wives of other members.'

Prostitution, in fact, was very hard to ignore. In a population of two and a quarter million, London boasted between 80,000 and 120,000 whores. At the top level there was quite a living to be made. The courtesans who were the queens of the trade dressed like the best, drove their broughams in the Park at the fashionable hour and openly competed with the finest and fairest Society had to offer. It was only in the novels of Dickens and Mrs Gaskell that they stumbled coughing through the ooze of the Docklands moaning for the river and beseeching their companions to stamp upon them and kill them. Many made considerable fortunes, married and turned to charitable works. In Paris in the early seventies, they were acknowledged if not positively encouraged. Accepted by a Society that was titillated by opulent sensuality, they were expected to put on an even more glorious show than ladies of the first rank. They gave dinners off gold plate, held levees at which they bathed in champagne, owned châteaux, kept racehorses, and drove out down the Bois de Boulogne in marvellous carriages. Cora Pearl, the London-born whore, was so rich and fashionable that she gave balls in her house to which the Princesse Pauline von Metternich and the Duchesse de Cadou were not ashamed to go.

London, however, was never quite so yielding. Courtesans were, in

general, not acceptable, though some did manage to marry gentlemen
and leave their pasts behind them. Agnes Willoughby married Lord
Windham; Laura Bell, Gladstone's great love, married Mr Thistlethwaite
and became a religious enthusiast. For the most part, however,
courtesans were to be found only by those who sought them out, in places
such as the Argyll Rooms, where they paraded their finery under
expensive gaslights, among the tat and tinsel of plate-glass and gilding.

In 1861 prostitution came to the Park in the person of Catherine
Walters. Her lover at the time ran a coaching stables and, thinking to help
his own trade with a little pimping, he fitted her out with a skin-tight
habit and a high-stepping hack and sent her into Hyde Park. The 'Ladies'
Mile' ran from the statue of Achilles down the northern side of the
Serpentine and was the place where ladies of rank and fashion exercised
their driving skills and impressed their society cavaliers. To have
prostitutes in open competition with them, plying for trade in their
midst, was a matter for public outrage but was not preventable. Women
like Catherine were no doubt very much more attractive than their
Society counterparts and many a girl's marriage prospects were impaired
by the rival charms of her professional sisters. Professionally, the gamble
paid off. Catherine, known as Skittles because she had worked in a
Liverpool skittles alley as a child, was so distinguished a horsewoman
that she caught the eye of the Marquess of Hartington. Soon the whole
of London had noticed her, and *The Times* ran a controversial open letter
on her appeal.

Early in the season of 1861, a young lady whom I must call Anonyma . . .
made her appearance in the Park. She was a charming creature, beautifully
dressed, and she drove with ease and spirit two of the handsomest brown
ponies eye ever beheld. Nobody in society had seen her before; nobody in
society knew her name, or to whom she belonged, but there she was,
prettier, better dressed, and sitting more gracefully in her carriage than
any of the fine ladies who envied her her looks, her skill, or her equipage
. . . As the fame of her beauty and her equipage spread . . . the highest
ladies in the land enlisted themselves as her disciples. Driving became the
rage. Three, four, five, six hundred guineas were given for a pair of ponies
on the condition they should be as handsome as Anonyma's, that they
should show as much breeding as Anonyma's, that they should step as
high as Anonyma's. If she wore a pork pie hat, they wore pork pie hats; if
her paletot was made by Poole, their paletots were made by Poole. If she
reverted to more feminine attire, they reverted to it also. Where she drove,
they followed; and I must confess none of them sit, dress, drive, or look as

well as she does; nor can any of them procure for money such ponies as Anonyma contrives to get – for love.

By 1872 Skittles had retired from her position of pre-eminence in the Park to a house in South Street, where she held salons that Gladstone is supposed to have attended. So Lillie would not have seen her, or her cohort of mounted cavaliers, but her effect, nevertheless, lingered. The Park had become an acknowledged place for intrigues, charged with the hint of the brothel, delicious with the confusion of tarts who might have been ladies and ladies who were probably tarts. Lillie could not have remained unaware of the desirability of riding or driving rather than simply walking among the crowd. It would have set the seal on her arrival in Society, and it would have been good for her following – nothing was so irresistible to the *fin de siècle* Englishman as a lady on horseback. Besides, she loved to ride. There was, too, a further dimension which Lillie could not have formulated but which *Vanity Fair* pinpoints in an article that compares the Park to a stage. Even before she became an actress Lillie responded to the elements of theatre that life in Society entailed. 'Entering Rotten Row', the article begins, 'in the crowded hours of the season's glory is, in fact, like stepping on the stage of a theatre . . . Bipeds and quadrupeds are alike conscious of the fact, and cast shy glances, toss their curls, square their heels and shoulders, essay curvets, and cock their hats, or their tails, as nature and vanity dictate.'

The stage was still a long way in the future for Lillie but there is a degree to which her success in society was a form of training for it and made it, when the time came, almost a natural consequence. In these early days of her first season, while she was still finding her feet, she was acting several parts, juggling her options and choosing who to become. In the studios of the painters, and now, in the great houses of London, she was by turns demure pupil, Victorian romantic heroine, flirt, iconoclast, foreigner and Le Breton. She was aware of the role that Society had cast for her, and though she was acting up to it, she was also making decisions about how much and in which directions she would really change. She was not yet indulging in the affairs that those around her found so diverting, but she had always enjoyed a dangerous game and Society's intrigues were just that.

Among her many admirers Lillie had two who were particularly insistent. They called on her separately at teatime, offered her joint riding lessons and claimed her on the dance floor. They were John Leslie and Moreton Frewen, who coincidentally married the sisters of Jennie

Churchill, Leonie and Clara. Of the two, Frewen appears to have been the more colourful. He was an adventurer, the son of a Sussex landowner of moderate fortune, who spent most of his life and all of his money on elaborate and unlikely projects. Known to his more waggish friends as 'Mortal Ruin', he embodied that particular late Victorian mix of brilliance and physical daring sunk, as so often, in a life of stupefying unproductivity. He ran the Varsity drag at Cambridge in 'the days when a master of hounds preceded a master of arts'. His claims to fame, when Lillie knew him, were his winning of a midnight steeplechase, run against Mrs Cornwallis West's Lord Rossmore, and his hunting exploits. He rode with the Wodehousian gods of the field, Lord Lonsdale, Bay Middleton, Chicken Hartopp and Whyte Melville. The most dashing of his rides were immortalized, or intended to be so, in *The Cream of Leicestershire*, on the cover of which he is seen riding through the railway cut on the great Ranksborough run of 1877. He was, as his biography describes him,

> fairly gifted with physique. He was one of the best gentlemen-riders in England. And he had a first class mind untroubled by second thoughts. He had a lightening range over the world of theory and a certain arrogance towards facts . . . His mixed philosophy was gathered partly from the green fields of the chase and partly from the greener tables of gambling. He believed that with the best of friends, as with the best of horses, he could get anywhere.

Lillie would have been impressed by his *Boys' Own* hero status but she was not so blinded as to be unable to tease him when they first met. He arrived late to dinner, preceded no doubt by his reputation, and her opening gambit was to ask solemnly, 'What are your spiritual beliefs?' He noted in his diary that evening that she was 'too small and slight of throat and neck, little Greek head all perfect', adding, 'but I felt that I required direction'.

It was not long before Frewen and his friend Leslie were calling at Eaton Place for direction and diversion. Most of their courtship of Lillie was done as a double act and she took neither of them seriously. Their first objective, which matched her own, was to get her into the Park. Frewen presented her with a magnificent chestnut hack called Redskin and offered to teach her to ride. Lillie, who was to adore the horse, did not bother to correct the donor's naïve assumptions. Riding lessons were part of her role-playing, carried out presumably to her own huge but private amusement. According to Leslie, when Frewen first hoisted her on to her mount she fell off the other side in a suitably feminine dead faint, straight into the arms of Leslie, who had to catch her and revive her. It is a Laurel and Hardy scene. She also had to be caught when they came to visit her singly for tea. Again Leslie solemnly recorded the effect of an unattended male in her drawing-room. She would wait until the maid had left, fix her guest 'with her huge blue eyes and appear to swoon, the idea being that the charm of his person had rendered her senseless'. All this was an amusing way of treating the inappropriate sighings and protestations of young unattached men. It was naughty and it meant a great business of supporting her in her affliction, fanning her face, loosening of clothes and fussing, but it was a joke for Lillie. Whether or not they knew that she was laughing at them is difficult to tell. They went on calling and she went on enjoying their attentions, but she was sensible enough to see that they had nothing serious to offer. What she was also doing, of course, was dipping her toe in the waters of adultery. Her hesitation had less to do with morality than it did with the practicalities and limitations of her new position. She had grown up with her father's example, after all, and was presumably unshockable. Her scruples were few and her appetites frank and free. It could not be long before she fell.

Chapter VIII

Fallen Angels

If admirers were for laughing at, her husband cold, and her family far away, Lillie needed people with whom she could relax and to whom she could really talk. She had her older, father-figure confidants, Millais and Watts, but now for the first time she began to enjoy the company of female friends. Lillie had never really known women in the way she knew men, and her relationships with her own sex were different from those she was enjoying with the painters and the cavaliers. This was new ground for Lillie and she was treading carefully. Characteristically, she chose her friends from the wildest Society had to offer, but she treated them with a strange deference. They were the old-hands; she was the new, and she was aware of the hierarchy. It was also useful to her. These society gad-abouts were the nearest thing to a role model in her new life, and whatever else they might have been they were not prim like her island peers. Sometime during this first season she and the slighted Mrs Cornwallis West became what Lillie described as 'great friends, almost sisters'. The Wests lived at 49 Eaton Place, a few doors down from the Langtrys. On the ground floor William West had a studio in which he toyed with a few paintbrushes and made a gathering place for upmarket Bohemia. Millais and Leighton were among his more frequent guests. The rest of the house was open to Society. The wicked Beresford brothers came calling, the Duke of Fife, who had given Mrs West a ptarmigan feather hat that she particularly prized, Lord Rossmore, even the Prince of Wales came, all to sit at the feet of the 'beautiful Irish savage' as Mrs West was known. Lillie's description of her looks is disappointing. She remembered her as

> petite, with a vivid complexion, golden hair worn short in the manner of to-day, and flashing hazel eyes; and equally attractive whether walking, on horseback, or in a ball gown. She was high-spirited, vivacious, and extremely witty, sometimes audaciously so, and the possessor of a fine singing voice.

What Lillie fails to convey is her daring and her scorn of convention. Lord Rossmore's account of their first meeting is more instructive. He had noticed her, 'the loveliest woman I have ever set eyes on', dressed in white with a huge white hat, surrounded by half a dozen men, and asked her name. Later the same day he had seen her again, at a ball given by the Prince of Wales, and recorded, 'I simply couldn't take my eyes off her.' He waited until she was talking to someone he knew and then went up and requested an introduction. ' "Hmmm," ' he was told, ' "I don't know whether Mrs West wants to know you." "Never mind," ' he countered, ' "I'll introduce myself." So,' in his own words, 'I turned to Mrs West and said with true Derry-daring, "Come on, let's have a dance." "Well, and I will, yer honour," she replied with the most tremendous brogue. Off we went. I was in seventh heaven, but I noticed that the floor seemed strangely empty.' Their heaven was shattered when they bumped into the Prince and Princess of Wales, for whom the floor had been cleared to open the dancing.

For a small woman Mrs West had a large number of names. She was Mary Adelaide Virginia Thomasina Eupatoria Cornwallis West, known to society as Patsy. Temperamentally she was very like Lillie, combining ambition with a spirited unconventionality. Her daughters made the two best marriages of their generation, one to the freezing Prince of Pless, and the other to the Duke of Westminster, who witnessed Patsy, at fifty, tobogganing down a flight of oak stairs on her skirts and remarked laconically that there were 'not many mothers-in-law like her'. There were probably not many wives like her, either. She had married at seventeen, and by the time she and Lillie met she had three children and was thoroughly bored of her husband's unflagging and vigilant adoration. Lillie gives a heartless account of a dinner at number 49 that is probably characteristic. Billed as an occasion on which this 'audacious Irish beauty bested her devoted husband', the story goes,

> going one evening to dine at their house with five or six congenial spirits, I noticed that his place at the table was unoccupied. No apology was offered nor allusion made to the circumstance until later in the meal, when the wine came to an end, and our hostess thereupon gaily informed us that we could not have any more as, having had a difference of opinion with our absent host, she had watched her opportunity and locked the poor man up in the wine cellar.

Presumably she taught Lillie a lesson or two about how to deal with a stale marriage, and if Lillie was not yet fashionably adulterous it would not be long before she was.

Lillie had two other close girlfriends. They were Augusta Fane and Gladys Herbert. Augusta was married to a Lincolnshire squire and seems to have been sensible and fairly ordinary. Gladys, who was her particular friend, was not. She was the sister of Lord Pembroke and was dangerously flamboyant. Over six feet tall, she was very beautiful. The French dress designer Worth remembered her being brought for her first fitting when only seventeen, and called her a 'lovely, slender, stately girl'. To an Englishman standing by, he mistakenly remarked, 'Of course she is very beautiful, but really she is a bit too tall.' The Englishman was outraged, drew himself up to his own full height, glared down at Worth and observed, 'But it is just such women who make the mothers of our fine tall men.' Motherhood for Gladys was still a treat in store. In due course, by a second marriage she was to have one daughter, to whom she was unrelentingly vile. When Lillie met her, she was a year away from marrying her first husband, George, the fourth Earl of Lonsdale and brother of hunting Hugh, whose time was devoted mostly to the consumption of alcohol and the enjoyment of actresses. He died, not long after they were married, in the squalor of a drinking bout, undertaken at a rented house in Bryanston Street, to which he was in the habit of taking his women. A drunken husband was only one of the things Gladys and Lillie were to have in common. The good Augusta wrote a shrewd sketch of her in her memoirs:

> Gladys had a fine character, and a broad outlook on life. She had, however, one fault – and that was an overwhelming curiosity to know everything and experience every sensation, and this inquisitiveness led her into dark places and amongst undesirable people, but fortunately it neither altered nor depressed her mind.

Lillie would have seen Gladys surrounded by a posse of admirers, all of whom were encouraged and most of whom were made ridiculous. Not the least among them, once she was married, was Alfred de Rothschild, who was unable to decide which he wanted most, the giantess or her renowned collection of pictures and china. He would arrive early in the morning and hammer on her bedroom door, calling out, 'My lady, my lady, £20,000 for the Boucher portrait of Madame de Pompadour, and a pair of pearl earrings for yourself.' The *pourboire* of his cousin Baron Ferdinand must have been larger, as he got the Boucher in the end. Lady

Lonsdale herself slipped through both their fingers and went on to become Lady de Grey, wife of the best shot in England, who had a fine moustache but little conversation. Lucy Cavendish, who was never nasty, wrote that Lord de Grey could be 'pretty nearly summed up as a shooting machine; kills double anybody else'. These were the days when the bag for an average day was 4,000 brace. This dazzling qualification for matrimony, however, quickly palled and Gladys turned her energies to other channels. These were, essentially, lovers, music and teasing her husband. She had the cheap tea service dropped behind his back so that he would think the best one gone (a joke Lillie would have revelled in). She became the single most important patron of the Royal Opera House, and she took Nijinsky and Sir John Lister Kaye as lovers. She also had an affair with Harry Cust, one of the most sought-after of the self-reverential Souls. It was she who, finding that she was sharing Cust's favours with Lady Londonderry, broke into his apartments and carried off the prize of her rival's love letters. These she read out loud at tea parties, and when tired of that she sent them off to Lord Londonderry with the terrible consequence of his vow of silence. Music was her serious interest and invitations to her musical soirées were highly prized. Needless to say, she had an unconventional technique of inviting, as one guest recalled, 'wives without their husbands and husbands without their wives, picking out the better of the two in each couple'.

This glittering career, both musical and amatory, was a long way in the future. When Lillie and Gladys met, in 1877, they were both in their fledgeling flamboyance. They were further back on the road than Patsy, their ambitions soaring, but unformed, their appetites still in the fury of their first awakening. Temperamentally they were well matched. Lillie, too, was drawn to the dark side, to the 'undesirable people'. Together they befriended the loucher elements of Bohemia, toyed with Swinburne and with Decadence, indulged their interest in sensual gratification. They had Patsy before them, to show them that marriage was not a tie but an extra freedom, and they had time, with nothing to fill it but pleasure.

Lillie was keeping dangerous company. She was charmed by the ease and elegance of the men she met in Society but it was in these women, so very different from the women of her childhood, that she must have caught the glimmerings of a new hope. In them she saw embodied the power to attract and hold attention, to command even, and a determination to shape their own destinies. She admired their high spirits and their style, the charm of their social engineering, and their ease in the presence of the great and the good. Most of all she admired their instinct for survival. Society was full of lessons for those who habitually sailed too close to the wind. There were the Churchills, the Aylesfords, and poor Lady Mordaunt, half insane, weeping out the names of her many lovers before a packed divorce court. The danger was half the thrill. As she watched her two friends, always on the edge, always trimming their sails with light-hearted, last-minute expertise, Lillie must have wondered, as an outsider, how much time she had got at the top – just how far, in their footsteps, she could go. But she was not watching all the time. The watching and the wondering would have been more a question of chill midnight pinpricks, a glimpse of a chasm, than sustained contemplation. There was little breathing space between the parties, and the badgering of artists and admirers, before she was whirled off again, with Patsy and Gladys ahead, daring her to keep pace.

It was survival of the fittest. Patsy and Gladys really were friends, but they were also rivals. In befriending Lillie they were riding her star, and there is just a sense, particular with Patsy, who was the smaller in character of the two, that they took a vicarious enjoyment in Lillie's risks. She had no money and no social position to fall back on, and a foot wrong would have been fatal. For Lillie it was life and death and that was titillating for her friends. It was Patsy, for instance, who was finally responsible for the demise of the famous black dress. This was probably a practical joke. Lillie was surprised one afternoon in Eaton Place by Patsy's whirlwind arrival in her drawing-room, apparently in 'a fever of excitement'. According to Lillie,

> She had come up from Ruthyn Castle, her husband's country place in Wales, without an evening dress, and suddenly she wished to attend the opera . . . She implored me to lend her my well-known garment. She carried it off, and, being absolutely reckless of my property, not only wore it to the opera, but went on to a ball afterwards, danced all night, and the next day my maid (with a beaming face) exhibited the gown to me practically in rags.

The story does not ring true. A woman like Patsy would have had hundred of dresses both in London and the country. If for some reason she had not, the maid, who would have done her packing, would have made sure one was included on pain of her position. It is much more likely that Patsy was carrying out a bet or a dare. There may have been much speculation over whether or not Lillie really had only one dress and this was a rather unkind way of settling the matter. There was also the question of how Lillie, who was known to be poor, would afford another one. Invitations would have to be turned down while a replacement was made and everyone could have laughed over the excuses. It was cruel and it showed up Lillie as an outsider, but it was the sort of joke that Lillie might have played herself. What is remarkable is that she failed to stall it, but it may be that she could not afford to deny her new best friend. It was indeed a hard world that she had chosen.

No doubt Society was gratified to see that Lillie did have to replace her derelict sartorial talisman with a newer and stronger model. She used the Jersey dressmaker who had her measurements, so she was still presumably unreconciled to the fitting process. The new dress was to be made of sterner stuff in case more beauties should suddenly find themselves with nothing to wear for several consecutive occasions. 'Madame's artistry', Lillie records, 'found expression this time in a black satin of such substance that it was a menace to the community when I danced.' So Lillie, no doubt aware of its impact, was still choosing to wear black. At the end of June, Lady Dudley gave a ball to which Lillie was invited. Georgina Dudley was in the top flight of professional beauty. As a teenager in Jersey, Lillie remembered, she had gazed at her picture in the local shop. After the success of her first season she had married Lord Dudley, for no obvious reason, since he was doddering, except that he might soon die and she could have a second chance. Margot Asquith admired her and remembered crowds gathering round her carriage, whenever it pulled up, 'to see this vision of beauty, holding a large holland umbrella over the head of her lifeless husband'.

The invitation to the Dudleys' ball had a condition attached. Lord Dudley could not bear the colour black. 'It depressed him strangely', presumably because it reminded him of his wife's imminent freedom. He forbade the wearing of it in his own house, and therefore, Lady Dudley was at pains to point out, they very much hoped Lillie would not mind putting off her mourning for one evening. 'The letter was so kindly expressed', Lillie records,

> that I could not feel offended, and as I had met her very often, and I liked her as much as I admired her, I immediately began to consider the question of indulging Lord Dudley's weakness for colours . . . Having decided that the function at Dudley House was worth the harassing ordeal of being 'fitted', I gave an order to a fashionable London dressmaker, and appeared at the ball in a white velvet, classically severe in line, and embroidered with pearls. Looking back, and judging from the sensation it

caused, it must have been a striking creation. As I entered the ballroom the dancers stopped and crowded round me, and as I pursued my way to greet my hostess they opened out to allow me to pass.

Mrs Stratton was the 'fashionable dressmaker' and Lillie had presumably got her name from her friends, to whom expense was no object and pearl beading a routine. She did not, of course, pay for the dress. She was a good enough advertisement to be given almost unlimited credit, and so she first – so light and so unthinking – put her foot on the pecuniary slide that would end in ruin.

With the demise of the black dress, the dowd of Graham Robertson's putative milliner was sloughed off and Lillie stepped forward, shimmering in creation after creation, a fully-fledged socialite. It must, in a way, have been a relief to her that she could survive and be accepted without it. In fact her renown ballooned, and as it did so the photographers were quick to realize that she provided a new subject. Soon there were photographs of her on sale everywhere, in every conceivable pose, her hair down, her hair up, in riding dress, ball dress, semi-undress, writing letters, gazing at dead birds with Victorian pity, or pinning a rose on her corsage. 'Presently,' she recalled,

> my portraits were in every shop-window, with trying results, for they made the public so familiar with my features that wherever I went – to theatres, picture-galleries, shops – I was actually mobbed . . . One night, shortly after their appearance, at a large reception at Lady Jersey's, many of the guests stood on chairs to obtain a better view of me, and I could not help but hear their audible comments on my appearance as I passed down the drawing-room. Itinerant vendors sold cards about the streets with my portrait ingeniously concealed, shouting, 'The Jersey Lily, the puzzle is to find her.'

Mobbing became a regular feature of her daily life, to the extent that a fair girl in a black dress who was mistaken for Lillie in the Park was carried off to St George's Hospital having lost consciousness in the ensuing crush. Lillie's precious liberties, and many of her pleasures, were of necessity curtailed. When her new friend Lady Rosslyn came to fetch her for a drive Lillie was disappointed to find a rather tame hack in the shafts of the carriage in place of the well-known high-stepping horse. Lady Rosslyn apologized with the explanation that the combination of Lillie in the carriage and the spirited horse drawing it would have been too risky.

Now Lillie's every move was watched and noted. The smallest adjustments to her dress were copied. When she twisted a bit of black velvet into a toque and stuck a feather through it to go to Sandown it was a matter of days before 'this turban appeared in every milliner's window labelled "The Langtry Hat".' Not all of the attention was welcome and Lillie soon began to feel the strain. 'It was very embarrassing,' she remembered later,

> and it had all come about so suddenly that I was bewildered. If I went for a stroll in the Park and stopped a moment to admire the flowers, people ran after me in droves, staring me out of countenance, and even lifting my sunshade to satisfy fully their curiosity. To venture out for a little shopping was positively hazardous, for the instant I entered an establishment to make a purchase, the news that I was within spread with the proverbial rapidity of wildfire, and the crowd about the door grew so dense that departure by the legitimate exit was rendered impossible, the obliging proprietors being forced, with many apologies, to escort me round to the back door.
>
> Instead of the excitement abating, it increased to such an extent that it became risky for me to indulge in a walk, on account of the crushing that would follow my appearance.

The scale and rapidity of London's reaction were overwhelming. Lillie, struggling to keep abreast of so many changes, had no time to adjust. Contemplation or stocktaking were out of the question. Like her brothers in childhood, her Society friends demanded that she keep up or be excluded. There were new manners, new morals, new conventions (and the breaking of them) that all had to be absorbed, and though she was drinking it in, she was desperately muddled. Looking back on it all in her memoirs she observes candidly that

> It would be difficult for me to analyse my feelings at this time. To pass in a few weeks from being an absolute 'nobody' to what the Scotch so aptly describe as a 'person'; to find myself not only invited to but watched for at all the great balls and parties; to hear the murmur as I entered the room; to be compelled to close the yard gates in order to avoid the curious, waiting crowd outside, before I could mount my horse for my daily canter in the Row; and to see my portrait roped round for protection at the Royal Academy – surely, I thought, London has gone mad, for there can be nothing about me to warrant this extraordinary excitement.

It would be easy to attribute her remarks to a decorous mock modesty – easy but, in this case, wrong. Lillie was genuinely upset by her success. The word that recurs again and again in her accounts of the period is 'bewilderment'. Nothing in her family life on Jersey could have prepared her for what she was now undergoing. Though she had been led to London by her ambitions, even in her wildest dreams of their fulfilment she could not have anticipated such a response. It was, after all, unprecedented. The passage from the memoirs continues, 'I felt apologetic, and inclined to disclaim aloud any hand in bringing about the strange attitude of all classes in London towards me.' Guilt, incomprehension and loneliness now underlay the headlines of her triumph. A reporter asked her in her seventies whether she might have been happier without her famous beauty. Her response was honest but qualified, answering with a laugh,

> What a question to ask a woman! What woman would not be beautiful if she had the chance? . . . Life has taught me that beauty can have its tragic side. It is like great wealth in that respect. It promotes insincerity, and it breeds enemies. A really beautiful woman, like a very rich man, can be the loneliest person in the world. She is lucky if she knows her friends.

These were lessons that, even in the first months of her discovery, she was having to learn. But if she was already feeling the misery and complication of her position, she was feeling it alone. Ned's reactions were all too clear. He had been a reluctant enough chaperone but his new duties as a bodyguard were infuriating. In the same interview Lillie observed,

> I never wanted this publicity . . . I was shocked and bewildered when it came. I remember my husband used to be terribly annoyed at it all. He used to lose his temper and blame me.

Ned's temper was to be a feature of the following years, exacerbated, no doubt, by drink. It has even been said that on occasion he beat Lillie. Whether he did or not, his presence was now a threat rather than a reassurance. By the end of June, in the freshness of her triumph, Lillie found herself, in a foreign capital, a country girl, proclaimed a goddess, flattered, excited, disoriented, lonely and afraid of her husband. It was not the sort of cocktail to produce rational and carefully considered behaviour.

Chapter IX

The Prince of Wales

On 19 May 1877 *Vanity Fair* had officially recorded Lillie's arrival in Society with a brief flourish of condescension.

> All male London is going wild about the Beautiful Lady who has come to us from the Channel Islands. She is certainly the most splendid creature that has ever risen upon London from an unknown horizon, and so far beyond the pretty with which we are usually more than content, that it is as though some newer and more perfect creature had risen, like Aphrodite, from the sea. She has a husband to make her happy, but still awaits a poet to make her known.

The comparison with Aphrodite prefigures Wilde's later and more deftly turned image, but, Aphrodite aside, it is a rather demure paragraph in the context of so much attention and change. What *Vanity Fair* misses, with its portrait of calm seas and domestic bliss, is the storm, at once public and personal, that now caught Lillie amidships. In these strange hot months of early summer, before she had time to gather her wits, Lillie's private indecision and her teetering morals were swept away, and she herself, flung headlong on the consequences of her celebrity.

By her own account, late in June, just before the Dudley ball, Lillie and Ned were invited to a supper given by Sir Allen Young at his London house after the opera. Alleno, as he was popularly known, was one of the first arctic explorers, a bachelor, and a man about town. By the summer of 1877 he had made several abortive attempts to reach the North Pole and had just returned from an expedition to find the North West Passage. He was one of the new rich, the son of a city merchant, and something of a celebrity himself. As befits a man of action he was elegant and taciturn, known for his 'shrewd good sense', and not for his conversation, which was minimal. He 'talked very little and thought a great deal', as Augusta

Fane recorded. And one of the things he thought abut was women. He had a collection of the most beautiful whom he took with him on board his yacht for Cowes week, and to which he now added Lillie. She gives her description of him in her memoirs.

> He was a fidgety creature, already in the forties, and had in his grey eyes the curious, faraway look which one associates with an explorer. He had very little small talk, replying mostly in monosyllables when addressed, but he was chivalrously devoted to his friends.

The 'chivalrous devotion' manifested itself in the form of hospitality. When he was not exploring, but in London, he entertained in some style, keeping, as Augusta Fane remembers, an open house, 'in the most literal sense of the word, never allowing his front door to be closed night or day, as he declared he could not breathe if it was shut.' On this particular night in June, it was a small party of ten or so who waited, in the breeze, to dine, with Lillie wondering at the delay. She records,

> Suddenly, there was a stir, followed by an expectant hush, a hurried exit of Sir Allen, then a slight commotion outside, and presently I heard a deep and cheery voice say: 'I am afraid I am a little late.' Sir Allen murmured something . . . in reply, and the Prince of Wales, whose face had been previously unfamiliar to me except through photographs, appeared in the doorway of Stratford Place drawing-room.

The Langtrys were the only members of the party to whom the Prince was unknown, and Lillie records extreme nervousness at her introduction. His appearance was made more brilliant than usual by several 'glittering orders' that adorned his chest and the blue ribbon of the garter. Whether or not Lillie really was ignorant of the purpose of the evening, it must have been immediately and flatteringly obvious that the Prince had asked for the meeting to be arranged. She was, of course, seated beside him at supper. In her memoirs she describes her conversation as 'monosyllabic'. This was partly the result of nerves but partly, too, that she was too intelligent to try to impress. She was feeling her way, waiting to see which of her many roles the Prince would respond to best. Her own account gives a good indication of the speed and shrewdness of her perceptions.

> . . . though silent, I was immensely interested in watching the Prince, and soon realised that, while good-natured and pleasant to everyone, he

preserved his dignity admirably, in fact I decided that he would have been a brave man who, even at this little *intime* supper-party, attempted a familiarity with him.

She was right, and it was clever of her. Though he loathed intellectuals, the Prince liked clever people – liked brains, in fact, almost as much as he liked beauty.

How disingenuous was Lillie's account of her meeting with the Prince? Like all the incidents in her memoirs it suffers from her sense of the drama of her position. She was, after all, writing her story, and after a decade or so on the stage it would be strange if she had learnt no lessons about how to present her material and hold the attention of her audience. It is unlikely that Sir Allen had not warned her. But forewarning would not necessarily have dispelled her nerves. Meeting the Prince at his request was the final proof of her success. It was also, as she may have been aware, the best opportunity yet for ensuring that her success matured into something more permanent.

To see the Prince as Lillie must have done for the first time, we must forget the bullying analyses of his many biographers, and imagine him in the glory of his untried potential. Lillie was new to London and her knowledge of him would have come mainly from papers and periodicals and her Society friends. In the 1870s the Prince was the acknowledged head of a Society that was newly woken into a rainbow dazzle of activity. He was in London, he was charming, he was not in mourning as his mother had been for almost two decades, and he was happy to be seen by his public. His mother's reservations, that so colour the modern picture of him, were, if not private, then known only to a few members of the court. He was perceived as racy, and had had a period of intense unpopularity after his appearance in court as a witness in the Mordaunt divorce case, but in general he was liked. He was gifted, as Lord Morley later observed, with 'just the character that Englishmen . . . thoroughly understand, thoroughly like . . . He combined regal dignity with bonhomie, and strict regard for form with entire absence of spurious pomp.' Meeting him in the 1870s, only a few years before Lillie, Lady Frederick Cavendish drew an exact and unsentimental portrait in her journal.

He does not get on with me, nor indeed with any but chaffy, fast people, though always kind and delightful in manner . . . he is amiable and truthful, and has sense and good feeling; my conviction is that, when he succeeds to the throne and has *duties* to do, he will do far better than now seems likely; but the melancholy thing is that neither he nor the darling Pcss. ever care to open a book.

Lady Frederick was a clear-sighted observer. The Prince was indeed shallow and dissolute, but he was kind and warm-hearted too. Later he was to prove that in matters where his heart was engaged he committed himself with characteristic energy. As a member of the Royal Commission on the Housing of the Working Classes he was both effective and conscientious. Indeed on one of his incognito tours of the worst of London's slums, he was so affected by what he saw that his companions had to prevent him making contributions there and then out of his own pocket, rushing him away before his disguise was penetrated. Afterwards he broke precedent in the House of Lords to speak with vigour on the need for slum clearance.

For the most part the Prince's social activity was the result of frustration. His most serious fault, as far as the court was concerned, was his indiscretion. He had been known to pass official documents round the dinner table for the edification of the assembled company. As a result the Queen trusted him with no state secrets and few honorary positions. Mostly this did not matter to him since he was not in the least interested in domestic politics, and, though he was interested in foreign affairs, loathed bureaucracy. His talents, which were ambassadorial, needed a social context, in which his tact and his natural diplomacy could shine. Though government bored him, he had shrewd and unerring instincts for the sympathies of the people. While his energies, which, like Lillie's, were superhuman, were thwarted of a serious outlet, he sank himself in a ceaseless whirl of gaiety and recreation. When called upon to justify himself, he observed, with some acumen, that 'we live in radical times and the more the people see the sovereign the better it is for the people and for the country'. He was right. Even *The Times* had complained of the Queen's continued absence from the capital – not that she cared about the press. To her son she remarked with a chilling conditional, 'If you ever become king, you will find all these friends *most* inconvenient.'

Bertie, as the Prince was familiarly known, had indeed a great number of friends. He possessed beautiful manners and immense charm. In conversation he was quick-witted and equally quickly bored. Ponsonby, born into the Household, remembers him drumming on chair or table with irritable fingers, muttering the while, 'Quite so, quite so.' This made

Lillie with her mother, Emilie, and father William Corbet Le Breton, and one of her six brothers, outside the Deanery

Below: Lillie at 21, just before her marriage to Ned Langtry

Above: Reggie Le Breton, Lillie's favourite brother, who died in a riding accident

The young Langtrys, newly married and looking distinctly Hogarthian

'The Milliner's Assistant': Lillie at the dawn of her discovery

The Prince of Wales,
who became Lillie's lover in 1877

Alexandra,
the beautiful Princess of Wales

The Red House,
Bournemouth,
which the Prince
built for Lillie as
their special
retreat

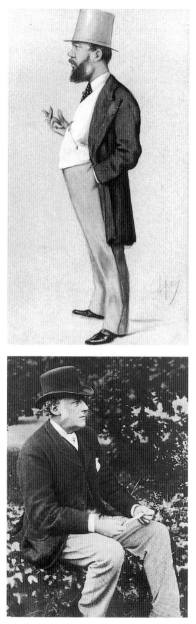

Lord Wharncliffe, patron of the arts, who became Lillie's trusted friend and confidant. Cartoon by Ape

Frank Miles

Sir John Everett Millais, Lillie's compatriot and favourite

James Abbott McNeill Whistler

'Jersey Lilies', by Frank Miles, one of the portraits that first spread Lillie's fame

Edward Poynter's portrait, reminiscent of Rossetti's 'Lady Lilith', one of the pioneering Pre-Raphaelite works of the 1860s, which confirmed Lillie's status as the ideal incarnate

Oscar Wilde, Lillie's friend and mentor

Prince Louis of Battenberg, Lillie's lover and possible father of her child

Arthur Jones, Lillie's childhood friend from Jersey and great love

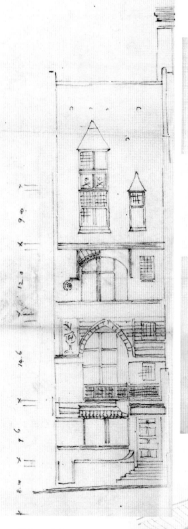

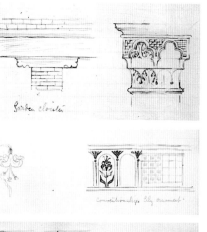

Garden cloister

Conventionalized Lily ornament

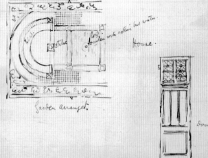

Garden arrangement

House.

Door

Edward Godwin's drawings for a house in Tite Street, Chelsea, commissioned by Lillie in her first days on the stage, while she was still effectively bankrupt

him frightening to those who could not keep up. Added to which, though he was not tall, he had, like many sensual men, an overpowering physical presence. Even Ponsonby, who knew him all his life, admitted to being 'perfectly terrified of him' at times. Fascinated by the combination of love and fear in which the Prince was held, he observed,

> I never quite understood why he made so many people frightened of him, but there can be no doubt that even his most intimate friends were all terrified of him. Abroad this was more noticeable, and on the many journeys I took with him I had only to mention his name and at once all resistance vanished . . . for he was by far the biggest man and the most striking personality in Europe . . . In spite of all this [he] had that indefinable quality of making all his staff devoted to him. All his personal Household loved him and his friends were deeply attached to him. The reason was that he was intensely human and that he was a great enough man to show his friends his true self with all the weaknesses of a human being. He never posed and never pretended to be any better than he was. The upper and lower classes loved him, although the middle class were often shocked at his actions.

If boredom and impatience were his Achilles heel, the Prince was particularly susceptible to those who could stand up to him. He loved people who spoke their own mind and did not flatter, and his closest friends were expected to balance on a tightrope between deference and high spirits. All this would have been obvious, and even intimidating, to Lillie at her first meeting. What she would also have known was that he was a renowned womanizer. It should not be forgotten that Patsy Cornwallis West had been one of his more recent lovers and she no doubt had primed Lillie. As far as Society was concerned the Prince's interest in Lillie was a foregone conclusion, and Lillie herself did not need to be a genius to work out the consequences of that first supper.

Not surprisingly, given the conscientious discretion of the private secretaries, there are no records of exactly when, how or where Lillie and the Prince began their notorious liaison, but we need not suppose that the Prince wasted time. He was in the habit of making his intentions fairly plain. When Daisy Warwick needed Royal help with her own emotional tangles, she saw, halfway through her story, that the Prince was looking at her in a way 'that all women understand'. Once the look had been made plain it was up to its recipient to indicate her acceptance or rejection. If she chose the latter, he would move on quickly and quietly to fresh pastures.

After the dinner at Allen Young's the Prince would probably have called on Lillie for tea. She would be expected to have her decision ready.

In the absence of proper sources, it is difficult to know just what Lillie's feelings for the Prince were. She was not ever in love with him, that at least is clear. But if at first she was nervous in his presence, she soon found that she liked his company; liked his warmth and his sense of humour. With his flashes of boredom or impatience he was titillatingly difficult to amuse, and Lillie enjoyed a challenge. She was attracted by the glamour that surrounded him, the glitter of royalty, the grandeur of Buckingham Palace (debarred to her since she had not yet been presented) and his evident power over the rest of Society. To be his mistress was to share in all of these. It would give her position and it would open doors. In short, it meant excitement of the headiest kind, and excitement was what Lillie was after. She would have had to be a great deal more fastidious than she was to turn him down just because he fell short of her emotional ideal.

Once their relationship was established it progressed at speed. The most obvious and immediate indication of change was in Lillie's daily ride in the Row. Now instead of her usual cohort of admirers, popularly known as the 'Langtry Lancers', she was accompanied only by the Prince. They rode either first thing in the morning, often straight from a ball without going to bed at all, or at seven in the evening, just before dinner. Sometimes the Prince was so engrossed that the evening's engagements had to wait. London hostesses were tolerant and amused. To Ned, dressed for a dinner he did not want to attend, it was simply infuriating. There is, in her memoirs, a cool account of one such occasion.

> . . . etiquette demanded that I should ride on so long as His Royal Highness elected to do so. Mr Langtry and I were, as usual, dining out, and when I arrived home I found him impatiently waiting on the doorstep, watch in hand, and in all the paraphernalia of evening dress. After a scrambling toilette we eventually arrived at the Clark-Thornhills, in Eaton Square, where we were due, to find it was nearly ten o'clock. Everyone was waiting, of course, but, before I could apologise, my hostess greeted me pleasantly, saying: So and So on his way here saw you riding in the Park, and, as we knew you couldn't get away, we postponed dinner indefinitely.' After the very natural grumbling of my husband, these words served as balm to my troubled soul. It is so difficult to please everyone.

It is indeed difficult to please all the people all the time, but Ned's pleasure was clearly no longer much of a concern.

Taking late rides with the Prince was a public statement. There was no possibility of their excursions going unnoticed. The Park, as we have seen, was a stage and, in Lillie's own words, the Royal red brow bands of the Prince's and his equerries' horses never failed to 'occasion a certain commotion'. Always before, the Prince had been discreet about his loves, but in the case of Lillie he positively paraded his affection. Presumably, like the rest of London, he too had lost his head. Lillie was, after all, everything he most enjoyed. She was high-spirited and physically daring, clever enough to keep him amused, beautiful, indefatigable and irreverent. By the end of 1877 he would go nowhere without her. Hostesses who were planning to entertain him in the coming winter months had to submit guest lists, and if Lillie's name was not already among those invited he would add it himself. Most significant of all, he started, before the year was out, to build her a house in Bournemouth.

Building houses for mistresses is not unusual in the annals of royal intrigue, but for Bertie it was a new thing. There were two obvious reasons behind his decision. The first was the strength of his feeling for Lillie, and the second was practical. She had nowhere that she could entertain him except Eaton Place. This was small, which need not necessarily have mattered, but it was made oppressive by Ned's constant and vigilant presence. Ned still had no more to do in the day than he had when he and Lillie first arrived in London, and he probably spent much of it at home, either recovering from the hangover of the day before or preparing for the one to come. There was no question of him going tactfully to his club like many another husband before him, because he did not belong to one. It is possible that the hopelessness of Lillie's marriage provided Bertie with a third motive for building. Like her he was far-sighted, and he must have been concerned about what would happen to her in the event of a separation. Bournemouth was the perfect place for a retired mistress to eke out her existence. It sounds, now, a desperately provincial exchange for the riot of a life in Society and, in a sense, so it was. But it would not then have seemed a complete backwater. In 1870 when the railway was extended down the coast, Bournemouth became a rising seaside resort. Russell Cotes, the American connoisseur, was to settle there in the nineties, building a villa on the seafront to house his collection. Wilde was to include it among the venues for his lecture tours. When Lillie and the Prince were looking for suitable building sites it was just beginning to be fashionable in a quiet way. Lord Derby was said to have a hideaway there already, and it was from him, in 1877, that they are meant to have bought the land for Lillie's house. The plot was in the Derbys' garden and completely stole their sea-view.*

It was a strange suburban dream home that Lillie and the Prince designed together. From the outside, many-gabled, half-timbered and of bright red brick, it looked comfortable rather than costly. The entrance was through a small porch with lead lights, not unlike her mother's private door in Jersey. Perhaps, too, Lillie kept her porch full of flowers. Beyond it was a hall, small and unpretentious, giving on to a parlour. Overhead, on the beam running across the ceiling, Lillie had carved, 'And yours, my friends'. It had the feeling on arrival of a folly, a cottage *ornée*, something simple and homely. This was deceptive. The house stretched away from the hall lengthwise, so that guests, coming in by the porch, on the house's shortest side, could have no idea of its actual size. The drawing-room and dining-room at the other end were immense. The latter, more dining-hall than dining-room, was vaguely mediaeval in feel. It was two storeys in height with a huge bay window at one end, and a giant fireplace of dark wood, complete with inglenooks. The top half of the window was stained glass, in the pattern of which were hidden twin swans, their necks curved in the shape of love hearts. Opposite the window at the far end was a minstrels' gallery and another inscription. This time, rather wantonly, it was, 'They say – What say they? Let them say.' It was a new decadence for a royal mistress to entertain in a house that her favours had bought, and Lillie must have done so alone, for there is no evidence that Ned ever knew of its existence. Presumably, with her provocative quotations, she had decided to brazen out her courtesanship, rather than keep up the usual simpering deception.

Upstairs the house was rather more gracious. There was a wide colonnaded landing with rooms giving on to it on all sides for Lillie's friends. The largest of these was, of course, for the Prince. Like the dining-room it was dark, with another huge fireplace, more inglenooks, a vaulted ceiling and bare beams. The bed was massive and Jacobean, and on the walls either side of it there were long panels, painted with sunflowers and red-hot poker. These were stylish and rather surprising. Somewhere between Arts and Crafts and the newly fashionable Japanese decor, they were amateurish in their execution and were probably done by Lillie herself. Around the fireplace, in Japanese blue and gold, there were tiles showing scenes from Shakespeare. The effect was distinctive. Lillie

* Langtry Manor, as the house is now called, is in Derby Road, Bournemouth, an area that is assumed to have belonged to the Derby family, with the nearby Derby Lodge as their retreat. This information was passed down by word of mouth through the various generations of tenants to the family who currently run the house as a hotel.

was obviously enjoying her house, and feeling, too, the first stirrings of a lifelong interest in decor. Off the Prince's room, but hidden from view, ran a series of passages and stairways that went behind the landing and connected with Lillie's room on the third floor. Interestingly, Lillie's bedroom was very simple. Light and airy, its main features were the windows, which were to the ground on two of the four walls. They bathed the room in a cross-light and would have given her the best sea-view in the house. The larger of the two opened on to a balcony above the garden. From it Lillie could sniff the salt breeze, alone, and be reminded of her island home, or watch her friends on the lawn below as they took tea or played croquet. It must have been an uneasy juxtaposition. Straining to combine these two incompatibles – the new life and the old – was to be the hallmark of her next five years. With no money and an alienated husband, her place in Society was only tenable so long as she remained Royal favourite. There was no question of her supporting herself. Nor was there any place for her family. Society preferred her out of context. So her position was in many ways a false one. Lillie, we must not forget, was bred to a horror of falsehood, and more particularly to a horror of pretension. Perhaps this room with a view, so kindly intended by her lover, was the place where she first shivered in the chill of the gap that now yawned between her past and her future.

When Lillie left her bedroom she found herself in the connecting passage that led to the Prince's room. To today's visitor, this feels curiously intimate, almost as though they were sharing a room. To go downstairs she would have turned off it through a pair of double doors. These gave on to a balcony that overlooked the landing and meant that she could make an entrance above her friends gathered below. She would then have descended the stairs to them and led them in to supper. It was all very neatly designed. She and the Prince made a practical team.

It is not clear exactly when the building was started and finished. The Derbys, from whom the land was supposedly bought, have no records of the transaction nor of Lillie's and the Prince's many visits to Derby Lodge to plan and oversee the work. Sometime before the year was out, Lillie and the Prince went down to Bournemouth and laid a foundation stone. On it were carved the initials E.L.L. (perhaps for Emilie Le Breton Langtry or perhaps for Edward and Lillie Langtry), and the date 1877. If so, they were playing with the initials, since Lillie had by now dropped the named Emilie. The monograph on her writing paper was simply LL. There was no reason for using Emilie here except that she shared the initial E with the Prince (and also, ironically, with her forgotten husband).

Chapter X

End of a Season

With August, the season of Lillie's discovery came to an end.

Society (and that now included the Langtrys) left London and did not officially return until the following May, when the climate was healthier. The capital became intolerable in the heat, as in the cold and the wet, but, worse than discomfort, there was, at either end of the seasonal spectrum, the danger of disease. For those who could afford it, escaping to the country was an imperative as much as a luxury. By July and August the summer heat turned the river into a breeding ground for a variety of life-threatening illnesses. The MPs in Trollope's *Phineas Redux*, kept in London for a late session, complain bitterly of the hazards fermenting in the Thames. 'I shall never get over it,' Mr Ratler announces, as he bakes on a bench behind the Cabinet Ministers. 'Think what it is to have to keep men together in August, with the thermometer at 81, and the river stinking like – the very mischief.' Trollope observes drily that Mr Ratler survived, but many did not. In the winter, conditions were just as dangerous with the city's workforce labouring through Dickens's smog-filled, slime-bound streets. Not so the rich – they went to Cowes for the yachting, to Scotland for the grouse and the stalking, and then home to their estates and on to the winter round of shooting and house-parties. It is impossible to imagine that Lillie did not do some, or all, of these. Society would not have relinquished its new toy so readily, but the records for this period are scanty. She must have gone to Goodwood in July and she did, as her memoirs record, go to Cowes.

Cowes week was a summer holiday and Society's amusements were more light-hearted and less ponderous than they had been during the London Season. Everyone stayed, either on board their yachts or in houses nearby, and there were tennis parties, fireworks and dancing. Those who had wilted under the pressure of the season found refreshment. The sea breeze that animated the bunting and the ladies' country dresses also revived the bloom in London complexions. It whipped up a forgotten sparkle in the gambler and the roué, and it gave back the port-soaked patriarch the skittishness of youth. For a contemporary flavour of the whole event we have Augusta Fane's description. The whole of Society would have been there, the Cowes roads filled with every kind of boat, and, as she recalls, 'it was a glorious sight to watch the big racing yachts come swooping down the Solent with every stitch of canvas set'. She continues,

> Cowes was a quaint little town in the 'seventies. Everyone walked out to dinner, as carriages would have been thought ostentatious; the simple life after the London Season. The whole day was spent on the sea, and the Club gardens were empty until the afternoon, when everybody collected there for tea. An old lady called Mrs Cust had a summer house opposite the entrance to the Club gardens, which was called 'the seat of the scornful', as it required some courage to pass under her scathing glances as she sat looking through her pince-nez from her point of vantage. Mrs Paran Stevens and her daughter, who became Lady Paget . . . were always in evidence. Mrs Stevens was a most amusing old character. She declared she preferred 'terra-cotta' to being on the sea, and never minded how much people laughed at her mistakes.

There were high spirits and plenty of jokes, some more innocent than others. In fact, though Augusta's nerves clearly were not strong enough, some people found Mrs Cust's cottage the perfect place for letting off steam. There was, in the seventies and eighties, a craze for the paranormal and, accordingly, when Louis Napoleon, Prince Imperial of France, joined the company that summer, a session of table-turning was organized in the disapproving Mrs Cust's sitting-room. The company, according to Lillie, sat round a table and joined hands,

> but immediately after the lights had been extinguished there were such violent upheavals that they seemed too good to be true, and on someone's striking a light, Prince Louis Napoleon was discovered hard at work throwing the furniture about . . . After this philistine interrupter had been respectfully put out of the room, the door carefully locked, and calm restored, we again waited expectantly in absolute darkness and silence for something to happen, and in about ten minutes it did . . . matches were struck again suddenly, disclosing the undefeated Prince Imperial, who had climbed the side of the house with the aid of a wisteria growing thereon and re-entered the room through the window. There he stood with several empty paper bags in his hand, while most of the

'investigators', and especially the Prince of Wales, were literally snowed over with flour.

Mrs Cust had much to complain of. Not content with the flouring of her sitting-room, the Prince of Wales and Louis Napoleon had a donkey hoisted into the bedroom of her amorous son, dressed it up and persuaded it to get into his bed. It was the sort of atmosphere Lillie revelled in, and so, for a change, might Ned if only things had not been as they were. 'The daily sailing competitions . . .' as Lillie recalls, 'the cruises in floating palaces by day, and the dances on shore by night, was a whirlwind of gaiety.' It was everything he had most enjoyed before the move to London. Now it was no longer. The sailing and the gala atmosphere would only have been painfully reminiscent of their early married life on board the *Gertrude*, the differences in their joint life highlighted by this forcible reminder of how it had been. For Lillie was the acknowledged mistress of the Prince of Wales and the toast of Society, and Ned, instead of winning prizes in his own yacht, was forced to be the guest of Allen Young on the *Helen*, his intolerable schooner full of beauties. Moreover, the inescapable Waleses, with their children, lived close at hand, on the Royal yacht *Osborne*. This year, 1877, their guests were the parents of the Princess of Wales, the King and Queen of Denmark, and their own Danish family, known for their pleasant lack of affectation, though the Prince of Wales found them intolerably dull. Every night there were dinner parties on board the *Osborne*, to which in Lillie's words 'a favoured few were invited', and after dinner there was dancing on deck. Lillie and the Prince, who were in high spirits, are supposed to have danced a cancan together for the amusement of the assembled company. The Prince had enjoyed plenty of discreet dalliances with married Society beauties but Lillie was different. He had made no secret of his admiration for her during the season, and now here she was dancing with him, the latest, most risqué dances, in front of his wife. It is one of the more remarkable aspects of their affair that Alexandra appears never to have felt threatened by Lillie, in the way that she was to feel later with Daisy Warwick and Alice Keppel. This had much to do with the fact that Lillie was the first of the public mistresses. It was something that Alexandra had not had to face before and besides she had a horror of jealousy. It was, as she said, 'the bottom of all mischief and misfortune in this world'. But it was also true that she had a genuine liking for Lillie. She too found herself unable to resist Lillie's openness, her energy and her unpretentious acceptance of her role. Lillie was too tactful ever to let her feel ousted. Lillie kept the Prince happy; she talked to the little Princes; and she was frank in her admiration of Alexandra herself. In some ways she made a valuable addition to the family.

In the day, Lillie joined expeditions and lunch parties. Often Sir Allen Young 'had the honour of entertaining the royal party for tea and a sail'. So the Prince was not stinting himself when it came to enjoying Lillie's company. What Ned found to do it is hard to imagine, except Lillie remembers that one day the affable Denmarks 'much enjoyed being rowed about the bay by Mr Langtry in the *Helen*'s little dinghy'.

Not all the fun, however, was innocent. Lillie also remembers the time they spent out of sight of the Royal yacht on HMS *Thunderer*, under the command of Charles Beresford. Apart from the many impromptu dances given on board there was one memorable and racy practical joke. In her words,

> All the cabins being below the water line, it was necessary to supply them with oxygen artificially, through air-shafts. One afternoon, while Lord Charles' small cabin was being inspected by royalty and others, his love of mischief caused him to switch off the supply of air and to watch the effect of his practical joke with great delight. Very soon our faces became scarlet, our breathing grew difficult, and we began to go through the uncomfortable sensation which must be experienced by a fish out of water.

Just how many 'others' were in the small cabin with the royalty is not clear, but Lillie enjoyed the Beresford brothers' lack of ceremony, and was clearly not the least bit troubled by the public nature of her position. To Ned, with the taste of gall never out of his mouth, alcoholic oblivion was the only effective solution.

When Cowes week came to an end Lillie and the Prince parted for a while. He went to Balmoral and she, with Ned, to stay with the Rosslyns at monstrous Easton Lodge in Essex. The young Daisy Warwick was beside herself with delight, remembering,

> Soon we had the most beautiful woman of the day down at Easton and my sisters and myself were all her admiring slaves. We taught her to ride on a fat cob. We bought hats at the only milliner's shop in the county town of Dunmow, and trimmed them for our idol, and my own infatuation, for it was little less, for lovely Lillie Langtry continued for many a day.

So, for Ned, adrift among those who saw him as 'fat and uninteresting', there was more salt in the wounds. For Lillie, there was more worship, more sartorial silliness and more riding lessons. Yet again, despite a whole summer of accompanying the Prince down Rotten Row on a fancy thoroughbred, she had 'forgotten' her riding skills. But this time the lapse of memory was due to a desire to make friends. Had she galloped off on one of Rosslyn's hunters, as she certainly could, the Warwick girls would have been impressed but there would have been no room for the pleasure and intimacy generated by her feigned incompetence. It seems now that she never switched off her charm. There was no one, in this new world, who was too young or too insignificant to be worth winning over. In the space of a few months Lillie had become adept at giving people just what they wanted.

As the year came to an end, in November or December, the Langtrys went home to Jersey for Christmas. They arrived in style on the Prince of Wales's yacht, the *Hildegarde*, lent to them for the duration of their stay, but if Ned had hoped for peace and normality he was disappointed. Even here, among the scenery of her childhood, they could not escape Lillie's new status. Her success was the talk of the Island. Her photograph would have been on sale in the shops, alongside those of the Countess of Dudley and Mrs Cornwallis West, and if she walked about the town in her old way she must have been pointed out to children in the street. The formal recognition of her position came when they were bidden to dinner at Government House, the island's most coveted invitation. Here, as Lillie left her cloak and made a last-minute check of her appearance in the mirror, she was surprised by two small, red-headed girls peering out at her from under the lace skirts of the dressing-table. Someone had smuggled them in to have a look at the famous beauty. One was the future Elinor Glyn.

For Lillie, returned for the first time since her 'discovery', everything was altered, and nowhere was this more apparent that at the deanery. Here she would have found a diminished party, with no Reggie, her mother bleak and neglected, and her father apparently unconcerned. Three of her brothers were dead, the circle broken, and Clement, married to a childhood friend, was happy and absorbed. There was little for Lillie now. Here, where she should have felt most secure, and most surrounded by those who loved her, she must have been shocked by her loneliness. The Le Bretons were not the family to make a fuss of her, or be impressed by her fame. She would have been expected just to pick up the old threads, to join in with their island life, now so confusingly different from her own. With Ned for company, and time, at last, on her hands, it would have been very hard for her to avoid taking stock of her position. She had no one she needed to please or charm, she was among people who knew her intimately, and she could, in theory, be herself again. If she tried to be so, she would have noticed, for the first time, that she had lost sight of who or what that self was. For the first time she would have seen how very far she had drifted from her old safe haven. Her stay, which should have been a rest and a reassurance, was to prove deeply unsettling.

Lillie was no longer simply the beautiful daughter of the Dean. Even if she had taken up again her old parish duties, her life in London had carried her too far from her origins for her to be able to return as though nothing had happened. It had given her a hunger for something she more than half-despised, and it had bred a discontent that made her old life impossible. She knew fame and she knew fashion. She had tasted leisure and pleasure, and the sophistication of illicit love and sexual power. She had lost her innocence and found her appetites. So her old paradise was barred to her, and yet she had little or nothing to put in its place. Did she realize, in December 1877, how precarious her life was? In fact, her position in Society was good only so long as she could sustain its, and more particularly the Prince's, interest. Her position as Muse for Bohemia was the same. Soon another beauty would arrive, with new or more paintable proportions, and she would be forgotten. The worlds she had chosen were both savage and fickle. Imagining that she could simply transplant herself, without the support of money of her own, relying only on continued favour, was desperate and wholly impractical. She had felt, as yet, nothing of the harshness of her adopted environment and she was full, still, of silly optimism. Nevertheless, as she walked her old walks, or rode, on a borrowed horse, the rides that she and Reggie had so enjoyed together, she must have realized her unmistakable and complete displacement.

Lillie's struggles with her own identity were one thing. She also had to contend with Ned. In the confines of the deanery, where there were so few distractions, his company must have been impossible to bear. Was she proud about admitting the failure of a marriage that her family had tried so hard to stop? Did they know about her affair with the Prince of Wales? Did they see how much and how desperately Ned was drinking? He, at least, must have made it clear to her, and to everyone else, that he was not happy with their London life. Presumably, too, he tried to persuade her to relinquish it, to regard it as a chapter that was now complete, and to move on to something that suited them both better. We cannot know their private wrangles, nor is there anything to tell us what Lillie thought on those winter days, when she walked her old cliffs and waited for the season to begin. She was tired. That is certain; tired by her success and its effects, physically tired by the rate at which she had been living, and tired by fighting with Ned. But she was dogged – that we know. There was no doubt, in her own mind, that she would return to London, whatever identity she chose to adopt. She had cut her moorings. Her winter trip home had the effect of casting her loose on her new life, with an abandon bred of knowing that there was no going back.

How Lillie persuaded Ned that they must return to London is another matter. He hated the city and he loathed her success, but his feelings towards her were still possessive. Lillie was later to complain loud and long of his jealousy. Alcoholism had killed his pride, and made him vindictive and self-pitying. All that was left to him now was to spoil her fun.

Chapter XI

A Dream

In January 1878, back in England, the Langtrys rejoined the Prince of Wales on the house-party circuit, with Lillie in a mood of fierce and abandoned gaiety. Her behaviour over the next two years was to be that of someone wholly given up to pleasure. She used her success, whether sexual, aesthetic or social, like a narcotic; to numb, to satisfy, to reassure, and to cocoon her from the crisis that she began to see was coming. As the financial and emotional stakes mounted, so did the fury and compulsion of her hedonism.

On 27 January the Langtrys went to stay with the Alingtons at Crichel in Dorset. Princess Alexandra hated weekending and refused all invitations, so Lillie had the Prince to herself. Consummation of their affair, restricted to early evenings during the season, was made easy within the discreet geography of the well-planned house party. The absence of the Princess combined with an atmosphere of licence to escalate and to heighten the physical side of their relationship. Lord Alington had been waiting to entertain the Prince since December. Crichel had been entirely fitted out for his arrival, though the visit had been expensively postponed several times. *Vanity Fair* noted cattily that Alington had been down to Marlborough House himself to interview the housekeeper 'as to what kind of towels were chiefly used in the Royal Establishment'. In an environment where worries of this kind were paramount there was, surely, little help for Lillie's sense either of proportion or reality.

After Crichel the Langtrys returned to London, but not to Eaton Place. Lillie's position as royal favourite demanded a rather more splendid context. They settled on Norfolk Street, Park Lane, an address that was both fashionable and expensive. Lillie describes it rather defensively in her memoirs as 'so small, so modest, so blushing, just one of a row of red-brick abodes forming one side of Norfolk Street'. In fact it was a ten-room house with stabling in the mews behind. To run it, they increased their staff, from the loyal old maid Dominique, to a butler and housemaid, and found that the butler drank and the housemaid saw ghosts. The house was said to be haunted (which Lillie would have liked) by Tyburn victims executed on that spot. The butler, who slept in the basement, reported 'repeated apparitions . . . who devoted the witching hours to such rollicking sports as rolling over his bed with their heads in their hands or rearing gibbets at its foot'. Finding Lillie unsympathetic and inclined to attribute his horrors to the effects of too much whisky, he packed his bags and his bottles and left. The housemaid, who was sober and truthful, reported that a man with 'long and beauteous curls, and the profusion of lace associated with the cavalier, barred her way down-stairs one morning in broad daylight'. But she may have been new to the sartorial quirks of Bohemia. It was just as likely to have been Joaquin Miller delivering an early morning ode. Lillie herself was unperturbed, her only complaint being that the chimneys smoked and the pub next door was too noisy.

The furnishing of 17 Norfolk Street, Lillie's first official home, was fun. Later Lillie referred to it as a 'little house of bizarre effects'. It was a combination of borrowed quality, bought sham, and original artwork. For furniture, Lillie went out and was comprehensively hoodwinked by the antique dealers, returning with plenty of artificially worm-eaten and blackened oak for her terracotta dining-room. On the walls she had hung a collection of rare old prints given by Lord Malmesbury, an old diplomat and friend of the Prince's, who lived at Heron Court very close to the house they had built in Bournemouth. The drawing-room she swathed in plum-coloured velvet. None of these, the house, its contents, its ghosts or its servants, were extravagances the Langtrys could afford. Later Lillie was adamant that she had been misled about just how much money her husband had, but this was not the case. The Le Bretons' pre-marital investigations had made it abundantly clear that Ned had next to nothing, and Lillie, as time would tell, was naturally financially astute. The truth is that she no longer cared. If she felt anything at this stage it was fury at Ned's apathy in the face of disaster. Her frustration made her cruel. She scorned his inadequacy and she goaded him into collapse.

Whatever Lillie was feeling in private would have gone unremarked in the eyes of Society. The only change it noted was that now, as a veteran in her second season, she was expected to sing for her supper. Her presence at all the most important events went without saying. It was, like that of the other Society beauties, as much a part of the decorations as the table arrangements, so much so that in some cases hosts had no compunction about dictating to her in matters of dress. In the first week of February Baron Ferdinand de Rothschild gave what *Vanity Fair* called 'a faultless dinner', followed by a ball for four hundred. There was an arrangement of blue Sèvres and orchids on the table and the nineteen-year-old Crown Prince Rudolph of Austria, for whom the event was staged, made a scene until the seating was changed to allow Lillie to sit beside him. The dancing after dinner took place in a white ballroom. Ten of the professional beauties had been asked to lunch beforehand by the Baron and offered new gowns from Doucet at his own expense. The dresses were all to be in pastel colours to compliment the freshness of the paintwork. Lillie's was pale pink, clinging crêpe de Chine, heavily fringed. Those who were less beautiful were warned by their host to make sure their dresses were clean, as the white background would show up anything that was less than pristine.

Of course Lillie's dress was beautiful, so she was hardly likely to complain, but that did not alter the fact that she could not have done so had she wanted. With her acceptance in Society, her autonomy was lost. She had to do her duty like everyone else. Nor could she complain about the other guests. Prince Rudolph's bad manners had to be smiled away, his attentions gracefully received. During the Rothschild ball he continued to monopolize her, dancing so energetically that the pastel pink gown was dark around her waist with the sweat from his hands. When she requested that he put on his gloves, he lisped a delicate rejoinder, 'C'est vous qui suez, madame.' It was probably the first time that the business of remaining charming was really irksome to Lillie. Possibly Prince Rudolph felt that as visiting royalty he would be given seigneurial rites with a favourite courtesan. Lillie was never precious but her delicacy was offended. Prince Rudolph had made her feel cheap. Remembering him later, she described him as 'a callow youth'. Among such carefully orchestrated beauty in the Rothschild ballroom he was rude, ugly – with the Habsburg lip and deep-set eyes – 'a thoroughly spoilt child'. After the ball Prince Rudolph made a nuisance of himself at Norfolk Street where he called at all times of the day and night. When once he arrived alone and excited, having left his constant chaperone in an overturned growler in Oxford Street, Lillie was forced to call upon the 'ever-watchful' Ned for protection. Life was becoming complicated. She had married and left Jersey looking, among other things, for freedom, and for a moment, watching Patsy Cornwallis West and Gladys Herbert, she had thought that she had found it. Now, as the Prince's mistress and London's new toy, it seemed that things were not going to be quite so easy.

Prince Rudolph's overtures were short-lived, however, and soon forgotten. The season officially began and ball followed ball, with Lillie 'much remarked' everywhere 'for beauty, as well as for success in dress'. In her memoirs she describes the round of her activities.

> . . . the . . . orgy of convivial gatherings, balls, dinners, receptions, concerts, operas, etc., which at first seemed to me a dream, a delight, a wild excitement, and I concentrated on the pursuit of amusement with the whole-heartedness that is characteristic of me, flying from one diversion to another from dawn to dawn, with Mr Langtry in vigilant attendance. I included the round of the clock in recording my social gambols, for there *were* times when, after dancing until sunshine confounded me, I felt wide-awake instead of sleepy, and consequently, changing directly from ball-gown to riding-habit, would mount my hack Redskin and take him for a breather in the Row . . .

The early morning rides, as well as soaking up the excess of high spirits, gave Lillie a rest from the 'vigilance' of her husband. As her popularity grew, so did his displeasure and his jealousy. And outwardly, at least, Langtry mania continued apace. In May *Vanity Fair* asked archly, 'Why do all our ladies dress in black this season?' Langtry accessories were all the rage. The Langtry bonnet, the Langtry shoe, the Langtry knot, even a mysterious article called the Langtry dress-improver, were everywhere on sale. Where Lillie went the world of fashion followed. A year from his first anonymous sight of her outside the park, Graham Robertson saw her again. The place, poetically, was the same; the person was not.

> In the spring of the next year I was wandering in the Row one Sunday morning when I became aware of a commotion among the solemn promenaders; a crowd collected, women scrambled on to chairs to get a better view, from all directions people converged towards some hidden centre of interest. As the hustle surged past me I suppose I must have stood open-mouthed and obviously interrogative, for a total stranger gripped my arm in passing and panted: 'Mrs Langtry – run!'
>
> I had heard of Mrs Langtry and I ran. Being very slender and compressible, I wriggled easily through the struggling throng and peeped into the clear space of enchanted ground at its midst.
>
> There, conversing with a tall and distinguished man (I feel sure he was

tall and distinguished, though naturally I did not look at him), stood a young lady in pale cream colour. Her back was towards me, but, as she talked, her head in its little close bonnet drooped slightly forward like a violet or a snowdrop – Good heavens! No wonder that I had all but sat down under the Barnes bus! My dowdy divinity of Hyde Park Corner, my pathetic nursery governess, had been the world-famous Jersey Lily, the Venus Annodomini, the modern Helen.

Robertson was stealing a march on Miles, who always claimed to have discovered Lillie. The description may be fanciful but it does show how natural, to her contemporaries, Lillie's elevation appeared in May 1878. She wore her new identity seamlessly and well. There is no hint of her being anything other than at home in Hyde Park, under an expensive parasol, and at the side of some Society blade. As presented here, Robertson's original sighting was a failure, not, as Miles might have seen it, to grasp the opportunity of a new face, so much as to recognize one incognito. Lillie, in her dowdy mourning, '*had been*' Helen and Venus already. Robertson had simply failed to penetrate a disguise.

Robertson was not the only one to see nothing strained or unnatural in Lillie's adoption from poverty into the world of privilege. For the moment Society did not either. If Lillie herself was unsure, London was still captivated, the Prince of Wales still adoring. Whatever midnight prickings of unease she might, from time to time, have felt would have dissolved with the warmth and the radiance of the morning. So the round went on. Easter found her at Cowes again for a holiday, with *Vanity Fair*, her shadow, at her shoulder. Its report detailed that the Yacht Club had been opened for what seemed 'quite a preliminary season . . . While Mr and Mrs Langtry, and Fred Burnaby, in a tall hat, have embellished the town.' There was plenty of fun to be had, of Lillie's favourite kind. *Vanity Fair* continued, 'Withal, the Thunderer is in the Roads, with Lord Charles Beresford on board, as ready, as ever, for anything.'

After Easter it was back to London again. There was the Royal Academy show in May, for which Lillie's portrait by Millais, the Jersey Lily, had to be roped round for protection. More importantly, in the second week of May, Lillie was made officially acceptable, when the Prince of Wales had her presented at Court.

Society ladies were routinely presented in their first season, before they 'came out'. Since this was Lillie's second, and she was married, it was done as a favour. Lillie had presumably begged her lover for recognition. She wanted to be distinguished from the actresses who were Society's only comparable toys. It was a testament of her arrival, but also of her right to be there in the first place. In some measure, too, or so she thought, it was an insurance policy, since it made her position good for years to come. Carrying the project through, however, involved unflattering quantities of tact and diplomacy on the part of the establishment. Ned had to be presented first, and this was done at the first drawing-room, by the Prince of Wales himself. In order to be presented, it was necessary first to have a 'presenter'. In the case of society debutantes this was usually their mother, or an older lady who had been at Court herself. Lillie's presenter was the Marchioness of Conyngham, who was part of the Royal Household, and who was therefore easy for the Prince to press into service. Her duties in this case were nominal as she would be needed on the day itself by the Queen, so Lillie had Lady Romney, 'cheery' and 'charming', as an escort. The drawing-rooms were held at three in the afternoon and Lady Romney, advised that it was preferable to wait until the very end of the drawing-room, rather than sit 'in full costume, with low neck and bare arms, in bright sunlight, for the edification of the surging crowd'. There was an element of playing it safe in her advice, as the public attention would have been overwhelming if Lillie had made a spectacle of herself in an open carriage and evening dress in broad daylight. But there was another reason for delay. As Lady Romney warned Lillie, the Queen rarely stayed to the end of a drawing-room as she found the standing so tiring, so that Lillie would most likely have made her curtsey to Princess Alexandra in her stead. Lillie records that she was relieved at this decision as she was afraid of the Queen, but so, in fact, were most of the Court. In the veteran eyes of the ladies of the Household, Lillie was a provincial. There was no guarantee that she would be fittingly dressed, that she would be able to carry off the curtsey, the complicated exit which involved catching a full train over the left arm before retreating elegantly backwards out of the presence. Above all, she was being presented as the Prince's acknowledged and publicly proclaimed mistress. It seemed much safer therefore to wait until the Queen had left, when Lillie's wish for acceptance could be granted without her breeding, or lack of it, causing any discomfort or embarrassment.

To Lillie the presentation was a challenge. Much hinged on it passing off without a hitch. She wanted Society's official seal of acceptance, a tangible proof of her triumph. But more than this, she knew the Prince well enough to realize that his stickling for decorum was offset by a measure of her own iconoclasm. If she could look beautiful and polished, carry off her presentation like a real lady, she would have secured her catch. The cocktail of her anonymous background, her current position as favourite and her success at a court drawing-room would thrill and engage him in a way he had never known before. On the other hand, if she bungled, she knew that the scales would fall from his eyes overnight. Lillie rose to the challenge and prepared herself accordingly. Her dress was sumptuous but understated, an ivory brocade gown, and matching train, hung, as was fashionable, from the shoulders. Both the gown and the train were garlanded with Marechal Neil roses, their pale yellow picked out by the lining of the train. On the day itself the Prince sent her an 'immense bouquet' of the real roses to carry with her and, no doubt, to give her courage.

To prepare her for the ordeal she dispensed with the services of a mere maid, relying instead on her mother and her aunt. To Emilie Le Breton it must have seemed a far and glorious cry from their first joint visit to London when Lillie was sixteen. They fussed and gloated over Lillie as they dressed her, competing with each other in their advice.

> My aunt thought I ought to have lunch before I started, or I should surely faint, but my mother affirmed that if I ate anything I should certainly have a red nose . . . the latter gained the day and I starved accordingly.
>
> They rehearsed me in the catching of my train as it would be thrown to me by the pages after my presentation, and also made me practise the royal curtsey until my knees ached. They warned me on no account to glance over my shoulder to see if my train was being properly spread by the pages in attendance, for that would be a sign that I was a country cousin, and so on and so on.

The delicacy of her sponsors had not gone over Lillie's head. She would have been more than aware of her own appearance in the eyes of the stony little Queen, as the lover of her eldest son and heir. How she dealt with it was entirely characteristic. Court dress was incomplete without a headdress. This was traditionally feathers, though the fashion when Lillie was being presented was for only the smallest and most unobtrusive plumage. The Queen had made it known that she preferred something more conspicuous and accordingly an edict had been given out by the Lord Chamberlain that the feathers must 'be at least visible to the naked eye'. Lillie seized on this peculiarity of the Queen's and made it an excuse for decorating her own head with three of the largest ostrich feather plumes she could find. The reference to the Prince's crest was quite brazen. Like the mottoes carved around her house in Bournemouth, it was a refusal to blush or to go quietly. But this was not a place of private entertainment for the fastest elements of Society; this was the Victorian Court. Lillie was no fool. She knew what she was doing. She was testing her friends, defying her sponsors, making sure that no one was admitting her into Society without their eyes open. No one was going to be able to pretend that they had thought she was simply a beautiful and virtuous wife. If she was at last triumphing, it was to be on her own terms. It was the first time she had dared sail quite so close to the wind and it was the herald for a bout of similar incidents that pushed at the boundaries of acceptable behaviour with a recklessness that bordered on lunacy.

Feathers aside, Lillie's first drawing-room passed without a hitch. She was patriotic and she loved the sight of the aristocracy pranked out in all its ancient finery. As she herself described it, it was a spectacle that was quite indigestibly gorgeous.

> . . . the superbly gowned women, wearing magnificent tiaras and shining with jewels, sitting waiting their turn in St James's Park in state coaches that were brought out only on these full-dress occasions, were a joy to behold. The bewigged coachmen, sitting in solitary glory on the resplendent hammercloths, and the powdered footmen in liveries heavy with silver or gold, standing on ledges at the back of these historic carriages, clinging to embroidered straps, were also part of the show. The entrance court of the palace, with the guard of honour of Household Cavalry and its braying band, and the beefeaters in their quaint Elizabethan costumes, showed . . . conspicuously in the daylight.

Once inside the palace, things were a little less ceremonious and stately. The ladies were 'penned like sheep' in the crush-room, arms aching from carrying their heavy trains, faces veiled in tulle and heads pulled by the weight of their headdresses. It was a long wait for a brief moment of glory. Expecting only to be received by the Waleses, Lillie went in, last but two, and found that she was to make her curtsey to the monarch after all. She was overwhelmed. She recorded later,

> It seemed to me an amazing thing to be shown into the presence of a sovereign one had heard of and prayed for all one's life, and to approach near enough to bend forward and kiss her hand, and, though the experience lasted but a second, I thrilled with emotion, loyalty, and pride.

The Queen, as people always are in the flesh, was smaller than Lillie had realized, though this in no way detracted from her impassive majesty. Lillie's description continues,

> She was dressed quite simply, in black, of course, with low neck and short sleeves, and her train was of velvet. Across her bodice was the blue ribbon of the Garter, and diamond orders and jewels studded her corsage. She wore many strings of beautiful pearls round her neck, a small diamond crown, tulle veil, and black feathers forming her headdress.

Victoria looked straight in front of her, extending her hand in what Lillie saw as a 'rather perfunctory manner'. She communicated neither pleasure, nor surprise, 'not even the flicker of a smile on her face, and she looked grave and tired'.

In fact, as Lillie learnt later that evening, she had stayed on at the drawing-room, against her custom, and despite the fatigue of standing for so long, in order to satisfy her curiosity over Lillie. Whatever else she felt, Queen Victoria loved a beauty.

Later that same night, when it was all over, and Lillie was back in the Prince's arms, dancing a Royal Quadrille at Marlborough House, it was clear that her success had been complete. The Prince was enchanted with her and her reckless style. Not only had his mother broken her custom and seen the drawing-room out, but, he teased, she was annoyed that Lillie was so late.

As to the feathers, once they had triumphed, he could enjoy the joke. It was, after all, just the kind he liked best, private, risqué and demanding more than a dash of bravado to carry it off. Lillie must have been elated, but she knew perfectly well what a close race she had run. Musing later, in her memoirs, she remarked,

> As to my appearance, I wondered what Her Majesty thought of my head-gear. I am afraid the waving ostrich plumes may have looked overdone, as the Prince of Wales that evening chaffed me good-humourdly on my conscientious observance of the Lord Chamberlain's order. At all events, I *meant* well.

Generally, people who really mean well do not find it necessary to highlight their intentions with italics.

Chapter XII

Waking

The immediate result of Lillie's presentation at Court was the false sense of security that being officially accepted as a member of Society gave her, along with a new-found confidence in her sartorial style.

But she knew the rapidity with which Society made and abandoned its idols, and she needed to find a way of sustaining its interest. Black, thanks to her initial success, was the colour of the season. Were she to continue specializing in understatement she risked going unnoticed. To be different and to maintain her profile, she embarked on a fantastic expansion of her meagre wardrobe. Emulation of the Society belles was her own excuse, but with it was mixed an unhealthy portion of necessity.

Constantly mingling with bejewelled and beautifully clad women, who changed their gowns as a kaleidoscope changes its patterns, created in me a growing desire to do likewise. For the first time in my life I became intoxicated with the idea of arraying myself as gorgeously as the Queen of Sheba, and, being accorded unlimited credit by the dressmakers, who enjoyed designing original 'creations' for me, I began to pile up bills at all their establishments, heedless of the day of reckoning that must eventually come . . . I indulged unrestrainedly in a riot of coloured garments. Indeed, the question of clothes became of paramount importance, and temporarily filled my mind to the exclusion of most things . . . Now I required a new outfit for every occasion, and, my husband aiding and abetting me by his approval, I became more and more reckless, allowing insidious saleswomen to line negligees with ermine or border gowns with silver fox without inquiring the cost, until the Christmas bills poured in, laying bare my colossal extravagance.*

*There was another reason, unstated, for Lillie's extravagance and this was the Prince of Wales's insistence on constant change and variety in a woman's wardrobe. Later she remarked that she had once worn 'a dress of white and silver at two balls in succession. I did

As far as Society was concerned, presentation had normalized Lillie. It had stripped her of some of her mystery and made her indistinguishable from any other professional beauty. Goddesses should not need the Queen to validate their position and make them secure. For those who had worshipped, Lillie's change, from the pure ideal of the beauty in black, to putting on all the outward show of a countess, was almost a sacrilege. The old guard, who had allowed Lillie her pedestal so long as she fulfilled their fantasy, began slowly to desert her. Others, mostly women who were envious, sensed the shift of mood and took advantage of it to declare Lillie unsuitable. London was no longer unanimous in her praise. Lillie, alive to the least tremors of disapproval and rumour, felt the change. The cautiousness of the ladies of the Household had not been lost on her. It was the first time she had come up against anything like the treatment she had received on her first visit to London, with her mother, all those years ago, and she felt again the prickings of the old fury.

Lillie had set a trap for herself with her presentation in Court. After it, there was nothing left to achieve, nowhere else for her to go, except downhill. She could, and did, enjoy the flunkeys in scarlet livery at Buckingham Palace balls, weaving in and out of a gorgeous throng, with their gold tazzas full of hothouse fruit. As she later observed, it 'completely realized my girlish dreams of fairyland'. But the tazzas were no nearer her grasp than they had been when she was simply the daughter of the Dean of Jersey. The truth was that she was not the same as the aristocrats she emulated and, thus, was a danger to Society; the tactful engineering of her presentation told her that much. The accident of her birth, which could not be undone, barred her invisibly from her goal, and was insurmountable. The usual solution to the problem of background was marriage, and she was already married. Divorce, should she choose that route, meant scandal and opprobrium, on a scale that would both outweigh and confirm her present position as an outsider.

Of course, in 1878, the change in Society's approach to Lillie was only atmospheric, the equivalent to a drop of a few degrees on the social thermometer. In responding to it all, she was doing so at the promptings of her pride, not, as yet, from necessity. But her pride was an important factor in the choices she was about to make. It alone prevented her from settling for a half measure, a position of comfort, bought with her

not know', she continues, 'that he [the Prince] was going to be present at both balls, but he was. He came up to me on the second night and exclaimed: "That damned dress again!" He walked away in a temper . . . It took me a long time to make it up.'

reputation, as the wife of a disgraced aristocrat. Her longing for acceptance was as strong as her need of the luxuries and the pastimes it guaranteed. She wanted to belong, if not by birth, then by right – through her own merits, not on sufferance, through the purse or position of another. This, as she was to find over the next year, was to become increasingly difficult.

Even if Lillie made no dramatic changes; if she and Ned were just to go on as they were, bankruptcy, which was unavoidable, would force them into retirement in Jersey or Ireland. Whichever way Lillie looked, she must choose between scandal and obscurity. No wonder, behind the gaiety and the extravagance, she began to feel like a rat in a trap. Nor did her relationship with the Prince make things any easier. After her gamble at Court had paid off, the Prince, as she had known he would be, was enthralled. Now she found that in order to keep his attention she must take more risks. To please him and tease him, she was wilder and more reckless by the moment. Their affair was public property, and as the public nature of her position was confirmed, so the tide of opinion continued to change. By May of 1878, in the court and social columns of the daily newspapers her name always followed his. Her photographs on sale in the penny-postcard stalls were pinned up underneath his, a lewd comment on their relations that deeply offended the more precious elements of Society.

By the middle of the season Lillie knew with certainty that her position in Society, far from being cemented by her presentation, was in fact bogus.

Vanity Fair, always a useful barometer, was the first to register public notice of the change. Now it began writing about her with that mixture of disapproval and jealous snobbery that was to become the currency of the following years. Towards the end of May, reporting on a ball at Buckingham Palace, it described in glowing and deferential terms Princess Alexandra's dress of pale blue covered with geraniums, fresh and feminine in inspiration. It also remarked on the splendour of her diamond necklace and tiara. Mrs Langtry, the only other lady mentioned, was dressed, by contrast, 'gorgeously' in white and gold and with no jewellery at all. The implication was that Lillie had decked herself out in borrowed plumage, that her appearance was more sumptuous than her position allowed. The Princess could afford to dress with restraint because her taste, like her beauty, was the product of her background, and therefore faultless. Also she had jewellery, and fine jewels were the outward indications of fine breeding. Not to have them was unacceptable. A naked neck was the badge of the parvenue. It was more than just rude; it was somehow immoral. On 25 May *Vanity Fair* confirmed its change of tack about Lillie with a thinly veiled attack on female ambition.

> Women never seem able to regulate their ambitions. I have seen a woman who when dressed plainly and simply shone among her fellows as a bright particular star, and who not content with this has allowed herself to form and endeavour to carry out the project of competing with all London, not in beauty only, but in dress. She did not reflect that to vie in the putting on of apparel with women of unlimited allowance requires at least an equal fortune; and above all she did not reflect that her chief charm lay precisely in that modest simplicity which she was so anxious to abandon for rich trappings. The event proved that she was wrong – for people, instead of admiring her beauty, which was undoubted, took to criticizing her dress – and so she lost credit for her face because she had elected to seek it for her gowns.

Imperceptibly, as the summer wore on, Lillie's fame slipped into notoriety. If she was not yet seen as wicked, she was beginning, in the eyes of some, to be ridiculous. Lillie herself laughed at the transition, and of course, instead of trying to make it better, made every effort to make it worse. When she felt the breath of dissenting whispers at her back she reacted with scorn, and her scorn was shocking. She was a natural iconoclast, and she hated the hypocrite and the snob. Their disapproval sparked a defiance in her that, smouldering in the timber of a desperate disillusion, ignited, at last, into a blaze. At least, she reasoned, if she fell from her pedestal she would fall in flames.

LIMBO 1878–1882

Chapter XIII

Prologue to the Death of a Goddess

Lillie was a survivor, and she never gave up. Looking down as her pedestal became her pyre, she weighed up the options before her. She was twenty-four, and the friends who, only months before, had seemed so welcoming were already sliding away. Defiance and insecurity drove her on. Had she been single, a suitable marriage would have brought her protection and position in one. Married as she was, it was a desperate step. It meant either divorce or elopement, and therefore all the horror of a public scandal.

It is easy to assume, in the light of her later notoriety, that Lillie was immune to public opinion. This is very far from the truth. She hated convention and petty decorum, it is true, but the flouting of small rules from within society was very different from being 'hooted at' from outside, as a pariah. Victorian Society was sensitive about the moral outrage of a mass it saw as common and in some way savage. Prince Albert's horrified injunctions to Bertie after his first romantic misdemeanour were not as fastidious then as they seem today. Picturing the furore that a commoner's illegitimate pregnancy would create, he urges Bertie to imagine himself in court. His mistress, he threatens,

> will be able to give before a greedy Multitude disgusting details of your profligacy for the sake of convincing the Jury, you yourself cross-examined by a railing indecent attorney and hooted and yelled at by a Lawless Mob!

These were fears that much of the aristocracy, and all of the clergy, would have shared. Lillie may have behaved as though she did not care, may, on the face of it, have been courting disaster, but she was still the daughter of a dean, however liberated. She was afraid of the publicity of the divorce court, afraid of being cast out, of proving Society's caution just.

Privately, too, she was afraid of meriting the scorn of the aristocracy in her own eyes. If her goal was a place in Society, it was now becoming clear to her that there were some prices she could not afford to pay. Nevertheless she did want protection, and that, in male-dominated Society, was something that only a husband could provide.

Marriage being out of the question, what were Lillie's other options? In Bohemia women could, and did, carve out their own niches. There were painters such as Louise Jopling, writers such as Violet Fane, singers such as Madame Patti, and actresses such as Ellen Terry, Mrs Patrick Campbell and Sarah Bernhardt. But a career depended on drive, motivation and resilience, all qualities that Lillie was to find in herself later on, but none of which were much in evidence in the shifting social sands of the 1870s. It is no surprise that, in her own mind's eye, her choices were, literally, personified – individuals, rather than anything so abstract as a course of action. In other words she looked to some*one*, rather than some*thing*, to save her. For the next four years all her energies were to be invested in people, more often than not in the form of an affair, sometimes as an intense and dependent flirtation. These men – lovers, confidants and mentors – were run simultaneously. Each one, in her eyes as well as his, was the most important thing in her life. He alone could help her. He alone had sole charge of her welfare – held her happiness and her security in the palm of his hand. Although the choice in the end would be hers, the destiny that went with it was another's, to be adopted and shared by Lillie as her own.

Broadly, Lillie's choices grouped themselves under the three old headings: Society, Bohemia and Jersey. Society was embodied in her affairs with the Prince of Wales, his friend and favourite Louis Battenburg, and the baby Lord Shrewsbury. These were just the most serious, or time-consuming, of Lillie's Society lovers. There were others, more casual, such as the unnamed gallant in Frances Warwick's account.

> During my first season [1880] a certain Lord X professed love for me. I was very attracted and not a little inclined to listen to his plea, but one night at a party I happened to overhear him call Lily Langtry 'my darling' as he helped her into her cloak. Then I heard him make an assignation with her. Naturally I was furious, and never again looked at him.

In Bohemia she had the painters Millais, James McNeill Whistler and Frank Miles, and her Svengali, Oscar Wilde. Jersey and her past were represented by Arthur Jones, the bastard son of the rakish Lord Ranelagh, and childhood friend of her brothers.

Lillie's involvements were not consecutive but simultaneous: occasionally one gained over another as Lillie grew less or more involved, but for most of the next three years, from 1878 to 1881, she maintained all the separate threads of her relationships, plaiting them in and out of each other, investing in each of them with apparently total commitment.

At this distance, in an age where we are used to the concept of cake being simultaneously kept and consumed, the sexual freedom and the whining manipulation of these years is hard to forgive. Lillie seems to have lost any kind of integrity. Nowadays we have forgotten that old ultimatum, career or marriage. We talk lightly of fulfilment and our own happiness, and we take it for granted that, if we cannot always be kind, we can at least be true to ourselves. Lillie's behaviour, as she vacillated and promised and vacillated again, looks weak and self-indulgent, her reliance on a man for direction and salvation nothing short of idiotic. But our freedoms are very new. It was not always so, and, besides, Lillie was psychologically and emotionally in turmoil. She had been presented as the season opened. She had been formally recognized, formally adopted by her chosen sphere. She should, or so she reasoned, have continued, through the parties and the race meetings, in a blaze of glory. Her standing should have been enhanced and underpinned by her recognition. She should have been secure. Instead, she felt herself to be staring into an abyss, her longed-for success on the point of turning into public shame and private degradation. It must have seemed to her, as the season wore on, that there were no choices open to her at all, only a series of damaging compromises.

Only very rich or very motivated women had, in those days, choice and freedom of expression. Lillie in the absence of either was clutching at straws rather than pulling strings. Her feelings, though fuelled by despair, were always genuine. When she gave her frantic assurances of commitment to five different men at once, it was not as an exercise of her power so much as a need to persuade herself that the option they embodied was the solution. She did feel everything she professed to feel and, more than this, she wanted passionately to believe in her own assurances. If at some level she felt the conflict of loyalties or the falsehood of her position, she did not recognize it with her conscious mind, and eventually, of course, the strain told.

Some of Lillie's vacillations were the product of a nature that was instinctively headstrong. Putting her life in the hands of another was not something she found easy. She was naturally independent and she could not give up her freedom lightly. Besides, her marriage to Ned had failed and there was no guarantee that a second one would not be changing one trap for another of a different kind. Experience had taught her to be wary, and she was by nature sensible. Her decisions, whatever they were, were therefore bound to be constructive. She wanted to be able not just to enjoy her life, but to believe in it, to feel that the energy she poured into it was well invested.

As it was, fame, an alien context, and the coming crisis had eroded her personality to such a degree that she had lost more than confidence in her own abilities. She no longer even had any knowledge of where or what those abilities might be. Her whole identity was subsumed in a determination to please. She became a mirror for whatever it was her companion of the moment wanted to see, unaware of the contradictions or incompatibilities this sometimes involved. For those on whom her attention was focused she made flattering company. For herself, it meant the constant strain of secrecy, keeping her various lives separate and unaware of each other's existence, a schizophrenic determination to keep her few escape routes open. To do so she had, at all costs, to keep up the façade of light-heartedness. Whatever it thought about her society must not see her desperation. If she could delay the crisis by her nonchalance, she would.

Turning tides are invisible to the bathers that splash in their shallows. They are evident only in undercurrents, and so it was with Lillie in 1878 and '79. To follow her progress through her second season, it looks as though her position was confirmed and established. To follow it with the knowledge of the spreading web of her emotional commitments makes for very different reading.

The season of 1878 had made a slow start. Discontent, like a plant, grows in wet weather, and the spring and early summer had been rainy. In June, at last, the sun came out, and with it most of the ill humour evaporated. Lillie's life appears a breathless catalogue.

In mid-June there was Ascot and the Derby. Lillie rode down the Royal Mile in the Prince of Wales's carriage, the acknowledged, and now flaunted, favourite. At the same time there was Hurlingham, for pigeon shooting, and Wimbledon, shooting for the Elcho shield. Lord and Lady Wharncliffe, as Commandants of the Camp, lived *in situ* for a fortnight in large tents, entertaining, as Lady Randolph Churchill recalled, every night, 'in the most sumptuous manner'. Ladies drove down, after the racing, 'in coaches in Ascot frocks and feathered hats', and stayed to dinner, driving back by moonlight. Lillie went too, presumably in someone else's coach, and tricked out in feathers and froufrou, all on credit. On 27 June there was a party at the Royal Academy and 'Mrs Langtry', as *Vanity Fair* observed, 'was seen standing before her own picture, the centre of an admiring circle'. The following Sunday there was another dinner at Baron Ferdinand's for the Prince of Wales. On 6 July, Lillie's friend Gladys Herbert married Lord Lonsdale at St Paul's. On the 27th there was the first polo match played by electric light at the Ranelagh club, at ten o'clock at night. Two days later there was a party at Goodwood House for more racing, at which 'Mrs Langtry embellished a pink gauzy fabric'. On 10 August Lillie was expected in Homburg with the Prince but they went instead to Cowes in the company of Christopher Sykes. Then there was Henley and a brief respite, before it was north to Scotland for the Northern Meeting at Inverness.

Keeping up the appearance of gaiety and insouciance was not the least of Lillie's problems. As the London Season closed, *Vanity Fair*, in an account of the 'Beauties of the Season', devoted a paragraph to Lillie and her new style. It started with a tribute to her as she was when she first arrived: 'the most wonderful eyes of a limpid, transparent blue, which always wear a winning expression'. It continued,

> She was observed to be extremely modest in her dress, very quiet and unassuming in her manner, and discreet in all her actions ... Mrs Langtry has indeed somewhat changed her style. She is, as her high position demands, far more splendidly dressed than when she first appeared as 'the little Jersey beauty'; she has a house in Norfolk Street; and she rides in the Park on a highly trained walking chestnut, on which indeed she looks admirable, having a splendid figure well set off by a habit without a fold.

Behind the cool compliments are the questions that the article begs but does not voice. How has this transformation been effected? At whose expense? And just who is she, this woman who now occupies so 'high' a position – the little Jersey beauty or the *grande dame*?

Chapter xiv

Back to Bohemia; Whistler

In her first season, though she spent so much of her time in the artists' studios, Lillie's attention had been entirely taken up by the demands of Society. Society was her goal. Only with her presentation at Court out of the way, and all her immediate ambitions fulfilled, did she turn back to Bohemia. Searching for role models, Lillie was unconsciously drawn to those whom she saw as self-made. Among the first serious influences on her was the painter James McNeill Whistler. In many ways he was an obvious choice. Like Millais (Lillie's favourite of the year before), and like Lillie herself, he was foreign. He had a tantalizing whiff of the outcast about him, a quality that Lillie was increasingly to look for in her men. He was American, flamboyant and had diabolic looks, and Society despite his undoubted genius had responded to him warily and with hesitation. It was puzzled by his paintings and outraged by his personal style. It was piqued by his indifference to the graciousness of its patronage and threatened by his professional self-confidence which, despite often lukewarm critical response, continued gargantuan. Whistler, in return, refused either to compromise or to flatter. This, of course, only made him the more appealing to Lillie. Anyone who could hold the limelight while cocking a snook at convention had lessons that she wanted to learn. To her, Whistler was a doyen of the psychological and social limbo that she was beginning to feel was her natural milieu.

Like Lillie herself, and like Miles and Wilde too, Whistler toyed with his outsider status. He loved to tread the fringes of acceptability. He took what he wanted from the Aesthetes and the Decadents and the Orient, acknowledging nothing, and produced a cocktail of his own that he published as the only possible or permissible artistic truth. He flew in the face of the establishment critics. He threw public tantrums. He believed in the cult of the personality as art. He took infinite pains with his hair and his sharpened beard, and he was monstrously vain. In short, he had opinions on art, on dress, on furniture, architecture, gastronomy, interior decoration, all of which he expounded with volubility and venom, and all of which were irrefutable in his eyes. To the establishment, he was at best controversial and at worst insufferable. And fuelling all this was an almost demonic energy. The architect Edward Godwin recorded in his diary a Sunday breakfast in Whistler's studio, at which he had seen Whistler paint a full-length portrait of Louise Jopling in an hour and a half; 'an almost awful exhibition of nervous power and concentration'. Energy of this kind was a quality to which Lillie was always susceptible. In Whistler, she found it mesmeric.

As always, beneath the veneer, things were not quite what they seemed. Small, precise and dandyfied, Whistler, to his familiars, was something between tyrant and child. His charm, which was legendary, and his waspish intelligence belied extreme insecurity and a passionate devotion to his art. He needed not praise so much as worship, and he surrounded himself with a coterie of pupils and friends all of whom referred to him as the 'Master'. Tremendous amounts of energy and emotion were wasted in the endless turnover of his friendships. A thousand times, attachments that began with a snowstorm of ornately worded notes ended in acrimony, the former soulmate being dismissed with a bilious little card. Friendships were forged with intensity, almost overnight. But they were consumed just as soon, as though in the fire of their own begetting. Not surprisingly, the bullying heat of Whistler's acquaintance was often more than the average person could bear. Friends were expected to keep up, to agree, enthuse, adulate and sing for their supper. Even then there was no guarantee of survival. Part of this was tyranny, and part of it was a hugely heightened sensibility to life as a whole. Nothing, to Whistler, was irrelevant, nothing unimportant. Graham Robertson described him as one of the 'most vital people I have ever known . . . Life was to [him] an art and a cult, [he] lived each moment consciously, passionately'. Whistler was the first person to teach Lillie that life itself could be art.

Whistler liked to dominate. His conversation, mostly monologue, was rapped out in a series of explosive rhetorical questions, a style so defined as to be open to parody. George Moore left an amusing send-up of him, comparing the Elgin Marbles with the work of a contemporary sculptor. Moore was a friend, so the pastiche is affectionate:

> . . . the relation of Art to Nature – which is the prerogative of the artist –
> art which is not Nature because it is art – Art which is Nature because it

is not art – Nature which is not art because it is nature – Nature which is
– Art which is not – the spontaneous creation – oh, come along my dear
fellow – come along – Lunch, bunch – lunch, bunch – lunch, bunch.

Talk was something Lillie would have heard a great deal of in Whistler's
studio. It was the currency of Bohemia, its lifeblood. A large part of the
necessary exchange of artistic opinion, of the cross-fertilization of ideas
and of stimulation took place socially, in these studio gatherings. In
Society this was not the case. Here conversation had no purpose to it
beyond the fulfilment of the 'high and holy mission . . . to amuse itself'.
This, as we have seen, consisted mostly in the saying of 'How do you do?'
as many times as possible within an hour. We have, as a reminder, *Vanity
Fair*'s pertinent, if exaggerated, assurances that it was considered bad
manners in Society 'for anybody to make a remark exceeding twenty
words in length, or including more than one idea'.

Some of these differences would not have been evident at Whistler's
famous breakfasts, for here he dominated the conversation. As one friend
recalled, 'he was never so brilliant as at his table but it was always stories
and small talk, nothing ponderous'. This must have been a relief, as witty
small talk was Lillie's speciality. If the subject was to be serious or
intellectual she lost her footing, but if it was the cut-and-thrust of gossipy
banter she was every bit Whistler's equal. A year of entertaining the
Prince of Wales had sharpened her naturally quick wits and given her a
healthy appetite for the anecdote. This was the kind of exchange that
Lillie could excel at and enjoy. But if Whistler liked trivia and was sensible
of the capacities of his various guests, others may not have been quite so
indulgent. Among his most intimate friends in the years '77 to '78 he
counted Swinburne, Decadent and drunk, who addressed Whistler as
'mon cher père'; Wilde, who needs no introduction; Godwin, the
architect; and Louise Jopling, painter and intellectual. The conversation
in their company would have been sprightly and extremely wide-ranging.
Jopling, recalling a later, but typical, evening's entertainment, recorded,

Mrs Langtry came yesterday, and looked very beautiful. A lot of people
came. Oscar Wilde, Pellegrini, Captain Carnegie, and Trendell stayed to
dinner. We had amusing discussions – Oscar Wilde maintained that in
poetry and painting the idea, or matter, was secondary to the execution,
'workmanship', as he called it – Pellegrini and I raved against him.

While Lillie was stepping into the artists' studios from the carriages of

Lady Lonsdale or Mrs Cornwallis West, and while she was coming only for tea and diversion, the conversation would have been tailored to suit the tastes of the patrons. If she was taking a longer view, if, that is, she was going to make her life in Bohemia, she would have to find her level in these voluble, aesthetic punch-ups. Raving was not really her style, and she probably found the company at these gatherings rather testing. Her letters over the period show her to be touchingly lacking in confidence. She uses the pet names common among the coterie, 'Godwino', 'Oscarino', but is deferential and grateful, as though she knew herself to be there on sufferance rather than merit. Insecurity, since he suffered from it himself, and more particularly since in this case it was that of a pretty woman, was something to which Whistler was very sensitive. Despite his own vitality and his occasional venom, Graham Robertson also noted in him an 'old world courtesy' which smoothed away all awkwardness in others, and an ability to exercise 'an almost hypnotic fascination such as I have met with in no one else'.

Lillie was indeed temporarily hypnotized. Whistler's effect was potent. He was a natural Svengali to both men and women, and so he very nearly was for Lillie. Just how close they were it is impossible to tell. They were fascinated by each other, that is clear, but Whistler's time and energies were being very much exercised by his law suit against Ruskin, and by his own financial problems. It seems unlikely that they did more than dance round the possibility of an affair that summer. But dance they certainly did. After that, they were swept apart by Whistler's bankruptcy, which resulted in his leaving the country for fourteen months. The pace of Lillie's life waited for no man and by the time he returned their moment had gone.

The beginning of Lillie and Whistler's friendship is something of a mystery. They had met at the Sebrights' fateful At Home in Lowndes Square. Whistler had formed part of that impromptu court around her chair in the corner and he would have vied for her attention with the other 'cavaliers'. So it is surprising that the first recorded sittings for a portrait are not until 1881 and that there is no evidence to suggest that they were even friends in Lillie's first season. He, of all people, did not need Society's sanction to admire unknown beauty, but there is nothing to suggest that he followed up his attentions that evening with invitations to sit or to breakfast. Nevertheless, by June of the following year (1878) Louise Jopling, who was convalescing in London, makes it clear that they were well acquainted. She was interested in painting Lillie, whom she did not know, and recorded, 'Whistler asked me to come to tea to meet her on Tuesday, but, alas, I cannot.' By this time, at least, they were friends enough for Whistler to be able to offer her as artistic bait. Clearly, like Miles before him, he was enjoying showing her off to fellow painters.

Besides tea and admiration on weekdays, Lillie was also attending Whistler's famous Sunday breakfasts. These took place in his studio, at twelve o'clock, and were a form of brunch. Between ten and twenty guests would be invited and all kinds of American specialities were served, often prepared by Whistler himself. Lillie remembers buckwheat cakes, popovers and corn muffins. She also noticed his taste in decoration which, like Wilde's, was fashionably oriental. The table was strewn with blue and white Japanese plates and coffee cups. There were 'queer little dishes' everywhere containing 'mysterious relishes and compounds' and in the middle of it all stood a bowl filled with water, on which a single lily floated. This was a far cry from the luxurious and orthodox abundance of hothouse plants that Society favoured for its centrepieces. Lillie took note, and soon her Norfolk Street dinner parties were ornamented with an antique blue glass bowl in which a yellow water lily floated. Openly she admits to this being 'cribbed from Whistler', and to it having subsequently become *de rigueur* as decoration in fashionable circles. At the time she remembered it causing 'much frankly expressed derision from my philistine guests'. The laughter of Society weighed with her not at all. She was genuinely interested in the artistic and the avant-garde and prided herself, if not on her cultivation, then at least on her lack of philistinism.

On Lillie's first visit to one of these breakfasts, she met George Smalley, art critic and newspaper correspondent, who recorded his impressions of her in an article some years later. When he arrived Lillie was sitting alone by Whistler's fireside. Smalley paints an intimate and sensual portrait.

> When the door into the parlour opened, this lady was sitting in a low chair in the corner by the fire, and the light of the fire shone on her face. A vision never to be forgotten; the colouring brilliant and at the same time delicate; the attitude all grace. There was a harmony and a contrast all in one; the harmony such as Whistler loved; the contrast such as it pleased her Maker to arrange; between softness and strength; the lines of the woman's full body flowing gently into each other, but the whole impression was one of vital force. There was no one else in the room . . .

Lillie was obsessively punctual so there is nothing overly significant about her being alone in Whistler's house. In fact the relationship was new enough, evidently, for Lillie still to feel the need to charm. The painting of Connie Gilchrist was hanging in the studio for the delectation of the breakfasters, and Lillie, catching sight of it, sighed, 'Oh Mr Whistler, what a lovely portrait. I have seen Connie Gilchrist but once, but I am sure it is hers. Nobody but you could have done it so beautifully.' Smalley, who thought it inadequate, was relieved. He was also amused by her grace and command of the situation. Smalley's account continues after she had left.

> I stayed on after the company had drifted away, and Whistler began at once with his explosive questions: 'Of course, you knew Mrs Langtry?' 'I had never seen her.' 'Then you had never seen the loveliest thing that ever was. Don't tell me that you don't think her perfect. It doesn't matter what you think. She *is* perfect. Her beauty is simply exquisite, but her manner is more exquisite still. She is kindness itself.'

Obviously the flattery and the quiet harmony had done the trick. Whistler was fired with excitement. Moreover, Lillie, like his favourite model mistresses, Jo Heffernan, Frances Leyland and Maud Franklin, had Titian hair. More interesting than Whistler's admiration, which was no more than to be expected, is Smalley's impression, with which his article ends, that Lillie and Whistler were two of a kind. Commenting on Whistler, though it could just as well be Lillie, he observes,

> In social life, as in art, conventions were to him so many objects of contempt. He, too, like Mrs Langtry, passed private Acts of Parliament for his private use. The Acts of Parliament of these two were for our use too, we were to obey them. None of us minded, only it was sometimes difficult to know when they were passed and what they were, and when they were repealed and when a new act came into being.

So their affinity was marked enough for others to notice it. Spiritually and temperamentally they seemed twinned. Whistler, with his evident genius, confirmed Lillie in her impatience of convention, and encouraged her to treat life as others did art. Art, after all, was not to be had without artifice, and there was no reason to draw a line between the expression and the reality, or, for that matter, to be any more prosaic in the one than the other. No one should be afraid of a pose, nor, having struck one, should they be afraid to dictate to others the conditions for its preservation. He taught Lillie how to capitalize on her instincts, how to make something of her life, to dress it, orchestrate it and arrange it, with autocracy, bravura and what one contemporary called 'a conceit so colossal that it is delightful'.

The breakfast with Smalley is datable by the Connie Gilchrist portrait, and by the fact that it took place at Tite Street, the house that Edward Godwin had built to Whistler's specifications. The house was finished enough for him to move into on 25 June 1878. Between that time and 26 November when the Ruskin law suit left him bankrupt, his friendship with Lillie grew fast. Soon they knew each other well enough for Whistler simply to arrive at Lillie's Norfolk Street house with an extravagant scheme of redecoration. As Lillie recalls,

> The drawing room . . . I draped with some plum-coloured material, which made it look prematurely funereal. To the rescue of this gloomy room came Whistler unexpectedly one morning, bearing bundles of palm-leaf fans and a tin of gold paint. It seemed strange that the apostle of the demi-tone should advocate garishness, but, feeling that I had missed my expected effect, and that he realized it, I listened gladly to his suggestions of gilded trophies to brighten the walls. So we set to work to burnish the fans, but the gold paint rained on us, and splashed us with such animate persistence, that, by the time our work was finished, our eyelashes glittered, and destruction sat upon our clothes. Still the addition of a painted ceiling, dimly representing the firmament, with a pair of birds (prophetically) depicted in full flight thereon, made the drawing-room, at all events, original as regards decoration . . .

The birds were Lillie and the self-styled 'Master' lording it over their aesthetic heaven, he the creator and she the Muse. In fact the image was a combination of defiance and wish-fulfilment. The person who is not in the picture, but whose negative presence they must both have been trying to exorcise, is Ned. For Lillie and for Whistler, life was not everything their buoyancy proclaimed. Somewhere upstairs Ned must have been sleeping, or nursing a hangover, or just his resentment. The Norfolk Street house was way beyond their means and the pace of their life furious. Like the Langtrys, Whistler too was balancing on a knife-edge of insolvency. Finessing their way through ball dresses, servants, and a specially commissioned house in Chelsea, both must have been alive to the horror of having their bluff called.

Besides the subtext of wish-fulfilment, this is an intimate picture of Lillie and Whistler physically absorbed in their shared project. The speed and effort of their work, the joint fantasy, which escapes debt and disillusion, the gold paint that rains equally on both, transforming and uniting them at once, are charged with an erotic intensity. If their relationship was unconsummated, it was nonetheless physical in nature. They were bound by misfortune and their eye-to-eye approach to it, but also by their indomitable vitality. Energy and showmanship were Whistler's trade marks and neither would have gone unnoticed by Lillie. Where others saw affectation and vanity she saw the overspill of an artistic temperament. Though she was naïve in her judgements on Society, there was nothing superficial about her grasp of the complications of Bohemia. In 1878 she was twenty-four, a year younger than Julian Weir, an American and the son of Whistler's old drawing master. Writing home to his parents from London he describes Whistler's lifestyle with barely disguised contempt.

> Whistler is a snob of the first water and a first-class specimen of the eccentric. His house is decorated according to his own taste. The dining room is à la Japanese with fans on the wall and ceiling. His talk was affected and like that of a spoilt child, his hair curled, white pantaloons, patent leather boots and a decided pair of blue socks, one-eyed eye-glass, and he carried a cane the size of a darning needle . . .

To set against this passage we have Lillie's own description of her friend, which refers loyally to his 'unquestionable genius',

> In personal appearance . . . Whistler reached the high point of eccentricity. He was a small, thin man. His face, deep lined (the skin resembling parchment in colour and texture), was lit by alert, beady, black eyes, and oddly emphasised by oily, curly hair, wholly of midnight blackness and with the exception of the one famous, carefully trained, snow-white lock on the forehead, which added a final weird touch. His expressive hands, with their delicate, tapering fingers, were thin almost to transparency, and he wore his nails so extraordinarily long that they produced a sense of discomfort. To estimate his age was impossible, but from his wrinkled face he might have been positively antiquated. Not an Adonis by any means, but of so unusual a type that his appearance was oddly arresting.

The most interesting thing about Lillie's description is its concentration on the man himself. She is struck not by his clothes, as so many others were – and Whistler was a dandy – but by his restless eyes, the oiliness of his hair, his delicate hands. It is his physical presence that is conveyed to the reader, and her final comment contains both an apology for her fascination and an attempt somehow to unravel or explain it, as though, even from the world-torn distance of her sixties, she was puzzled by the hold he had over her that summer.

Chapter XV

Heaven and Hell

At the same time as Lillie was being disturbed by Whistler she was drawing nearer and nearer to an acquaintance from childhood. Arthur Jones was the catalyst for her downfall. He was a friend from Jersey, one of seven illegitimate children that Lord Ranelagh had with his long-suffering mistress. Bachelor and rake that he was, the keeping of a loyal common-law wife was not the least surprising of his many quirks. On the birth certificate her name is given as Mary Edwards Elliott, of 4 Park Place, St James's Parish Westminster, though she seems to have called herself both Mary Elliott and Mary Edwards when the occasion suited. Otherwise we know very little of her except that she must have loved Ranelagh to bear him so many offspring, with so little hope of the official status of a wife, and also that her charms must have been persuasive, since she subsequently found a man prepared to overlook all seven of her indiscretions, and make her an honest woman at last.

Mary married soon after the last of her children had been born. There were four girls, Alice, Adelaide, Constance and Emily, and three boys, Arthur, Charlie and Reggie. Mary's husband, Thomas Weiss, carried her off to Worthing, where he installed her in number two Lennox Villas, by the sea. It was not convenient for the seven children to accompany them, and Mr Weiss, though tolerant, was not willing to bear the financial burden of their upkeep. Instead they were brought up for the most part by a nurse, in a large house in Richmond, funded by Ranelagh. In the holidays they went to Worthing to visit their mother, or to Portelet, Ranelagh's small but idyllic Jersey estate. Ranelagh, for all his vanity and his dislike of commitment, was a loving and interested father. He occupied himself with the smallest of their domestic arrangements, had decided opinions, which were strongly expressed, and expected regular reports on the children's health and welfare from their nurse. Arthur, known as Artie, was the eldest son and the darling. He was also, as a child,

weak and sickly, and therefore doubly indulged. In her letters to
Ranelagh, his nurse referred to him disparagingly as 'Your simple
minded son Artie'. Simple-minded he may have been but his affections
were strong. His own letters to his father are touching, full of passionate
but misspelt endearments, and solemn statements of good intent. Some
things do not change and, even grown-up, he was never what Lillie
would have called 'over-burdened with intellect', his interests being the
traditional ones of a Society buck – horses and hell-raising.

It was at Portelet, in the long Jersey summers when they visited their
father, that the Jones children would first have got to know the Le
Bretons. Ranelagh, as we have seen, was acquainted with the Dean and
his own sizeable and unruly family. The thirteen children would have
been natural playmates. Arthur quickly became a friend of Clement and
Reggie. Born in 1854, he was a year younger than Lillie and, given his
later tastes, must have joined in happily with the rides and the knocker
stealing and the practical jokes. If, at first, the tomboy Lillie was scornful
of the Jones girls and friendly with Arthur alone, for his part in her
brothers' games, she made, when she grew up and married, a fast and
enduring friend of his sister Alice. So much so that, later, when Clement
and Alice fell in love, Lillie was happy to be used as the excuse for their
frequent meetings.

The first record we have of a grown-up acquaintance between the two
sets of children is from the period of Lillie's dangerous attack of typhoid,
soon after her marriage in 1875. Arthur then was close enough to know
of her illness and send her a cake to speed her recovery. Languid, but
convalescent, Lillie wrote back, addressing him very properly, as a
married woman should, as 'Dear Mr Jones'. She thanks him for his kind
thoughts and apologizes for not having written before, excusing herself
on the grounds that she was 'so ill at the time with fever'. The formality
was only skin-deep. As the letter goes on she shrugs it off in favour of a
half-flirtatious, half-sisterly familiarity.

> I hope you don't mean to spend the whole winter in Jersey. Do write and
> tell me all the news and the engagements. How does the drag answer?
> What do you ride? Your new horse I suppose. Are the Bells nice and how
> does dear old Noirmont look? . . . I expect *all* my questions answered
> mind.

'Dear old Noirmont', where the Langtrys had started their married life,
was across the headland from Portelet, a walk or a short ride away. This,

then, would have been where their grown-up acquaintance was cemented. Here Alice and Lillie laid the foundations of their friendship; and Arthur Jones, on the sunny headland walks, learnt, if not to love, then at least to admire the young Mrs Langtry. This little letter about the cake, asking for Jersey news, was found carefully preserved among Arthur's papers. So it was precious enough at the time for him to keep it safe.

Lillie made a dashing and encouraging chaperone to Alice and Clement and their affections were quickly engaged and pledged. When their courtship was at its height, news of it reached Ranelagh, who had rather more ambitious ideas for his girls, partly in the hopes of boosting the family's dwindling fortunes. He wrote angrily to the Dean, accusing Lillie, with her Noirmont newly married ménage, of providing a screen for Clement's lovemaking. He demanded that Clement stop what he saw as a secret correspondence with Alice and tried to extract a promise from him and his father that the meetings between the young couple would cease. Clement was forbidden to communicate again in any way with Alice, and Alice was forbidden to go to Noirmont. Not surprisingly, the Dean refused to oblige Ranelagh with his interference, and eventually the links between the Joneses and the Le Bretons were cemented, in 1877, by Alice's and Clement's marriage in St George's Church in Pimlico. The fact that this was the year of Lillie's 'discovery' must have gone some way towards mollifying Lord Ranelagh, who had in any event helped give Lillie her entrée into Society. If Alice and Clement had married without his consent, it cannot have been long before he relented.

With Reggie dead shortly before Clement and Alice became man and wife, Lillie looked to Clement to replace something of what she had lost. He was her next closest in age. Now married to her friend, and with an establishment and solicitor's practice in London, there was all the more reason for their intimacy. For Ned, too, the friendship must have seemed refreshingly innocent, the simple and familiar company of Alice and Clement a relief from the gilt and gingerbread of Society. Over the next few years the young Le Bretons and the Langtrys were to spend as much time together as Lillie's social life could spare. She must, therefore, on the occasions when he, too, was in London, have seen Arthur. The next time Lillie was to write to him there were no barriers of etiquette between them. Her letter is unaffected, intimate and enthusiastic. Clement and Alice were clearly planning a Whitsun holiday at Portelet and Lillie, hot and disenchanted in London, begs to be allowed to join in. She writes,

> Dear Arthur, I wonder if you will let me come over with Alice and Clem. If it would bore you please say so – I will only come on condition that you will let me contribute my mite towards the expenses. *Do* let me come. Yours very truly, Lillie.

A few days later, still having heard nothing, Lillie begs a second time:

> Dear Arthur, I am *dying* to come over with Clem and Alice next week. I'll sleep in the cottage or on the terrace or in the boat if you'll only let me come. *Please* say yes and I shall enjoy it so if it really won't inconvenience you. I am longing to get out of town.

Jones represented her childhood and her brothers, and she writes to him in the language of that forgotten time, easy, eager and lacking in affectation.

After the gracious, doctored, anecdotes in aspic of her memoirs, her letters to Jones are like spring water. Here she is as she really was – in that moment, on that hot day, beset by the problems of adult life, and longing for her old landscape, for the respite of her old and easy intimacies. It is Lillie's own voice, clear and immediate, that rings at last in our ears; her hand that brushes the page, her feelings that animate the girlish loop of its characters, prompting its flow of careless and unpunctuated lines. Gone are the embalming fluid and the scalpel. These are the parts of herself that Lillie did not want us to see. True, much of what she wrote was hasty and regrettable. Much of it showed her to be weak or, worse in her eyes, warm. But in depriving us of it, she left us something flattened and dehumanized, a Frankenstein of improbability, where we should see the colour and the round of character. Keeping her secrets close, she lost us the vitality of these years in her mid-twenties, lost her unthinkingness of youth, her rapid affections, her partial vision, and her efforts at control. Mistakes are what give us our third dimension. They prick us into life. They are the proof of our humanity and always the key to our psyche.

All this Lillie knew, but flawlessness, even if it was only in two dimensions, was what she wanted. The real and the probable were not her concern. Her letters to Jones, which have slipped so fortunately through her net, are the best means of unravelling her later fictions. They give us back the breathing woman, with all the immediacy of their composition. Now, where posterity saw only the chill of unflagging ambition, we can see muddle and conflict. Where it assumed that she calculated on her influence, where it thought that she milked her royal lover for cash or protection from scandal, where it saw no qualms, no compunction, no genuine fondness for anything other than her own immediate comforts, we can see otherwise. The warmth of her impulses, the depth of her confusion, are laid bare in her letters. Here she stands as she really was – flawed and inconsistent and alive. We see her, at all times and everywhere, both everything and nothing. She was the Society beauty, dressed in lace, and the shoeless tomboy of her youth. She was both loved and scorned, corrupt and bemused, spoilt and unspoilt. She wanted to please and charm, and she spoke naturally to everyone in their own language. She slipped, without noticing it, from the affectation of her talk in Bohemia to the schoolboy spirit of her youth and, as it was in her language, so it was in her behaviour.

In the case of Jones, however, Lillie was driven by something more than an instinct to charm. She wanted a reprieve. What Arthur could give her was her girlhood back. She wanted to start again, to make her choices with the preparation of a clearer head. She wanted not to have tied herself to Ned, to have tried a second season in London unmarried, to be able to make a true choice of a proper companion for life. All this of course was impossible, but Lillie's longing for a second chance was so strong as to amount to belief in its existence.

Not surprisingly, Lillie must have got her way and gone to Jersey with Clement and Alice for the Whitsun weekend. Since she did not date any of her letters it is impossible to tell when exactly she and Jones became lovers. But in the letters that follow the spell in Jersey, Lillie is no longer boyish. Whenever it happened, it happened fast. By the time she writes again a great divide has been crossed. Now we see her trying not only to keep the lid on her own growing commitment, but coping too with the constant threat of rumour. These letters are feverish and demanding, exhibiting a rather desperate veneer of control. Mostly they are arrangements to meet, scrawled in pencil on scraps from a pocket book, or two lines penned on her own fancy paper, a gold lily embossed in the left-hand corner. After the purchase of a green writing case, she wrote, and it is typical,

> Darling, come up for a minute when you come. Ned is actually gone out for half an hour so if you come soon I shall see you alone. Do you like the letter case. I hope it isn't too large. Your lover ever, Lillie.

> I am so delighted you are coming over on Saturday with me. I wanted you

to understand this afternoon that I would meet *you* at Alice's at 4.30 but you didn't tho I went there in case you might.

The note would be written as Ned closed the door, and someone such as Lillie's trusted maid Dominique would run with it to Jones's lodgings. In the meantime, Lillie waited in agitation, hoping that Jones would come, aware of the possibility of Ned's return, or the arrival of the Prince of Wales – aware but no less careless of the risks she ran. Disgrace, ruin, the loss of her few remaining chances, nothing seemed to count any more. She ran the gauntlet of the Prince's displeasure and of Ned's battery almost without thinking. Again she writes, the haste tangible,

> Dearest Artie, There is a train at 12.30 which I shall catch. Please go down by the train before and wait for me at the station. Ever, Lillie

> If I *can* escape Ned I also will come down by the 12.10. Therefore if I am not there in time you will know Ned is seeing me off by the 12.30 which I am afraid he will insist on doing.

These meetings must be during the autumn of 1878, or spring of the following year. It was still only the beginning of the affair, but there is a sharp urgency to Lillie's tone that is new. There was something in Jones that Lillie needed for herself, in a way that she did not feel with the Prince or her admirers in Bohemia. Whether it was the salvation of her childhood, or reinstatement in the bosom of her family, or simply a chance to turn the clocks back, to start again untrammelled, she fell rapidly and desperately in love. She lost the balance between her other protectors, lost the ability to make a cold decision. We feel her, almost despite herself, focused increasingly on this shadowy figure from her past, rushing to meet him at an assignation that she has failed to make clear; pretending indifference while watching for him, even in places where he could not be; missing him in rooms full of the wrong people. We see her, in Norfolk Street, sitting at her writing table in the early evening, grasping a rare moment of solitude to scribble a plea for his company; watch her, as she paces the room in her tea-gown, her eye on the clock, calculating, hoping, delaying dressing for dinner, against his chance arrival. Always she is distracted by the demands of her career in Society. Always there are people between them: Ned, her friends, her lovers, even her family, from whom her love must be kept. Frustration and secrecy are her constant companions. She worries about gossip. She juggles lovers and social engagements. She smiles and dresses and entertains. Then, suddenly the path clears and they meet – her reward, a few snatched moments of deceit, lighting the dark landscape of her hope and despair with the beacon of a passion.

Arthur's love, and the life he seemed to offer, became talismanic to Lillie, and she clung to it all the more strongly because she knew all along that it could not be true. As his declared lover Lillie was importunate, and rarely, if ever, in the driving seat. Jones was, in more ways than one, her Achilles heel. Though she was to love again, and despite the fact that she was never stingy with her favours, he was the last man on whom she truly relied, the last man in whom she placed all her hopes and all her trust. As the love affair developed, hope upon hope was heaped on his shoulders. She wheedled and bullied by turns, demanding that he provide her with the longed-for salvation. She expected him to provide a refuge from the hounds of scandal at her heels, to love her, shield her, fight for her. Never again was she so desperate, never again so dependant.

By the time he came to fail her she had learnt her lesson. She never again relinquished the controls.

After Jones, Lillie's lovers were for diversion and financial exploitation. Since he had no money at all, and since she knew it, Lillie loved Jones without ulterior motives. Of all her lovers he was the least used, and therefore the purest, the most deeply felt. In recognition of this, of his being the only chink in her armour, she destroyed all his replies to her letters. If her voice has been handed down to us, rich and complex; his is silenced. All we can tell is that he returned her love for several years and that, even when it faltered, he could not bear to destroy its written record. Though his letters to Lillie are gone, hers to him were kept in a green case that she bought for the purpose, kept long after the affair had ended, through both their marriages to others, and through many deaths, until they were found, as he had left them, still in the case, in an attic in 1978. It was a long time to keep a secret.

Chapter XVI

Oscar Wilde

Before 1878 closed there was one more player to enter Lillie's stage. In December Oscar Wilde had arrived in London from Oxford and moved into the shambolic Salisbury Street house in which Miles had his studio. Wilde took the floor below Miles, the ground floor being occupied by Harry Marillier, a Bluecoat schoolboy, who had fitted it up as a library. Various descriptions of Wilde's rooms survive. All agree that they were marvellous not just for their avant-garde aestheticism but for the incongruity of their location. Though Wilde rather affectedly called it 'Thames House' (on account of its view) it was, from the street, a nondescript building. Once inside, there was a crumbling dirty warren of staircases which gave no hint at the light and sophistication to which they led. One account called it 'one of the most remarkable apartments in London'. It describes a long room,

> . . . panelled principally in white, and on the panels were inscribed many autographs of famous men and women. Sarah Bernhardt's name was scrawled with a carpenter's pencil right across one panel. Those of Ellen Terry and Henry Irving were on another. The furniture, rugs, hangings and blue china were a revelation to the eyes of one on whom the new aesthetic movement was yet to dawn. Lilies were everywhere, and on an easel at one end of the room, like a sort of altar, stood Edward Poynter's great yellow portrait of Lillie Langtry . . .

Miles and Wilde were in fact in the process of having a house adapted for them by Godwin. As early as 1878 plans had been submitted to the Works and General Purposes Committee, and after one rejection and some modifications, work was begun in Tite Street, Chelsea, close to Whistler. The building was ready by July 1880. It was suitably rarified in design – red and yellow brickwork, with balconies and a green slate roof.

Wilde called it 'Keats House', either after the two women named Skeates from whom the property had been bought, or to fit with Shelley House around the corner.

The informal gatherings that Society had enjoyed in Miles's studio Wilde now shared, acting as joint host among the startling blue china and the Tanagra figures. They had no maid to perform the offices of a hostess for them so one of Miles's models, a flower girl off the streets, was pressed into service. Miles, always affable, would lend a hand, but not Wilde, who considered tea-pouring, like cricket, an unclassical activity, and therefore beneath him. Two of their regular guests were Lillie's friends, Augusta Fane and Gladys Lonsdale. Augusta remained unimpressed by their domestication, though she was fooled by the flower-seller. The two young women would drive down together, in Lady Lonsdale's carriage, to have tea 'in their quaint little old house', where, Augusta remembered, 'we were waited on by one maid dressed in sage blue and holding a lily in her hand – which got very much in her way when arranging the tea table'.

Lillie, who was still intimate with Miles, would quickly have resumed her acquaintance with Wilde. Again, as with Whistler, she was disturbed by his physical presence and no doubt, in this case, also by his nebulous sexuality. She had not forgotten her first meeting with him two years before. 'Vividly', she recounts in the memoirs, 'I recall the first meeting with Oscar Wilde in the studio of Frank Miles, and how astonished I was at his strange appearance.' Now, again, she saw

... a profusion of brown hair, brushed back from his forehead, and worn rather longer than was conventional . . . His face was large and so colourless that a few pale freckles of good size were oddly conspicuous. He had a well-shaped mouth, with somewhat coarse lips and greenish-hued teeth. The plainness of his face, however, was redeemed by the splendour of his great, eager eyes.

In height he was about six feet, and broad in proportion. His hands were large and indolent, with pointed fingers and perfectly-shaped filbert nails . . . The nails, I regretfully record, rarely receiving the attention they deserved. To me he was always grotesque in appearance . . . That he possessed a remarkably fascinating and compelling personality, and what in an actor would be termed wonderful 'stage presence', is beyond question, and there was about him an enthusiasm singularly captivating. He had one of the most alluring voices that I have ever listened to, round and soft, and full of variety and expression, and the cleverness of his remarks received added value from his manner of delivering them.

By comparison the ordinary Augusta found Wilde's appearance shocking, indeed 'revolting'. 'He had,' she remembered, 'a fat, clean shaven, pallid face.' Worst of all were the green teeth, stained by the mercury he had taken as a cure for syphilis. Like most of Society she was not seduced by cleverness, and she was positively disgusted by anything that departed from the accepted mould for manhood, as defined by straightforwardness, muscularity and facial hair. Lillie had had more than her fill of Society's ideal male and was intrigued by Wilde's difference. To her, as with Whistler, he was a fringe figure, and she was fascinated by his insouciant capacity to outrage.

Wilde was twenty-three. He had, as Lillie rather unkindly pointed out, not done anything to deserve the reputation he was undoubtedly beginning to enjoy. He had written a handful of poems but no great work. His plays, his stories and his provocative lecture tours were all in the future. He was a prize-winning Oxford graduate, no more, and yet when he went to the theatre he was already pointed out as 'that bloody fool Oscar Wilde'. What he had done, early on, was to fulfil what he later termed 'the first duty in life', which was to assume a pose. Innate character was not for him. It was not artistic. Instead he cultivated his already overblown sensibilities and affected a camp boredom. This was not the full-blown style of his prime by which we tend to remember him now, not yet the knickerbockers, or the green carnation, or the lilac gloves that were carried but never worn. He was still young, like Lillie, just setting out on his career, but he had had a coat cut for himself in the shape of a violin and he was searching for a mode of expression, for a vehicle for his views.

For inspiration, Wilde looked to Whistler, to France, to the Decadents, and to Ruskin and Pater, trumpeting their rival philosophies of the aesthetic. For himself, he believed in beauty, in the senses, and in contentiousness. He had the same appetite as Lillie for experience, the same delight (though his was more conscious, more intellectually formulated) in the contradictions of life. Nothing for him was taboo. In his mind's eye, the tree of knowledge, as he saw it, 'with its staring fury', stood next to the tree of life, whose 'blind lush leaves' mingled with the leaves of its neighbour, so that their fruits hung side by side. He made no distinctions between them and gorged himself equally on both. In its more sensual aspects, he had a strong susceptibility to religion. Worship was, to him, a form of art. At Oxford he had toyed – and he was never more serious than in play – with Catholicism. He also had a serious and enduring preoccupation with morality. All this, and yet he lacked a motive for writing or speaking. Like everyone else, he was looking for a Muse.

At Miles's tea parties, Wilde quickly gained a reputation for wit in conversation. He appeared easy and self-assured. His tastes were sophisticated. People began to point him out and to expect something of him. It was widely known that he had won the Newdigate prize for poetry (though he himself was reticent about his triumph), so it was as a poet that he was expected to make his mark. The cult of personality, with its overtones of publicity and self-invention, was not an art form that Society recognized. It, at least, expected something more, and Wilde was aware of this. When Miles introduced him to 'the most beautiful woman in the world' he was quick to hail her as the Muse he lacked. Ronald Gower, homosexual friend of both men, was told by an enraptured Miles that he, with his pencil, and Wilde, with his pen, would make Lillie the 'Laura and Joconde of the century'. In other words they would make her into a goddess and disseminate her cult.

All this was flattering to Lillie in her first flush of recognition, but no more than anyone else was offering. Two years later, in 1879, with her cult already fading, she was less blasé and she was looking for mentors. Wilde was a year younger than Lillie, born the same year as her lost brother Reggie, though it was not as a brother that Lillie saw him. He was brilliant in a way that she particularly admired and he was dangerous, not to others so much as to himself, in a way that she found, if not attractive, then at least compelling.

What did Wilde see in her? Much later he left a careful exposition of her classical attractions that has the solid feel of the statuary it describes. What he saw as the 'grave low forehead, the exquisitely arched brow; the noble chiselling of the mouth, shaped as if it were the mouthpiece of an instrument of music; the supreme and splendid curve of the cheek; the augustly pillared throat which bears it all' were the features of the boy Antinoos made flesh again in female form. He recognized and revered the classical precedent, seeing Lillie herself as in some way responsible for its magical appearance. Her beauty was to him a form of genius. That it was not marble, this time, but flesh, enhanced with the attendant complexities of decay and compromise, made it perfect. Added to which, her following was beginning to desert her. The taint that was beginning to corrode her was like a magnet for him. He could fly in its face, vindicate her, be the last clarion of her dying cult. Whole avenues of religious postures opened before him, including, exquisitely, those of self-sacrifice and martyrdom.

Behind the pose of a goddess and her prophet or priest, there were two people. Wilde and Lillie, whatever their motivation, were friends. Indeed Wilde may even have felt they were more than that. His biographer, Richard Ellmann, makes a case for their having had some kind of affair, in which Wilde's affections, for a moment, were truly engaged. At any rate, he made his admiration for her public from the first. Lillie records that,

> he always made a point of bringing me flowers, but he was not in the circumstances to afford great posies, so, in coming to call, he would drop into Covent Garden flower market, buy me a single gorgeous amaryllis (all his slender purse would allow), and stroll down Piccadilly carefully carrying the solitary flower.

Punch's mocking title the 'Apostle of the Lily' was more perspicacious than it first appeared. But Wilde turned out to be a demanding admirer. If Lillie looked perfect she must have the mind to match. He began to tutor her in Latin and Greek, and took her regularly to the British Museum to acquaint herself with all her stone siblings. They went together, at Wilde's instigation, to hear Newton's lectures on Greek art, arriving in the same carriage to a crowd of cheering students, who gathered every morning to watch them disembark. He introduced her to Ruskin, his great mentor, though Ruskin was not impressed. And he took her to tea with his mother, Lady Wilde, otherwise known as 'Speranza' the poetess, in Onslow Square. Soon Lillie was relying on Wilde for instruction in every area of her life. That her few surviving letters to him are confiding and flirtatious means little on her side, since it was the currency of all her communications with men. She was, however, playing Wilde and Miles off against each other, so there must have been something, on Wilde's part, to play with. Staying at Beaconsfield in 1879 she wrote to Wilde cancelling her next tutorial. The letter give us a flavour of their friendship.

> Of course I'm longing to learn more Latin but we stay here till Wednesday night so I shan't be able to see my kind tutor before Thursday. Do come and see me on that afternoon about six if you can.
>
> I called at Salisbury Street about half an hour before you left. I wanted to ask you how I should go to a fancy ball here, but I chose a soft black Greek dress with a fringe of silver crescents and stars, and diamond ones in my hair and on my neck and called it Queen of Night. I made it myself.
>
> I want to write more but this horrid paper and pen prevent me so when we meet I will tell you more: *eadem* (only don't tell Frank).

Lillie may have been flattering herself with Frank Miles's jealousy. Wilde's distress, on occasion, was very real. When he heard Lillie attacked by a Society lady he referred to her attacker publicly and in anger as 'that old lady who keeps the artificial roses on her bald head with tin tacks'. At some point during the summer he began a poem to Lillie called 'The New Helen'. Lillie, though flattered by the poem, began to find Wilde's persistence irritating. He was, she recalls,

> . . . so obsessed with the subject that he would walk round and round the streets in which our little house was situated for hours at a time, probably investing me with every quality I never possessed, and, although Wilde had a keen sense of the ridiculous, he sometimes unconsciously bordered thereon himself. For instance, one night he curled up to sleep on my doorstep, and Mr Langtry, returning unusually late, put an end to his poetic dreams by tripping over him.

If Lillie liked admiration she found worship tiresome and ridiculous. She did not believe in goddesses and, besides, Wilde was probably better company when he was not lovesick. She goes on, in her memoirs, to record another incident, when her irritation finally got the better of her.

> There were times when I found him too persistent in hanging round the house or running about after me elsewhere, and I am afraid that often I said things which hurt his feelings in order to get rid of him. After a frank remark I made on one occasion, I happened to go to the theatre, and, as I sat in my box, I noticed a commotion in the stalls – it was Oscar, who, having perceived me suddenly, was being led away in tears by his friend Frank Miles.

Goddesses have boxes at the theatre, even if they are on the verge of bankruptcy, and their acolytes must brave both the crush of the stalls and the agony of rejection. This account must be taken with a pinch of salt, however. Lillie wrote it in the 1920s, after Wilde's public disgrace. A declaration of her friendship with him was daring enough for her; she did not want to admit to more intimacy than she need.

Later on, one of the major deceptions of Lillie's life centred round her failure to stand by Wilde when he was in trouble. She maintains in her memoirs that she lent him money in the last years of his life, for which there is no evidence, a clear indication that she felt uneasy about her desertion.

Plenty of other and older friends vanished, once Wilde was a bankrupt and a jailbird. Almost all his former intimates shunned him, either because they could not tolerate his sexuality or because they disliked him begging for money. As for Lillie, perhaps, in this case, she did have something to deny. To many others who suffered trouble or disgrace, Lillie was a loyal friend. Augusta Fane, for one, was to write of her that 'all her life she kept her women friends', and elsewhere, with Lillie in mind, that,

> Women have more moral courage than men, and are far more loyal. When great troubles and difficulties beset one's path in life it is our women friends who stick by us and hold out the helping hand.

Lillie's friendship with Wilde lasted through and beyond her affair with Arthur Jones, and was close enough to make Jones jealous. He wrote, years later, when Lillie was in a patch of convalescence, accusing her of being too ill to come to London but not too ill to enjoy the society of Wilde, who was staying in the same house. Wilde himself, whether his love for Lillie was a love of the imagination, or something that was, however briefly, realized, was quite aware of Jones as competition. The feelings he describes in all of the three extant poems to her are those of anxiety, pain and jealousy. Ellmann quotes tell-tale references to 'the arched splendour of those brows Olympian' and the 'too perilous bliss' that his lips had drunk at hers. He also quotes from a poem entitled 'To L.L.', in which a girl with grey-green eyes ran from the poet's kisses, taunting him characteristically with the reproof, 'You have wasted your life. You have only yourself to blame that you are not famous.' 'The New Helen' was chaster and more circumspect in its references. Wilde brought a presentation copy round to Lillie at Norfolk Street, bound in white vellum, with the inscription 'To Helen, formerly of Troy, now of London.' Lillie liked it well enough to include it, in full, in her memoirs. Mostly it concerns itself with the usual classical caravan: Helen, Semele, Calypso and Aphrodite herself. Only towards the end does it become biographical, when Wilde bemoans the possibility of Lillie leaving the country in favour of the 'red lips of young Euphorion' and the isle of her birth. He begs,

> The lotus leaves which heal the wounds of Death
>   Lie in thy hand; O, be thou kind to me,
> While yet I know the summer of my days;
>   For hardly can my tremulous lips draw breath

To fill the silver trumpet with thy praise,
    So bowed am I before thy mystery,
So bowed and broken on Love's terrible wheel,
    That I have lost all hope and heart to sing,
    Yet care I not what ruin Time may bring,
    If in thy temple thou wilt let me kneel.

Alas, alas, thou wilt not tarry here,
    But, like that bird, the servant of the sun,
Who flies before the north wind and the night,
    So wilt thou fly our evil land and drear,
Back to the sower of thine old delight,
    And the red lips of young Euphorion;
Nor shall I ever see thy face again,
    But in this poisoned garden-close must stay,
Crowning my brows with the thorn-crown of pain,
    Till all my loveless life shall pass away.

O Helen! Helen! Helen! Yet a while,
    Yet for a little while, O tarry here,
Till the dawn cometh and the shadows flee!
    For in the gladsome sunlight of thy smile
Of heaven or hell I have no thought or fear,
    Seeing I know no other God but thee;
No other God save him before whose feet
    In nets of gold the tired planets move;
The incarnate spirit of spiritual love,
Who in thy body holds his joyous seat.*

The poem has all the usual tangle of flesh and spirit, of gods and bodies, religion and eroticism, that were the hallmarks of Wilde's love. Lillie, though she played the goddess so well, had more than a touch of tantalizing androgyny. Her appetites were pronounced and dark. Her looks were heavy and sometimes masculine. She had the physical dash and daring of her brothers. She could swim and row and ride. She had a frankness about her and a boyish grace. And yet she was a woman. Part of her fascination for Wilde must have been that she combined the feminine and the masculine in a way that offered a much needed rescue

* 'The New Helen' was first published in *Time* in July 1879.

from his muddled and illegal leanings. There is an underlying urgency to the poem that is hard to ignore. He needed her not just as a subject for worship, to inspire his poems, but also to liberate him from the 'poisoned garden-close' of his own sexuality. The taint of perversion carried with it, as he was to find, terrible retribution and disgrace. Without the salvation that androgyny extended, his life would have to be passed in lovelessness, so he pleads to Lillie as though she were his only hope.

Wilde's worries about losing Lillie to 'young Euphorian' and her 'island home' were not unfounded. By January of the following year Lillie was contemplating elopement and was discussing it with Lord Wharncliffe. Whether or not Wilde, too, was in her confidence, he was no fool. If Jones was jealous of Wilde, then Wilde was returning the compliment. In fact neither need have lost much sleep. Their roles in Lillie's life were so separate as to make it impossible for either of them to threaten the tenuous happiness of his rival. As she lost no opportunity of telling him, Lillie could not live without Jones, but then neither could she have lived without Wilde. He was absolutely necessary to her in the limbo of her lost self and fading popularity. If she did not tell him so, it was only because she did not realize it herself. In contrast, Wilde was only too aware of how much he depended on Lillie. His fears of loss stemmed from needs that were artistic as well as emotional. Lillie was his self-professed religion, a fertile source of inspiration for his poetry as much as for the development of his aesthetics. 'Seeing I know no other God but thee' has behind it the assumption that he cannot function artistically without a god of some sort. Because of his sexual ambiguity his love poetry relied on the tradition of enshrining the beloved with the language of religious observance rather than celebrating it in a secular context with language that was either passionate or straight erotic.

To Wilde, then, as to so many others, Lillie was irresistible, but she was more than irresistible, she was necessary. A goddess in distress is a rare opportunity and Wilde needed to worship. Their relationship, while it lasted, was profound, but Lillie was only one in a succession of Wilde's enthusiasms. At Oxford there had been Pater. Then 'La divine Sarah' Bernhardt. Now Lillie. And so it would go on. It was hard for a deity to escape him, whether it was a question of simple appropriation, or whether the deity needed help with its own creation. In Lillie's case he elected himself something between prophet and PR agent and he set out to proselytize. Worship after all was a career move. It gave him a subject for his highly wrought extravagances, and it forced both himself and it into the public's notice. As a sophisticated form of dual publicism it would not have worked without the devotion being, in some way, real. He could not have done it for someone he did not like. In this instance, clearly, he liked a great deal, and, complications aside, his feelings were reciprocated.

Wilde was an entrancing companion. Despite Lillie's occasional irritation it was an equal partnership. In their strange symbiotic friendship, a matching opportunism and talent for showmanship screened, for both, what was still unresolved or inconsistent. In different ways they were raw underneath and each, while brilliantly cresting their wave, was aware of the imminent danger of drowning. From Wilde, though she never had the grace to acknowledge it, Lillie learnt more than from anyone else. He was her Svengali. He caught her on the brink of chaos, saw both what she really was and what she could become. He set her on the course that she was to take up and steer so valiantly, and if he did not quite invent her he certainly gave her the means of inventing herself.

Whatever form their relationship took, Wilde loved Lillie well enough to know her in a way that Jones was incapable of, Whistler too preoccupied for, and that the Prince's position forbade. He is the best key to her mind and its true workings that we have.

Chapter xvii

Society

How quickly, if at all, the Prince knew of Lillie's double infidelities in Jersey and Bohemia is hard to tell. Had she continued to allow him his privileges it is unlikely that, even if he did find out, he would mind very much. Appetite amused him, so long as he still got his share. What he found harder to stomach was a marked preference for someone else. In any case, Jones and Whistler and Wilde were not part of his world, a fact which made the erosion of his sole claim both less noticeable and less discomfiting, and, most important of all, Lillie's behaviour towards him remained unchanged into 1879.

Ned, however, was less tolerant. In December of 1878 *Vanity Fair* had a brief entry in its gossip columns which ran,

> A lady well-known in society is said to have been seen with two black eyes, *not* the result of self-embellishment. The question asked is, who, or rather which, gave them?

Ned had reached the end of his tether. On top of the multiple infidelities there were the debts, and he was beginning to find that, even if he closed his eyes to his wife's lovers, he could not make her creditors disappear. He now began to mark his sense of outrage and loss with appalling bouts of recrimination and battery. Heavy nights of drinking and long days of brooding resulted in abuse that was both verbal and physical. He also began, for the first time, to threaten Lillie with divorce. This probably had more to do with the bills than with his rivals but, whatever the reason, it was leapt on by the Fleet Street rags. Both *Vanity Fair* and its nastier, tattling counterpart, *Town Talk*, ran stories about the coming case through December and the New Year. *Vanity Fair* was first, with a tongue-in-cheek disclaimer against the rumour of divorce that must have been circulating in the salons before Christmas. In February of 1879

Town Talk asked whether it was true that London was

> shortly to be regaled with a highly sensational divorce case, in which a well-known beauty will play a prominent part? And is it also true that someone occupying a very high position in society will be called upon as a witness?

Two months later, like a dog with a bone, it returned to the subject, this time with a little more authority in its tone.

> About the warmest divorce case which ever came before a judge may shortly be expected to come off. The respondent was a reigning beauty not many centuries ago, and the co-respondents – and they are numerous – are big 'pots'. The poor husband is almost frantic. 'Darn this country,' he says, 'nothing belongs to a fellow here. Even his wife is everybody's property,' Oh that woman! I myself loved her. I bought her portrait . . . in thirty-five different positions, and wept over it in the silent hours of the night.

Lillie had lost her battle against rumour. She was, imaginably, desperate.

If Ned knew about Jones, and it is likely that he did, he might have relished the prospect of Lillie's future life, dunned by her London creditors and shunned by Society, living in obscurity with her penniless love. As it was, he found that it was one thing to be cuckolded by the future King of England and quite another to be usurped by the bastard of a minor peer. Besides, Lillie's affections had never been wholly engaged with the Prince. She admitted in old age that she had always been a little afraid of him and that 'he always smelt so *very strongly* of cigars'. With Jones, it was different. Her feelings were simply not controllable. For the first time, she too became possessed by the idea of divorce – though she preferred that it be managed privately and without scandal, for, unlike Ned, whose motives were sour and vengeful, she had the prospect of a fresh start ahead of her, of a new and hopeful life with Jones. Ned had become too problematic. She was afraid of him and tired of fighting. And besides, she too now knew that they were staring at bankruptcy. Lillie was never one to stay on a sinking ship. Slowly, almost unconsciously, she had geared herself over the winter months towards separation, building a structure of help and support for herself, outside her rejected domestic life. Emotionally and psychologically she packed her bags, heaping them on Arthur Jones, on her confidants and on her remaining friends, until, by the beginning of 1879, she had moved out, and left their marriage empty.

At the season's close, in August 1878, the Langtrys had gone to Scotland, Lillie's first trip north of the border. They stayed first with the Millais in a rented house, for a peaceful month's fishing, which Ned had clearly enjoyed. It was the last time Ned had her to himself. There is no record of where the Langtrys spent Christmas but by January of the following year they were in London again. Roller skating, newly invented, was the latest craze and Lillie was spotted at Prince's Club, skating 'most gracefully' on her brand-new wheels. Then they hit the house-party trail again, going north to stay with the Wharncliffes at Wortley. Lillie was now writing regularly to Lord Wharncliffe, leaning on him for advice and emotional support. He was integral to her new extra-marital system of props. For his part, he was probably unhappily in love with her, like so many others. Ned and Lillie spent a week at Wortley and then it was on to stay at Brantingham Thorpe, with Christopher Sykes, whose scalp, for diversion, Lillie was idly contemplating. Sykes was a bachelor friend of the Prince of Wales. Lillie would have met him countless times in Society, and had stayed with him, and the Prince, that summer at Cowes. He was not Lillie's type, a solemn dandy of the old school, spectacularly bearded, and temporarily very rich, though he bankrupted himself entertaining the Prince, to whom he was devoted. Loyal in a rather lugubrious way, he suffered cigar burns, sticking with billiard cues and the regular emptying of the brandy decanter over his head, to all of which his only reply was, 'As Your Royal Highness pleases.' This was greeted, by the Royal set, with thigh-slapping and howls of laughter, a guaranteed pep for any moments of longueur. Probably, too, it amused the Prince to see Sykes enamoured of his favourite consort. He may even have suggested it to Lillie as a possible match. In her letters to Wharncliffe Lillie refers to him frequently and familiarly as 'Xtopher', or simply 'C'.

From Brantingham, Lillie at last got round to thanking Lord Wharncliffe for his hospitality and telling him her news. There is an intimate confidentiality to her tone that, if Wharncliffe was in love with her, must have been a torment. She had been, since she saw him, to three balls, and apologizes for not having written sooner but skating and dancing had left no time for anything else. Her letter closes with a breezy injunction to 'write to me occasionally'. Wharncliffe must have taken her at her word for she was promptly answered. He invited both her and Ned back to Wortley, on their way south from Birmingham, on 7 February.

They came and stayed another week. On their departure Lady Wharncliffe noted in her diary, 'Ed. very low.'

The conclusion of the Langtrys' northern tour coincided with the publication of the rumours of divorce in the *Town Talk*. Ned, despite their foundation in truth, reacted with fury, threatening prosecution for libel. Wharncliffe wrote again in sympathy and Lillie replied with a flood of relief.

> Dear Lord Wharncliffe, Yr kind heart prompted you to write to me just the letter I longed for & shows me that I have not wrongly appreciated yr. true friendship. You will know that Ned has at last decided to prosecute the Editor, not I must admit without considerable opposition on my part, my horror of being dragged before the public being great, still I think he is right. Indeed after hearing the atrocious statements circulated thro' the medium of Town Talk, I became so morbidly sensitive that I dared not walk in the street & I am still utterly miserable. I shall be in London all the month. I think you said you would come to see me on the 22nd. The morning will be the best about 12. By then I hope this tiresome business will be settled.

Lillie knew full well that she could not be 'dragged before the public' in a divorce court and survive, but she must have been counting on the protection of the Prince, whose interests were possibly more fragile than her own. To Lord Wharncliffe she was hoping that her bluff would not be called. But the 'tiresome business' showed no signs of being settled, as London moved towards another season. By the end of May *Town Talk* was happy to name names, observing on the 31st,

> I am informed that Mr Langtry has announced his intention of breaking my neck. Now, if the brave gentleman wants to go in for neck-breaking, surely he can find plenty of his friends (?) who have injured him more than I have.

After this, in the week that followed, there was a second report, this time a disclaimer. It was probably the result of pressure put on the editor Rosenberg, but it had the effect, as he knew it would, of keeping the matter in the public eye. It ran:

> There has been lately a rumour that Mrs Langtry was about to appear in the divorce court, with more than one illustrious correspondent. The rumour is, like many others, without the least foundation.

The main result of these continued attacks was to stamp Lillie, in the eyes of the public, as an adventuress, whose notoriety was purchased at the expense of her own morals and her husband's peace of mind. She was well aware now of her unpopularity, and her letters contain many references to her 'enemies'. To Lord Wharncliffe, her loyal champion, she wrote in triumph on a good day,

> I am sure you will like to know that the Princess of W. who was riding this morning sent for me to ride with her in the row. Wasn't it nice of her. I dont think she has ever ridden with anyone before, so I felt very proud and hoped all my enemies could see me.

Poor Lillie, so trivial and so embattled, manipulating her way through her solitary campaign as the summer wore on. When in London, she kept Lord Wharncliffe at her beck and call. 'Are you never coming again to see me. I shall be at home tomorrow at 4 & probably alone.'

The letters to Jones himself dry up in her third season. This was not because Lillie was any less dependent. He and she were for the moment matched in their devotion, and had, too, found a way to be more constantly in each other's company. Jones would base himself, when not in Jersey, with his mother at Worthing and Lillie would make long visits to Brighton. She would stay, with or without Ned, in the rather grand house of a Baron Grant, a crooked property speculator, also on his way down, after a decade of success which had included the development of Leicester Square in London. Grant's title was self-styled, a rather loose interpretation of the gratitude of the Italians for his fund-raising efforts towards the Galleria Vittorio Emanuele at Milan. He was typical of the kind of man to whom Lillie found herself increasingly drawn: personable, 'of agreeable presence and enthusiastic manners', and an habitué of the criminal fringe, that shadowy no-man's-land, stretching between honest enterprise and felony.

Brighton had become fashionable during the Regency, most obviously with the building of the Royal Pavilion. By the end of the century many of the rich still had houses in the sparkling butter-coloured seafront squares, or on the wide avenues that divided them, to which they retired at the close of the season. The Reuben Sassoons, who became Lillie's close friends, and the Alingtons of Crichel, among others, were regular visitors, and would have made Lillie feel that she was not in exile. With the London season still going, it was a quiet and genteel front for Lillie's affair with Jones, near enough to the capital for Lillie to return on the train for social engagements that were obligatory. To anyone who asked, her reason for leaving London was a feminine sensitivity to the atmosphere created by the cruel attacks of *Town Talk*.

Surprisingly, the person who took Lillie's erratic attendance hardest was the Prince of Wales. Relations between the two of them were, by the summer, beginning to be strained. In June the Comédie Française arrived in England for a theatrical season. They brought with them the new star of the French stage, Sarah Bernhardt. With Lillie's pedestal crumbling and her deity in question, London was ready for another craze. Sarah was already famous in France. She was waif-like in appearance, determinedly decadent in the best French *fin-de-siècle* manner, and already several steps ahead of Lillie in the creation of a saleable self. She travelled, it was rumoured, with a circus of pet cheetahs and pythons and took a daily rest in a coffin lined with pink silk. It did not matter whether the details were true or false. London was hungry once again and letters back to France from her entourage were frank in their amazement at the extent of her success. 'Nothing,' wrote Francisque Sarcey, 'nothing can give an idea of the craze that Mlle Sarah Bernhardt is exciting. It's a mania.' And this time Lillie was to be a spectator.

Lillie was not by nature envious. She recognized Sarah's genius and admired her beauty. Moreover, Bohemia had taken up the Bernhardt cult and since Lillie increasingly saw Bohemia as her guiding light she joined in its adulation. As an added spur there was the carping of the middle-brow elements of Society and the man in the street who had not. Lillie would have been keen to distance herself from their bourgeois disapproval. Her praise, in her memoirs, of Sarah was both astute and unstinting:

Bernhardt's personality was so striking, so singular that, to everyday people, she seemed eccentric; she filled the imagination as a great poet might do.

Her beauty, frankly, was not understood by the masses. It was a period of tiny waists, large shoulders, larger hips; and this remarkable woman, who possessed the beautiful, supple, uncorseted figure . . . was called a skeleton. She gowned herself beautifully, wearing mostly long, trailing, white garments, richly embroidered and beaded . . . Around her throat she tied the large bow of tulle made familiar in Georges Clairin's painting, in which she reclines on a couch, all in white, with a Russian wolf-hound at her feet . . . Painters and poets admired her. Oscar Wilde enthused over her likeness to coins of the ancient Romans, and carried me off to the British Museum to hunt for her profile in coins, intaglios, and vases of the period . . . Like all great beauty, however, it did not blaze upon one's vision, but grew upon acquaintance. And hers, being a combination of intelligence, of feature and of soul, remained with her until the end of her life.

Of course there is a hierarchy being established here: Lillie was compared to Greece in the golden age of Phidias, Sarah only to Rome, but Lillie's admiration was nevertheless real. Here was a woman who was fêted in the same way as Lillie had been, with a son but no husband and without any of the normal trappings of respectability. She was a siren, brilliant, egotistic, independent, illegitimate, and yet still *sortable*. She had as many lovers and as many cheetahs as she wanted and Society did not seem to care. True, the old guard clicked their tongues, but they could not turn the clocks back.

Lady Frederick Cavendish wrote in a diary entry at the end of June,

London has gone mad over the principal actress of the Comédie Française who are here: Sarah Bernhardt – a woman of notorious, shameless character . . . Not content with being run after on the stage, this woman is asked to respectable people's houses to act, and even to luncheon and dinner; and all the world goes. It is an outrageous scandal.

Times were changing, and Lillie was not slow to notice. Lillie and Sarah met soon after Sarah's arrival in England at a breakfast given by Sir Algernon Borthwick, editor of the *Morning Post*, and patron of the theatre. He was particularly keen on French drama and this season for the Comédie Française had been his idea. Sarah wore white and the famous tulle bow and she and Lillie sat on either side of their host and, presumably, weighed each other up across the divide. They appeared to get on pretty well. Like Lillie, Sarah was shrewd, however eccentric or affected she chose to appear.

Lillie noted,

In private life, she seemed as natural as a child, and was quite unspoiled by the adulation of the world. She had an enormous sense of humour, and a quickness of perception which enabled her to grasp a speaker's meaning and reply before he was halfway through his sentence.

Here was a new goddess, and since the old one was beginning to prove difficult, the Prince of Wales solaced himself with obeisance at the rival shrine. In part this must have been intended to sting Lillie into repentance. In part he was simply following the trend. Bernhardt's first appearance at the Gaiety was, in the second act of *Phèdre*, greeted with hysterical applause. The *Standard* recorded that, 'A scene of enthusiasm such as is rarely witnessed in a theatre followed the fall of the curtain.' Watching, possibly with Wilde at her elbow, Lillie would have been astute enough to see how all this was managed. Sarah, it was made known, had overreached herself on her first performance. The curtain call revealed her too weak to stand, supported in the arms of her leading man. According to the papers, she then spent the night vomiting blood while doctors put fragments of crushed ice between her lips. Death was feared. Her own doctor from Paris was summoned post-haste, and arrived to ban her from all further exertion. She had his orders published abroad, disguised herself in a cloak and a lace fichu and went to the theatre as planned. Unfortunately the opium she had taken as medicine veiled the audience and her fellow players in 'a luminous mist' and she cut two hundred lines, closing the scene and causing her co-star Croizette to collapse in shock. Yet again the effect on the audience was electrifying.

Nor did Sarah limit her conquest to the theatre. In the daytime she dressed herself fetchingly in white overalls and brandished the paintbrush and the chisel. She produced enough to stage an exhibition of her own paintings and sculpture. Not surprisingly, she sent out her casual invitations to a hundred people and was rewarded with the presence of twelve hundred. Among them were the Prince and Princess of Wales, and Lillie. The money she raised went towards the purchase of two baby lions, which were substituted, when she reached the zoo, for a baby cheetah, a dog-wolf, and seven chameleons, all of which were housed, at great inconvenience to her neighbours, in her London lodgings. Blood, passion, art, opium and wild animals, there was nothing that anyone could teach Sarah Bernhardt about publicity. Lillie, like the rest of London, watched spellbound and took note.

It would be easy to polarize them, these two rivals for Society's attention: Sarah the wilful, decadent artiste, Lillie the beautiful, sensual adventuress. Of course in reality there was a more complicated cocktail of qualities, some of which they shared. Neither cared a fig for convention, both liked the danger of the edge, both had a natural instinct for managing their own public image. Although, for each of them, the iconoclasm was unpretended, they were aware of its contribution to their standing and nurtured it or suppressed it accordingly. Sarah wore her nerves and her passion on her sleeve, flaunted her son, dressed with decided theatricality, but spent the first hours of every day enthroned on an exercise machine. By contrast, Lillie, when her turn came, would screen her illegitimate child from the world, posing as her aunt. Similarly she would squash her own nervous sensibilities and stage-manage her own every movement. She would learn Sarah's lesson of the possibilities presented by judicious self-publicity and give to the world, not the wild bohemianism of her rival, but a front of sphinx-like politeness, something that, to Society's irritation, was more the *grande dame* than anything its salons could produce. It is easy to forget that Lillie's unconventionality was as deep-rooted as her ambitions. She had learnt it from her father at her mother's knee. Recklessness and impatience of petty decorum were innate. They were part of the air she breathed. When she saw the same qualities flaunted by the writers, painters and actresses of Bohemia it was only one more reason for choosing this as her final refuge rather than the stifling drawing-rooms of the aristocracy.

Later, when Lillie too was an actress, she and Sarah saw more of one another, recognized in each the steel below the surface, and became friends. There is a good account in Lillie's memoirs of a boxing match they held to please Sarah's illegitimate son Maurice.

> . . . there were breakfasts with her at her hotel, sometimes alone with her and her son. The latter was crazy about *la boxe* and Sarah and I were once beguiled by him into trying a 'bout'. We entered into it with great gusto, Maurice giving timely aid to one or other as it was needed, and we were both much the worse for wear at the finish.

It is an incongruous picture – two single mothers at fisticuffs over breakfast in a New York hotel room – very different from the graceful Society charm Lillie showed to the reporters who interviewed her,.

This fearsome scene was a long way in the future. In 1879 Lillie and Sarah were official rivals – rivals for London and rivals for the Prince of Wales. *Vanity Fair* reported that Sarah was 'at once very witty, very ready, and very fearless in her remarks'. At any rate she was fearless enough to rebuke the Prince for failing to remove his hat, in accordance with French tradition, when he visited her backstage at the Gaiety. She is reputed to have told him, 'Seigneur, on n'ôte pas sa couronne – mais on ôte son chapeau.' The Prince was duly enthralled and it was not long before Sarah was missing rehearsals, with the excuse that, 'I have just come back from the P of W. It is twenty past one. I can't rehearse any more at this hour. The P has kept me since eleven.'

In July, just before the Comédie Française returned to Paris, there was a fête at the Royal Albert Hall. The money raised was to go towards providing a bed, in the French hospital in Leicester Square, exclusively for French actors who fell ill while on tour in England. Both Lillie and Sarah stood behind stalls. Sarah sold her own paintings and her own animals. Lillie, according to *Vanity Fair*, sold 'relays of tempting little flowers'. According to popular myth, she also, and more mundanely, sold cups of tea. The tea, it is said, was priced at five shillings a cup, or a guinea if Lillie took the first sip. The Prince with Alexandra and daughters patronized both of the rivals' stalls. From Sarah he bought a portrait in oils while Alexandra bought two white kittens. From Lillie he bought tea. Having poured the cup, she put it unasked to her lips. The Prince left it untouched, saying deliberately, 'I should like a clean one, please.' Lillie, publicly rebuffed, served him again in silence. No doubt, in part, this was the Prince's old friend decorum raising its head. Even to him, with his wife and family marshalled behind him, it must have seemed bad taste to share a cup with his mistress while they watched. But it was true, too, that his relations with Lillie were becoming strained. Rumours always come from somewhere. Fact or fiction, the story shows that tensions between them were now obvious to others. Lillie was too careless of convention, too desperate. She had begun to challenge the Prince with his lack of intention, his inability to do anything to save her. If he could not help her, then he could not expect exclusive rights to her favours. Far from keeping her other affairs private Lillie was using them as a taunt. Sarah was a taste of her own medicine. The exchange in the Albert Hall was only the first in a series of similar confrontations, all with the same whiff of rumour about them. The patience of the Prince was fraying.

Chapter XVIII

A Gay Light-hearted Nature

With the Prince of Wales disgruntled, Arthur Jones to be kept secret and Oscar Wilde's demands to live up to, it would seem that Lillie had her hands full. In fact her life was neatly compartmentalized. Since neither Jones nor Wilde were really a part of Society Lillie left them behind when she set off, in the Indian summer of 1879, on her usual stately home circuit. Even Wilde, fashionable though he was, would hardly have been an asset on a shooting weekend, and his views on fox-hunting are well known. He went to the houses of patrons of the arts, and to the Lewises and the Sassoons, who were trade, but his path would not have crossed with the Prince's.

As Lillie left London, holiday-bound, her romantic interests shifted again, and widened. She went first, in July, to Oakley Court, Lord and Lady Otho Fitzgerald's house at Taplow. Among the house party was the nineteen-year-old Lord Shrewsbury (one of the candidates for Wilde's 'young Euphorion'), with whom Lillie had struck up a serious flirtation. He, that is, was serious; she was flirting. The event was a water party recorded in a rather muddled way by Augusta Fane, who remembered Lillie, in the throes of a new affair, deliriously happy. In fact the emotion that Lillie was dressing up as delirium was most likely relief. The season, with *Town Talk* and a tetchy Prince of Wales, had been a terrible strain. Also, hiding Jones, when Lillie's every movement gathered a crowd, was impossible. It was a blessing to be out of London, in more intimate surroundings; to be away from Jones, whom she could not resist; most of all, to be able for a moment to deflect attention from her real concerns. Here, with Shrewsbury, was a romance that could be completely public. She had been introduced to him during the season by the root-eating Violet Fane. She had even been asked, by his mother, in the best Society tradition, to look after him. 'An attachment to a married woman would keep him out of mischief.' Lillie was doing her duty, educating the next

Earl, and preventing him from marrying someone he had found in the Park. The couple were beautiful. The affair was sanctioned. Throwing herself into it with gaiety and passion that was, at least in part, pretended was an excellent screen for Lillie's growing obsession with the unfashionable Jones. She may even have hoped to trick herself out of her infatuation. She did not at all like being ruled by her emotions. It was dangerous both to her position and to her comfort. If she could have persuaded herself that she really loved Shrewsbury, she would have been doing herself a favour.

In her recollections of the affair, Lady Augusta appears unshocked by their love. She was indeed delighted at its effect on Lillie, noticing

> a charming personality and naturalness. She had no affectations and no make up, either of face or mind; she was just herself, so no one could help loving her, with her gay, light-hearted nature. Above all things she was no snob; indeed had she possessed more worldly wisdom and less heart, she would not have quarrelled with her most illustrious friend for the sake of a handsome young *peer of the realm*! For a short time she was very happy as her youthful lover was devoted to her, and then he suddenly left her and eloped with the beautiful wife of an elderly man . . .

Elopement was in fact not how it ended, and was for Shrewsbury a long way in the future. Lillie's more immediate problem was the 'illustrious friend', who could not have been often jilted.

After Taplow the Langtrys, with Shrewsbury in attendance, moved north. Gladys Lonsdale, newly married and, increasingly, Lillie's chosen friend, was also party to the affair. She too was receiving press attention for her unorthodox domestic arrangements. She and her husband had barely been in the same country since their marriage. He lived mostly on his yacht, drinking and whoring, and she pursued her own various interests in London. Their lives were apparently completely separate. At the end of August Lonsdale left on another cruise, this time to Iceland, and Gladys went alone to Lowther to entertain the Langtrys. Unlike the rest of Society, Gladys had Lillie's interests at heart, and thought Shrewsbury might well be the answer. He was rich and noble and extremely good-looking. More to the point, as she had probably spotted, he was young enough to act on his passion regardless of the conse-quences, and would make a practical match for Lillie if he chose to elope.

Whatever plans Lillie and Lady Lonsdale were laying, disaster threatened again, as August ended, in the form of Ned's divorce suit. As soon as Society had left London for the grouse moors *Town Talk* took up the cudgels again. On 30 August it announced with authority,

> A petition has been filed in the Divorce Court by Mr Langtry. HRH the Prince of Wales, and two other gentlemen, whose names . . . we have not been enabled to learn, are mentioned as co-respondents.

This time it was confident enough to follow up with an article entitled 'Who is Mrs Langtry?' This accused her of insatiable vanity, attacking, among other things, the constant posing for photographs, practised by all the Professional Beauties. It ran:

> Mrs Langtry herself cannot assert that there is any modesty in posing to photographic artists in, to say the very least, suggestive attitudes, to leer and wink and simulate smiles that can only be ranked one degree beneath lewdness. The daughter of a family who certainly cannot rank with the old and stable nobility of our country has, by some means, been raised to a fictitious popularity by means of the photographers' camera and lens, and for what purpose? To be exposed in the windows of shops with her name attached to the picture, to have her points criticised as if she were a horse for sale, to give 'Arry and Hedward an opportunity of passing indecent remarks about her, and to disgust all respectable thinking women at the public exhibition she makes of her charms.

This time, it seemed, *Town Talk* was in earnest. A week later, after Society, and more particularly the Household, had failed to react, it made a second announcement. It observed:

> No attempt has been made to contradict the statement published in these columns last week as to the Langtry divorce case, and my readers may be assured that it was no invention. I now learn that a few weeks ago an application was made that the case be tried in camera, and I believe the learned judge acceded to the request.

Presumably Lillie was kept informed, as she moved from house party to house party, of the accusations levelled against her. Ned, for once, was with her and it must have been difficult to maintain a front of civility for their hosts. From Lowther, as though nothing at all was happening, the Langtrys followed the fashion and went north again. This time it was not to Millais and his wife, for quiet domesticity, but to Glen Tanar in Aberdeenshire, the home of the businessman Sir Cunliffe Brookes.

Shrewsbury was not of the party. He went to London, where he was fêted in club-land before departing for the Zulu wars. Without either him or her real love, Jones, Lillie was not a little bored by life on a sporting estate. It rained almost continually and, with *Town Talk*'s taunts ringing in her ears, she was again in dangerous spirits. Later she recalled,

> There was a large house-party assembled – the men eager for the massacre of grouse and the stalking of deer. They, no doubt, enjoyed themselves hugely killing things, but there is nothing much for women to do . . . so I invented what I thought a very engrossing sport . . . Procuring a large tea-tray, I sat in it and tobogganed from the top of the stairs to the bottom! The sport was so enthusiastically taken up by the girls staying in the house that Cunliffe Brookes quietly ordered his butler to lock up all the good-looking or silver trays during my visit.

The evenings with their impromptu dances compensated for the dreary days. Lillie was captivated by the romance of the real Scots in their kilts, the young Lords Gordon doing sword dances for the entertainment of the other guests. These house parties were forcing grounds for adultery and she probably did not suffer much over the absence of her favourites. If she was not consoling herself in the arms of another man, Lillie would have had plenty of opportunity for whispering confidences to her girlfriends. Everyone loved an intrigue. A young and illicit love affair was to be enjoyed at second hand as well as first. As always, Queen Victoria, her moral antennae quivering, was quick to spot the temptations presented by these out-of-season entertainments. She wrote in horror to her favourite daughter, Vicky,

> Is it not the one thing I have always been so anxious and distressed about? It is what has done dear Bertie so much harm – and it is a most unfortunate tendency in the upper classes. That visiting is . . . the worst thing I know and such a bore. The gentlemen go out shooting and the ladies spend the whole day idling and gossiping together.

For Ned, at least, the sport would have provided a welcome distraction from the range of his wife's activities.

At the beginning of October someone had taken the first steps towards contradicting the rumours that *Town Talk* was gleefully publishing abroad. On the 4th there was a brief disclaimer. It was not much, but it ran,

I am now informed on authority which I have no reason to doubt that Mr Langtry has withdrawn the petition which he had filed in the Divorce Court. The case of Langtry v. Langtry and others is therefore finally disposed of, and we have probably heard the last of it. It is useless for the sixpenny twaddlers to deny that Mr Langtry ever filed a petition. He did, and as I have said before, an application was made to Sir James Hannen to hear it privately, and he consented.

By the end of October the Langtrys were back in London and facing the music. Things for Lillie must have looked bleak. That she survived, as she did, was due to an eleventh-hour combination of good luck and Royal muscle. Flown with the success of its scoop on the Langtry divorce, *Town Talk* turned its attention, still on the subject of the immodesty of posing for photographs, to Lillie's friend Patsy Cornwallis West. She had such a mania for supplying the demand for her image that she had installed, so it said, a little photographic studio in each corner of her garden in Eaton Place. Between them Patsy ran, changing her clothes as she went, to gratify their insatiable desire for her pictures. Before the week was out, her husband was suing Rosenberg, the paper's editor, for libel. The Langtry camp saw their chance. When Rosenberg arrived on 11 October, for a preliminary hearing, he found he was to stand trial for a further charge of libel against the Langtrys. Furthermore, the case was to be heard by Mr Justice Hawkins, a notoriously vindictive judge.

The case came before the court on 25 October. The Langtrys' counsel was a high-powered team of three, paid for, no doubt, from the Royal coffers, and Ned himself, sober and immaculately turned out, appeared in the witness box. Asked whether there was any truth in the *Town Talk* libels he replied, 'Not one single word.' He maintained that he had never filed for divorce, nor considered doing so, and, further, that he had 'always lived on terms of affection with his wife', and that he was 'living with her still at Norfolk Street'.

Rosenberg did not get off lightly. He was forbidden to name his sources, found guilty and sentenced to eighteen months in prison.

It was not Lillie's finest hour.

Chapter XIX

Storm Clouds

Once the *Town Talk* libel case was won Ned gave in to his despair. He had no money. He was expected to go out night after night in Society, where he was tolerated but not respected. He was shackled to a wife who was both scornful and unfaithful. Worst of all he had made a fool of himself in the law courts. He had publicly gone back, under pressure from Society, on his accusations of adultery. Seeking a divorce now would be, at best, nonsensical, and, at worst, admitting perjury. He disappeared constantly on fruitless money-raising expeditions to Ireland, and he drank.

On Lillie, the case had quite a different effect. Vindicated in the law courts, her reputation now shone with unblemished brilliance. She was seen, at the end of October, with Gladys Lonsdale at the Strand Theatre, where *Vanity Fair*, in an indulgent mood, noted, 'Recent malicious falsehoods have not apparently affected their intended victims . . . I never saw either look better.'

Far from turning over a new leaf, Lillie took her survival, not as a lesson, but as proof of her invulnerability. She threw herself with undiminished vigour into her various intrigues. The removal of Ned gave her at last a taste of real freedom. She could return to Norfolk Street at the end of the day without the prospect of his drunken accusations to greet her, or, as she left again to the entertainments of the evening, to speed her on her way out. At first she found her liberation an unlooked-for delight.

Towards the end of October, in the middle of this window of enjoyment, the news filtered back that Shrewsbury had been injured in Africa. Lillie played out the part of distracted lover.

My Dear Lord Wharncliffe,
    Thank you so very much for writing. I am so wretched about this

horrid news but you *don't* think he is very badly hurt do you? It is so much worse because I cannot say how anxious I feel about the poor boy. & I have to go everywhere all the same. Could I telegraph to him to St Vincent and so catch a steamer there? I want to see you so much. Could you drive me to Watts tomorrow on yr way to Wimbledon as you proposed doing the other day. I said I would be there at 3 or if not will you come to see me at 6.30 on my return. Fancy I have promised to take a young woman to lunch at Sandown today and to the opera this evg. & I can't get off it without saying why. So I must go. Yrs very truly.

The letter is by no means desperate in its concern. The affair, in its ups as well as its downs, was light relief rather than anything more serious, and there is the sense that Lillie was enjoying the drama. It was glamorous to have a young hero for a lover, and, besides, 'the poor boy' was not hurt at all. At the same time, *Vanity Fair* ran a jaunty and irreverent little rhyme among its Society columns, which put the accident in perspective. It went,

> He was ordered off to Zululand
> We gave him a farewell dinner and
>   Enlarged his tum.
> He bravely got to Zululand,
> Then tumbled off his war horse, and
>   He sprained his thumb.
> So he packed his things in Zululand
> Took the first steamer homeward and
>   He home did come.

Whether or not Wharncliffe was reassuring, Lillie did not let the Zulu wars bother her for long. She was too busy enjoying her life *en garçon*, as the Prince of Wales called it, with Gladys Lonsdale. Her activities were being regularly and uncritically reported in the gossip columns and always without her husband. Most of the time, it seems, she was not even aware of Ned's movements. They were now communicating only intermittently and by letter. So she and Lady Lonsdale, whose husband was equally invisible, more often than not chaperoned each other around the town. Otherwise Lillie was again in Brighton with Jones.

She came to London in November, and went alone in a red 'tightfit' to the wedding of Millais' daughter on the 28th, taking with her a silver coffee pot as a present. Then she disappeared again. Her few days of freedom were almost over, for money matters were pressing. The bailiffs had moved into Norfolk Street and it was simpler to stay away. Before she left she wrote once more to Wharncliffe, her father-figure confidant, on whom she continued to lean for help and support.

Dear Lord Wharncliffe,
    I rather hoped to have seen you at the Millais Wedding this mg. But I suppose you were unable to be in town. I came up yesterday to find that Ned had been up for a day during my absence and had left probably for Ireland. I wrote to him from Brighton but he took no notice of my letter. It is really the most extra-ordinary proceeding on his part dont you think so? My brother tells me that he met him accidentally the day he was in town and thought his manner more than strange. I am so sorry not to have seen you. I had looked forward to our meeting and had hoped you might have advised me. I shall return to Brighton on Monday for a week or 10 days. After which I am going to Derby to the Alsopps. The Wilmots have asked us to Chaddesden in January. Very kind of them isnt it? But Neds proceedings are so depressing that I dare not look forward . . . Give my best love to Lady Wharncliffe. *Is she better?*

As usual the innocence of Lillie's tone was pretended. If Ned's behaviour to her brother was 'more than strange' on the rare occasions when they met, then it was because Ned had noticed, through the veil of alcohol, that Jones was more to Lillie than just another of her passing fancies, a fact for which he held Clement and Alice, as sister and brother-in-law, partly to blame. Before the court case, this would not have worried Lillie, but now even she was aware of the depth of Ned's despair, and she found it frightening.

So far, Ned was the only person Lillie had neglected to charm, or to cajole into forgiveness and tolerance. Strange as it sounds, she had not wanted to make an enemy of him, and she was, despite her apparent insouciance, extremely anxious about his intended course of action. She saw that he was desperate, and that in his madness he had lost any instinct for self-preservation. She did not want to watch him destroy himself, and she did not want his destruction to be hers. She was warm, and she was capable of love, but she was not, at this point, able to be unselfish. She was frightened of Ned, for both of them, but she was also both injured and uncomprehending. She had been thoughtless, and she was beginning to see that the consequences of gaiety and lightness of heart were a good deal more serious than she could have imagined. As always, it was to the long-suffering Lord Wharncliffe that she expressed her sense of injustice and her confusion. On 2 January, just back from Brighton where it seems she spent Christmas without Ned, she wrote again. Now she was at Norfolk Street, alone, and facing financial ruin. 'I arrived', she tells him,

> in the middle of the night from Brighton. I shall be very glad to see you at *one* tomorrow. I cannot unfortunately be at home at 12. It seems to me however useless to discuss my unfortunate affairs. Mr Langtrys present intention is to be amicably separated but my impression is that he is not quite sane.

Separation, however amicable, was to prove a lonely business. With Ned there beside her, Lillie at least had someone to blame for her predicament, someone who officially protected her from her own responsibilities. For all his faults, Ned had been a buttress and his continued absence made her feel for the first time what it was to be running her own life. She found herself woefully insecure. She had no income nor any immediate means of providing one, and Norfolk Street was now occupied constantly by bailiffs. It was increasingly difficult for Lillie to carry on her normal social life, and, with Ned away, it was she who had to explain to the creditors that they had no money. It was she who had to negotiate another two days' grace and then, when it was refused, she who had to entertain her Society callers in the presence of the bailiffs, as though it were all an amusing game. Of course she did it very well. She made light of it, as she describes in her memoirs, diverting her friends with a picture of gaiety and mischief – Beauty triumphing over Poverty, and poking fun at the dirty tradesman. She writes,

> . . . our financial position grew worse and worse. Creditors became stony-hearted and deaf to our entreaties. At last the crisis came. Bailiffs invaded the little Norfolk Street house, and Mr Langtry frequently found it convenient to go fishing, leaving me to deal with the unwelcome intruders as best I could.

So successful was she at dealing with her unbidden guests that, far from being shunned as she had thought she would be, she found herself never without the company of one or other of her Society friends. The picturesqueness of her circumstances, though it upset her staff, was not wasted on her callers. In this new role, they flocked once more to see her. Her account continues,

The same faithful maid, an Italian named Dominique, had been with me all through my astonishing London experiences. This devoted woman took the matter of the bailiffs' sojourn much more keenly to heart than I did, and during this harassing time she never missed an opportunity of cramming my few trinkets and other treasured trifles, and, indeed, anything portable, into the pockets of anyone who came to visit me. In this way some very distinguished friends departed from the beleaguered house with their pockets full, all unconscious that they were evading the law.

She escaped to Brighton whenever she could and thought desperately of what course of action to take. She had, it seems, never really believed that Ned would leave her and was distressed and amazed that he had done so. For his part, Ned did not know what he had done, or even what he should do. He too was escaping, but whether it was from his wife or his life or his creditors he had no idea. He ran away, and he returned. He made one plan, and changed his mind a moment later. He was unable to decide whether it was punishing Lillie more to leave her alone, or to bully her along with him. His inconsistencies, to Lillie, were nothing short of crazy. She sat waiting for his decision, dizzy with his vagaries, and, every now and then, he would appear unannounced at Norfolk Street, wild with injustice, to demand that they move, or sell something, or simply to get drunk – and to abuse his wife.

For all her shrewdness and powers of perception, Lillie was obtuse over Ned. She could see no reason for his bitterness, and she deplored his drinking. She had loved him when they married, and she still could have loved him as a friend (their separation, after all, was to be 'amicable'), but she felt no possessiveness towards him, no jealousy, and she could see no reason why these emotions should feature in his feelings for her. What she found hardest, all her life, to forgive in her former lovers was an inability to remain friends after the end of the affair. For her husband to be guilty of this smallness of mind was to her incomprehensible. After all their vicissitudes, when asked in her seventies how she wanted to be remembered, her answer was, and it was not political, 'As a woman who loved her husband, her child, and her friends.' She could not understand the violence of Ned's despair. She could not see that the life she had created for them was one that he did not want. And she could not imagine his jealousy and his sense of hurt. Other Society husbands managed, why couldn't he? And why could they not continue as companions? What she wanted, of course, of her husband, as of her lovers, was more brothers.

*

But Ned was not the only one whose behaviour was inconsistent. Despite being unable to 'look forward', as she had complained to Lord Wharncliffe in November, when the time came, Lillie's spirits lifted again on the house-party circuit. This was partly because the Alsopps, who had invited them, had also asked the battle-torn Lord Shrewsbury. On 11 January 1880, Wharncliffe received another letter, altogether different in tone, in which she breathlessly asks his opinion about eloping.

> I found the letter I wrote to you from Chaddesden was never posted. I am so sorry and ask yr. forgiveness for what must have seemed dreadfully rude. It was so very kind of you to write and I was so glad to get it but I dont understand yet whether they could prevent our remaining together after we had bolted. He is staying here and I am more in love than ever. I think I shall be in town the end of next week, but I will let you know. I had such a delightful week at Chaddesden, they were so nice to me.

This, then, was Lillie's solution, to run away, since Ned had left her, and place herself in the hands of another protector. But to run off was a crazy plan, and one that Lillie would never have contemplated had she not been so frightened of Ned or so hard-pressed financially. The age gap between them was eight years, and they had known each other for a matter of months. Shrewsbury was a boy. He had no experience of the world and no knowledge of the extent of her debts, or the desperation of her husband. It must have been clear to Lillie, almost from the outset, that Shrewsbury would not have made much of a protector. If she had played along with it, against her better judgement, it was because it had provided a screen for Jones that was both convenient and timely. Also the adulation of a younger man was flattering, and she had needed reassurance. Wharncliffe was in favour of this particular match and it must have been a relief to have Society's universal approval. That the approval would vanish as soon as she took the relationship beyond a summer affair, she also knew. She was not committed emotionally, but she had precious few choices, and time was not on her side.

Underlining Lillie's lack of commitment is the silliness of her declaration of affection in the letter to Wharncliffe. It is uncharacteristic and its tone is Society's. She does, in these unsettled years, slip in and out of different conversational styles. To Society, as to Bohemia, she talks its language. Here, it is part of her attempt to be accepted, and it contrasts strongly with the sincerity of her urgent and entirely secret communications with Jones of the same date. She was unafraid of being flattering, or straight manipulative, but she was never vapid.

Whatever Lillie's reservations, Shrewsbury was determined. Lillie followed up her first request for guidance with a second letter as soon as she arrived back at Norfolk Street. 'Dear Ld. Wharncliffe,' she writes,

> I am hoping to see you about 12 tomorrow. It will be so good of you if you will find out for me what would happen if we carried out our present intention. I hope we shouldn't be cast into prison.

Her caution makes the imbalance between them as a couple all the clearer. Shrewsbury was young and impulsive and she was, by nature and now by experience, wary. She was having to do the thinking. She did not want to find herself, once she had taken the plunge, parted from her protector, or subject to the law. Scawen Blunt, politician, libertine, and man of letters, whose acquaintance with Lillie was slight, observed unkindly in March that her 'only idea now is to get a divorce and marry him', but that Ned would not hear of it. One reason for Blunt to be malicious was that Lillie was temporarily out of favour in Royal circles. His diary entry continues with an account of a muddle Lillie had made over her afternoon callers. She had tried to put the Prince off with an excuse, but he, 'not having received the note, came and found her with Shrewsbury'. Blunt closes with the cool observation that the Prince was 'easily ruffled'. The ruffling did not last, and he was seen riding with Lillie in the Park a few days later, in what was clearly a public show of reconciliation.

Wharncliffe's answer to the urgent question of elopement must have been lukewarm. Probably he marginally preferred divorce to running off, but having just successfully sued for libel it was unlikely that Lillie could now persuade a jury to believe in the Langtry marriage as anything other than idyllic. There is no further mention of elopement in her correspondence. What is clear, however, is that Lillie's spirits stayed strangely buoyant into the following season. The winds of change were blowing again, and Lillie was busy trimming her sails to catch them. As though she knew this season to be her last, she sat it out, despite the bailiffs, at Norfolk Street from February.

The main reason for buoyancy was Louis Battenberg. He was the Prince of Wales's friend and particular favourite. Young and irreproachably handsome, he had the *frisson* of royalty about him, without the encumbrance of any of its usual privileges or constrictions. His father's morganatic marriage had given him the title of Prince of Hesse but had freed him, despite being the eldest, from the duty of succession. Left to follow his own course, Prince Louis had broken the family tradition of soldiering in favour of a career in the British navy. The Prince and Princess of Wales adored him. He had long legs, hooded eyes, a naval uniform. He was a spirited raconteur, a gallant rider and he danced with the grace of a gazelle. What more could Lillie ask for, in the season of 1880, as she spiralled into her abyss of unprotection?

Usually Battenberg was out of the capital, on service, which was what he preferred, but in April 1879 the Prince of Wales had persuaded him to take a position on the Royal yacht *Osborne* as an officer under Charles Beresford. His duties, imaginably, were negligible. For most of the time, when the Royals were not on board, he was in attendance at Marlborough House and madly in love with Lillie. Their affair was conducted with absolute discretion and with the apparent permission of the Prince of Wales, but it was of course universal in its renown. This had its uses, since Battenberg's popularity meant that Lillie was once again beyond public reproach. *Vanity Fair* was polite in its notices and Lillie was again Society's darling. Wilfrid Blunt, whose own affair with Violet Fane was sanctified by the 'feu sacré', watched her hooraying in the London drawing-rooms to a crowd that was once again more sycophantic. Her 'latest witticism', as recorded by him, was to remove her shoe 'and hit her lovers' heads with the heel'. Sneer as he might, no doubt there were many who queued for this privilege.

Yet again, things were more complicated than they looked. Her relationship with the Prince of Wales was still proving troublesome. He played an uneasy second fiddle and, although he was too sophisticated to object to sharing her favours with his protégé, Lillie was finding it harder and harder to keep him sweet. She worked tirelessly. She was seen at Sandown, racing in March, where it was observed that 'the Prince talked much with Mrs Langtry'. She even, so rumour had it, accompanied him to Paris in April, where they travelled incognito and the Prince was seen to kiss her on the dance floor at Maxim's. By May she was back in London again, and again the centre of attention. The Freakes, who were new rich and part of the Prince's set, held a series of evenings at which tableaux of the Waverley novels were presented to an enthusiastic audience. Lillie of necessity took part. She played Effie Deans in a set designed by Millais, after his first picture of her, and she was rapturously received. When the curtains rose it showed Lillie in a short blue dress and flowered bodice, her hair flowing free over her shoulders, and her face, as one review marvelled, 'inexpressibly sad and beautiful'. Her lover, Robertson, was played by Godfrey Pease, who leaned over a wall and 'gazed at her with unutterable affection', probably genuine. The event was such a success it was repeated twice more by popular demand, and Frank Miles was commissioned to engrave it for *Life*.

Her success gave Lillie a new taste of triumph. Here, in play-acting, was the admiration that she craved but without all the usual attendant problems of reciprocation. To keep an admirer, as Lillie had discovered, it was necessary to fan the flame. Without a return of his affection, a lover soon grew cold or turned his attention elsewhere. When she came, years later, to write her novel *All at Sea* she allowed an exchange between her heroine, the irresistible Lady Verulam, and a disappointed lover that is her own experience in a nutshell. After the rebuttal of his declaration the lover indulges in all the usual threats of suicide and eternal suffering. Urged to forget the past he moans, 'I can never forget it,' to which he is offered the tart rejoinder, 'You will be a phenomenon if you don't . . . It is the thing men find easiest to do – to forget a woman they imagined they loved.' This was written in Lillie's sixties, with the mantle of cynicism heavy on her shoulders. It was not a lesson that she had fully learnt by the summer of 1880, but she was nearer to it than she knew.

As always Lillie was moving towards a conclusion that was as yet unformulated in her conscious mind.

Before the season had begun, in late February, her constant friend and companion Lady Lonsdale had contracted measles. Their friendship was such that Lillie is supposed to have acted as her nurse, sitting up with her through the nights and watching her through her fevers. When she was recovered again, she and Lillie were closer than ever. They continued, in the absence of their respective husbands, to chaperone each other to all the amusements of the season, a partnership unusual enough, and yet so evident, as to inspire an article, in *Vanity Fair*, entitled 'The Semi-Detached Wife'. This was a surprisingly perceptive and sympathetic account of the problem, particular to marriages in the nineteenth century, of freedom and its effects on women. The husband, whom the writer calls 'Benedict', has, it observes,

> sown his wild oats: he is exchanging the reckless life of bachelorhood, of which he has tired, for the calm joys and peaceful rest . . . of matrimony. She, on the other hand, is entering, from the monotonous routine of the schoolroom, upon a life she has just seen and heard enough of from elder

sisters or novels to value a great deal above its worth. Even though she loves the man she gives her hand to at the altar, marriage is to her a door to all the pleasures of existence. The intoxicating bowl is about to be put to her rosy lips, at last she is to show what beauty can be made of when maternal restraints are withdrawn; and lo! she is offered, by a man who has had all his fun, a cup of gruel and a nightcap. So she revolts – if she has 'a spirit' – revolts at once and decidedly; and then he has to make up his mind equally promptly. There are two courses open to him. Either he can . . . bravely enter again upon the bustle and struggle of which he has long ago sickened; or he can . . . permit her to become what we have called a semi-detached wife. He chooses the latter course. From that moment their lives get into different grooves, and daily go further and further apart.

Despite its shrewdness and its unbiased tone the article has only Victorian conclusions to draw. The sacred 'home' becomes a place of misunderstanding and intolerance. The husband, 'being an Englishman and unable to put strong emotion into words', cannot express his misery and heartsickness. The woman, we are warned, finds her pleasures away from home, grudges the affection she cannot help bestowing on her own children as an interference to her socializing, and grows 'daily harder and more cynical'. Then, too late, she finds that she has 'thrown away the substance for the shadow; and that even the successes of a few London seasons do not make up for a long after-life without a home'. Behind the Victorian moralizing lies the implication that a woman who does not make her home the centre of her life will fail in her marriage. It is not possible to have one's cake and eat it: a happy marriage and the enjoyment of freedom are mutually exclusive. So the old hierarchy of the father as figurehead, and the mother as adoring and home-bound helpmeet, is reaffirmed. Attempts to subvert or circumnavigate it are automatically doomed to failure.

Whether Lillie read the article or not, it sounded a warning knell, as she moved into another season, with her ambitions focused on a second marriage. Her bosom friend, chosen out of all that society had to offer, was Gladys Lonsdale, the woman Augusta Fane had described as having a 'fine character, and a broad outlook on life', but whose one fault, an insatiable curiosity, 'led her into dark places and amongst undesirable people'. Wilfrid Scawen Blunt, who had seen her out riding in March, and was less charitable, observed that she was 'much improved in looks' since marriage but 'given over to vanity'. (His own vanity and promiscuity knew no bounds, though he could not see it.) He went on, primly, to remember her governess predicting, while Gladys was still a child, that she 'would go to the devil in a coach and four'. 'This', Blunt's entry closes, 'is what she seems to be doing'. And, if so, Lillie was doing it with her. She shared with her friend the same inquisitiveness of spirit, and the same refusal to rule anything out without experiencing it first. By now she had drunk deep from the cup of freedom. Renouncing it would have been an impossibility; nor was there any hope of her suddenly becoming the home-loving little woman on which, it seemed, a happy marriage depended. But if she could not clip her wings she might, or so she was beginning to think, be able to fly in a different direction.

Chapter xx

The Storm Breaks

The Freakes' tableaux vivants had tipped the balance of Lillie's outlook on life in the summer of 1880. Of course there was still the possibility that Louis Battenberg might fling his position to the winds and marry her, but Lillie was realistic enough to know that it was an outside chance. Her attitudes were changing now as fast as her hopes died. For a while, she had been asking her friends in Bohemia what she should do, and they had offered various suggestions. Wilde, of course, wanted her to act. Miles had thought of market gardening, which Wilde had dismissed, partly because he was possessive and it was Miles's idea not his own, and partly because he found 'muddy boots' unaesthetic. Whistler had been impressed by the caricatures she made of her friends and thought she should paint. So, it seems, did Poynter, who had also been surprised by her evident talent. After his first visit to Norfolk Street he had been struck enough to write to Wharncliffe, observing,

> I had never been in her house before: her drawing-room is very quaint, like a magician's cave; her paintings on glass surprised me. I had no idea she could do so well.

Millais, altogether more practical than his fellows, had used his influence to persuade Heinrich Felberman, editor of *Life* magazine, to find her a job as a columnist. Felberman was tempted. As he recalled in his memoirs, Lillie's various portraits on his pages had already done wonders for his circulation. In particular the picture of Effie Deans had been what he termed a 'phenomenal hit'. 'Before that', he remembered,

> she had narrowly escaped becoming my society editress. Sir John Millais, my neighbour in Kensington, who took the deepest interest in Mrs Langtry's future welfare, just at the time when her financial crash came,

approached me through the Rev. Compton Reade . . . to give the famous beauty employment on my social staff. He believed that she had a talent which could be developed and would be of great use to me in the world in which she moved. The price asked was 800 guineas a year, which, although I was of a speculative disposition, I considered too high. I offered half and eventually increased it by another hundred . . . After a good deal of persuasion I was prevailed to go as high as six hundred pounds, but the very same day I received a telegram saying that Mrs Langtry had decided to go on the stage.

She did not, in fact, finally decide on the stage as a career until late 1881, but she did, in the June or July of the year before, take lessons in diction as a means to that end, engaging a Mr Cauvet as a tutor. This she kept under wraps. It was more elegant to appear to have bowed to popular demand than to have elbowed her own way into the limelight. Later she said of this last season – and though the sentiment is true the details are magnificently vague –

Looking back on this period, I find a difficulty in placing the exact moment when I felt a changed attitude toward the undreamed-of social maelstrom into which I had been swept. Most of the people with whom I associated were either persons of importance in the land, with duties and responsibilities towards their country, or they were artists working hard to become rich and great, while I was absolutely idle, *my* only purpose in life being to look nice and make myself agreeable.

Nevertheless, very likely I should have continued to flutter flimsily along, spending money, but that by now our waning income had almost touched vanishing point, and, although I do not wish to lay stress on the fact, Mr Langtry also enjoyed the pastime of quiet squandering, so that, as time went on, we began to find ourselves un-pleasantly dunned by long-suffering tradesmen. All this made me generally unhappy, for when one lives beyond one's means, with money troubles as constant companions, there can be no compensation for the intolerable worry and anxiety. My anomalous position once realised, I began to lose interest in my daily round of amusement till it became unendurable.

In fact Lillie's change of heart happened at last quite suddenly in June 1880.

The Waverley tableaux were mounted on the 1st and then again on 8 May. Somewhere around the 24th or 25th Lillie wrote her last letter to Lord Wharncliffe in her 'Society voice'. She was whirling around the London dance floors in the arms of Prince Louis. As usual, when she was happy, she had been too busy to answer Wharncliffe's letters and questions. Now she writes with a catalogue of the balls she has attended; Christopher Sykes's, 'most successful', Lady Cork's, 'over-crowded and badly run'. In short there was 'so much gaiety . . . that we are all quite worn out'. She was just starting for the Bachelors' Ball as she signed off, and then she was planning a week at Goodwood. In her own account of her decision-making, it was only the money troubles that forced her out to work. 'Very likely,' as she says, 'I should have been content to flutter flimsily along' had it not been for the bailiffs. This is engagingly disparaging and it could easily have been true, but as things worked out, it was not the money that decided her. Financial ruin threatened in May, but did not strike until much later in the year. Besides, Lillie was never happier 'fluttering' than when it was in the face of disapproval or snobbery. She had the much-tried Prince of Wales, and she had Louis. She was indispensable again at Marlborough House, and, while the Indian summer of her popularity lasted, she would enjoy it.

She was, as it happens, sicker at heart than she realized. When she went out to these parties that so hampered her correspondence with Lord Wharncliffe, it was, like Lady Lonsdale, with the devil driving. Once again she was pushing at the boundaries of decorum. Twice in the space of a month she overstepped the mark with the Prince of Wales. First, at a fancy-dress ball she arrived dressed as Pierrette, knowing that he was planning to be Pierrot. This was about as public a statement of her position as she could have made and it was designed to embarrass and to outrage. It was also an insult to Princess Alexandra, whom Lillie particularly admired. The Prince was angered, and Society was horrified, but she survived. But the second time she was bent on destruction. With the ink on her last letter to Wharncliffe barely dry, she found herself cast out at last. The story goes that the Randolph Churchills gave a ball at which Lillie, who was normally only a moderate drinker, broke her habit and drank champagne with abandon. During dinner she and the Prince were both seen to be in high spirits, their teasing and laughter holding the table. The Prince enjoyed her in difficult form but he was precious of his dignity. At some point after dinner, with the teasing escalating into taunts Lillie forgot herself so far as to put a spoonful of strawberry ice down the back of the Prince's neck. This was not acceptable. He turned on his heel in silent rage and left the ballroom.

Lillie was dropped overnight. Invitations were withdrawn, parties mysteriously cancelled, and she was cut when she rode in the Park. In its speed and effect her ex-communication mirrored her discovery. When she awoke, the morning after the party, it was to a different world.

The incident, whether fact or fiction, was widely and variously reported. Lillie herself always denied it, and when writing her memoirs she attempted to lay the ghost of her indiscretion by retelling the story with Patsy Cornwallis West and her husband at its centre.

Lillie's banishment was not long-lived, and it was not comprehensive, but it taught her once and for all who her real friends were. Bohemia stood by her, Wilde, Miles and Millais, as did Gladys Lonsdale and Patsy Cornwallis West, and indeed, in the end, the Prince himself. Perhaps she wrote an apology to the Prince; history does not relate. In any case, before the end of the week, he had relented. With it, the invitations started up again, not this time in a flood, but enough at least to count. His forgiveness was, for the moment, kinder than heartfelt. He knew what ruin his withdrawal of favour would call down on her head, so he spared her. However, when July came and Alfred de Rothschild gave a dinner in his honour, Lillie was not among the favoured few. The Prince chose the guests himself. He invited Lady Lonsdale, her bosom friend, but Lillie he only asked in, with the crowd, after dinner was over. A month ago, this would have been unthinkable.

Only when Lillie was reinstated, albeit at a lower level than before, did she find the energy to make a change in her direction. Of course, when she came to write about it later, in her memoirs, she made it seem a single, dramatic, instant of revelation. She went, on 12 July, to a ball at Grosvenor House, given by the Duchess of Westminster. Halfway through the evening, in front of a portrait of Sarah Siddons, she had her road to Damascus. She felt, as she says, that she must

> forthwith cut adrift from this life, which we could no longer afford to enjoy, and, prostrating myself in admiration before the wonderful portrait . . . I recalled the fact that the artist had signed his name on the hem of her gown, and had declared himself satisfied to go down to posterity that way. Then from the Siddons portrait I passed on to other great works of art, and became filled with the desire to become a 'worker' too. Impulsive as I was in those days, I did not wait for my carriage, but, pushing my way through the throng of footmen clustering round the hall door, I walked, in spite of my white satin shoes, through the wet and muddy streets to my house, happily not far distant, eagerly considering how to remodel my life. But it is not an easy matter to change suddenly from the butterfly to the busy bee. Besides, I had no confidence in my ability to earn money in any

profession or even trade, so I was forced to face the fact that my chances of success were remote.

It is such a poetic picture, Lillie with the light of revelation in her eye and mud on her satin slippers, that it seems churlish to carp about detail. Her feel for her own story amounts, like her beauty, to a form of genius. The facts, of course, were a deal more prosaic. On 26 June, a full fortnight before the Grosvenor House ball, *Vanity Fair* observed, 'There is a rumour that a lady celebrated for her beauty in London has conceived the ambition to go on the stage, and that she is now studying elocution with that object.' If she had hoped to keep Cauvet's lessons a secret she had failed, but she had, it seems, been canvassing for opinion among her friends in Bohemia. The idea of the stage as a career had been suggested to her by Oscar Wilde and Wilfred Scawen Blunt, both of whom had seen it as the best means of employment for her peculiar talents. Lillie, of course, did nothing without consulting the Wharncliffes. They went abroad on 18 June, in an attempt to restore Lord Wharncliffe's health and happiness, and Lillie wrote before their departure, probably in the first week of her forgiveness by Society, around the beginning of June. In contrast to her last, this letter was full of purpose. She had reached the decision that marriage to a member of the aristocracy, even to someone as young and biddable as Lord Shrewsbury, would be intolerable. She was going to manage on her own, or not at all. From Norfolk Street on a Monday morning, her recent crushing exclusion unmentioned, but only just behind her, she writes,

> Dear Lord Wharncliffe,
>   What I am going to write is entirely a secret *please* don't hint or breathe it even to Lady W – The truth is, that I have come to the conclusion that if I carried out my intention of marrying Ld. S. my last state would be worse than the first, he is quite as uneducated & much more jealous than Ned, as I have lately had opportunities of seeing & he gets worse every day – In fact I should despise him in a month – I know you will be rather angry with me for being so changeable but I doubt if I could ever be devoted for long to a man to whom nature has been kind only in physical gifts and who has no intelligence at all. In four words I *am sick of him*. Now for my plans as you will see it is necessary for me to do something. Why shouldn't I act. I don't mean without previous hard study for I should love it as an art & should wish to excel – Do you think I should succeed. After all look at women like Neilson making 100 a night in America, & you will admit that she is not over-burdened with intellect.

I am very persevering really & would work hard. I am going to write to Nellie Terry to come & see me & advise me. But I should like to have yr. opinion. Tell me exactly what you think & write as soon as possible. I should live with my brother and sweet little sister-in-law.

Yours very truly

Lillie Langtry

I am so tired of being made love to.

The letter was written in haste, with little punctuation and a great many crossings-out. It was not the letter of a Society lady so much as that of the child the Wharncliffes did not have. It was also the kind of letter Lillie might have written to her own father had her charmed family circle not dissolved. Poor 'Lord S', the patient Wharncliffe's choice, was relegated, for being nineteen no doubt, and too handsome, and too stupid. Instead, Lillie plans to 'excel' as an actress. There was never, of course, any question of mediocrity. Also, in this new idyll, she will, she says disingenuously, live with Clem and Alice. This meant with Jones. Just as she had been a cover for Clement and Alice before they married, so she assumed they would be a cover for her. She was to be disappointed. Clement, now that he was a respectable London solicitor, had become stuffy and would not condone adultery even in his sister.

Lillie's excitement in her letter to Wharncliffe fell short of the mark. The idea of independence and of a career on stage, as visualized through the eyes of Wilde (who first suggested it) and Sarah Bernhardt, who epitomized the successful diva, was very different from the practice. Lillie, despite her success in the tableau of Effie Deans, had less confidence than enthusiasm and it was a good many months before she settled, with any purpose, on acting as her chosen career. We do not know how Wharncliffe responded to her letter, but in the ensuing weeks, while Lillie wavered and worried, something else, a disaster both terrible and unforeseen, gathered out of the horizon and broke about her head.

Chapter xxi

Secret Lives

Lord Wharncliffe left on a tour of the Continent at the beginning of the third week in June. Just after his departure Lillie wrote a letter, ostensibly to thank him for strawberries and plovers' eggs. In fact it was a remarkably cool *tour de force*, designed to allay suspicion over her health. At the end of June Lillie had been dining at Marlborough House, when she had been overcome by stomach cramp and fainted, either at the table itself or soon after the completion of dinner. She had been sent home and Francis Laking, the Royal physician, followed her round to Norfolk Street, to produce a diagnosis. She was, of course, pregnant.

Whether Lillie was surprised by the news, or whether she already knew it, it is impossible to tell. Her pregnancy, at the beginning of July, was not more than a month advanced, so she could not in any case have known for long. She had, it is true, filled out since her arrival in the capital. Society's heavy diet had put paid to the corsetless days of her first season, and it may be that the discomfort of the tightly laced dresses she now wore contributed to an early discovery. Had she known, it would perhaps go some way towards explaining why she had, as she put it later, 'gone so far as to forget my manners' with the Prince of Wales at the Churchills' ball. She may even have told the Prince of her suspicion, hence the speed of his forgiveness and the prompt dispatch of Sir Francis Laking. For Lillie, the knowledge of her condition was only the beginning. There were two far more pressing problems to be addressed, in the form of Ned's reaction and the question of paternity.

It is evident that Lillie herself did not know which of her legion lovers was the father of this unwanted child. The only thing she did know was that it was not Ned. And she knew, too, that if he found out – and how could he not – his rage and disgust would be terrible and very public. Here was a disaster indeed and Lillie sat in her Norfolk Street drawing-room blank with fear. To whom could she turn in her calamity? Who was there who could hide her, forgive her, provide for her? – not the bachelors of Bohemia, and not Royalty, that was sure.

If the Prince of Wales was solicitous, his position barred him from the provision of any kind of real support, and Lillie knew better than to ask for it. Certainly, in the early days he did not offer her any practical help beyond providing her with a physician. It may well be that he did not realize the impossibility of Ned's fathering her child, or that he hoped, as she did, that it could be aborted.

At first, it seems that Lillie informed no one, and asked for nothing. When she found herself too vulnerable to cope alone, she told Jones, and, true or false, she told him the child was his. So it was he who went to the chemist and bought the potions to make her miscarry, and it was on his shoulder that she wept out her terror and her shame.

When they were not together, she wrote frantic notes on any piece of paper to hand, and it is these that show us the depths of her misery and her dread of discovery.

> My own darling,
> I am *not* yet, but it is awful. I am sure there must be something wrong or what I took would have made me. Please go to a chemist and ask how many doses one ought to take a day as I must go on taking it and come to see me at 11 tomorrow morning. Please darling as I am so wretched.

Once Lillie had told him, Jones became indispensable to her. So great was her fear that she did not dare to move without him. When he threatened to leave London for Jersey she reacted with utter despair:

> My own darling,
> I am quite as wretched as you. Ned will drive me quite mad if he never leaves you with me for a minute. What *am* I to do darling? I am so worried I don't think I can tell Ned do you? and if not how am I to get away? for four months. Why couldn't Ned and I come over to Portelet instead of the Broadwoods – and I could make an excuse and get away from him at last. You *won't* go back my darling till you know what I am going to do. *Please* promise not to. If you love me you can't be so unkind as to leave me. You *dear* you know I care for you *only* in the world but I hardly dare look at you. My dearest Artie I will arrange tomorrow with you to see you alone on Saturday. *Swear* you won't go back yet or I shall die of worry.

This is a new Lillie, tragic and dependant, but the old one was not yet altogether lost. While, to Jones, Lillie tore her hair and beat her breast, to

Wharncliffe she wrote letters of breezy disingenuity. He was still on the Continent, and longing for news of home. Her next letter to him is datable by its references to Daisy Warwick, whose engagement was announced on 26 June. It must therefore have been written in the first weeks of July – that is, in the first throes of her horror and despair. It is a monument to her determination. 'Dear Lord Wharncliffe,' she writes,

> Soon after you left Mr Strudwick dined with us and seemed much pleased with my offer to sit to him which I have since done, but I dont think he has succeeded in making a likeness. *Nausicaa* has been very much liked as a rule but tho Poynter must have worked tremendously to get it as forward as it is still it is very far from being finished. I have been so seedy again lately indeed at this moment I am suffering from cold and headache and it was so unfortunate that I felt so unwell after dinner that Sunday at Marlboro House that I had to leave an hour before the rest. I tell you this because no doubt you will hear as I did that I fainted *at dinner* because the Prince wasn't civil enough!!!
>
> The Princess and Miss Knollys came to see me before they left town and had tea and stayed for an hour. I was so puffed up about it that I was quite disagreeable for two days after. more especially as she kissed me when she left.*
>
> That hateful Vanity Fair published an announcement of the impending marriage of Brookie and Daisy Maynard wh. made Lady R. naturally furious and sent Brookie in hot haste to Paris. It is so wicked and I am so sorry for *him* as he cant help being very much in love with that pure, lovely girl and now he maynt see her. My head aches so, I must give up, tho' I have a great deal to tell you.
>
> Give my dear love to Lady Wharncliffe.

Set side by side, Lillie's letters to Jones and to Wharncliffe could be written by two different people; the one so dependant, and so afraid, and the other gracious, long-suffering, and so interested in Society and its doings. Did she count, among the 'great deal' that she had to tell Lord Wharncliffe – her adviser and her confidant – the news of her pregnancy?

---

*Lillie's gratitude to the Princess for the kindness of her visit and her (Lillie's) pride in their friendship was such that she risked the telling of this story in her memoirs.

'The honour of the unexpected visit brought me at once to my feet, ill though I felt, but the Princess insisted on my lying down again, while she made herself tea, chatting kindly and graciously. She always used a specially manufactured violet scent, and I recall exclaiming on the delicious perfume, and her solicitous answer that she feared possibly it was too strong for me.'

Most probably she did not. The impossibility of Ned's being the child's father, and therefore the need, at all costs, to prevent him from finding out made secrecy paramount. Plenty of women had children by their lovers and no one batted an eyelid, but they were usually well versed in the practical aspects of such cases, denying their husbands nothing, in order that nothing should be suspected. The fact that Lillie leans, in her letters, so heavily on Jones for advice and support indicates that she had as yet involved no one else in her dilemma. If she could abort the baby, or get rid of Ned for the critical months while she gave birth, then no one need know. If she could not, she would need help.

Time ticked by, and still Lillie was undecided. Somewhere towards the end of the season, she told Prince Louis. He was a serious candidate for paternity, and she knew that his feelings for her went deep. He, in turn, informed his parents and probably told them that he intended to stand by Lillie. Certainly, later on, Society knew that he had offered to throw up both position and career for her sake. He did believe the child to be his, but he was being naïve; marriage to Lillie, if it had ever been a possibility, was now out of the question. The establishment machinery ground into action and Louis was found employment on board a ship called, poetically, the *Inconstant*. It was commissioned to make a journey round the world under nothing but sail, a project designed to keep him out of harm's way for a long time.

It was left for the Prince of Wales to pick up the pieces. He may, of course, have believed that the child was his. In which case he was honour-bound to help Lillie.* That he did so, with speed and efficiency and secrecy, was a generosity she never forgot. Despite her infidelities to him, which looked so like ingratitude, and despite her undecorous public taunts and humiliations, he had stood by her in her darkest hour. She had not asked for his help, and she had not expected him to give it. When it was all over, her regard for the Prince was deep and enduring. All her life afterwards, she felt herself to be emotionally in his debt.

For the time being, Lillie's debt to the Prince was material as well as emotional. Through the offices of Sir Allen Young she was lent £2,000,

---

*He also presumably felt a degree of responsibility towards his protégé, whom he knew to have little in the way of capital. Providing for Lillie during her confinement and keeping Ned away was going to be an expensive business and one that Louis had neither the funds nor the influence to cover. There is a story, years later, of Louis and the Prince tossing the paternity, while staying at Regal Lodge, Lillie's racing box. Louis won and the Prince, as a forfeit, is supposed to have presented Lillie with a golden statuette of herself naked, which she kept in the middle of her dining room table.

which was generous. This was to clear her immediate and most pressing debts and to enable her to leave the country.

More important than the money, which he may have supplemented as the months went on, was the fact that the Prince took the management of the problem on to his own shoulders. Invitations for Ned to fish and shoot in Scotland throughout the autumn flooded into Norfolk Street, at his command. All Lillie had to do was organize her own lodgings out of sight of Society and keep quiet. She stayed in London, to allay suspicion, until the season had well and truly ended. Towards the end of July she began to hint at the possibility of going back to Jersey for good and on 7 August it was reported that she was not at Cowes and was 'on the point of returning to her native isle'. The way that the information was circulated made it clear that her leaving was a matter of choice, not necessity. For the cynical few who doubted her motives, Lillie was helped by her impending bankruptcy. This had been a matter for public speculation for some time and to Lillie's relief now provided a perfect smokescreen.

So as not to slink away, but to make her exit seem graciously unhurried, Lillie took a house with Lady Lonsdale for the racing at Goodwood. All their friends were entertained, and all their friends were told that Venus Annodomini had had enough of Society and was returning to Olympus. It was all beautifully managed. At last Lillie left, escorted to the train by Patsy Cornwallis West, leaving Norfolk Street to be sold up, 'the sheriff's dismal emblem "the carpet flag" flying from the drawing-room window'. Possibly the bankruptcy, like so much else, was stage-managed to coincide with her departure.

In her absence the house and all its effects were sold at auction. The loyal Lady Lonsdale wrote to Lillie after it,

> I only heard by the merest chance that Norfolk Street was being 'sold-up'. Why didn't you tell me? I was lunching at—House, and the Duchess and I drove there at once. Unfortunately, the *black bear* had already been snapped up, but we managed to get the *peacock*, which I will keep carefully for you till you return. Everything went for immense prices – your little tea-table with your initials on, down to your skates – so I hope your horrid creditors are satisfied.

Lady Lonsdale's finely developed, and aristocratic, sense of the necessities of life had a sad ending. Lillie became increasingly superstitious about the peacock as a bird of ill-omen and left it in Wilde's sitting-room, in revenge, after one of their worse rows. Miles, who knew of the seriousness of their disagreement, and was still sharing rooms with Wilde, assumed it was a present to him and took it away; whereupon, his father died, his betrothed broke off their engagement, and he himself became insane. If only Lady Lonsdale had thought to buy a bed or a chamber pot.

By the middle of August 1880, Lillie was at Portelet with Jones, and also Alice and Clement. Her cares, together with her formal dress, had slipped away from her and she was, for the time being, ecstatically and domestically happy. On 2 August the Wharncliffes had returned to Wortley, and Lord Wharncliffe and Lillie were again communicating freely. Still he was kept in the dark over her reasons for departure. From Portelet she wrote to him, soon after her arrival, in holiday mood.

> Dear Lord Wharncliffe,
> Your letter was only forwarded to me yesterday with a quantity of others which have been lying in Norfolk St. since I left – I had been wondering so much why you had never written a line. I was very sorry not to see you before I left town – I am enjoying a quiet country life with my brother and his wife and her brother in the latters cottage. It is far in the country and perched right over the sea which is certainly bluer than any sea I ever saw – & the surrounding hills are *red* with the most brilliant heather. It is *dreadfully* hot & I am writing this in a hammock on the verandah in a bewitching blue and red bathing costume with nice Greek sandals. Alice and I have an assortment of them & have abandoned petticoats entirely. Don't be shocked as there isn't a soul to see us & as we row, swim, or fish all day long we find it infinitely more comfortable. We have all sorts of fishing appliances and get every sort of fish & shell-fish but great big red mullets are the most plentiful & lobsters. Have you been at Simonstone this year. Ld Manners sent us grouse once or twice which were much appreciated so if you are shooting, do likewise. I am going to write to Pc. Louis today about Mr Frank Wortley & will say a word to the P of W if you like. Do write to me – & with love to Lady Wharncliffe,
> Yrs ever truly, Lillie Langtry
> P.S. Encourage people to believe that Mr L is here.

Lillie's postscript is interesting. Wharncliffe did not know that she was pregnant, but because of his position as father-confessor, even though many of her confidences were elliptical, he knew more than most about her relationship with Ned. He also, clearly, was trusted enough to be relied on for tactical deception. In return, Lillie would use her influence in his and his family's favour. None of the letters have survived but she was still communicating with both Louis and the Prince of Wales, though her easy references and her obvious pleasure at her surroundings indicate that she was suffering no heartache at their separation.

For a while, at least, Lillie had the charmed existence of her childhood back. She was living with Clement and Alice, in Jones's cottage, on the island she knew as Eden. She had her lover, and the sea, and the long summer days to fish and swim and ride. She had no debts and no Ned. Her house and furniture had been sold, her position, along with her extravagant borrowed plumage, put off. She was light-headed with liberty. Best of all, the pressure to make a decision about the direction of the rest of her life had miraculously been removed. For the next six months, until she had her baby, she was safe and provided for. Grounded by events and, like most women, suffering a hormonal rush of dependence and domesticity, she acted out a happy life with Jones.

Lillie's mood of euphoria, like the cloudless Jersey skies, lasted on into autumn, when Lord Wharncliffe's communications began to sound a more sombre note. In England the ladies of Society were crowing over her departure. Gossip began to circulate, fostered by the boredom of the shooting season. Shut into their country houses, watching the autumn rain streaming down the drawing-room windows, and waiting for their men to return, the more waspish of Lillie's acquaintances started to add two and two. Lord Wharncliffe had panicked when he heard them and, like the fool he was, wrote immediately to Lillie, to ask whether their calculations were justified. Lillie was outraged, as much by the intrusion of London into her haven as by any truth it might have stumbled on. She wrote back,

> Dear Ld Wharncliffe,
>   I certainly do not think it kind of you to repeat to me all the malicious and vulgar gossip you may hear & I shall hope that for the future you will contradict all reports of that nature on Yr own authority. I don't know who the *ladies* of yr acquaintance at Doncaster may be but I am quite sure Lady Wharncliffe didn't believe it – I quite expected that there would be disagreeable things said directly I left but I scarcely thought anyone would have ventured to say that I had returned to my *own home* for such a reason. I saw Mr Langtry the other day, he was here for a short time and is much more amiable & as soon as he can afford it he will take another house for me. In the meantime I am contented to be here with my books and fishing &

gardening. I am fully occupied – I am making Arthur a lovely garden, palms
& camellias & Marechal Niel roses & all sorts of lovely tropical things.

Yrs very truly, Lillie Langtry.

Ned's arrival was clearly a fiction. The postscript in her last letter tells us
as much, but Wharncliffe's eyes were scaled and he probably did not
notice. Her rebuke stung, but even here, in the tide of her invective,
Lillie's pleasure in her surroundings breaks through. She really was
happy – happier than she had been since a child – wholly absorbed in
rediscovering the life that she had run from so eagerly, only four years
earlier.

A large part of Lillie's pleasure was made possible by the fact of her
being on Jersey, at her old pursuits, but not among the wreckage of her
family at the deanery. Her last visit home had been unhappy, both
because of the realizations it had forced upon her, and because of the pain
of its memories. Portelet, across the bay from 'dear old Noirmont', was a
perfect mixture of the old and the new. To see it now, the house where
Jones once lived is changed beyond recognition. In Lillie's day it had the
solid look of the Victorian holiday villa, every window with a striped
awning to shade it from the summer sun. But the garden Lillie made, and
loved, is still discoverable along the approach and in some of the
remaining planting. Here she could weave a fiction for herself of normal
life, safe from the ambush of the deanery ghosts. She could garden, as her
mother had. She could play at housekeeping with Alice, or she could put
out to the sea she knew so well, and haul in the catches of her youth,
lobsters, shellfish, and 'great big red mullets'.

Portelet is a small, high headland, with the house itself sitting on the
side of the hill, looking out across sloping lawns, to the sea and the rock-
strewn bay below. Verdant and airy, it gives itself to gardening now, as
then. Everything Lillie touched flourished, and she discovered, in her
planning and planting, the beginning of what was to become a lifelong
passion. Tucked into one side of the hill, halfway between the house and
the sea, and among the gardens, was the cottage where Lillie and the
young Le Bretons stayed. To reach it, or the beach, there is a paved path
that circles the hill like a belt, steeply dropping to the bay and its tiny
landing-stage. On one side, as it runs, the path is protected by a low wall,
covered with red valerian, jutting out, halfway down, into a platform that
hangs above the sea. Even now it is a mysteriously beautiful place. Lillie
had many homes in her long life. London alone sports a rash of blue
plaques, all of which proclaim her residency at different times. But

nowhere, not even at the house built for her by the Prince in Bournemouth, is there such a feeling of her presence as there is on that path, with her garden around her, looking over the sea at Portelet.

Often, on her way up or down, in the evening, as she went to her lover, and at different times in the day, as she came or returned from fishing trip or garden making, Lillie must have stood on this platform, and contemplated the curious turquoise of the Jersey sea. Portelet was an emotional fulcrum on which her life balanced that summer. She was given, even if it was only for a month, the rarest prize that life can offer, a return to the paradise of her childhood, a chance to turn back the clock and start again. She knew that the gates to the Garden should have been barred to her. She knew herself to be blessed with unearthly fortune, and, as she looked at her landscape from the path to the sea, she knew that the choice – forwards or back – was her own. Here it was, in the end, that she sloughed off her old skin. Here she began the descent into her private purgatory, from which she would later rise, changed and compromised, sold for material wealth and world renown. No wonder that the place has held on to her shade, kept it, as it was in the suspense of indecision – happy, and for the last time, resplendent in all the flawed glory of its self.

Lillie's summer holiday, though heightened and intensely felt, lasted only a moment. Clement had to return to London. Even Jones had obligations elsewhere. And Lillie, as her pregnancy advanced, was growing. Jersey was not the place for a secret birth. She was too well known, and besides there were too many of her London friends whom the milder climate might have tempted to a winter visit. But before she found herself a retreat, she needed to squash any rumours circulating among Society. In October, five months pregnant, she crossed over to England and booked into the Bath Hotel in Arlington Street. From here she wrote again to Wharncliffe.

> Dear Ld. Wharncliffe,
>   My fit of sulks is over & I am ready to be friends with you again. I have given myself rheumatism walking in a tight costume to disprove the report you told me of, and I feel highly displeased at being routed out of my nice warm island on account of it. – I am very fond of you really & consider you as one of my very best friends but I fear you are very easily influenced by what you hear & very apt to believe these hateful stories. I saw the Prince on Friday. He says he hopes it will be alright about yr. nephew. but I had written as soon as I received yr first letter to both him & Pc. Louis on the subject. I wish Ned could get something to do so that

we might settle down again & be happy – We are dreadfully hard up just at present. It seems I am the only pretty woman in town in sound health so perhaps that accts. in some measure for the report.

With this letter, Lillie's uses for Wharncliffe were almost over. He had come dangerously close to discovering her secret, and in his suspicions had shown no broadness of mind. Only the cool of head and heart were any good to Lillie now. So his dismissal was revoked and he was graciously reinstated (as the Prince had taught her in her own moment of disfavour) at a lower level than before. He was read a small lecture on his faults and was condescendingly forgiven. There were no more confidences, only deceits, for he was now to be held at arm's length with lies about Ned and the possibilities of their future happiness. Nor were there any of the old appeals for help. On the contrary, Lillie made it clear that she, with her superior connections, was the person to whom the world turned in its hopes for advancement. She managed it all with surprising skill and control.

Chapter XXII

A Voice from the Underworld

Her mission in London accomplished, Lillie loosened her stays and returned to Jersey, but summer was over, and the blue skies were gone. Arthur was away on the mainland. He had a commission as a Lieutenant in the King's Royal Rifle Corps, mainly through the offices of his father, who was the regiment's Lieutenant Colonel Commandant. She comforted herself with his dog Chance, and she tried to keep busy, but the spell was broken. Thus began Lillie's dark age. There is no reference to the next six months in her memoirs. There is no trace of her whereabouts, and no record of her thoughts or feelings. No letters to her friends, if she wrote them, have survived, and her correspondence with Wharncliffe was ended for a time. But we do have the letters she wrote to Jones, preserved in his little green case in the attic at Portelet.

These letters to Jones, gauging, as they do, her loneliness, her anxiety, and her periodic and suffocating depression, are a chrysalis, from which we see her rise, iron-winged with determination. Every day she wrote to him, long, clinging letters, full of domestic news and pleas for reassurance. Gone are all her old voices, the gracious, unruffled tones of the Society diva, the vapid self-absorption of her letters to Wharncliffe, the breezy boyishness of her first few to Jones. Instead we hear only the dark of disorientation – her pain, her misery and her abject dependence. Often, too, we hear her fighting with her own internal demons, for she was afraid of complaining too much, of frightening Jones away with her needs and her anxieties. She tries hard to persuade both him and herself that she has things to do and that her old energies are intact. She organizes for Cauvet, her elocution teacher, to come and join her on Jersey, in order that she can keep up her lessons. She tries to keep her eye on the future, to look beyond the arrival of the baby, and she tries to busy herself on Jones's behalf. But it is a thin skin of control that she stretches over her seething self, and more often than not it fails to hold. Thus, in

October of 1880, alone at Portelet, she wails,

> Darling Arthur,
>   It seems ages ago already since you went away. I am *so* dull without you. You really must come back soon . . . drill or no drill. The cares of house keeping weigh Alice and me down. How you got through it so quietly is a marvel to us . . . It is blowing a hurricane here. I don't know how Mr Cauvet will be able to cross. Chance mingles her groans with mine at your absence and has been indulging her grief on my red sofa to its utter destruction but as we are companions in misfortune I haven't scolded her – We have an idea of getting up a fête for your hunt in the terminus at St Aubyns – a sort of bazaar – and we want to have one stall of Japanese things with men dressed as Chinamen. So you might bring over all the Chinese dresses you have. Mr Arbuthnot will help us and you must too. It won't be much trouble as the shop will send us things marked cost price and then we can sell them rather dear and pocket the difference and then they will take back what we don't get rid of . . . If you don't like it please telegraph but I think you will. Dearest boy, I hope you miss me. Please *please* hurry back, I want you so much.

Often Jones was not as tender or as prompt in his reassurances as Lillie would have wished. Only days after writing this last, the bazaar and all its delights are forgotten. The veneer of preoccupation is gone and she is desperate again.

> My darling Artie,
>   You are very unkind not to write to me. I have written to you every day . . . *Please* do come back on Tuesday night. I am so miserable I can't stay here if you don't. *Please* come and do your drills some other time. You would come if you knew how dull I am. Cauvet must have had such a bad passage. Today it is blowing harder than ever and the sea is dreadfully rough. Do come Artie for Heaven's sake if you care for me.

Deprived of London, and made vulnerable by pregnancy, Lillie craved attention. When Arthur was with her and the weather mild, Jersey was an idyll. Without him she was sometimes unable to rise for exhaustion and anxiety. It was clear that, in this state, she could not be left alone, so she took the risk of allowing her garrulous mother into her confidence. This gave her something else to worry about, since Mrs Le Breton was a stranger to the secret, but it solved the immediate problems of loneliness and incapacity. When Clement and Alice had to return to England, Mrs Le Breton duly arrived and took on the business of caring for Lillie. This was a mutually convenient arrangement since she and the Dean had finally parted company. He was living in Marylebone in London, semi-disgraced on account of his philandering, and she, the Londoner, had remained alone in Jersey. Lillie's return must have been something of a godsend. She had, at last, something to do and someone who needed her. It must have taken all her little energy and ingenuity to keep up Lillie's flagging spirits. Together they worried about Ned, and walked about Lillie's gale-blown garden. Together they planned for the baby and puzzled about Lillie's future. For Lillie, the time was punctuated and made bearable only by Arthur's dilatory communications. She lived from one letter to the next, writing with a flood of gratitude by return of post.

> My darling Arthur,
> I was glad to get your letter this morning. You dear boy to write. Imagine how dull I am without you. Mother has had a very bad cold and has gone to bed and they all left for London this morning so I am all alone and so miserable. Cauvet has just given me my usual lesson which has occupied me a little but I am deadly dull. I hope you miss me too my darling. I walked with Dominique this morning and last evening but it wasn't very lively. Those people have never sent the flowers. I am going off to say I don't want them. Write me everything you do my darling you know how it interests me and although I feel I have been very disagreeable please know it is because I have felt ill, not because I don't love you. More than ever [   ] I am going again to try to get your letters at the post office but you didn't leave me an envelope and I don't think they will give them up.'

Eventually Lillie and her mother, with or without Jones's help, decided on the Continent as providing the best refuge for Lillie's remaining months of pregnancy. They left together for France sometime towards the beginning of November. They went first to Paris, where they booked into the Hotel Castille to wait while the Prince sent someone from England to find them permanent lodgings just outside Paris itself. Lillie hated the secrecy and resented the boredom. Daily she sent back her paper wails to Jones at Portelet.

> My darling,
> I was so glad to get your letters last evening. I *am* so wretched. Pratt won't let me go out excepting in a brougham with two or three veils on and I am bored to death. I have had a headache ever since I came to this stuffy

hotel and am getting quite ill. He has promised to fetch me to see some apartments and I have been waiting an hour for him. It will be too dark to see what they are like. I think it too selfish of him. I went to the theatre one evening but I hated it without you. You *will* come over as soon as you can won't you. I have read your dear letter over and over. *Please* write as often as you can. Goodbye my own darling boy . . . I am wretched without you.

Besides the boredom and frustration, there was still the more serious problem of Ned and his suspicions. Clearly he had found out that Lillie and her mother had left Jersey and wanted to know where they had gone. Jones telegraphed Lillie in alarm and she replied,

What a frightening telegram. How can Ned know I am away? and what can he have to write to me about. I am so frightened about it. I can't sleep and don't care to go out or move. I have taken an apartment in the Champs-Elysées for 1100F a month. I don't think it is much do you? You must try to get back to help me more . . . won't you darling. I always have you at all events darling haven't I? to care for me whatever happens. Goodbye my darling boy.

So Lillie solaced herself with hopes of Jones's constancy. She told herself that, despite his long absences, his love and his commitment still equalled her own. She consulted him rhetorically about rent, preferring to believe that he could and would care for her once it could be so arranged. On practical matters, however, he clearly fell short of the mark. The accommodation in the Champs-Elysées was being paid for by the Prince of Wales, through the offices of George Lewis, solicitor to Society and a friend of Lillie's.

Lillie must also have written either to Lewis or to the Prince himself. Someone acted promptly and Ned was sent on invented business, as far away as possible. On 27 November *Vanity Fair* noted that, 'Mr Langtry is about to go to America on business, and proposes to remain there two months.' Lillie was reassured and able, for a rare moment, to resume a more commanding role.

My darling boy,
I cannot understand my letter not reaching you yesterday. I wrote in time for post on Monday and yesterday. I do hope it will reach you darling. I have been thinking again over my address and I wish instead of saying *Berlin* you would say that you have at present no address and that you are expecting to hear from me where to forward them so that you may be able

to show them to him. say that you let us Portelet but that my mother was not well and you think we went to France. If you say Berlin it will be so difficult to explain why we went so far etc. and we might be in 100 towns in France besides Paris. I do hope we shall know something settled and before Saturday so that you can come back.

While Lillie worried about secrecy, and found her own solutions, Jones had been hunting, and wrote, with sublime unconcern, of the scrapes he and Redskin had encountered. Lillie was still at the Hotel Castille.

My own darling boy,
    I *was* pleased to get your letters this mg. I have been in bed all day. I can't sleep at all at night and am getting so ill from it – I believe it's missing you so much. I am so miserable and have been *longing* all the day to telegraph to you to come over but I am so afraid you wd be angry if you came and found I wasn't very ill. How I *do* wish you wd turn up. How can you imagine that I can be happy anywhere without you my darling sweetheart. Thank goodness I have found an apartment and I hope we shall get into it tomorrow or Tuesday but you had better write here once more. Write by return *please* darling – I am so sorry you have disabled Redskin and so horribly nervous at the idea of your riding any of those horrid Jersey horses wh. I am sure can't jump. *Please please* be careful for the sake of the little girl who loves you so. Oh do come over and go back for a fortnight later if you *must*. When you come will you bring a pair of spectacles belonging to mother. She left them at le Gallais in Bath St. in her work table. Also a bottle for me of Larbalestiers eau-de-Cologne as I like it so much better than any other. I bought such an odd little white dog the other day. It is tiny and likes being always carried about. I believe from your letter you thought I was flirting with Batt! Oh Artie Artie what a *bad boy* you are to imagine these things. I never see anyone without thinking of you and wondering if you would like it. Goodbye my own love. Do come soon there is a little room for *you* waiting. My head is throbbing so I can't write any more – Goodbye my darling heaps of love . . .

When he could spare the time from hunting Jones would cross to France for a few days to be with Lillie. 'Darling,' she wrote on one such occasion,

I *am* so delighted you are coming. If I am awake as I hope to be I shall come out but I have been so bad with a cough and want of sleep that I have taken an opiate tonight. But I think I shall awake. Please have some breakfast dearest and look after yourself.

Always Lillie swung between happiness, when he was with her, and
worry and depression in his absence. More than once his visits had to be
cut short because Ned was becoming suspicious. Then Jones would rush
back to Jersey, and telegraph America on Lillie's behalf, to set his mind
at rest.

> My own darling boy,
>   Have you been a good boy and written to me from Granville? It is so
> wretched your having to leave me just now, I *do* miss you so my darling.
> You must not be frightened if I tell you that I fell down this morning in
> the Avenue flat on my side. but I don't think I hurt myself. I feel a little
> stiff that's all. Wasn't it unlucky? I didn't see the pavement and tripped
> over it so it was entirely my fault and I fell so quickly no one could have
> saved me. If you had been with me my own darling, I should probably
> have had hold of that strong little arm. I am going to have my bath
> presently so you see I am not bad. I heard from Lewis yesterday. Don't
> forget all these *important* instructions darling and come back *soon*.

It did not take long, once Jones had left, before Lillie's demons reasserted
themselves. A confident letter, written in the flush of security generated
by Jones's recent presence, would be followed the next day by a cry of
anguish; so quickly did her moods oscillate.

> My darling,
>   the boat arrived at Queenstown at 1.00 yesterday but as yet I have
> heard nothing from Geo Lewis. I am *utterly* miserable and upset and I
> don't know how I shall get through the day till I hear more . . . I haven't
> courage to move or go anywhere. My fall didn't hurt me. Wasn't it lucky?
> Your letter was so nice. I had it by my bedside last night and read it
> whenever I woke. You didn't worry me my darling. It is only my peevish
> temper that makes me complain. You dear boy, I *wish* you were still here
> – yet I know you must stay where you are – till something is known.
> Darling, darling I do want you here. No one cares for me except you. I am
> too miserable to write more and besides I am afraid you won't get this
> letter before Thursday.

Slowly the time passed and Lillie inched towards the birth of her child.
Occasionally, when the overwhelming lethargy lightened for a moment,
she took an interest in the outside world. *Nana* was playing in Paris, 'that
disgusting novel of Zola's wh. you have probably read', as Lillie
described it in a rare Dean's-daughter moment, though she did not go to
see it. She asked often about Jersey, where she longed to be, and which

she now associated with all that was healthy and hopeful. Were the ladies in the market, the ones she knew from childhood, 'old Esther and the others', well? 'Will you see them,' she asked in one letter, 'and *scold* them *well* if they don't wear their shawls.' Ned was less of a worry now that he was out of the country, more particularly as the Prince had stationed two men in Queenstown, to watch the boat and make sure he did not escape. This left Lillie room to think instead about her garden at Portelet, for which she filled her letters, as the year turned, with directions. 'Be very busy', she urged Arthur, 'and look after the farm and everything and have some seeds planted in yr frames. You will see which ones require heat and you are to have something put across the garden to prevent the donkey making his supper of my pet plants.' Never did she mention Society, or her friends in London. All her preoccupations, in her good moments, were domestic and centred on life at Portelet.

When Lillie was stable, it was as though her fame, and her marriage, and all her life among the whirl of the season, had been erased, or simply dreamt. Nothing mattered any more except their garden and their happiness together. 'Darling Artie,' she confessed once, 'I am so ashamed but I have a dreadful fit of jealousy about Miss Le Brocq and the Wests. *Please* promise in yr next letters not to speak to them.' They might, in fact, have been any normal, happily married couple were it not for the strange taboo of their supposed child, unmentioned in any of Lillie's letters, whose arrival was awaited with no excitement and no joy, and whose negative presence broods like a storm cloud over their correspondence.

Part of the reason for Lillie's preoccupation with Jersey in her letters was that she needed something for herself and Jones to share, something to feel that they were jointly creating. There was so much that they could not talk of together, so much of which she was afraid. The garden, in her tender care for it, her preparations for the new year, and her cosy planning, took the place of the baby. Everything that, under normal conditions, she would have put into waiting for the birth she put instead into Portelet. For it was the case that, while Jones believed the child to be his, Lillie was not so sure.

In her eyes, pregnancy had been the last straw in a life that was already impossibly fraught with difficulties. It was a source of shame and of endless worry. She was terrified of Ned's violence if he should find out and terrified of the public disgrace. She worried about where to hide the baby once it was born, and she worried about how to provide for it day to day. Her insecurity was such that she could barely face these problems herself, let alone discuss them with Jones. Most of all, she needed his support and his love, and she was afraid, every moment that he was away, of his hearing something decisive against her, of his finding someone else – someone younger, gayer or with fewer worries. The unhappiness that she showed him in her letters, and her clinging dependency, were only the tip of the iceberg. Many days she must have spent, lying on her bed in her apartment in Paris on the rue de Naples, listening to the bright, busy sounds of the world around her, of people celebrating Christmas and the New Year, while she stared, alone, at the blackness that was her future, and felt her baby stir inside her, and wondered how to go forward.

The winter of 1880 was a bitter one, and the baby was due in March. Lillie's usual robust health was gone and she caught a series of colds. Jones was back in Jersey again and did not plan to return until the due date. In February she wrote to tell him the doctor thought it could not come before 18 March. Clement had found her out and was outraged at her predicament. She begged Jones to come to her sooner than planned.

My own darling Arthur,

I am laid up with a very bad cold which all this horrid frost and snow has given me and cannot get out and am also afflicted with all sorts of worries. Clem has written me today a long and disagreeable letter, principally full of abuse of my mother in consequence of a letter she wrote begging him to be careful not to say anything. I am really quite tired of him. My darling I think I shall be quite grey-headed soon with worry. How I do wish you were here to console me. I go sighing about the house in the most miserable condition. You *can't* be so dull as I am. I think if I get an angry letter from Ned it will kill me. *Please* write to me very often. I count the days till I can hear from you. The two letters you forwarded were both from Col. V about the offer he had for my chestnut mare and begging for an immediate answer. However I don't meant to let her go, so if he should telegraph before he has time to receive the enclosed letter please write to him to that effect. I owe you *pounds* for that American telegram. How I do wish you could come over even for a short time and then go back and come again . . . Chantreuil says *not before* the 18th and perhaps not till 3 weeks later. It is dreadful I have been feeling better lately, but am very seedy again with my cold. I *do so* want you. I *can't* wait ten days more, and you *can't* plant potatoes yet. Yrs ever darling Artie

This time Arthur came directly and must have stayed with her until after the birth, since her next letter to him announces her return to England.

The baby arrived very promptly on 18 March, a girl whom they named
Jeanne-Marie. There is no way of telling whether Lillie found the birth
easy or difficult, and whether she and Jones were happy, despite their
circumstances, once the child was in their arms. Certainly, for both of
them, the birth cemented their relationship. Privately, in letters after it,
Lillie refers to herself as Jones's wife, and their plan, clearly, was
somehow to live together on their return to normality. In the meantime,
a nurse was found, and the baby baptized in the English Protestant
Church, and Lillie and her mother returned to England. Mrs Le Breton
was to take Jeanne, with the nurse, down to the house in Bournemouth,
designed, so conveniently, by the Prince, as a hideaway. Lillie was to
make her own way back to London, alone.

Chapter XXIII

Letters

It was early in April when Lillie and her mother, with Dominique, the nurse and little Jeanne set out from France on their return to England. Jones travelled with them as far as Guernsey, so it was quite a family party. Lillie was not yet recovered from the birth. She was weak and still very depressed. The parting, when they reached the Channel Islands where Lillie was to leave Jones, was desperate. As soon as she set foot on English soil she wrote,

> My darling,
>   Just arrived and so horribly tired. A lot of live ohs came on board at Guernsey and sang and screamed all the way across which made sleep quite out of the question. We got in at two and went to the Marine Hotel which turned out to be a *pot* house of the lowest description in which people shared beds between six and the proprietor was quite drunk and would not show us our rooms and kept on asking us to drink champagne with him. I was so frightened that I couldn't sleep. I hope my sweetheart you weren't very miserable all alone at Guernsey. I missed you *dreadfully* and when I reached Weymouth felt inclined to come back to you. I am never happy without you.

Mrs Le Breton went on to Bournemouth the following day and Lillie, debilitated and utterly miserable, was fielded by the Lewises. George Lewis, solicitor to both Lillie and the Prince of Wales, had managed the finances of her confinement, and probably too the logistics of keeping Ned busy and under observation on the other side of the world. He was the only person, apart from the Prince, to know of the real reason for Lillie's departure, and he and his wife took her in on her return, and nursed her back to something like health and spirits. She stayed with them first in their house in London and then, for the sake of her health, in their cottage at Walton-on-Thames. They were kindness itself, and sophisticated enough to pity her and to refrain from judging, but it was not easy for Lillie. Lewis, like the Prince, assumed that the child was royal, either his or Battenberg's, so there was no question of Arthur visiting during Lillie's stay. Lillie by now had become so dependent that separation from her lover was unbearable. Besides, back on English soil, and with the birth over, the whole question of her future now became an immediate concern. She needed Arthur for support and she needed him for protection against any possibility of a return to the life she had been living the year before. Naturally she consoled herself with a flood of letters.

There was another threat that hung over Lillie in the first month of her return, a threat worse than any problem of insolvency or occupation. Ned was returning, and expected to be reunited with his wife. Seven months of hiding had taken their toll, and whatever residue of fondness she had felt for him, before leaving, had staled into abhorrence. She dreaded their first encounter. Moreover, since they were still married, she knew that as soon as she was well enough, she was expected to return to life with him in London. After so long with Jones, and after the emotional upheaval of the birth itself, the idea of returning to Ned filled her with horror. She knew herself to be too changed for any convincing pretence at tolerance and too vulnerable to cope with the money worries. She shrank from the vicious circle of rows, and drinking and beatings. Yet every day Lewis briefed her on her story against Ned's arrival, and every day she duly passed it on to Jones.

> My own darling,
>
> I am so sorry I couldn't write yesterday but there was no post. I *was* glad to get yours but today have had none, on account of the post too, I suppose. We are momentarily expecting a telegram from Ned as he must have arrived this morning at Liverpool. . . I am to say I was in Paris three weeks in January, that I had not been away when he telegraphed but had expressed my intention of going to Paris, that since my return to Jersey I have been at Portelet with my mother and that I crossed last week – I am still feeling very unwell no better or stronger than I was in London. It is so provoking. I think most likely I shall come to town on Tuesday. Shall you be up by then. My darling I miss you so much. We must never quarrel must we? Goodbye my darling many kisses from Lillie.

This letter was written on Saturday. On Tuesday they were still waiting to hear from Ned, when she wrote again,

> I have been hoping for a letter from you today but I suppose you hadn't

time yesterday to write. We have had *no* telegram or news of Ned. It is most extraordinary and Lewis can't make out why. Today I have remained in bed as I am so afraid of making myself ill however it is delightful to think that after this I shall be alright – I suppose my darling I shall come up to town Friday or Saturday the former if I can and if I have heard from Ned. If *you* hear of his whereabouts please let me know. The Comyn Carrs are staying here and Oscar Wilde came last night . . .

Then, at last, Ned materialized, and seemed unsuspicious, and happy to believe Lewis's carefully concocted stories. Lillie breathed a sigh of relief to Jones.

Darling Artie,

I waited to write to you until I had seen Ned as I knew you would be so anxious to know. Well he is in very good humour and seemed quite satisfied at my telling him I had been in Paris about a month and that I crossed with my mother and you from Jersey the Monday before I came here. I told him we stayed at Portelet with you after our return from Paris. He is staying with Reg at present so you may come across him. I am most anxious to get him to settle something, so that I may come to town on Saturday, wh. you may be sure my own darling I long to do. I am dreadfully weak and am going to send Dominique up tomorrow to get me some wine so that I may take a little nip privately now and then but I do long to be where I can do as I like tho they are kindness itself. I am quite alone now here. The others went up to town today. I don't know how I could enjoy the society of Oscar Wilde as you wrote, as I have been in bed all the time he has been here. Goodbye my own darling boy. Ned only got my telegram yesterday as the fog prevented them landing . . . He had received endless letters saying I had not been in Jersey but I said mother was so excited at the idea of going to Paris that she talked to all her friends.

Clearly there had been plenty of friends, during her confinement, who had discovered pressing loyalties to the formerly 'fat and uninteresting' Mr Langtry, and had been zealous in their attempts to disabuse him over Lillie's whereabouts. Though Lillie was temporarily reassured by their failure, Jones was unhappy. Now it seems it was he who needed her, and who most resented Ned's appearance. He wrote her his disappointment and she replied,

My Darling Arthur,

Your letter made me *so* miserable my own boy you know not to be in the blues. I am coming up *quite* early on Monday and you shall see me as soon as I come. The Lewis' are going up to town tomorrow afternoon and I am going to telegraph to you tomorrow if it's fine to come down. I don't think it would do for you to come to the house but I will meet you outside. I did not write earlier as I wanted to see Dominique first. Don't trouble about houses darling I really think an hotel is better . . . I wish I could always see you. Please try to see Ned. He is at 25 Kensington Gate.

Whether Arthur came down to her or not, Lillie was in town as promised, at the beginning of the week. She booked into the Alexandra Hotel and immediately sent round for Jones, who was staying in his father's lodgings at Albert Mansions, in Victoria Street. Ned, it seems, was with her, as she worries in her note about Arthur's reply being indiscreet. Once again, meetings had to be arranged in secret. Jones came, but before he did so Lillie was writing again, in haste, to arrange a meeting in Ned's absence.

Writing this in case Ned is here when you come to tell you that I must try to see you alone and will therefore come to Victoria Street as soon as I can get there after you leave here. As Lord R is away I suppose it will be quite safe. It *is* nice to think that tomorrow we shall be together again isnt it. I am feeling so seedy.

They were together again only for a moment. Ned was no clearer about what he wanted to do. He seemed to feel that he and Lillie should continue to live together, and to this end they took the lease of a house in Berkeley Street. Jones set off again for Jersey, and Lillie turned to pen and paper for solace.

My *own* boy,
         I was dreadfully vexed when Alice told me I had missed the post. I was longing to write but I *hope* you got my telegram. I fear I shan't hear from you at least till Tuesday. We have taken the little house in Berkeley Street I told you of and we hope to get in by Tuesday. I shall be very glad to be settled tho London seems *so* dull now you have gone but I suppose any place would be the same to me without you. George Lewis had Clem to meet me at his office the other day and we 'made it up' in a way, but I feel we shall never be the same again. He said he would never forget *your* having been with me. . . . How I wish my darling you could make some money; enough for us to be happy I am so miserable tonight, I feel I can't live without you. I will finish this letter tomorrow. Goodnight my precious boy. Monday morning. My darling I have just got your little letter. I am so glad as I was afraid I couldn't hear. I am so bothered trying to get

servants etc. It is such hard work isn't it? and I don't know what to do about Redskin and a brougham. You need not be jealous of anyone my own boy, I can never care for anyone but you.

Money was an abiding problem. Neither Lillie nor Jones was frugal in their tastes, and Jones was often in debt. Like Ned he did no work, relying entirely on Ranelagh for income. This appears to have been erratic and often negotiated by his mother on his behalf. When there was talk of Jones's sister Emily marrying Lord Napier she wrote to Ranelagh,

> Arthur has received his cheque but it is not *nearly* sufficient to pay all the back debts that have been accumulating during the last year. He lives quietly enough and has only dined out twice since I have been here – and *I* pay all the butcherbills weekly, so that takes a great deal off his usual expenditure – but there is quite £50 owing, so try to think of him also and don't buy any more diamond rings just yet.

Ranelagh's excitement at the prospect of a boost to his failing fortunes was understandable. He encouraged Emily in letter after letter, and attempted to put on an encouraging show for his daughter's prospective in-laws, by supplying her with a handsome ring. Napier's father, however, was not taken in and stopped the marriage by threatening his son with penury. Ranelagh was disappointed and he and his children returned to their former financial brinkmanship.

It is easy, among the clinging domestication of Lillie's letters to Jones at this period, to forget how rakish a lover Jones really was. His background was louche enough, with Ranelagh and the tight-fitting tailcoats, and the seven illegitimate children, and the retinue of ballet girls. But besides his inherited colour, Jones was cutting a small swathe of his own, on the hunting field and in the Jersey gentlemen's clubs. In 1879 he had been banned from the Victoria club for causing a drunken disturbance, and now, despite Lillie's dependence, he was in trouble again. Lillie's last letter had been written on Sunday. The next day she wrote again, desperate and disapproving.

> Darling,
> 	I am utterly miserable and your letter makes me still more so. Ned is drinking and behaving so badly. I don't think he will stay with me. We quarrelled just now about the amount of drink he consumes and he has rushed off to . . . get money to pay the bill. I don't know *even* if he will

come to Berkeley Street where we go today. I wish you wouldn't make me still more wretched by being rowdy. You know how I hate anything of that sort. *Please*, please don't. I shall write again tomorrow but my whole future looks very black today and I can't write more.

Jones's response must have been huffy (and, to be fair, Lillie had changed – from the girl who slid downstairs on other people's silver salvers and struck her lovers' head with her slipper, to this woman who whimpered and worried) for in her next letter Lillie complained of his indifference.

My darling,
      Your cold letter made me miserable. I hate that sort of letter please don't write so any more – I want to come over at Whitsun tide do tell me if it will be safe – Ned is rather better today thank goodness. We are at 3 Berkeley St. but have no servants yet. Pinchon must remove all the cabbages. I will *not* have them planted in my flower garden. It is too bad of him. I have been nowhere since I wrote but have been busy getting the house in order. Alice is at Fulham. I heard from her yesterday. I hope you will get away for a week and then we could go back with you. What is the use of staying if the potatoes are not ready. Goodbye my own darling. *Please* don't drink or be rowdy it makes me more miserable than anything else.

Once she was in her own house again Lillie addressed her mind to the question of her future. She had sacked Wharncliffe from his position of chief adviser, and had put no one in his place. But she had made contact with her old friends in Bohemia, and it was to them that she now chose to listen. When she dined out it was with the Lewises, to meet Wilde, Millais, Louise Jopling. Whistler recorded her presence at a breakfast he gave at Tite Street, and began a portrait, now lost, called *'Arrangement in Yellow'*. She also put her toe back into the waters of Society, mostly to show herself and to allay suspicion. She did not go to much, but she attended some of the old events of the season, private views at the Grosvenor Gallery or receptions at Marlborough house, among others, to meet the King of Sweden. She wanted, for a number of reasons, not the least of which was pride, to show that her exile had been chosen not imposed. She also wanted to keep her options open and her instinct told her that, if she kept up her contacts, they might be useful to her in time to come. Some of her real friends she entertained at home, albeit on a small scale. To one of these events Whistler was bidden and left the jottings for a rehearsed reply upside down on a sheet that also, appropriately, recorded his views on clothes. It ran,

> O! most lovely Lillie, I am indeed flattered and delighted to be present at your rentrée of triumph and success. Long before now would I have been to renew my allegiance and to declare my joy at seeing you more beautiful than ever – but I have been ill like an ordinary mortal – though always your devoted JW.

The 'rentrée of triumph and success' was a tender loyalty from one who had been through the mill himself, and was worldly enough to guess at the troubles that Lillie had to keep hidden. Although her real friends pretended it was all as glorious as ever, Lillie's life was not, through choice, the whirl that it had been the year before. There were plenty of reminders of her old occupations, some more galling than others. Shrewsbury, her former fancy, was in London, but she had no inclination to take up again with him. Besides he had moved on to pastures new himself. He had struck up with another married woman, the wife of Alfred Miller Mundy, a Derbyshire squire, with whom he did manage to elope later in the year. Blunt's unkind claims about Lillie's determination to catch him had been short of the mark. Shrewsbury had had his heart set on an elopement all along, and it must have been she, a year ago, who had dragged her heels to stop him.

Once again, since there was nothing to tempt her back to her old life in Society, Lillie was considering the options before her. Now, with Jones penniless, and herself, for the moment, constant, she was casting about for a solution that would keep them both in comfort. Acting was still the favourite, but despite Cauvet's lessons and the success of the Waverley tableaux, she could not commit herself. As the season approached, she wrote again to Jones, in brisker tones than she had done so far. Even if she was no nearer her goal, she was beginning to feel her health returned. This was a more stable letter than she had written for quite a while. It contains all the usual geographical and horticultural touchstones, but it shows, for the first time, a complete confidence in Jones's commitment to her. It also shows her returning to the idea of trying out the stage.

> My own darling,
>   I wish you wouldn't think I *flirt*. I assure you nothing is further from my mind. In fact I am moping far too much and never care to go out. I fear people are horribly ill-natured about me. However I don't mind the wretches. I saw Ellen Terry two days ago and we had a great talk about the stage. I am going to learn the part of Hero in Much Ado About Nothing

and rehearse it with her first to find out if I have any talent . . . My dear Artie, Pinchon *must* take his cabbages away – I am quite horrified. I am also sorry all the bulbs have been planted in the new garden, as if there are rabbits about, they will eat the lilies even sooner than uninteresting cabbages . . . We lunched at the Sassoons today, but there was no one there. I am bored to death with the people and with Society, I do so want to do something. Ned has endless creditors sitting in the hall again. Quite like old times. Are you a dear good little boy really? and really missing your wife? You sweet I *wish* we were together *now*. I think your letters to me are pretty safe, as long as you enclose them to Dominique. If you get a good offer for Portelet dearest, I think you had better let it as we can always be together somewhere else. We could take a cottage together on the Thames wh. would be heavenly. Goodbye my own boy. Write often to your devoted Lillie.

The visit by Ellen Terry is also recorded in the memoirs, where Lillie magnificently translates the offer to rehearse Hero as a test of ability into an offer to take the part of Hero in a Lyceum production under the fabled Henry Irving. Terry was, in fact, always kind about Lillie's abilities as an actress but on this first visit, as Lillie herself admits, she was discouraging. 'After the financial crash,' Lillie's account runs,

> I appealed to the great and enchanting Nell to give me her views. She came and spent a precious hour of her time, outlining the different aspects of the vocation I was being so persistently advised to follow. The difficulties and disappointments that I might encounter, and what she termed the 'rough side', seemed to her almost insurmountable for one who had been so petted and spoiled and idle as myself.
>
> On the whole she was discouraging. Yet, a few months later, when I appeared . . . in other roles, and was on the eve of my departure for the States, I went to the first night of Much Ado About Nothing at the Lyceum, and, at the supper given afterwards on the stage . . . Ellen Terry . . . confided to me that she had had me in mind for Hero and that Henry had intended to offer me the part . . .

The confidence of the voice in Lillie's later account, the easy familiarity with 'Henry' and the 'enchanting Nell' come from the other side of the rubicon and are unrecognizable in the context of April 1881.

Her letters to Jones are more than just another cache of love letters, they are a minute record of a mind being made up. Written daily, with no premeditation, they are almost a stream of consciousness. Though she appeals to Jones often, to take some of the burden off her shoulders, to find a solution that will be a refuge for both of them, she knows at the back of her mind that what she is asking of him is impossible. The love affair is as much with Jersey, with an old way of life, a turquoise sea, a house and garden, as with Jones himself. Slowly now we see her relinquishing her only dream of domesticity. We watch her, in her letters, becoming the voice on the other side of her choice, dipping her toe in the water, and then retreating. And each time she comes back to it, it is with a grain more certainty, a grain more realism.

For the moment Ellen Terry's discouragement hit home. Lillie's next letters have dropped the preoccupation with the stage and are eager only for news of Portelet and the garden. 'Darling,' she writes, 'I do wish we could make money in the country. I feel such a longing for it and hate London so. Couldn't we have a poultry farm? Do try and think of something.' She was thinking only of her next visit to Jersey, which she hoped could be at Whtisun, blocking out the creditors who paced her hall waiting for an interview, and losing herself in the irrelevant business of cuttings, manure and seedlings.

> Darling boy,
>   I am so delighted you are improving my garden but do tell me *much* more about it. Where the new beds are and what you have planted. Also whether there are lots of things coming up. Is there any clematis coming up in the lower garden on the wall behind the strawberries? As if so it ought to be trained and there are roots round the house. I hope you don't let that green favourite of yours overrun everything. I should like you to get a few sunflower *plants* and put them in that high bed in our new garden as they cannot have too much sun and when I come over I shall bring a lot of plants which I *hope* I shall do at Whitsuntide. I want you to have the big bed in the new garden planted where there is room with *low* growing seeds as I want the lilies to seem to come out of a carpet of flowers and the shady bed may have nemophila, and also plant all that piece at the back of the garden – the cliff, with all sorts of bright things. I forget what seeds you have but they must be things that like the sun.

The instructions go on and on, a desperate pretence at making something of her life, something that was, at once, a project to be managed and an escape. And there were, after all, so many things to escape from – London, her debts, her husband, and his drink and his suspicions, Society, her own inadequacy, her dawning realization of Jones's inadequacies too, Clement's disapproval, and the whips of her twin furies, ambition and regret. She tried to be busy and to make Jones busy, and she tried to be constructive. Slowly she was attempting to piece together a life for them, and if she had not yet settled on exactly what it should constitute she did know that it meant turning over a new leaf for both of them. To silence her furies, she had raised up for herself two new gods. These were industry and discipline, and to them she now turned. She redoubled her efforts at preparing herself for the stage, adding, to her regular lessons with Cauvet, the services of a second tutor, Mrs Stirling.

> My own boy,
>   I am so glad you are so good but so am I. I went to Mrs Stirling's and had a lesson today and she said she was immensely surprised at my powers so I am rather pleased; but en revenche there has been a bailiff in the house for two days and I have had to pay him and also have had to go round to Ned's creditors this morning asking them to wait. *One* of them was so rude. Yesterday I was vaccinated as the small pox is awfully bad here. Ned has been rather a brute lately but I will try to keep him with me tho it is killing work. I hope you aren't flirting and if I ever find out you have done so I shall lose all confidence in men . . . My lilies are still fresh and scent the whole room. Have you any wallflowers? I should so like some if anyone is crossing and could bring a hamper. I am afraid they could not come by post.

The tone is refreshingly assertive. Inching towards her professional goal Lillie had, for the moment, recovered some of her old optimism.

As the summer arrived Lillie made plans to escape, for real this time, on holiday to Portelet. Ned would go with her but it is clear from her arrangements for accommodation that they were not expecting to share rooms. She writes to Jones,

> Darling Artie,
>   I am so sorry you can't find any sunflowers. I must try to bring some over. Ned says now he won't go out to the cottage. So can you make that attic room habitable either for him or Dominique. I am so longing to come over my darling, you don't say how delighted you are at the idea. You are a dear good boy to work hard at Portelet instead of hanging about that grimy little town. I hope to goodness mother is keeping her tongue quiet. If you see her tell her she must be very careful. Alice and Clem dined here last night. Poor Alice reminds me of an unpleasant phase in my existence. London is dull as ditchwater. Everyone is on the river Lady L included. Goodbye my darling.

Alice, who was provoking so many unpleasant memories, was in the last stages of pregnancy. Clearly Clement's disapproval had subsided and Lillie and the young Le Bretons were again much in each other's company. Along with her new-found belief in work, Lillie was shoring herself up by constructing a family. Realizing her relationship with Jones in a context of sisters and brothers-in-law, and nephews and nieces, was a way of making it concrete. Longing for their affair to be formalized, she held on to those things around them that were permanent or part of their shared life. The only person left out of her carefully created circle was Jeanne. She worried about Alice and her health, or her mother and her state of mind, about Jones and whether or not he was working. She ordered plants and planned the garden. She talked of Portelet as 'my home' and, in organizing her visit, her instructions about accommodation were less those of a guest than of the mistress of the house. Whatever her plans for the future (and it was surely one of the reasons that she took so long to commit herself to the stage), the focus for her whole being was still unquestionably Jersey.

The plan to escape to Portelet at Whitsun, however, fell through. The creditors were threatening and Ned was unable to leave for fear of bankruptcy. He was still involved in various business schemes set up for him by Lewis. This was simply a way of the Prince making sure that Lillie had money. Their sudden income was easier to explain away if Ned appeared to be earning it. As far as Lillie's affair with Jones went, it explained too why she needed to keep Ned with her for the time being. 'My darling', she apologizes to Jones,

> Indeed you must write again for I have not good news for you. Ned says now he can't possibly get away before the end of the week. It's *too* annoying but I can see he *really* can't or we should be made bankrupt. They have threatened to make him one in a fortnight if he doesn't get some money so you see it is very serious. My own boy some of the flowers you sent me are still fresh but you should have tied them in bunches and put wet moss around the stalks and underneath and over them. The stocks smell quite delicious. I see a great deal of Alice – she still looks very well. Don't forget your little girl my darling. She doesn't forget you and hasn't flirted with *anyone* in the *very* least.

They did not go to Jersey, and Ned, to avoid a second collapse, was kept very busy by Lewis. Lillie and Jones struggled to maintain their affair by remote control.

Darling Artie,
        I thought you had quite forgotten me as I had no letters for two days.
I am afraid the Broadwoods make themselves so pleasant you haven't had
time to think of your little girl. Lord Yarbert was here last Mon. He is
going to Jersey at the beginning of July in his yacht for a week and rather
wants me to go but Ned is such a man of business now I don't know if he
will – He is going to make £300 a year out of the Ostend thing and I hope
will get made a director of some other companies. He has to go to Brussels
on Wednesday next. I wish you could come over then. I think darling
there is every chance of our coming over to Portelet if it isn't let in August
but I am afraid I shan't be able to get rid of Ned.

In both letters, the 'little girl' is, of course, not Jeanne, but Lillie.

While Lillie and Ned tried to right their finances, Lady Lonsdale's
peacock, now installed at Berkeley Street, leaked out its bad luck, this
time in the form of the death of Maurice Le Breton. He had been asked
by the natives of a neighbouring village in India to rid them of a man-
eating tiger. Having the Le Breton love of a challenge, he had set out on
foot, wounded the animal, and, turning to his servant for the second rifle,
found himself deserted. The tiger clawed him as he made his escape up a
tree. The wound turned bad and Maruice died of blood poisoning. In
Lillie's vulnerable and domestic frame of mind the blow was prostrating.
Jones, of course, shared her sorrow.

My darling Artie,
        I was so surprised to find from your letter this morning that you had
not yet heard of poor Maurice's death. We also recd. such an
extraordinary telegram from mother that I think poor woman she must be
off her head with grief. I do so wish you would go and see her. I am quite
miserable and hate London so. I should like to get over to Jersey if I could
but Ned is so extraordinary I cannot make out what he intends to do. He
starts for Brussels on Sunday and will be away for about a week I suppose.
Darling you really might come over. I suppose you will have to anyhow in
time for the review at Windsor. Alice is doing so well . . . and the baby.
The latter was also quite black haired when it was born so I suppose it is
the manner of babies. A is so strong and has such a colour it is quite
wonderful. Goodbye my own darling boy.

Dutifully Arthur came within the week. Lillie's last letter was written on
Thursday and on Monday she was eagerly awaiting his arrival. Already
just the promise of his presence had steadied her.

My own Artie,

    I shan't have to write again after today as you will cross I suppose on Wednesday. I hope you won't put it off. It is so good of you darling to go and see my mother. I am sure you cheer her up. Poor thing it must have been a dreadful shock to her as well as to us. I have tried to write to her as often as I could as it gives her something to think about. I see Alice every day, she is very well – How I do wish darling, I was at Portelet in this lovely hot weather with you – I am so miserable here. Ned went on Sunday to Brussels but I fear he won't be long away. It is such hard work living with him, sometimes I feel I must give it up. Goodbye my own sweet boy. I am *longing* to see you. You are very naughty to have weeds in the garden.

Maurice's death was the perfect excuse for Lillie. It was her duty to go home and see her mother, even if it was only for a fortnight. When the season finally ground to a halt Lillie made her arrangements, this time without Ned. Now she was busy and happy and had time only for the briefest scrawl.

Missed post yesterday. I *am* sorry but I suppose you were so occupied racing that you did not miss my letter *quite* so much. The heat is awful so that the ink dries as I write. I cross Thursday, darling, Ned is going to fish for ten days in Wales and then comes to fetch me so that's perfect isn't it. Clem seems sulky at my crossing and keeps making hints that he cannot go to Portelet as he used. But you know he always grumbled didn't he. I have just come from your dentist who stopped my tooth beautifully without hurting me and I am to go again on Thursday . . .

As always summer at Portelet and Jones's unstinted company were all that Lillie loved and longed for. Away from the prying attentions of her Society acquaintants, from London and its noise and its cruel expectations, Lillie found Jersey a balm to her battered soul.

Not surprisingly, when she returned to England again she suffered another crisis. Clement and Alice had not thought it right that she should be at Portelet and were publishing their disapproval. Ned had refused to come and collect her as planned and she had travelled back alone, staying at Kingston Lacy on her way. At Berkeley Street, when she arrived, all the old demons were waiting. Abandoned by Alice and Clement, on whom she had projected her own involvement with Jones, she was forced to recognize the barrenness of her existence. The myth of a family that she had so carefully constructed had dissolved. She was alone with her gadfly creditors, stifled by marriage, prisoned in the rented house that she and Ned could not afford, watched by the London she had come to hate. If she looked for something to blame, she found that it was money, and its absence, that tied her hands; Jones had none, and Ned, while Lillie stayed with him, had only what Lewis paid. If she left she would have nothing. Meanwhile, Ned came and went as he pleased, unpredictably at all hours of the day and night, drunk. Even her few friends were no help. They expected her to be able to shift for herself, to make something of her life, and she could no longer face their expectations. As autumn approached, she sat in her tiny drawing-room, limp with longing, the buzz of the city around her a torment, and her heart and soul in Jersey with Jones.

> My own boy,
>   I am so dreadfully depressed at not hearing from you today. I have only had two letters from you since I left, one of them such a cross one. You must have known I wouldn't write at once and that it was the post and not me you ought to blame. I wrote the instant I arrived and they told me the post went at 5.30 so I can't think how you didn't get my letters. I couldn't write at Weymouth as I had no paper or pens, besides it being such a scramble in the morning. Ned came up on Saturday and was in the most *horrid* humour and the next morning seemed to have forgotten that he had been so. I expect he was so drunk. I don't believe I shall ever be able to live with him. I very nearly rushed back to you. I would if you had enough for us to live on. I *wish* you could make some. One of the people at Kingston Lacy told me that an agent buying potatoes in Jersey had told him he had made 40 a week commission for eight weeks this year. I wish you had. Ned tells me Clem and Alice were both equally cross at my being at Portelet. Have you seen anything of them? My darling *do* come over . . . I am so miserable, I don't care what happens to me when you are away. I couldn't write on Saturday as I didn't get up in time and there was no post there. *Please* do come I am longing for you. I don't know what to do. I am sure I can't live with Ned and yet I dread being left to my own resources. Ever my sweetheart your loving and devoted Lillie.

This was one of the strongest pleas Lillie ever made to Jones, and still he was unable to find an answer to their problems. Had he been more decisive, had he come and taken her away, and protected her from Ned, and made a home for her on Jersey – had he thought of even one scheme to make money for them, she would have gone to him. As it was he was too weak, too directionless, too indolent, to take charge. He failed her, and after this, in some measure, Lillie was aware of the hopelessness of waiting for him. Slowly, wearily, she turned herself around and faced her future alone. Though she had not by any means given up Jones, she knew from now on that, if there was to be a solution to her problems, it would have to be she who found it. If Jones was what she wanted, then she would have to do the providing. She would have to make the decisions and she would have to run the risks. Ironically, the independence and the strength she had to find, in order to do this, was what finally stifled their love.

Meanwhile Ned found that he could not afford Berkeley Street and announced that they should look for somewhere out of town. Much as Lillie hated London, the country, with Ned, was worse. She wrote to Jones,

> My own darling,
> I am afraid I shan't have time to write tomorrow as Ned is going to drag me to look at houses in the country. He is so irritating . . . I *am* wretched without you my own boy. I do hope you will come soon. Are you sure it would be no use to give Portelet to a French agent as well? I can't tell you what I feel when I am away from you and how I long to be back at Portelet. It *is* my home isn't it? Lord Wharncliffe came to see me today. He came up on some business so I promptly asked him for Neapolitain violet roots. I know he has some. He said he would send them straight to Portelet so if they come, will you have them planted *facing* the west. They tell me that is the great secret with violets and they ought to have leaf mould mixed in with the soil but I am afraid we have none. I love to hear about my garden, so please tell me about it – and if it isn't giving you too much trouble could you put in half a dozen cuttings of the hydrangeas I wish we hadn't forgotten them the blue ones would do. I have taken lots of exercise since I've been here. There really isn't a *cat* in town. I never saw it so thoroughly empty. I am going on Thursday to see the rooms for Jeanne and I hope to settle her there soon. It will be such a blessing – Good night my own precious sweetheart. I can't tell you how I love and think of you. Your own loving L.
> Are the seeds up yet? I have sent some red petticoats to you for my old women in the market.

If Ranelagh was a doting and interesting father to his illegitimate progeny, it was not an inherited trait. Jones seems to have involved himself very little in Jeanne's upbringing. Lillie, however, was different. It was quite normal for children to be brought up by remote control in the nineteenth century, particularly among the aristocracy. Besides, the stigma attached to illegitimacy was such that Lillie would have known, from day one of her pregnancy, that she would not have been able to keep Jeanne herself. Nevertheless, she must have missed Jeanne and worried about her in Bournemouth more than she was letting on. Having her nearer at hand in London was both risky and expensive, but it was what Lillie wanted. Why Lillie did not mention Jeanne, in the hundreds of letters that streamed from Berkeley Street to Jersey, is a puzzle. Some of them are incomplete and it may be that Jones destroyed pages that referred to the child. It is also quite possible that they agreed on silence in case their letters were intercepted or read. At any rate, Jeanne was moved to lodgings in London in the autumn. Who paid for them was another matter, and whether it was money coaxed out of Ranelagh or the Royal coffers is impossible to know. It was, however, a firm indication that whatever Ned felt, Lillie was not contemplating a move out of London. Ned's house-hunting was not a success, but its cause sparked a revival of Lillie's interest in a career.

> My own sweetheart,
>   I was glad to hear from you today. Ned has gone down to his cousins to shoot so I am alone today. I suppose he will be back tonight. We went down to Windsor but I am rather glad to say saw nothing the least suitable I can't take any interest except in Portelet. My darling read the enclosed letter from old Cauvet and tell me what you think. You see he seems to have an idea I should succeed also – Do tell me what to do. You see sweetheart if I did live alone I should see so much more of you we could always be together whilst if I remain with Ned it will be much more difficult. I have made no plans anyway yet. I suppose if I stay with Ned we shall go for a little to Brighton after next week – on Tuesday we are going to Sandown races and to sleep the night at East Sheen, so please let me know when you will come over. Lewis is not back yet but I think I have found suitable rooms for Dominique so that is something done. I *do* so want to get rid of Ned, he drives me wild. You darling boy I wish we were married. Ever you own little girl.

This last was written on Friday and Lillie and Ned spent the weekend fighting. On Monday she was low again.

> My own darling,
>   I was so furious with myself for forgetting about that stupid early post. I wrote the letter and then had to tear it up. I am perfectly miserable about everything. Ned is odious. We are not going to Sandown after all. I

do wish darling you would come over and let us try to settle something. I don't like to stay in this house much longer . . . and I don't know what to do and where to go. I want you to help and advise me so much. I have toothache again which is maddening with all my other worries. I do long to fly over to you my sweetheart.

Desperate as she sounds, Lillie was nearer a decision now than she realized. This was the great moment of change, undersold, in her own account, by her refusal to acknowledge the toil and misery from which it sprang. In the context of the dragging days of her confinement and convalescence, it is dramatic.

According to her memoirs Lillie went alone to Sandown and, as she grandly records, to stay at East Sheen with the Duke of Fife. As far as her own account is concerned, she and Ned had separated soon after the financial crash. The chapter that concerns the long-awaited switch from socialite to actress opens with a jaunty and largely fictitious account of her state of mind and domestic arrangements. It is in marked contrast to the real voice of the Jones letters. She writes in the brisk tones of her professional life, her motto 'let us not fuss, please' unsaid but evident in every line. It is as though she is still ashamed of her once terrible weakness, disgusted in retrospect by her fears. Instead, she reads us a little lecture on the unimportance of money, splendidly stonewalling the fact that it was the leitmotif of her letters for this period.

> Parenthetically, I may say, money has never had an exaggerated value in my eyes, nor have I counted on it for happiness. I have considered the ups and downs of life as the hills and vales of experience, and learnt early to accept the unluckiest turns of Dame Fortune's wheel with equanimity . . .

This may have been true later on, but in 1881 money was an insuperable problem. Certainly she went to some lengths to make sure she was never short of it again, and although she became hard-headed and phlegmatic, the phlegm and the hard-headedness were acquired; they were not innate. Looking back on her shambolic former self from the discipline of her later life, she chose not to see this period at all. As she tells it, she lost her money. She left Ned, and she went on the stage. It was all very simple and very clean. Six months are gone, waved away. Twenty-four weary weeks since Jeanne's birth – weeks of pleading and longing and desperate uncertainty, not to mention the endless lessons in diction, the consultations about the stage, the possibilities of poultry farms and potato agents – all are erased at a touch. The chapter opens,

> Being young and of optimistic tendency, my nature quickly rebounded from the shock of misfortune, and I soon ceased to take our financial tumble greatly to heart, and presently returned to London, where I took a quiet apartment. Shepherded by my faithful, white-haired Dominique, who daily gave further proof of her devotion, and appeared to have unlimited resources at her command, I had not been permitted to feel any acute need of money, although I saw little or nothing of Mr Langtry, who now fished perpetually.

As Lillie would have it, she had just returned from several days' racing with the Duke of Fife, and was settling down once more to what she rather stylishly termed 'the mutton chop of adversity', when the card of Henrietta Labouchère, the wife of a prominent politician, was presented to her, and – hey presto! she was bundled on to the stage. Her mind, in her own words, 'was still quite unsettled with regard to the future, and it is a question what twist my life might have taken, had I not chanced to meet Henrietta Hodson, a quondam actress, who had become Mrs Henry Labouchère . . .' Chance, in this case, was actually Oscar Wilde, who was one of those stage managing Lillie's transformation into an actress, and who effected the introduction, probably after much discussion. Mrs Labouchère had retired from the stage, as befitted the wife of a politician, and was now offering her services as a coach, in which capacity Wilde enlisted her help. Needless to say this is not how Lillie would have it appear. Here is how she records their first encounter:

> Without having the least idea of the identity of my visitor, and little dreaming the important role in my life for which Fate had cast her, I gave orders that she should be admitted. Before me stood a woman in the forties, with a rather pugnacious cast of features, a square jaw, short, curly grey hair, a plump figure, a musical voice, and a dominating personality. She plunged at once into the subject of her visit. A rumour that I was studying for the stage was her excuse for coming to ask me to take part in a semi-private amateur entertainment being organised by her for some local charity at the Town Hall, Twickenham . . . When Henrietta Hodson's breath failed, and I partially recovered mine, I told her that rumour . . . had lied; but, quite undaunted, she persisted in her request with so sweet a smile, and so ingratiating a manner, that I finally gave way and agreed to 'try'.

In Lillie's letters to Jones there is no reference at all to this surprising appearance of an unknown figure. She did, after her last, in which she had said so pathetically, 'I don't know where to go or what to do . . .' move out of Berkeley Street, leaving Ned. She went to their mutual friends the Broadwoods' house, which was empty while they were out of town, and from here she wrote again, purposeful and with the Labouchère amateur dramatics in view.

> Dearest Artie,
>   This is the tiresome early post. I heard from mother yesterday that you are looking very ill. I do hope you will take care of yourself darling, as it makes me unhappy to think you are ill. I go down to Twickenham on Wednesday till the Saturday to rehearse and the play is on Saturday. I am going to send up to Ld Ranelagh today to find out when he is going to Jersey now goodbye.

The Broadwoods were returning to London and needed their house, and it is a measure of Lillie's new sense of direction that she took the problem of her lodgings so much in her stride. The same day, she wrote to Ranelagh,

> Alas Lord Ranelagh, I must ask forgiveness in anticipation for what I am going to write but as the Broadwoods return on Monday next I stand a fair chance of being homeless on that day and therefore must leave no stone unturned. I have been wondering if you had any idea of going to Jersey or anywhere and in that case whether you would let me your flat till the end of April for 10 or 12 guineas a week which is what I should have to pay for a furnished flat in the street. Please don't be angry with me for asking but I thought it possible you might be going away.

Ranelagh was most accommodating. He had no plans to go away but Lillie was given her own room in his apartment, 18 Albert Mansions, Victoria Street, with the proviso that he came and went as he pleased when he was in town. No doubt between them they negotiated a businesslike price.

With the matter of her lodgings settled, Lillie set off for Twickenham and the stage. She was to stay with the Labouchères, who had bought Pope's villa as a retreat, and rehearse daily with her new mentor. The play was in fact a trailer for the more serious business of the evening, a drama called *Plot and Passion*, by Tom Taylor, with Lady Monckton, a popular amateur actress of the day, in its leading role. Lillie, in her 'little comedy' of twenty minutes, *A Fair Encounter*, would thus be broken in to the business of the stage very gently. If she was proved to have no talent there would be no great loss of face, and they could think again. The evening was set for 19 November and in the meantime they worked and worked. Even in her memoirs Lillie makes no bones about how difficult she found her new career. She had a quick and retentive memory and getting her lines by heart was no problem. 'Finding the right inflection', as she recalls, was a different matter. This 'was such a constant worry that I began to wonder if it could be my native language I was engaged in speaking'. Back and forth she and Mrs Labouchère tramped, often under the critical eye of the MP himself, who, according to Lillie, 'invariably made some disparaging remark about my gestures, and, holding his arms and fingers in a wooden manner, he would say, "Why do you do this?" which cruelly wounded my susceptibility.'

Along with her first lessons in stage business Lillie also learnt resilience at Pope's villa in Twickenham. If Labouchère's criticisms seemed unkind at the time, she had reason to thank him in time to come. It was one of her greatest assets later on in her career that she was able to submit to criticism with a good grace.

At last the great day came and Lillie, in fear and trembling, and unwatched by any but a handful of locals, stood on the tiny stage of the Twickenham Town Hall. Needless to say she took stage fright and had to be prompted out of paralysis, from the wings. 'Alas!' she records,

> 'not a word of the opening soliloquy could I remember. There I stood, a forced smile on my lips and a bunch of roses in my arms, without the vestige of an idea of what was to happen next. Fortunately, after several promptings from my coach, who was listening anxiously for her cue behind the door, I recovered my wits and my words, and the 'encounter' proceeded to a languid finish without further incident.

Insignificant as it was, both as a piece and as an event, *A Fair Encounter* was Lillie's rubicon. Once she was over it there was no question of going back. She was motivated suddenly in a way she had never known, full of determination, thrilled at the vistas of possibility opening up before her. As though to make up for all the time wasted in reaching her decision she threw herself into organizing her next appearance. Henrietta, the agent of her transformation, was forgotten. Even Jones had to content himself with second place. When Twickenham was over and she was back in her room at Albert Mansions she wrote to him,

Darling Artie,

I think my little play was a great success. I have decided to have another performance in town if it can be arranged at Xmas time. Mrs Labouchère thinks I have talent and might do a good deal. I hope you saw the notices in the Morning Post and Observer. They were very flattering considering how slight a play it was. I saw Lord Ranelagh yesterday and he says he can't go over till the end of this week.

He admired this room very much and after I was gone brought that woman to see it. He said I might show it to anyone.

Jones had not been to the performance, but he was expected to have been studying the review pages with his heart in his mouth. Lillie assumed that her progress would be as important to him as it was to her. She had, it seems, learnt no lessons from marriage to Ned. Jones was not interested in the stage, and although unable to provide for the two of them himself, was not prepared to hand over supremacy to Lillie. For the moment Lillie was both unaware and unconcerned. A few days later she wrote again,

Dearest Arthur,

You will by now have read that I was successful and I am indeed thankful it is over. I was *so* nervous that I didn't even hear any applause tho' oddly enough I didn't show it. I have made an engagement at the Haymarket and am going to begin rehearsing almost immediately so I shall again be dreadfully hard at work. I fear I shouldn't see much of you if you were here as I have now to think only of my play. I can't think why Ld R hasn't gone to Jersey. I never see or hear of him. I am just going to be photo'd in my dress and will send you some – they have given me £50 for a sitting.

To Jones, receiving the letter in Jersey, in their shared world, with the garden she had planned around him, it must have felt as though Lillie had slipped from him already. It contained nothing of their joint concerns. Portelet, the garden, her poor sad mother, the network of family she had built up to house their love, all were gone, like a mist. In its place, spread out in her letters from now on, lay an unfamiliar landscape, barren of anything save this one, new, all-consuming interest – an interest that bordered on obsession, to which all time and all energy must be given, and to which, in the end, even love was sacrificed.

Chapter XXIV

The Stage

The theatre was not an acceptable profession – actresses in Lillie's day were seen as immodest and unladylike. At worst they were often prostitutes. If the Victorians had qualms about the propriety of portrait photography it is not surprising that they were unable to contemplate the stage. To smile to order, to make an exhibition of charms that should have been discreet, to simper through love scenes that should properly have made her blush, compromised a lady's integrity, her innocence and her virtue. The prejudice of the times is well summed-up in the letter that Mrs Patrick Campbell's aunt wrote to her, on hearing that she was planning a career on the stage. Page after page, in near hysteria, she pours out, as to a lost soul:

My dear Beatrice,

Since I received your first letter I have felt almost unable to write. The shock it gave me I could never explain to you, nor would you understand it. Nor did I quite realize before *how* dear you were to me. I should hardly have believed that losing you would, after all, have caused me such infinite pain.

Poor, unfortunate child, may God help you, if, as you say, the die for evil is cast. I can only pray, as the only chance to save you, that you make too decided a failure ever to try again.

Good God, how could you think I could write and wish you success? . . . When you were the first-rate musician which I have never doubted your becoming, I hoped you might have played with glory at concerts, and over here, what a joy to have heard you – and your praise. For *that* would have been honest and reputable praise. Whilst gaining which you could have held up your head in any society. Oh, my poor Beatrice, you can form no idea – you have yet to learn – the shame, the humiliation of seeing yourself despised by decent people.

Even the admiration of the mob will not make up for it to you. You have too much intelligence for that and, I thought, too much pride . . .

How can a woman bid with pleasure farewell to her best and happiest heritage – name, reputation, affection – to allow her every look and movement to be criticised by all the common jeering mouths and minds of the public . . .

A painful effort this letter is. But I would not write until a day or two had a little cooled and calmed me. I am anything but strong yet . . .

I must bid you goodbye, Beatrice, believe me with much sorrow and sympathy with you and your ill-governed impulses . . . You know my disgust for that class to which you are going to ally yourself – our disgust, I might say – and to think that one we loved, and had lately in our midst, goes, and with pleasure, into such a set – to be one of them! . . .

No one exhibited such horror when Lillie made her announcements, but she did have to brave some disapproval. As she recalls, 'there was a mixed feeling among my friends and relations, and none of them received the new departure with pleasurable anticipation . . .' It helped if she could lay the blame on someone else and the patient Henrietta made a good scapegoat. To her friends Lillie insisted that she had been dragged on to the stage by her hair, that she was the unwilling victim of Henrietta's determination. Though she told Jones (the italics are mine), '*I* have decided to have another performance in town' and '*I* have made an engagement at the Haymarket', the memoirs tell a different story. After Twickenham, she records,

I felt truly thankful when the curtain fell, and I then and there resolved never again to tempt Fate on the stage. But I 'reckoned without my host', or, rather, my hostess, who ordained otherwise, in spite of my lukewarm co-operation.

For some reason, kindly, I am sure, she determined to do her best to make an actress of me . . . I knew it was useless to protest, and therefore resigned myself to what seemed a brazen experiment.

The next step in the 'brazen experiment' was to play Kate Hardcastle at the Haymarket, in *She Stoops to Conquer*. Like Twickenham, this was to be a benefit gala rather than a professional run, but this time it was in London, and playing to the whole of Society. In case Lillie's name was not enough of an attraction, the supporting cast was drawn from the best that the professional stage could offer. Kyrle Bellew, the matinée idol whom Lillie and Lady Lonsdale had worshipped in the old days, from the other side of the footlights, was to play her lover. Arthur Pinero, Lionel Brough, Nellie Farren and Charles Brookfield were just a few of the popular extras. Almost immediately Lillie plunged into a rigorous rehearse schedule. She had just short of a month to prepare herself. Jones, who had no such pressures, was losing himself in more rakish pursuits and Lillie, deep in her work, returning late and alone to her room, was, briefly, intolerant.

> Dearest Artie,
>   I did get a letter from you on my return. I wish you wouldn't be so silly my dear boy. I really can't see the fun of wasting your money gambling when it might be much better employed – I am going to play in London in 'She Stoops to Conquer' on the 17th December and I am obliged to work very hard and must keep quite quiet or I shall be ill. I am in a very nervous state about everything. Of course you have seen the criticisms in the weekly papers they were very kind weren't they. Dearest Artie do write sensible letters.

Arthur was chastened, and her next letter was fonder and less self-absorbed.

> Darling boy,
>   I hope you did get my letter yours has only just come, detained too by the fog, I suppose. I am so glad to hear you are hunting, you will like that won't you, as for me I am worn out with rehearsing, tho it is great fun. I think I should like it I am sure. I am just going to lunch with the Sassoons and am afraid of not having time to write between my rehearsal and post time. The pampas grass has arrived, I am so much obliged to you for it, darling goodbye, write often to your very loving Lillie.

This, despite its settled warmth, was almost the last of Lillie's letters to Jones. Their paths were diverging.

When 17 December came there were crowds outside the theatre queuing for seats in the pit and the gallery. Some had even thought to bring sandwiches and camping stools. The fashionable seats had been bought long in advance by one of the grandest audiences in the history of theatre. 'And what an audience it was!' Lillie reminisces with pleasure:

> Packed with the rank and file of London. The Prince and Princess of Wales were in the royal box, and in the opposite one sat the Duchess of Manchester and a large party. My best friends, too, with their attendant swains, were anxious to get as near as possible, and crowded into the front

rows of the stalls, all more or less tittering and amused, and not at all inclined to take me seriously. That, of course, was a trying ordeal, for I had not yet learned that most necessary accomplishment which only comes by practice – the habit of looking into the auditorium without seeing the audience, and I must admit that all the familiar smiling faces in front considerably disconcerted me . . . Happily, the afternoon passed without a hitch; countless bouquets were thrown to me, and everything seemed like a dream when it was all over.

'Like a dream' was exactly how Lillie had described her first success in Society. The stage, besides giving her the attention she craved and the money she needed, was a second chance, a new world. Unlike the real world of Society, Lillie could, with dedication, belong completely to the theatre, and best of all it was a place where the aura of magic that surrounded her would be invulnerable. Under Wilde's tutelage Lillie had come to prefer the unreal. She wanted to be allowed to construct her myths without Society tearing them down at every turn. And she was happy to be criticized for her professional ability if it meant that her self, her breeding, her morals, her ambition were protected from censure. By offering her career to the world for judgement she was deflecting attention from what touched her most nearly, from all that was vulnerable or precarious in her private life.

The reviews were mostly gentlemanly. Abraham Hayward, nonagenarian Society gossip, admitted in private, 'I am not prepared to say she has the requisites for a great actress except the voice.' In public, once he had been pressed into service, he wrote kindly and at length in *The Times*. Most of the article was about her beauty – 'the finely shaped head, the classic profile, the winning smile, the musical laugh, the grace of the figure'. We have heard it all before, but he went on to observe, more astutely, that these were qualities 'which the public in a theatre can appreciate as well as the privileged admirers in a drawing-room'. He was right, as Lillie herself knew. For the moment, the world would throng just to see her dressed in different costumes. What she was offering was the portrait photograph in three dimensions. Acting was only a small step from being represented, in her Society days, holding a dead bird, 'with an expression of grief on my face . . . which . . . was designed to touch the heart of the sentimental public'.

Lillie had a healthy amount of borrowed time before anyone expected her to produce passion or real dramatic art. Louise Jopling, who went to the gala first performance, wrote that, 'The house was crowded to see the fashionable beauty. I remember nothing of her acting. I recall only the lovely lines of her throat.' It was a back-handed compliment. Had the acting been worth looking at, she would no doubt have noticed.

Also among the audience on Lillie's benefit night were the Bancrofts. Squire Bancroft, as he was known, and his diminutive wife Marie were prominent in the theatrical world. She had been an actress who had given up the stage in order to manage and direct with her husband. They were known chiefly for bringing what was then called 'cup and saucer' drama 'to absolute perfection'. The words are Ellen Terry's, and it is she too who has left us a description of the couple as Lillie would have seen them. Mrs Bancroft was 'a smart little figure . . . above all things *petite* – dressed in black – elegant Parisian black'. Her husband, no less distinguished and always visible on first nights, was 'a remarkably striking figure of a man with erect carriage, white hair, and flashing dark eyes – a man whose eye-glass, manners and clothes all suggest Thackeray and Major Pendennis, in spite of his success in keeping abreast of everything modern'. It was the Bancrofts who had the lease of the Haymarket at that time and who had lent it for the evening of Lillie's performance. They saw the following Lillie could command, felt that her acting was passable and engaged her, for her first professional run, to play Blanche Haye, in a comedy called *Ours*. They were to open in the second week of January and Lillie would work through Christmas to be ready.

With professional acting, rather than one-off performances, 'the dream' dissolved. The Bancrofts had engaged her at what she later called 'a very high salary', and with money for the moment taken care of, she had room to look about her. She had, by January 1882, been in harness for three months. Nor was there any respite in sight. This was quite a change from her former life of leisure. Her recollections of this period are stark, and truthful.

To say that I was enamoured of the profession I was entering would be untrue. I had never been stage-struck, and after all the adulation and social *éclat* that had fallen to my lot since my arrival in England, there was nothing strange in it for me from the publicity point of view. Indeed, to appear on the stage in the same play, speaking the same words, wearing the same gowns at the same time every evening seemed a very dull and monotonous existence, after the various rounds of festivities which had, till now, been the only business of my life. I had loomed so large in the public eye that there was no novelty in facing the crowded audience . . . Thus the excitement of the *débutante* was denied me, and only the hard work remained. The dreary rehearsals, hour after hour, day after day, in a cold and darkened theatre, were often unnecessarily drawn out . . . by endless altercations about things that did not much matter and discussions irrelevant to the subject in hand . . . Though the Bancrofts were excessively kind to me, I did not feel very happy at the start.

Lillie always understated unhappiness, and if she says she was 'not very happy', we can take it that she was miserable. What had happened to Jones is a mystery. She was still living at Ranelagh's house but in the green case there are no letters at all that refer to her début on the professional stage. Obviously she and Artie still saw one another, but what Lillie needed now he could not provide. Once again, taking her first uncertain steps in a new world, she needed father-figures not lovers. She had struck up a friendship, partly self-serving, with Abraham Hayward, the author of *The Times* review of *She Stoops*. She did not, by her own admission, particularly like him, remembering him in the memoirs as a 'small shrivelled figure' with a reputation as a raconteur. Nor did she enjoy his company – 'to my mind he was too appreciative of his own jokes and giggled and wriggled in a tiresome manner as he retailed the latest gossip'. But he was useful, and he had the added advantage of being very friendly with Gladstone.

Gladstone was one of Lillie's stranger choices, selected because he embodied the unlikely combination of extreme susceptibility and rigorous moral standards. Lillie thought that his approval would help her cause and she asked Hayward for an introduction. On 8 January, before she opened, he wrote to Gladstone telling him that Lillie admired him and asking him to call on her at Albert Mansions any evening at around six. Lucy Cavendish, Gladstone's niece, who often acted as a secretary, docketed the letter on the back, 'Recommends you, if you have time, to call on Mrs Langtry, who is a great admirer of yours. (You are aware that she has gone upon the stage)'. She was the one who had reacted with such outrage to the lionizing of Sarah Bernhardt.

Gladstone's family and friends thought that the acquaintance with Lillie was undesirable and unnecessary. Notwithstanding their cautions, Gladstone did call. He had a weakness for ladies of precarious virtue, enjoyed the tension of their company and was titillated by the cocktail of sex and shame that their correction involved. It was a peculiarly Victorian predilection. He had gone so far as to set up a programme for rescuing prostitutes, that involved him going out into the streets at night and engaging them in conversation, before enticing them home for soup and

Bible-reading. Hayward knew all this and in his first letter about Lillie apologized with the aside, 'I tell you this, although I fear you have other more pressing corrections just at present.' That he put Lillie in the category of fallen women needing salvation was interesting enough. Before he called, Gladstone wrote back to Hayward to find out just how far Lillie had fallen, and was told:

> Mrs Langtry has recently adopted the stage as a profession and she told me that all her thoughts are now absorbed by it. She was much pleased by the passage in your letter relating to it which I read to her. Her only engagement for the present is for a piece called *Ours* to be revived at the Haymarket on the 19th. There is no formal separation between her and her husband but they are little together and he has as good as told her to shift for herself. His fortune would not admit of their living any longer in London . . .

Hayward's second letter was written on 14 January, and Gladstone must have made his first visit soon after. It was apparently the first of many. Lillie recalls his kindness with effusions of gratitude in her memoirs. 'Now,' she says,

> he often came to see me, and would drop in – he was Prime Minister at the time – to find me eating my dinner before going to the theatre . . . His comprehensive mind and sweet nature grasped the difficult task that lay before me, the widely different orbit in which my life would henceforth move, and he knew how adrift I felt.

Lillie was indeed lonely, as she sat down, day after day, to the 'mutton chop of adversity', before setting off for the Haymarket. She was debarred from Society now by much more practical questions than simply the desirability of her profession. 'When I went on the stage,' she recalls,

> I knew that I had burned my ships behind me, for an artist's life necessarily cuts one off a great deal from the events of society – one's hours, meals, work, and rest being all apart from other people's.

Her old friends still kept in touch, and called to find out how she was and how she liked the stage, but they came in ones and twos. The parties and balls and lazy Bohemian teas were over.

Gladstone, like Millais and Wharncliffe and others before him, provided advice and protection. He helped her with the interpretation of her parts, read aloud to her from Shakespeare or the Bible, and interested himself minutely in her welfare. For extra information, he relied on Hayward, with whom he corresponded regularly, and who always included a paragraph about Lillie in his letters. Gladstone, for instance, had been unable to go to the first night of *Ours*, and was keen for news. Hayward, sitting in Lillie's dressing-room after the performance, was interested to note that Ned was among those backstage. Gladstone was duly informed.

> Lady Lonsdale was with Mrs Langtry when Mr Langtry came in and warmly congratulated her on her success. She told him that she was already making money and asked him if he wanted any. He said that whatever she made was her own, and nothing should induce him to take any of it (by the present law her earnings *are* legally her own).

It is a rare and fascinating insight into the remains of the Langtrys' relationship; Ned backstage, unstinting in his praise, and Lillie offering him money. Later, he did take payments from her, in return for a promise to leave her alone, so perhaps his proud refusal was only because of the presence of her intimates. More likely it was genuine, since the arrangement was very new. It is a surprisingly sad little vignette.

Habits of extravagance die hard, and whatever Lillie's arrangements were with Ned, she was still keen to spend what money she was earning. The question of where she could live was once again exercising her. Clearly she could not lodge with Ranelagh for ever, and her first thought was to throw in her lot with Whistler and Godwin, each taking a floor of Tower House in Tite Street. Lillie was to have the ground floor and the accommodation was to comprise three bedrooms, a bathroom, a studio 39' by 18' and 16' high, a large dining-room, a kitchen, hall, scullery, wine cellar, pantry and larder. This was all fairly luxurious. Lillie after some delay got as far as signing an agreement, with Alice Le Breton as witness, and paying a deposit of £225, but there was a problem with the cash flow of her co-lessees. On Monday 27 February, the day that all the deposits for Tower House were to have been paid, Godwin noted in his diary, 'Mrs Langtry and self only ready.' No one else, it seemed, could lay their hands on money with such speed. Where Lillie's came from we can only guess. However, by March she was tired of waiting and had backed out in favour of an even grander scheme. Lady Lonsdale had just had a house built for her, also by Godwin, and now Lillie wanted one too. She was working and performing and was very hard to pin down. Godwin, though excited by the commission, was dismayed at her elusiveness and regretted her pulling out of Tite Street. One 13 March he wrote to her,

> Dear Mrs Langtry,
>
>   I called yesterday and today but as usual all in vain. I begin to think we shall never meet again. I waited here the other evening for you and again today at my own place . . . still in vain. However to lose no further time I have set enquiries on foot for someone to take your place if that can be managed the rest will be easy. There will be something for you to pay (but not much) for the extra work made necessary by your withdrawal.
>
>   Now as to the house where is it to be? Next to Lady Lonsdale's? for which many thanks are due to you. If so we must lose no time about the ground. What do you intend to spend on it and how much house do you want? Please tell me the details by letter if you cannot meet me and whether I shall secure the land or not.

The house was never built, for a number of reasons. In her memoirs Lillie refers to it as 'inexpensive', but Godwin's plans, which survived, rather indicate otherwise. Her requirements, including her level of staffing, appear in his pocket book, dated 17 March. They were as follows:

> 1 double servants room
> 1 smaller do.
> 1 better for maid
> Bedroom 18×18 bath and dressing room out of it
> Spare bedroom smaller 1/2
> Dining room 18×18
> Drawing room (studio size)
> Hall and staircase
> Kitchen & 1
> Servants hall   Butler
> Butlers pantry and safe   cook – ho. maid
> Various   maid

Like Lady Lonsdale's it was to be the town house of a Society lady, not the discreet lodgings of the mutton–chop eater. Besides these notes, there are careful drawings for lily ornaments and a lamp, a drawing of a colonnaded garden of fantastic grandeur, sporting tiled and painted moorish columns and a fountain, as well as a front elevation of the house itself which was a riot of balconies, heraldic shields and cut brickwork. Even the colours for the rooms were noted, which were, like those in Whistler's house, 'grey-green-blue, old gold or matting colour and ivory and walnut'. Lillie's own excuse for the fact that the house was never built was that her 'triumvirate of counsellors, Oscar Wilde, Frank Miles and Whistler' had offered so much advice, all of which Godwin had tried to accommodate, that there was found to be no room for a staircase. Oscar Wilde was in fact in America so his role in the design must have been imaginary. Equally, for an architect as experienced as Godwin, to forget the stairs, in a house of three floors, was fatuous in the extreme. The project was simply too expensive.

Whatever commitments Lillie was making in London in March of 1882 were shelved in May, when she was released by the Bancrofts and set off on a tour of the provinces. If she had found the stage hard work to date, touring was even more so. She travelled without rest, performing as soon as she arrived, for the next four months. Her itinerary took her all over England and Ireland, on and off public transport, living in strange lodgings, dressing out of a suitcase. The strain of constant change and of uncomfortable travel was incalculable. Lillie was under more pressure than she had ever known before. In compensation she was, for the most part, rapturously received. With her went both her parents, an indication of their much needed support in her new venture. It was observed in Lancashire that Lillie 'appeared every morning walking with her father, her arm in his'. This was uncharitably assumed to be a PR move; 'the stately figure of the handsome old dean, with a loving daughter hanging on his arm, was well calculated to edify the provincial mind with its instinctive love of the decorous and the genteel'. It may have been so, though the affection was genuine.

She played in Manchester for a week, to abysmal notices and huge audiences, and at the end of the run her carriage was unhorsed and she was pulled by an adoring throng from the stage door to her hotel. Then it was on to Edinburgh and Glasgow, across to Dublin, where the audiences were 'unusually gay and boisterous', and Belfast. Here, as she recalls, 'my creature comforts were thoughtfully looked after' by some enthusiastic supporters,

> who lowered pheasants, hares, and other delicacies, from the gallery to the stage to testify their approval of my artistic efforts, and insisted on my receiving them at all sorts of dramatic moments.

Belfast, which was the home of the Langtrys, obviously felt it had a claim to ownership, and was therefore more lavish in its tributes. The university, not part of the pheasant-lowering fraternity, presented Lillie with a flock of fluttering doves, tied with blue ribbons to a floral cage.

All this was very gratifying, but the critics were still lukewarm. It was becoming increasingly obvious that her following owed too much to novelty. Back in London, it would not be sustainable for long.

In September Lillie was engaged by the Imperial Theatre for *As You Like It* and *An Unequal Match*. Though Ellen Terry sent flowers and a telegram, Lillie was given cordial but stern warnings by the reviewers. Clement Scott of *Punch*, later a friend of sorts, wrote,

> We are strongly and honestly reminding her that without positive genius there is no royal road to eminence, even in the histrionic art; and that a novice must stoop to pick up the rudiments and master them before she can conquer its difficulties. Mrs Langtry is of too solid a physique for any light skittish movement; her laugh not yet being under control appears forced and painful; and her action is as constrained and mechanical as that of an Eton sixth form boy on speech day.

It was far from complimentary. Her borrowed time was running out. All too soon, the theatre-going public's curiosity would be satisfied, leaving Lillie to fight for bit parts like everyone else. Instead, she and Henrietta Labouchère decided to try the New World. Wilde, Lillie's mentor, was already there, outraging the Americans with his wardrobe, his ego and his edicts. For Lillie it was a bold move. Henry Abbey, the famous New York impresario, was wired to engage her and came at once. Between them Lillie and Henrietta negotiated a fee marginally larger than Sarah Bernhardt had been paid the season before, and Lillie was left with nothing to do except order her dresses, pack her bags and say her goodbyes.

Lillie had now been working and touring without a break for exactly a year. She was exhausted, and she was having second thoughts about America. Gladstone and Hayward watched her every move. Hayward's letters chronicled her debility with conscientious solicitude.

> I saw Mrs Langtry at the conclusion of her London engagement . . . she looked ill and worn, and was suffering from a bad cough of more than six weeks standing, which she said was made worse by acting. It is to be hoped that the sea voyage will set her up.

Whatever the desirable and healthful benefits of a sea voyage, its contemplation was a different matter. Emigrating, however briefly, would be the final test of Lillie's independence – leaving her friends and family behind, herself unprotected by husband or lover, and out of reach of Jeanne. Whether or not Jones was one of those she dreaded leaving it is impossible to know. There is one last letter that it is difficult to date, which shows her relying on him for lodgings again, and for a short time. The beginning and the end of the letter are lost but she asks him 'to see about a house for us or get some lists – Brook Street or Grosvenor Street might have something. It is for such a short time that one might as well be comfortable don't you think so?' Most likely it was written at the end of the provincial tour, to organize things for her return. Since she would depart for America on 14 October and the tour ended on 26 June she had little time to enjoy whatever he found. She was, however, very much looking forward to seeing him.

> I have so much to tell you my sweetheart. I do miss you dreadfully much more than you can miss me. You haven't written me nice letters this time. Please do darling I am never tired of your telling me how much you love me . . . You guess what makes me ill don't you? and why I daren't travel before . . .

There is so much we do not know: whether or not Lillie and Jones had seen each other while she had been on tour, whether or not Jones still cared, who exactly the 'us' of the letter is – Lillie and her mother? or Lillie and Ned? or Lillie and Jeanne? or Lillie and Jones? Was it another pregnancy that was making her ill and unable to travel? So many unanswered questions. What is certain is that when Lillie left for America she was leaving for a long time. If Jones was not going with her, then was their affair over? Or did Lillie hope to return having made enough money for both of them?

As the day for departure approached Lillie's trepidation mounted. She was, as she put it,

> not wildly enthusiastic over the prospect, for the States, at that time, seemed to me to be about as far off as Mars, and nearly as inaccessible. I had travelled very litle, and England, to my limited vision, seemed a large slice of the world after Jersey. Moreover, my many friends and relations were within easy reach, and to leave them for unknown lands gave me a feeling of utter depression.

In a state of 'utter depression' Lillie made her arrangements. The Red House in Bournemouth was rented out, to some people called Holdsworth, and Mrs Le Breton took Jeanne back to Jersey. Henrietta Labouchère, who was sick of her life in England and had no regrets about leaving for America, swathed her house and her husband in brown holland, dismissed the cook so as to be sure Mr Labouchère went hungry, and cut the buttons off all his shirts. In London, tearful dinners were given for Lillie in farewell, and so in her own words we will send her off:

> When the time came to say good-bye to England, I . . . felt increasingly mournful. A crowd of acquaintances saw me off at Euston, my saloon-carriage was heaped with flowers, and everything was done to cheer me up. Nevertheless, after the train had started, I settled back in my seat, feeling very forlorn, and indulged in a good cry. Arrived at Liverpool, I still hoped to the last minute that something would prevent this undesired voyage – even a broken limb would have been welcome – but nothing intervened . . . and I went on board the *Arizona* feeling perfectly miserable.

It was two years before Lillie was to return and in time, of course, Jones, her 'own darling boy', married someone else. But, according to his descendants, there was a room always kept for Lillie at Portelet. In her rare breaks she would return to Jersey, coming and going, like an aunt to the children in the house, giving advice about the garden, and walking the old beach path, until Jones's death, a year before her own.

MRS LANGTRY AND HER

REPERTOIRE 1882–1900

Chapter XXV

Prologue to the New World

What was it that Lillie wept for, as the coast of England dipped below the horizon? Only the end of a life and the burial of one set of hopes. Her dream of belonging in the London salons had soured. It could not be had on her own terms, so she would have none of it at all. But even though she had kissed Society goodbye, it had been with mixed feelings, and she could not but mourn the loss of what she had so nearly known. Moreover, she had failed her husband and she had left her love, and she had neither her baby nor her family with her for comfort. She was only just twenty-nine, and though she was free, she was bruised, very bruised, by her recent experiences. She was also afraid of what lay ahead. If she had before her a fresh start and a second chance, nothing was sure. There was no security, no promise of success.

Lillie knew from the American first-generation heiresses, who came to England to trade money for blueness of blood, that America was the land of opportunity.* There were fortunes to be made, from cattle, from the railways and from real-estate. For the adventurous and the cash-hungry it was a new Mecca. Both Dickens and Trollope had addressed the subject in novels (*Martin Chuzzlewit* and *The Way We Live Now* respectively)

* Years later, Lillie wrote the following dialogue, with these trophy huntresses in mind. Clara Palk, the daughter of an American businessman, opines,

'Why surely you must know, Lord Vernham, that it is the ambition of every good American parent to have a son-in-law with a title? . . . America's greatness springs from her restless spirit of competition; and the men who defeat each other in business encourage their wives to adopt the same tactics in the marriage of their daughters.'

'But marriage should not be a business transaction,' he protested. 'Is there no true love in America?'

'Not much, I'm afraid. You see, our men are so busy.'

'Then you go to Europe to look for it?'

'To buy it – yes. We find we get a better return for our money.'

and, closer to home, among Lillie's own acquaintance, Moreton Frewin had gone to try his hand at cow-punching. But, as Frewin was to find out, there were no guarantees. Despite Lillie's natural buoyancy, the possibility of failure must have crossed her mind, and if she failed in this, having cut her ties with Society, what would become of her then?

If Lillie was unsure, as she paced the deck of the *Arizona* and contemplated her future, she was not wholly unprotected. Wilde was still in America, nearing the end of his lecture tour, and she knew how well he had been received. In the first days of his glory, a flurry of letters between the Tite Street coterie had kept her abreast of his successes. In February of 1882, he had written to Whistler, 'My dear Jimmy, They are "considering me *seriously*". Isn't it dreadful? What would you do if it happened to you?'

Whistler, who was longing to be taken seriously and who was not famous for his generosity over the triumphs of others, wrote back rather sharply, 'My dear Oscar – that you should be considered seriously was inevitable – that you should take yourself seriously is unpardonable.'

The two men were standing on the edge of their friendship, about to tip into acrimony. A little later a group of signatories, including Whistler, wrote an open letter to the New York papers, which ran in part, 'Oscar! We of Tite Street and Beaufort Gardens joy in your triumphs, and delight in your success, but we think that . . . with the exception of your knee-breeches you dress like "Arry Quilter".'

Sometime between the above exchanges, Whistler had asked Lillie to another of his breakfasts. She responded, 'I shall be delighted to assist at yr breakfast. Great fun – Aren't you sorry for Oscar? they don't seem to treat him very seriously do they? & *why* does he wear knee-breeches? Like Bunthorne? Yrs eadem Lillie'.

The tone of her letter was flattering to the Master. She would have known that relations between him and Wilde were strained. Lillie was politically astute, and when she was keen to please she always swam with the shoal. If to Whistler she laughingly took his part, it was not an indication that she had abandoned Wilde. In fact, it was more than likely that she was also communicating with Wilde himself, and that news of his success, although nothing between them has survived, had reached her by a more direct route. At least, when she decided on the New World, Wilde knew of her plans and had even been told the date of her arrival.*

---

* As early as 12 February 1882 Wilde knew of Lillie's plan to try the American stage. Writing to the wife of George Lewis, from Chicago, he observed, 'I am delighted about the Lily: she and I are facing great publics, and here I know she will succeed.'

Already, to interviewers, and to anyone who would listen, he was blazing her trail.

Once more, for Lillie, her sea voyage was a metamorphosis, but whereas, before, the change had come as a surprise, this time she was banking on it. Now, even her smallest effects were calculated. London had taught her a great deal, and everything in the New World depended on her lessons being well and truly learnt.

We know, from the novel she wrote in her fifties, that Lillie had absorbed the basic tenets of the London school of Decadence. Though hardly a manifesto for the movement, *All at Sea* contains elements that, in a light-hearted way, were a distillation of its influence, such as the studied artificiality of its dialogue, and the easy familiarity with neurasthenia, the trademark, morbid sensitivity of the true Decadent. There is, for instance, in its opening pages, an exchange between two friends which runs,

> '. . . Tell me something now about your ménage. How is Kit?'
> 'Poor Kit's not at all well,' answered Lady Vernham. 'I am afraid he is neurasthenic.'
> 'That means immoral, doesn't it?' inquired Mrs Renshaw.
> 'What are you thinking of, my dear? Neurasthenia is a complaint – a sort of constant complaint.'

As usual Lillie was not committing herself, so much as commandeering those aspects of the movement that particularly suited her way of thinking. Although her novel was not written until 1908, her exposure to these theories had been during her first seasons in London, at the feet of Whistler, Swinburne and Wilde. Any appropriations would have been from this earlier date, and therefore already a part of her mental landscape when she set off for America. Foremost among these was the concept of the cultivation of the self. As Matthew Sturgis describes it, in his elegant study of English *fin de siècle* Decadence, *Passionate Attitudes*,

> To Wilde and his admirers the word 'personality' carried a particular weight; it referred to that deliberately cultivated self which stood above, and against, rude, innate 'character'. The 'first duty in life', according to Wilde, was to 'assume a pose'.

For Wilde (and it was something that Lillie had fastened on to with alacrity) the creation of a personality was a form of artistic expression. In his life, he used it as a provocation and a means of attracting attention. In his works, it was an enduring and recurrent preoccupation, the implications of which were explored in changed identity, incognito, exchange and straight invention. Masks, lying, Bunbury, Dorian's portrait, the various different Ernests and Mrs Erlynne's unacknowledged motherhood were all the products of this fascination. For Lillie, whose successes and miseries had destroyed her sense of identity, and who wanted protection, its application was practical. To be allowed to start again with a new personality was a godsend, if not a necessity.

So when the first pangs of parting were over, and Lillie began to think constructively about the challenge before her, she turned for guidance to the doctrines of Wilde. With her then, amongst her mental luggage, she carried his London lessons, his precepts of personality, of management of the public, of striking a pose. In America, where no one knew her, they would be easy to put into effect. New York was a clean slate. She could be whatever she chose, and however sad she was on departure she quickly realized that the voyage was valuable choosing time.

So who and what exactly, were the identities in Lillie's skeleton, shipboard wardrobe? A strange amalgam of real people and characters from myth or fiction. From her London life she kept Venus Annodomini, though the poor Victorian heroine, Robertson's milliner, was long forgotten. Added to Venus she had the flesh-and-blood example of the most characterful of her friends: Wilde himself, Lady Lonsdale, Whistler, the Prince of Wales and Sarah Bernhardt. From these, she extracted various qualities – flamboyance, style, the exercise of power, royalty of demeanour, daring – and rolled them all up into her own version of the Society *grande dame*.

Not all Lillie's role models were taken from life. Some were literary. To complete her armoury, and to explain her status, she also adopted the role of mysterious widow. This persona was modelled entirely on fictional types, of which there were many examples in the novels popular at the time – Trollope's Mrs Hurtle and his Madame Max, to name but two, not to mention a character of her own subsequent invention, Mrs Renshaw, who was to feature in *All at Sea*, and who provides a valuable commentary on Lillie's interpretation both of the widow as an entity, and of the whole question of assumed identity.

It would be wrong to treat Lillie's different identities with too heavy a hand. She was only half conscious of what she was about in constructing personae for herself. Her self-invention was part tutored, it is true, but it was also deeply instinctive. In using the term 'mask' to describe her chosen poses, it is not my intention to depict something too concrete, too absolute in its construction.

These, then, were Lillie's first masks, already in place when she stepped ashore in New York. Later she would add to her repertoire, or have added by others, Mrs Erlynne, Wilde's version of her; Mr Jersey, her racing persona and most masculine side; and Lady de Bathe, her final and tragic incarnation, which came with old age and her second marriage. Many, if not all, of these masks were not distinct. There were elements of most of them in each of the poses Lillie adopted as her life advanced, but behind them, and in counterpoint, there was always Venus. This was Lillie's benchmark identity, the one that she could not relinquish, which hovered at her shoulder, sometimes, in the early days, as an added dimension, later as a ghost, a terrible indicator of how far she had travelled from her bourne.

All this makes it sound so easy – as though changing one's persona were as simple as changing a dress. And if at first, for Lillie, it was easy – was even a relief – the reality was to prove very different in the end. 'Those who want a mask have to wear it. That is their punishment.' So Wilde was to write much later, in his years of suffering, after trial, conviction and imprisonment. And he wrote it when his own masks had been stripped from him and he was forced to stand before the public, naked and ashamed. In their place, when the ordeal was over, he wore 'self-realization', not as a mask, but as a badge of honour, a vindication and a legitimate artistic goal. He consoled himself with the fact that the limitations imposed by a mask's immutability, the fixed nature of an assumed identity, were constricting – a punishment, no less. For Lillie, whose goals were not artistic so much as financial, a mask seemed a blessing. In 1882, ahead of her mentor, she was wounded, and though the damage was slight by comparison, she had no capital to make out of suffering. She preferred to hide it.

When Lillie faced her American public for the first time, no one could have told that her identity was anything other than innate, so seamless was her invention. She was charming, well-bred, effortlessly elegant – regal even – and untouchable. But Wilde was right. A mask is immutable and hers, once they were in place, did reduce the dynamics of her life. Like all his characters, for that is, in a sense, what she now was, she had overlaid the true element of affection and instinct, which were good, with the armour, first of her own pose, and second of her reputation. Protection was what she was after, hiding the true and vulnerable self from the unkindness of public scrutiny. She wanted, at this point, never to step off the stage. If anything had to be judged, she wanted it to be her professional skill, not her character. So long as this was so, so long as she could keep up the performance, then the world's opinion, since what it commented on was no more than a pretence, counted for less than nothing. 'What does it matter,' she said towards the end of her life, 'what people say, so long as they don't actually *know*?' Notoriety became just another layer of protection.

For the rest of Lillie's life, from now until she died, most of what she did was informed by this middle pretended layer, by the shell of her assumed pose, not the core of her real self nor the outer layer of public perception. Her actions and her reactions alike were the products of its disciplines and its demands. Her life, such as it had become, was lived at one remove. Only very rarely were the depths plumbed. When they were, when the mud was stirred, and the old agonies rose to the surface, they were dulled as soon as felt, with the consolation prize of pleasure.

So, if we reel forward for a moment, to view the rest of her life as a whole, we see how, time and again, when the need arose, she numbed herself with luxury and sensation. In Paris, at the house of Worth, or at Newmarket, Ascot or Goodwood, she shopped and gambled and raced away her pain.

Gradually, in the years that followed, Lillie came to feel that if she had lost England because of money and because of rigid social convention, if she was unable to live in the way she wanted with the man she wanted, and if it was only her birth and her poverty that made her adultery immoral while that of her friends was accepted, then she would fill the abyss of her loss with pleasure. She would make her money by any means, and she would have all that it could buy. She would solace herself with dresses, with jewels, with private travel, houses, land, racehorses and a yacht.

It would be a mistake for a biographer of the heart to chronicle every one of her performances, to enumerate her successes, her lapses of taste, her intrigues. They are, all of them, successes and failures alike, just the dirt that stuck to her chariot wheels as she passed. They neither reflect her inner self, nor change it. They are acted out at one remove, by an adopted self. For Lillie was set on her course. Her decisions were made and there was no going back. The events of the latter part of her life, though superficially dazzling, are the currency of her terrible exchange: money and fame for the security of self. As such, they are almost irrelevant. Their importance lies in the extent to which they became a distraction, a way of preventing herself from noticing how she had been short-changed. And so it will be enough, for the purposes of this book, to watch the phoenix as she rises, armour-plated, from the ashes of the last four years, to look at her several disguises, note the few reversals that touched her heart, and to let her die once more.

Chapter xxvi

Mrs Renshaw

Once Lillie had dried her eyes she found the crossing amusing. Her anecdotes about the voyage are lively and full of enjoyment. She had always been happiest at sea. She never suffered from sickness, had kept her boyish immunity to discomfort, and was unperturbed by the vermin that roamed the ship. For the *Arizona* suffered terribly from rats – rats that were long-coated and tame. Henrietta Labouchère, who had not Lillie's sea legs, kept to her cabin and woke one morning to find one of them sitting on her chest. Lillie's only remark was,

> 'Alas, I knew the fellow! He used to sit and listen while I read to the invalid, and, with unwelcome familiarity, would indicate his need of water by rattling the chain in the wash-basin.'

Nor was Lillie particularly bothered by the autumn gales that caught the ship halfway across the Atlantic. 'One night,' she recalls,

> the water swished about the corridors, and I think we were all more or less frightened. I waded along the passage ankle-deep, until I came upon a steward cleaning shoes at the foot of the gangway. On asking him in a terrified whisper, 'Is the ship going down?' he replied, 'D'ye think if the ship was in danger I'd be here brushing boots?' This seemed such a sensible process of reasoning that I returned, with complete confidence, to my berth.

Lillie was 'the acknowledged ship's belle'. Needless to say, she found herself sitting at the captain's elbow at dinner every night, fawned on by her fellow passengers for, beauty aside, the gentler members of her sex were mostly laid low with seasickness, and she had no rivals. Lillie practised what we would now call her 'networking skills' and found herself a posse of adherents and hosts for the first days of her stay in

America. She also had time and scope for developing her wardrobe of identities. Chief among these was the prototype for her fictional heroine Mrs Renshaw.

All at Sea, Lillie's novel, apart from its obvious debts to Wilde and his Society type, was based on her own experiences backwards and forwards across the Atlantic. It is slight but entertaining, centring on a sea voyage to New York, in which the heroine, Minnie Vernham, adopts, while the journey lasts, an assumed identity. Married, but travelling separately from her husband, she is persuaded by her friend, the racy Loo Renshaw (whose impending second marriage prevents her from making the crossing herself as planned) to take up her berth on the boat. Minnie's stated aim is to spice up her own marriage of seven years with a seasoning of jealousy and temptation.

> 'You see,' she explains to her husband, 'it would be such a huge joke, wouldn't it? I am not so very bad-looking, am I? And wouldn't you be proud if you saw men falling in love with me right and left? . . . and I should do everything in my power to make them fall in love with me just to please you, don't you see?'

Mrs Renshaw is a widow, and in adopting her persona Minnie Vernham finds that, just as she planned, all the men on board first fall in love with her, then propose, and then threaten suicide – 'such a huge joke'.

The story is, in part, about the problems of deception and flirtation, at both of which Lillie was expert. She had, by the time she wrote it, a lifetime's experience behind her. But its ending is happy, after a Victorian fashion, offering to everyone the quiet redemption of marriage. Even Loo Renshaw, the author of the deception, whose respectability, at the outset, had been questionable, and whose motives for marriage were impure, is allowed to love the husband she has made the butt of her repartee and whom she has married for his money. She is rewarded, in her own words, after five years of a 'rather Bohemian harum-scarum life' with 'a haven of quiet and content'. A Bohemian life was a euphemism for moral laxity.

When the novel opens, Mrs Renshaw is awaiting the arrival of her friend Lady Vernham, and while she waits she looks round her 'pretty little room in Green Street, Mayfair', and sighs – sighs because, as she puts it, 'nowhere could her eyes alight without encountering a portrait of the man she was about to marry; and the man she was about to marry was not beautiful to look upon'. Later, Mrs Renshaw passes Lady Vernham a photograph of her lucky intended, saying, 'Don't scream!' and is treated to the rejoinder, 'He looks like a man who will never cause you a moment's pleasure or give you a moment's pain.' 'Do you know', Mrs Renshaw asks, 'how many thousands Ernest has a year?' 'Something colossal, I suppose?' 'Yes, but I won't crush you with the amount of my future wealth; I am crushed quite enough by it myself.'

Here are two of Society's most delightful specimens. Stylistically the debts to Wilde are obvious, but Wilde would never have allowed either of them to live innocently ever after. Lillie's morals by the time she was sixty were so muddled and compromised that she could see nothing wrong at all with talking like this. After all, she had done it all her adult life. Her ending, therefore, with Mrs Renshaw's transition from brittle Society hostess to good little Victorian wife is uneasy, not to say ridiculous. It is not just in books that the worldly and the self-serving lose sight of true happiness. If it was Lillie's attempt to rescue herself from the censure she had suffered, it was a poor and jumbled effort.

The idea for Mrs Renshaw, 'most charming and insouciant of widows', was one Lillie had borrowed from the Prince of Wales. He had chosen, when travelling incognito, to do so under the pseudonym of Baron Renfrew. When he and Lillie had gone to Paris together, this was the name he had used. Lillie would have been in on the secret, and enjoyed her first taste of assumed identity. Now, on shipboard, like the pretended Mrs Renshaw, and through all her subsequent days in New York, Lillie sported with people's devotion, and then, when things were too hot to handle, pleaded the tie of marriage. She flirted, and more, while it suited her temper or her pocket, but when she tired, or felt trapped, she was Mrs Langtry again, whose husband was too ill to follow her across the sea, and to whom she was indissolubly linked. Having lost her own love, Arthur Jones, even if the fault was partly her own, she made fun of the loves of others. Nothing was serious any more. Intrigues now were 'such a huge joke'. Her desperate cry to Jones only months earlier ('I am so miserable tonight, I feel I can't live without you') was a thing of the past. Those who felt as she had done, that life was impossible without love, were fools and nothing more.

The voyage, besides giving Lillie time to harden her heart and practise her roles, gave her space to prepare herself. By the time they reached New York she had marshalled her resources. They arrived at daybreak, after a voyage of sixteen days, to hear, as she completed her toilette, the 'furious braying of a particularly brazen band'. Abbey, keen to make sure his investment payed off, had gone to work on the publicity for Lillie's tour. In Lillie's own words, she

> hurried on deck, and there found a tug alongside, with Henry E. Abbey, and his partner Schoeffel, marshalling a perfect army of reporters, while Oscar Wilde, torn from his slumbers at an unearthly hour, still had the spirit to wave a bunch of lilies in welcome.

The 'unearthly hour' was 4.30 a.m., but still Wilde had taken the time to dress for the occasion. He was not disappointed. On the following day, the *New York Times* gave a detailed account of the entire ensemble.

> He was dressed as probably no grown man in the world was ever dressed before. His hat was of brown cloth not less than six inches high; his coat was of black velvet; his overcoat was of green cloth, heavily trimmed with fur; his trousers matched his hat; his tie was gaudy and shirt front very open, displaying a large expanse of manly chest. A pair of brown cloth gloves and several pimples on his chin completed his toilet. His flowing hair and the fur trimming his coat were just of a shade, and they gave him the appearance of having his hair combed down one side of him to his heels and up the other side.

It is characteristic that what Lillie saw was people, not the harbour or the strange city. Ellen Terry arriving for the first time the following year, and so burdened with artistic sensibility, records by contrast,

> When I first saw that marvellous harbour I nearly cried – it was so beautiful . . . the vast spreading Hudson with its busy multitude of steam boats, and ferryboats, its wharf upon wharf, and its tall statue of Liberty dominating all the racket and bustle of the sea traffic of the world! . . . The sky scrapers . . . did not exist in 1883 . . . there was Brooklyn bridge though, hung up high in the air like a vast spider's web.

The difference did not stop here. Terry, who was observed by the press to stop acting once she left the stage, was considered 'a dowd', inelegant in her dress and manner, and irritatingly informal. Mrs Patrick Campbell, under the same conditions, was plain rude. 'The fool I felt', she recalls, 'was beyond words to describe – and I am afraid I said something like this: "How perfectly dreadful, why do you do it? Is it for

your living? It seems to me so insulting.'" Lillie, who had less talent to
fall back on, kept up the performance night and day. She knew she must
lose no time. Before her, on the landing stage, Lillie saw, not press
professionals, but the people on whose devotion she relied for success.
The power wielded by the London reveiwers was still fresh in her mind.

Alan Dale, who was among the reporters in Abbey's launch, noticed
that Lillie made it 'a point to be particularly and effusively kind to the
gentlemen of the press; to answer all their questions and to receive them
as friends'. If her attentions were transparently self-serving that did not
lessen their effectiveness. Dale remained a devoted admirer, remarking
after longer acquaintance,

> I have met Mrs Langtry a score of times at her house and at the theatre.
> On every occasion I have found her the same. Of course she is a clever
> woman. She calculates upon the effect of everything she does, but in an
> artistically imperceptible manner.

Artistic imperceptibility was the key to all that Lillie now did. Everything
looked natural, however calculated it had been at the outset. This was
what made her masks so impenetrable, what ensured their comprehensive and lasting success.

Only when she had dealt with the reporters did Lillie look about her.
The beauty of the harbour was acknowledged and dismissed in one line
– 'I had never seen so noble or picturesque a port.' Then they were
bundled into a landau and trundled over the cobbles, in and out of
potholes, to the Albemarle Hotel. Again, her observations were
characteristic.

> The first thing that struck me . . . was the sense of hurry around me. I felt
> that the crowd running to the cars and hurrying and jostling each other in
> the streets was literally exemplifying the adage that 'Time is Money'.

She was in the right place.

In the afternoon Lillie went for a drive and showed herself and was
'mildly mobbed'. In the evening she went to a dinner given in her honour
at Delmonico's. To this she wore her trademark black dress, this time
impeccably cut, and no jewellery. Black, now that she had not the
presence of Ned at her shoulder, had the added benefit of enhancing her
mystery. It made her look like a widow, without having to go to the

trouble of telling a lie. She was an avid reader of Trollope's novels and would have known *The Way We Live Now*, in which Mrs Hurtle, whose husband, an alcoholic like Ned, was safely enough on the other side of the Atlantic for her to contemplate a bigamous engagement to an Englishman. Mrs Hurtle's sensual beauty, we are told, was that of another age. Like Lillie she had luxuriant hair, a perfect complexion, 'her cheeks and lips and neck were full', her chin was dimpled, her bust 'full and beautifully shaped'. What is more, her dress was always black, 'always new, always nice, always well-fitting, and most especially always simple. She was certainly a most beautiful woman, and she knew it'. On the other hand, in the eyes of the virtuous she was 'an adventuress – might never have had a husband – might at this moment have two or three – might be overwhelmed with debt – might be anything bad, dangerous, and abominable'.

It was not that Lillie consciously modelled herself on Mrs Hurtle, that would be fanciful, but Mrs Hurtle was a type, a precedent, and Lillie was looking for roles, the more mysterious the better. Stepping out of Abbey's launch was stepping on to the stage of the New World. That was the main reason for taking such trouble with the press. She had a capacity that would now be called cinematic, to see the effect of her own entrances and exits. She knew how exotic the foreigner could look at the moment of arrival; the artistic value of the first step on land, of the morning light, the playful breeze, and the backdrop of the sea. If she could not quite step naked out of a cockle-shell, the launch full of reporters and the brass band were the next best thing.

Even so, Wilde's presence on the quay must have been reassuring. He accompanied her to dinner at Delmonico's, to hold her hand as she made her first faltering steps in a new world, to trumpet her beauty, as he had done in the old, to manage her masks, and to coach her on, in her guise of charm and insouciance. The result was a second season of Langtry mania. Years later, the *New York World* remembered the impact of her arrival in a long and glowing tribute.

'In New York's age of innocence, thousands of men and women waited on a dock one chilly October morning in 1882 to witness the arrival in America of Lillie Langtry. She proved to be no less and so much more than the expected, that wild demonstrations then began which lasted in the city for several days, broken only by proper intervals in which her weary admirers fell to sleep to dream of the fabulous Englishwoman. Shops displayed 'Lantry toques', tiny turbans of black velvet to be worn

rakishly; hairdressers advised dressing the locks à la Langtry, a great
twisted knob low on the neck with curled bangs on the forehead . . .

It was all reassuringly reminiscent of Lillie's London successes. The
following afternoon, returning from her rehearsal, she found four men
and two pianos blocking her passage up the hotel stairs. They asked her
to settle their wrangle, which looked like becoming a fight, by choosing
one of the two instruments then and there. When Lillie, who had no need
of a piano, answered that she wanted neither, one of them cried out, 'No!
but we mean you to have one. Everything that Langtry touches is gold!'
In the end, of course, both pianos found their way into her apartment. To
Lillie, with the memory of creditors pacing a rented hall fresh in her
mind, a country where grand pianos dropped into her lap in pairs must
have looked distinctly promising. Even without the pianos, she was full
of optimism. Langtry mania was alive and well. Everything seemed set to
succeed. She had a contract for a season and money worries, for the
moment, were a thing of the past. To cap it all, the boxes and stalls for
her first night, auctioned a few days later, fetched twenty thousand
dollars.

Lillie was due to play at the Park Theatre in New York. Dramatically, on
the day of her opening, it burnt almost to the ground. Pierre Lorillard, an
acquaintance from London days, rushed into her hotel sitting-room with
the news. From her window where they watched, the scene was
apocalyptic – flames leaping skywards through the theatre roof. The only
thing that looked like surviving the blaze was an enormous billboard
bearing the legend 'MRS LANGTRY' in suitably eye-catching letters.
So sure was Lillie of her good fortune that, as she watched the battle of
this sign for survival, she cried, 'If it stands, I shall succeed!' Then, in her
own words, as it teetered unpromisingly, she cried out again, 'And if it
burns, I will succeed without it!' Needless to say, it stood. In her
memoirs, the standing of the sign is highlighted with italics, and followed
by three exclamation marks.

Lillie as Rosalind in *As You Like It*, her favourite role

A rare image of Lillie in her first years on the stage. The signs of exhaustion and anxiety, and the strain of her chosen profession, are for once clearly visible in her face

Fred Gebhard, the young millionaire who became Lillie's lover shortly after her arrival in New York

Facing page: Success: Lillie in Boston photographed by James Notman

Posing for Lafayette in 1899.
Lillie was 46 when this
photograph was taken

Lillie's sitting room at Cadogan
Place, her last London home

Lady de Bathe.
Lillie photographed by
Bassano in 1911

Lillie as 'Goddess of Goodwood'

Merman, Lillie's prizewinning racehorse

Lillie's daughter Jeanne at the time of her presentation at court

The electric smile. Lillie in her sixties, still playing a principal boy

Mr Jersey, Lillie's domineering and masculine racing self

Below: Striding past Claridge's, the smile gone

Lillie in Monte Carlo with her faithful companion, Mathilde Peat

Lillie, the year before she died. Photographed by Cecil Beaton

Chapter xxvii

Down the Primrose Path

If Lillie's masks were comfortable and convincing, maintaining the illusion, on and off the stage, was a costly business. For her private life, as with her productions, Lillie needed props, and the props had to be lavish. Venus could not be expected to settle for ordinary surroundings and Mrs Renshaw's discreet elegance had its price. As long as the run and the tour that followed it went well, Lillie would make money, but to shore up her position, in case it did not, she found herself a young millionaire. He was Fred Gebhard, the only son of a rich merchant, whose death had left him the kind of fortune that Mrs Renshaw found so crushing. Before Lillie he had attempted to marry Leonie Jerome, the sister of Jennie Churchill. When it came to nothing, her father wrote to her in congratulation: 'it is well you escaped that match. He was a lovable boy that never grew up, and his weakness which was so attractive was his undoing.' Though Lillie was so industrious and so disciplined herself, she was no stranger to indolence or weakness in her men. Like Jones and like Ned, Gebhard's time was divided between clubs, yachts and horses, and like them too he was susceptible to love at first sight. When they met, he was only twenty-two, seven years younger than Lillie, and immediately began a programme of extravagant courtship. Great bouquets of flowers, with diamond trinkets hidden at their heart, arrived at her hotel. Lavish dinners in fashionable venues were provided. If Lillie did not immediately succumb to his charms, she did not hesitate over accepting his tributes.

The association of Lillie and Gebhard was conducted in a blaze of scandal. Despite the demure widow's black, Lillie was still married. Henrietta Labouchère, notwithstanding her own defection from the marriage bed, did not approve of Lillie's openly consorting with an infatuated bachelor much younger than herself. She began to make known her discontent, and soon the New York papers, who shadowed

Lillie's every move, were following the dispute with greedy interest. Each detail of the story was recorded, often with lavish embroidery, in the morning newspapers, until Mrs Labouchère announced her intention of returning alone to England, leaving her protégée to go to perdition, along with whatever gallant she chose. Gebhard, feeling called upon to defend Lillie's honour, recorded her innocence in a piece of ill-advised and semi-illiterate bluster published, the morning after Henrietta's departure, by the *Sun*. It is supposed to have run:

> Mrs Langtry could do no wrong, even if she wanted to, because she is watched by Mrs Labouchère, by a younger sister of that woman who is a better actress than she is a watchdog, which isn't saying much, by a Miss Pattison of Mrs Labouchère's staff who never stops spying on Mrs Langtry, and in my opinion she is jealous, by the manager of the hotel, by the hotel servants, and even by people on the staff of the Wallack's Theatre. I am willing to wagger [*sic*] that these spies are also on the payroll of the snooping Mrs Labouchère. I challenge her to produce her own marriage certtificat [*sic*], as proof that she has a right to criticize a lady who has done no wrong.

Box-office takings ballooned.

As time went on, and with Gebhard's enthusiastic help, Lillie found that the more flamboyant her style, the bigger the demand to see her. She made no change to the public nature of their friendship, and he was only too happy to make ample display of his adoration. Even if he could not turn a phrase, he was a swashbuckling figure to have in tow. He was dark-haired, over six foot, and built like a boxer, and then, of course, there were his riches. Once more, as fast as she could find it or make it, Lillie was spending her money. When her first Broadway run finished in December 1882 and she set off on tour, it was with twenty cartloads of personal effects and on a private train. The train had been lent by her new and outrageous friend, Diamond Jim Brady. It was called the City of Worcester and it ran to three bedrooms, a bathroom and an elegant saloon. At her side, on the footplate, when she waved her new public goodbye, was Gebhard. Neither of them were in the least troubled by the scandal that surrounded their open association. Lillie had never suffered much from scruples, and she was beginning to find that notoriety was an even bigger box-office success than well-bred beauty. Mrs Labouchère's 'somewhat peevish' departure was only the beginning. On tour, in early 1883, there was more and worse to come.

The City of Worcester's first destination was Boston, which had a reputation for morals that were both prudish in theory and stringently applied. Here, Lillie and Gebhard kept a low and tactful profile, but after Boston, it was on to Philadelphia, followed by Chicago and St Louis, and as they travelled, they grew more reckless. One morning, when they were breakfasting in Lillie's room, he fully dressed, she in a peignoir, they were interrupted by the editor of the St Louis *Globe-Democrat*, who pushed past the maid and proceeded to question them about their relationship. With or without their co-operation over details, he jumped to the inevitable conclusions, and went back to his office aflame with moral outrage. When his article appeared, Gebhard was so incensed that he sought out the editor at the hotel bar, denouncing him publicly and to his face. Once again Americans at the breakfast table gorged themselves with accounts of another 'Langtry Scandal'. This time there were even rumours of a duel.

The duel, if ever proposed, was never fought, but after St Louis Gebhard and Lillie parted company for a while. She went on to Memphis, New Orleans, Milwaukee, Cincinnati and Buffalo, where she was joined by Wilde, still on the lecture circuit. With Wilde, she took time off to go sightseeing. They rode in a carriage through the middle of a live sequoia and visited the Niagara Falls. Wilde fed the inevitable reporters with appropriately extravagant soundbites about his companion, and then, once more, they went their separate ways. Periodically, and, for once, discreetly, Gebhard would appear for the odd night here and there. For the moment they had had enough press attention. Needless to say, the scandal kept the box-office healthy.

It is difficult to get to the bottom of exactly how much money Lillie was making at this point. One American source states that in Memphis alone, where she played for two weeks, she made $31,539.80. It is a very precise figure to be taken from nowhere, but in the context of Mrs Patrick Campbell, the darling of the intellectuals, it looks a little fanciful. On tour a year before Lillie, Mrs Campbell's business manager had written home in ecstasies,

If I tried to explain how great her success was, I am afraid you would think I was exaggerating. We are playing in a small theatre to the same prices as charged only by Sir Henry Irving and Sarah Bernhardt, and you know the amount of scenery and the large company they travel; in our case there is only Mrs Campbell. Why in Chicago all records were beaten. Mrs C holds the record house, the record matinée, the record week, and the record for the city, for no star has played to so much money in two weeks as she did; the gross receipts for the two weeks were nearly £7,000.

Mrs Campbell's profits are in pounds sterling as opposed to dollars, but, even so, the difference is very great. At the end of the year, when she had finished her tour, and was contemplating a return to England, Lillie wrote to Abraham Hayward quoting her own figure for her takings. She had, she informed him, made £25,000 in eight months. She also wrote to her old friend Wharncliffe, quoting the same figure, but in neither case does she say whether this was gross or net, nor whether this was her own clear profit, after Abbey and the company had been paid off, and she does not mention the combined costs of scenery, costumes and hotel bills. The only thing we may be certain of is that Lillie's overheads were not inconsiderable.

A lecture tour was not as financially rewarding as a theatrical tour, but it is interesting to compare Wilde's success with Lillie's, given their promotional techniques. Lillie's management of her finances was untutored and unerring. When Wilde toured, his fortunes were the subject of many anxious letters between his friends. Dion Boucicault, the Irish dramatist and actor, who later worked with Lillie, wrote to the Lewises:

> Oscar is helpless because he is not a practical man of business . . . I do wish I could make him less Sybarite – less Epicurean. He said this morning, 'Let me gather the golden fruits of America that I may spend a winter in Italy and a summer in Greece amidst beautiful things.' Oh dear – if he would spend the money and the time amongst six-percent bonds! I think I told him so, but he thinks I 'take a painful view of life'.
>
> There is a future for him here, but he *wants management* . . . he might make a fair income – if better managed – and if he would reduce his hair and take his legs out of the last century.

Aside from his views of Wilde, Boucicault also records the takings from his own theatrical tour, an 'unprecedented' success which produced 'about eleven thousand pounds' – again, low by comparison with Lillie's twenty-five.

Characteristically, Lillie was quick to recognize just how and why she was so successful. Scandal, blatant invention, public notice, none of it touched her now, and when she returned to New York, late in March at the end of her tour, she did not in any way modify her behaviour with Gebhard. In this first year abroad she had gone through some of the greatest and most rapid changes in her life. Her movements were not yet vested with all the pomp of her later life, but she had set her course. The pace of her future was established. Moreover she had already developed the hallmarks of her mature style: an incredible grace and femininity, an elegance and an unruffled charm that were almost regal in their perfection, all maintained against a backdrop of the most outrageous scandal and rumour. It was a clever and unusual combination, and it kept up her public profile, in a constant oscillation between the unacceptable and the idolized.

Within two years of the end of this first tour, despite Ned's absolute refusal to grant a divorce, Lillie and Gebhard were living together in the house he had bought for her on West 23rd Street, one of New York's most fashionable residential areas. In her memoirs Lillie refers to it as hers, bought with the proceeds of her stage success. 'Possibly,' she muses,

> I have the bump of habitation abnormally developed, for it is certain whenever I like a place I feel an immense desire to acquire a house there; so it is not surprising that I lost no time in securing a house in Twenty-third Street, New York, for my head-quarters, and, happily, my mother, though advanced in years, was prevailed upon to cross the Atlantic to be with me.

As usual with Lillie's loves, there is no mention in her memoirs of Gebhard's presence in the house, but the reason for Mrs Le Breton's arrival was to provide the ménage with a veneer of respectability. Also unsaid is the fact that with her, from England, came little Jeanne, now said to be the orphaned daughter of her brother Maurice, and therefore Lillie's niece. Jeanne and her grandmother set up home with Lillie, to act as an eccentric, and not altogether convincing, dual chaperone.

Lillie's flamboyance escalated. Now she wanted a private train of her own. Plans were drawn up by Colonel Mann, the inventor of the boudoir railway carriage, and, unlike the house in Tite Street, this time extravagance of design presented no problems. The train was seventy-five feet long and too heavy for many of America's bridges. Lillie christened it 'Lalee', Indian for Flirt, a reminder of the racehorse that she and Reggie had bought and trained together as children – as well, no doubt, as a wry comment on herself and her dealings. In her memoirs she describes it in all its ostentatious detail.

Its exterior was gorgeously blue . . . and on either side were emblazoned wreaths of golden lilies encircling the name. The roof was white, and there was an unusual quantity of decorative brass, wrought into conventional designs of lilies. The platforms, which were of polished teak, brought . . . specially from India were very massive . . . Of the interior, the observation room calls for no special description, but the designer had certainly devised a wonderful sleeping room and bath. The former, upholstered in Nile green silk brocade, was entirely padded, ceiling, walls, dressing table etc., with the idea of resisting shock in case of collision . . . The bath and its fittings were of silver, and the curtains of both rooms, of rose-coloured silk, were trimmed with a profusion of Brussels lace. The saloon was large, and upholstered in cream and green brocade, made specially for the 'Lalee' in Lyons, and I was agreeably surprised to find a piano installed therein. There were two guest-rooms, a maid's room, complete even to a sewing machine, a pantry, a kitchen, and sleeping quarters for the staff.

Not for nothing did Edward Michael, her manager in the nineties, compare her to royalty. For if in outward show she grew ever more exotic, her manner remained impeccably ladylike. Her dignity and her calm were legendary, her smiles and her charm lavished on bellboy and suitor alike. Though her train was private, still she invariably commanded all the services that porters and station masters could provide. 'Gaunt, uncouth, loud-voiced porters and attendants all fell under the spell, and would almost fight amongst themselves for the privilege of serving the "madame" as they called her.' She was greeted with red carpets wherever she went, mayors dressed in their full regalia met her train when she toured, and she was showered with tributes that ranged from pistols to large tracts of land. Michael's picture of her procedure before departing is particularly evocative.

Mrs Langtry never hurried, never fussed, never flurried.
  When travelling, punctually about three minutes before the advertised time of the train she would appear on the platform, and at once the atmosphere became electric. The station-master would hurry to her to make obeisance; at a sign from him porters would open doors, and produce foot-warmers; newspaper boys would have papers ready, and my lady would progress gently and calmly along the platform to her carriage, bestowing a kind word here and a smile there. The guard would not start his train until he had looked in on his charge, and found all comfortable.

If Lillie's travelling arrangements were luxurious, her dressing-rooms in whatever town she happened to be playing were no less so. A Boston reporter covering her second American tour regaled his readers with her minutely observed splendour:

> Mrs Langtry insists upon having each dressing room arranged . . . as nearly alike as possible. This is one of the first things her stage manager attends to on reaching a city. Most of the paraphernalia is carried by Mrs Langtry when on tour. Her dressing table is of white wood, heavily enamelled in white. The table is elaborately ornamented with cupids and butterflies, delicately made and grouped and is festooned with old rose satin with muslin beneath, peeping through at the top. The mirror is electric-lighted to Mrs Langtry's own special design and by an ingenious arrangement, colour effects, blue, red, and amber, can be obtained at will. Thus the actress, when dressing, can always tell just how new gowns, hats etc. are going to look as to the blending of colour when she is on the stage.
>
> For the reception of the very numerous accessories of the toilette there is a sort of tray. Nearly everything on this table is of gold. Each brush, comb, scent-bottle, powder box and the like is engraved with Mrs Langtry's initials, the monograms being surrounded by a ring of turquoises. The wonderful cases of manicure instruments are all fitted with implements of solid gold. A cosy sofa of luxurious proportions, decked with alluring cushions of dantiest design, and a decidedly business-like escritoire are also included in the equipment of the Jersey Lily's dressing room . . . needless to say the general effect is truly magnificent.

The only people who surrounded themselves with such trappings were royalty, or, ironically, the cream of the French courtesans. But the detail of the description shows us that Lillie was answering a demand. Her American public lapped up her style and her luxury, in an orgy of shock and titillation. So much she had gauged correctly.

But what of Lillie herself – if this was the outward show of her life, who, now, was the person behind it? She had left her love and she had bartered her virtue for Venus's show. She could hardly complain that the world saw her as a fallen woman, but if she was not proud about her moral standing, she was proud about her acting. When she first contemplated the stage she had written to Wharncliffe, 'Why shouldn't I act. I don't mean without previous hard study for I should love it as an art and should wish to excel.' Though the box-office takings were more than healthy for most of that first year, there were some failures. And despite her careful work with the reviewers, not all had lost their wits over her charms. The notice in *Music and Drama* for her performance as Rosalind was crushing. It ran,

How did the British beauty appear before American eyes? A rather tall and plump figure, large feet; large hands; a large mouth; eyes too light in colour for her brown hair; a bad walk; one foot crossing over the other; a gentle graceful bearing; a genial, winning manner; a clear, sweet voice becoming harsh when it was forced . . . Why should the American people rush to see a court favourite? For the same reason that they rushed to see Jumbo. But let me do justice to Jumbo, even though I seem severe upon Mrs Langtry. He was not only a notorious elephant, but a very large one and the way in which he devoured things was thoroughly artistic. Mrs Langtry is not an extraordinarily beautiful elephant, she has no artistic skill. She is simply a pretty amateur playing a part pleasantly.

Though Lillie was changed in outward show, though London had left her damaged, though her mask-wearing and her ostentation had begun to corrode her, she had, underneath it all, some central aspects of her old self intact. The *Music and Drama* review would have stung her pride. It was a reversal – like her first visit to Suffield's ballroom – and reversal was always, to Lillie, a spur. She was still extremely determined, and if she bowed her head and suffered the criticisms for the moment, she was only biding her time.

Chapter XXVIII

Venus in Harness

In April of 1883, her first American tour behind her, Lillie began another run in New York, this time including *Pygmalion* and *Galatea* in her repertoire. A month later she received a letter from her old friend Wharncliffe, whose wife had taken on a maid who had once worked for Lillie – or this was the excuse for writing. Lillie was delighted to hear that she was not forgotten and wrote back, in high spirits. Wharncliffe wanted to know when she was planning to return, and she answers,

> I am going to stay over this side by the sea until the heat drives me away, as I want to do some serious study and think I have less cause for distraction here than in Europe. But I shall return some time in August when I shall go to Paris for six weeks work there. I am more than ever in love with my profession and am so delighted at the general verdict on my improvement.

Judging by the reviews, the 'general verdicts' were fictitious but, she was concentrating hard on improving her technique. She did indeed study hard that summer, and when the heat became unbearable returned, without Gebhard, to England and the Continent. By 1 July, she had registered at the Conservatoire in Paris for six weeks' intensive coaching under the guru of the French stage, Joseph Regnier. Her determination bore fruit, and if she was never inspired as an actress, by the time she left in October she was at least competent and professional.* Abraham

---

* Ellen Terry's views on Lillie's ability as an actress, though she never saw her act, were avowedly influenced by Lillie's good sense and modesty. She writes,

> I am aware that professional critics and the public did not transfer to Mrs Langtry, the actress, the homage they had paid to Mrs Langtry, the beauty, but I can only speak of the simplicity with which she approached her work, of her industry, and utter lack of vanity about her powers. When she played Rosalind . . . she wrote to me:

Hayward was impressed by her confidence, and wrote his last report to Gladstone,

> Mrs Langtry was in Paris with her mother, who accompanies her to the United States. After a three months tour there she is going to Australia. She told me that she had invested £25,000 – besides money reserved for her outfit . . . I introduced her to Coquelin, who was very much struck by her. We had an animated discussion on Molière in which she joined – speaking French fluently with a slight foreign accent.

The trip to Australia was nothing more than a fall-back, in case her American audiences deserted her, but the introduction to Coquelin was productive. They immediately became friends and, for Lillie, to count the stars of the French stage among her intimates gave her own art a welcome boost. If Coquelin and Bernhardt took her seriously, then the critics could hardly dismiss her. After stocking up on gowns from her favourite designer Worth, with whom she cleverly negotiated an acknowledgement in her programme as part payment, Lillie went back to England. On 1 October she was in Liverpool with Wilde, who had taken time off from a series of lectures in London, to wave Ellen Terry and Henry Irving off on their tour of the States. Terry recalled, 'Many people came to see us off at Liverpool, but I only remember seeing Mrs Langtry and Oscar Wilde.'

Once the world could see that Lillie was serious in her intent, and modest about her abilities, it was kinder in its criticisms. She took great pains to show the finicky old guard that she valued their opinions, whether good or bad, and was grateful for their criticism. Graciousness and meek submission became her trademarks. With Clement Scott, the perfumed and respected English reviewer, whose fur coat and expansive white waistcoat were watched for with dread at every opening night, she was painstakingly tractable. Writing to him after her spell at the Conservatoire, she observes,

> 'Dear Nelly – I bundled through my part somehow last night, a disgraceful performance, and *no* waist padding! Oh what an impudent wretch you must think me to attempt such a part! I pinched my arm once or twice last night to see if it was really me. It was so sweet of you to write me such a nice letter, and then a telegram too! Yours ever, dear Nell, Lillie.'
>
> Just at this time there was a great dearth on the stage of people with lovely speech, and Lillie Langtry had it. I can imagine that she spoke Rosalind's lines beautifully, and that her clear grey eyes and frank manner, too well-bred to be hoydenish, must have been of great value.

I shall always like you for the frankness with wh. you abused my Rosalind. I was on the verge of an abyss of vulgarity from wh. yr timely warning saved me . . . However I am glad to be out of leading strings and I trust when I play again in London you will tell me the truth with the same candour . . .

Though he saw through the flattery, meekness and submission proved powerful weapons. Scott was soon writing and translating plays for Lillie and she, for her part, continued to write to him with increasingly genuine deference and friendship.

However transparent Lillie's manipulation of her critics, it would be wrong to assume that she was impervious to bad reviews or that she found the eating of humble pie either easy or digestible. 'Let us not fuss, please' applied as much to herself as to others and if mostly she smarted in silence, with a smile, there were times when she was too tired or too strained to suffer the hurt and then she would, selectively, complain. Scott, whose comments she felt to be always fair-minded, became, for a while, one of her confidants, and in just such a mood of injury she wrote to him in 1885,

My dear Mr Scott,
    I am so eager to hear the play. When are you able to come? It is too bad of me to inflict such a journey on you and I wouldn't if I could possibly get up to town but I cannot get my strength up at all and am hardly up to playing. I think of going to the sea from Saturday till Monday. Next week I play Pauline Monday Tuesday and Saturday. I hope you will be here one of those evenings. The press here is most inimical . . . I don't want them to write what they don't mean, but there are ways of doing things and they are absolutely abusive I think Gordon Bennetts remark was a wise one. That 'actors and actresses should be cleaned with a feather duster not smashed with a meat axe' I won't write any more I feel hurt and angry at the injustice of the world. I don't know why I should write all this to you – but I feel that you are a true friend . . .

In general, however, Lillie's ability to take criticism in good part was both widely acknowledged and widely admired. The serious critics mostly came down on her side, and it was the provincials, who had axes to grind on the whetstone of morals or privilege, at whose hands Lillie suffered worst.

William Winter, the grand old man of American reviewing, when he came to write his recollections of the stage, *The Wallet of Time*, gave Lillie an entire chapter, in which he summed up her career in America from first to last. Though he was confessedly entranced by her beauty, it was a scrupulously fair and balanced account.

> Her acting at the first was marred by self-consciousness, but it possessed distinction and it evinced dramatic aptitude. From that time onward she labored with incessant energy, essaying part after part, and not flinching from any professional test, however severe . . . Mrs Langtry's adoption of the stage was fortuitous. She had attracted attention as a Beauty and had become a favourite in London fashionable society. Her circumstances necessitated that she should find employment, and she resorted to the theatre. Her choice of a pursuit was ascribed to vanity, and at the outset of her professional career, while she did not lack the encouragement of admiring friends, she encountered opposition and was constrained to endure both censure and ridicule. Her resolute purpose, however, prevailed, meeting all obstacles in a cheerful spirit and without resentment. She was not, in a high sense, a great actress and she did not pretend to greatness, but she was possessed of inherent dramatic faculty, combined with unusual advantages of person, of physical training, and of social culture, and in seeking the Stage she followed her natural bent. She was a born actress. The crudity of her early performances was obvious, but the freshness, charm, and promise of them were equally so. In New York, from the moment when she strolled on the scene, in 'The Unequal Match', no experienced observer could entertain distrust of her ability or doubt of her success.

Winter's account made several important points. The first was that Lillie herself never had any pretensions as an actress. About her abilities, she was always disarmingly honest. When asked in interview about her career, her response was, 'I was never a great actress. But I really loved the stage. I took it very seriously.' It was an irony that her box-office takings, combined with her private life, meant that her productions were always lavish and well publicized. She was, it turned out, a brilliant businesswoman, and it made financial sense for her profile to be as high as possible. As a result she was compared, not to the middle-ranking professionals, but to the stars, in which context, artistically, she fell short.

Lillie did, as she said, take her profession very seriously, and she never shirked. As she points out in her memoirs, for the rewards of fame and the notice of Society, many a talented provincial would wear away her youth for the sake of a successful stage career. But Lillie had tasted the sweets that success had to offer long before she began her life in the theatre, and without the slightest exertion. To Lillie when she started, life, as she recalls,

> seemed so narrow behind the scenes, and there seemed to be so many trifling but exasperating rules and regulations, and these, combined with harder work than I had ever thought myself strong enough for, made me often devoutly wish that I was sitting comfortably in the auditorium looking on, rather than taking part in the play, and, indeed, set me deploring the urgent need of money that had obliged me to abandon my previous mode of life, which, now that it was over, seemed so desirable and afforded me many pleasant recollections.

These were her feelings at the outset, and although after a year of success and financial reward in America, combined with what Sarah Bernhardt had described to her as 'the luxury and bohemianism of travel', she was more than reconciled, still the stresses and strains of her chosen life were great. Even Mrs Patrick Campbell, devoted to her art as she was, admitted that,

> The life of the stage is a hard one; the sacrifices it demands are enormous. Peaceful normal life is made almost impossible by the over-strained and necessarily over sensitive nerves – caused by late hours, emotional stress, swift thinking, swift feeling, and that odd *reculer pour mieux sauter* which comes upon all public performers.

Lillie had, unlike her sister actresses, left much that was pleasant and luxurious behind her. It is all the more extraordinary in her case that she managed to find within her such reserves of discipline and industry. For she worked the long hours, that were demanded of her, without complaint, and often at the expense of her health. Writing to Lord Wharncliffe in 1885, while on tour in England, she described her average day:

> Dear Ld Wharncliffe,
>   I am so glad to hear from you and that you are still interested in this strolling player. I am hard at it again and haven't a spare moment – but it is such a happy life especially when ones efforts are appreciated even by hypercritical Manchester – as I am led to believe they do from the immense audiences and the criticisms I forward to you – I may add the press was not favourable last time I was here. It is now half past nine and I am starting off for a rehearsal of 'As You Like It' wh. will be over about

one when I shall have to dress for a matinée of *Galatea* so that I shan't see food or hotel till 5 this afternoon when I dine and go off to play Rosalind – What would yr fine ladies say to a day like that. and yet I have sometimes a rehearsal at one a.m. as well. I am not up in news – I don't know since I left who has died, married, or bolted. Pray write sometime and post me . . . Now goodbye and excuse this pencil scrawl I am writing on my knee.

The voice is energetic but still soft. As yet the material comforts were being offset by the hardships of the stage's demands. It was early days, before experience had set her in a mould of iron discipline. Whatever the hours and the disappointments it is still 'such a happy life'.

There was one other important point that Winter's account highlighted. This was that Lillie had not taken to the stage out of vanity. He had noticed that, as someone who was given to role-play in her ordinary life, she was peculiarly suited to a life in the theatre. He had also commented on her financial position. This was closer to the truth. Lillie had accustomed herself to quite a standard of living and there were precious few professions for a woman that commanded an income large enough. She now had an insatiable appetite for money. It was her solace, her security, the proof of her ability. It opened doors. It made her able to snub Society, and if anything was lacking to her then it enabled her to buy it. For money, Portelet and Jones, and her chances of domestic happiness, had been sacrificed. She believed in money, in the eighties and early nineties, with a blind faith. So long as her faith was unchallenged she was happy, but when that god too fell, no one could help her in the blank of her disillusionment.

Chapter XXIX

Purchasing Paradise

After Arthur Jones, Lillie's lovers were all fantastically rich. Choosing Gebhard so soon after her arrival in New York (he had been at the dinner at Delmonico's on her first night) smacked rather more of opportunism than it did of romance. According to Somerset Maugham, who was taken into her confidence on one of her many transatlantic journeys, Gebhard was the love of her life. What Lillie is supposed to have said is, 'He was famous in two continents, because I loved him.' It is not perhaps the most romantic declaration but they were together for just under a decade, although their relationship was complicated by Ned's absolute refusal to grant Lillie a divorce. It is said that, as early as 1883, she was writing to Lewis about formalizing her separation from Ned, but Lillie was a great one for keeping her options open. It would be a mistake to interpret the fact of her inquiry as an indication either of intent or of commitment. It is likely that she was simply exploring the lie of the land.

Had Lillie been determined on a life with Gebhard, there was one route open to her. She could invest in land in America, thereby making her eligible for American citizenship, and a divorce in the American courts. This would leave her free to marry Gebhard and to live in exile. But there was one serious drawback. Lillie's divorce would not be recognized by English law, and England was where her friends and the remains of her family lived. She had no wish to sever her connections there. Her emigration, however pleasant, was temporary and financially driven, and, besides, she liked to be able to come and go as she pleased. Being her own mistress was the most precious of her new-found freedoms, and, as Jones had found out, self-sacrifice was not one of her qualities. She hated to compromise, to close doors, and she needed to love Gebhard a great deal before she gave up home and birthplace for his sake.

If we take Lillie's word for it and assume, as she says, that she came to love Gebhard with all the fire of which we know her to be capable, she must nevertheless, by nature and by experience, have minded less about formalizing their relationship than he did. Marriage now had very little to offer her. She was free. She was making plenty of money of her own. She was untroubled by the world's opinion of her domestic arrangements with her lover, and she was, as she had always been, unfaithful. Marriage, she was only too aware, would curtail many, if not all, of these precious liberties. Lillie was a colossus in character and she needed plenty of breathing space. It seems unlikely, whatever private promises she may have made to Gebhard, that she was in any hurry to tie herself a second time. If so, it is puzzling that, in 1888, they bought adjoining farms in Lake County, California. Their stated plan was to breed racehorses, a project that had always been dear to Lillie's heart, and it may be, in her usual barmy way, that while Gebhard assumed it would end in marriage, she thought their affair would end but their friendship survive, enough at least for them to remain amicable business partners.

The purchase looked like quite a commitment, but Lillie, as she always did, was hedging her bets. If for Gebhard there was only one reason for investment, for Lillie there were many. There was the possibility of added freedom if she obtained citizenship, there was the prospect of making money from the horses and eventually the land itself, and there was the question of their love and their future life, for which this would provide a useful testing ground. But whether it was any or all of these, or simply the 'bump of habitation' that impelled her, there was one more reason that was private; one that to Lillie was surely the most compelling of all.

When she had returned to England in '83, Lillie probably saw Jones. All her life she had a habit of assuming that old doors remained open, however many new ones she was opening at the same time, until she found them to be actually locked against her. She needed to be certain that there was no possibility of going back to Jones, now that she had the money and the means to support them both. She needed to talk to him. When she saw him – if she did – she might have found, either because he had lost interest or because she had moved on too far without him, that their love was indeed finally over.

Characteristically what Lillie minded losing most was the frame for this love, its geographical location, the house, the garden, and the beloved Jersey landscape. These were the anchors that had held her in the past. These were what she missed. In their stead, she might have reasoned, she would buy a replacement, and while she was at it, she would see whether the provision of a context for her affair with Gebhard made him more indispensable. They did, it is true, have their house in New York, but if she was seriously contemplating making a life with him she needed somewhere private and shared, where they could live in the country way she had always loved, somewhere that could be both a retreat, and a project. Still Lillie was haunted by Jersey, haunted by her summer with Jones. What she wanted was a second Portelet, a proof that nothing was really lost, that the poignancy of her memories could be matched by the happiness of the future, and that happiness could, as she had hoped, be bought.

Altogether Lillie and Gebhard's purchase ran to about 6,500 acres, comprising two arable farms, with large clapboard ranch-houses, pasture for horses and cattle, and a vineyard. It was going to be quite a concern. The land and its two ranches were bought sight-unseen, by a third party – in itself not a promising start – and Lillie spent a fortnight, in her spare time, furnishing her house in a 'simple and comfortable manner'. The furniture, once bought, was sent on ahead, overseen by Lillie's English butler, Beverly, who was to distribute it according to Lillie's instructions, before she arrived on her first visit of inspection, with a party of friends. He was not given much of a head start. Lillie and her guests travelled in the Lalee from San Francisco, until the railway ran out. The rest of the journey was made in two wild-west coaches, which the enterprising Beverly had commandeered from the ranch. The drive to 'Langtry Farms', as the ranch was called, was seventeen miles and Lillie had plenty of time to inspect the landscape of her blind investment. She was, or so she says, not disappointed.

> The huge plateau appeared a dream of loveliness. Being early July, vast masses of ripe corn waved golden in the light summer breeze, dotted here and there with the enormous centenarian, evergreen oaks. It was, without exaggeration, entrancing. In the distance were the boundary hills of the far side of my land, hazy and blue as the Alps sometimes are, and on which, the mindful Beverly informed me, my numerous cattle ranged. On and on we drove, each turn of the road making us gasp with the new picture disclosed, till, threading our way through my vinyards and peach orchards laden with fruit, which covered a great part of the near hills, we reached *home*.

As always, the picture is slightly misleading. It was in May, not July, that Lillie made her journey, so the image of golden corn and laden fruit trees was a fiction. Artistically, however, it was correct. Arcardia is always abundant, and Arcadia was – was it not? – what her money had bought.

The day after her arrival, Lillie and Gebhard rode into their home town of Middleton, on matching white horses, and cabled the lawyer who had chosen and spent so wisely on their behalf. The cable ran, 'Am delighted. Words don't express my complete satisfaction. Join me in Paradise.' Reporters for the *St Helena Star* were told,

> She is greatly pleased with her newly-acquired possessions and has laid out plans and given orders for the general overhauling and remodelling of things about her ranch. She has secured the services of a French Gardener who will lay out fine lawns etc., and otherwise beautify the premises. The lady seems to take great pride in the place and aspires to make it a second Eden.

No expense was to be spared in the creation of Paradise. As well as the French gardener, to manage the vineyards Lillie imported a man from Bordeaux. The 'simple' ranch-house boasted a different style of decoration for every room. There was a pink parlour and a blue parlour, a Japanese room, an English room, an American room. She had an army of administrative staff to whom she issued her instructions for improvement, besides a changing cast of Indian sqaws and cowboys to do her bidding about the house and grounds. To her farm manager in June 1888, she wrote,

> I received through Stewart your statement and hope everything is going on smoothly. I see you had already bought a bull – but it doesn't matter for we really need him anyhow. I have had a thoroughbred Jersey bull given me if I can manage to bring him out so far. I see three bales of hay bought does not Mr Stewart mean sold? We find the weather unbearably hot here and shall be glad to be back . . . Please have those bad places mended in the road to the vineyard before I come back. I hope Cheney has planted some vegetables. Please see that he does so – tell Hooper the venison was delicious. I sent some to friends here and they enjoyed it immensely. Catch up all the cows you can before I return as I am bringing rather a large party with me all looking forward to cream and fresh milk. With kind regards to Mrs Hamm.

In the event the large party found some other more pressing diversion, for Lillie never came. Nor did she visit the ranch again during the whole of the next year. In June 1889 she was still making improvements, none of which she had seen. To her assistant Dr Aby she wrote,

> You don't know how much and how often I think of the ranch and picture

the changes you have made. Please don't lose patience or heart because I can't come this summer, for I hope the day is not far distant when I shall spend six months in the year there, and I do want to feel that it will be pretty and complete. I am so glad you are getting up the chickens. I do love a poultry yard, and it will be one of my chief pleasures. Some day we must have geese and ducks as well. You ought to have those by the lake, and when we are up there we will be independent of Middletown butchers. How are the sheep? Are there any lambs? I am highly delighted at the advent of Eole's posthumous daughter, and I think she should be called Miss Eole after the old horse. Where is the windmill going to be? If you hear of any good brood mares out there let me know, and if I am in funds I will buy them. How different it must all be now, making your own butter and everything. How does the bakery do? I will be with you in spirit this summer anyhow. Are there any pigs left or have you exterminated them? Freddie says he is going to pay for the wagon, as it is for him.

The letters are similar in their instructions to her Portelet letters – but echoingly hollow in their emotional content. The last time she had been interested in vegetables it had been with Jones. To him she had written how she longed to be with him, how she ached for Portelet, and for news of their garden. To him she had suggested, 'Couldn't we have a poultry farm?', and it had been another dream that they would share, a touchingly naïve scheme for providing them with income enough to live. Now she says, with shades of Marie Antoinette, 'I do love a poultry yard . . .', and it is to be, not as before a necessity – just *one* of her chief 'pleasures'. The garden at Portelet, for Lillie and Jones, was the physical manifestation of their love. It was the vessel for all their hopes of a life together, a living context that had given rise to their passion in the first place, and that continued to feed it, uphold it, and frame it. Langtry Farms, however good Lillie's intentions, was the product of money not love. This time it was not two lovers building a shared escape, a private haven, where the world could not reach them. It was not Lillie writing passionately to the man she loved, asking for news of improvements that he had personally overseen, rewarding him with tender interest and praise. Her discussion in her letters is with a paid servant. It is he, not Gebhard, who is begged not to lose heart, not to despair of her arrival.

Of course, Lillie did, as she professed, think often of her ranch, but it remained a fantasy. It was a panacea for the ills of her life on the stage, a promise of happiness, as yet unrealized, with the man she had chosen on this new and foreign shore. While it continued to hold out its potential in her imagination alone, it was an effective anchor. What she dared not do was to test it, to run the risk of exposing its limitations by a prolonged visit. Unseen but once, it allowed her to believe that she had a refuge, and that could she only reach it, all would again be well, and she would be in Eden, with nothing lost, nothing broken, and the first promise of innocent pleasure intact. But there is only ever one Eden; Lillie knew that. And she knew, too, that the gates to it are locked and closely guarded. Once betrayed, it is never regained. Lillie's Eden had not been enough for her when it had been offered in Jersey. She wanted money as well as Paradise. So she had sold it, and now she thought she could buy herself a new one, bigger and better than the old.

California was not Lillie's island home. It held no memories for her, no ghosts. Her first and only sight of it had to be improved upon in the telling, not because it fell short in itself – it would, as she claimed, have far exceeded her expectations in its beauty – but because she needed to persuade herself of its perfection. She needed to believe in what she had bought with Gebhard, and when she looked on it she found its emptiness was modified only by the echoes of other, better known, domestic landscapes. Jersey, too, by her own description, had blue skies and plentiful orchards and 'soft-eyed cattle' browsing by crystal streams. If she could leave Jersey, which belonged to her both culturally and emotionally, then there was no hope of a new landscape providing an anchor that was stronger, a set of ties, ready-made, to draw her back and hold her as she wanted.

Nothing strikes at the heart like similarity. Nothing is ever so painfully different as the familiar in a foreign context. Like Ruth, Lillie found that the corn was not so much unripe, as alien. *'Home'*, as she calls it in the memoirs (and the italics are hers), is where the heart is, and though Lillie had left her purse at Langtry Farms, her heart she had lost.

Lillie and Gebhard bought their land in 1888. They did not part company until 1892, and though Gebhard sold his share in 1896 Lillie kept hers until 1906. That gave her four years in which to return with him and eighteen to return alone, but by her own account she never went back.

During that time Lillie had holidays, both with and without Gebhard, in England and on Jersey and on the Continent. They did, it is true, have one serious reversal, when the trainload of racehorses they were sending out to the ranch caught fire killing eleven of the horses. This was tragic but for someone as determined and phlegmatic as Lillie it was not insurmountable. Moreover the accident took place in June of '88. It was early days, and there were many subsequent successes and compensations.

The truth is that Lillie soon found there was a world of difference between having and holding. With her first sight of the ranch, the new and shiny god Mammon swayed on his pedestal. If he never quite fell, it was only because Lillie now had little else to put in his place. Interviewed at the end of her life she admitted to feeling that the 'pleasure of desire is greater than the joy of possession'. Mrs Renshaw, her model and her own creation, was more specific. At the end of *All at Sea* she writes to her friend Minnie Vernham, saying,

> Now that Ernest's great wealth has placed all kinds of amusements and extravagances within my easy reach I feel to care much less for them, and I realize that the real joy of life is not to be found in the perpetual search of excitement and new pleasure, but rather in the sympathetic companionship of some one who loves you and whose love you are able to reciprocate.

Life is no mirror of art. While Lillie shared the characteristics and much of the outlook of her creature, the soft reward that Mrs Renshaw's insight earns was not allowed to her author.

Chapter XXX

Venus Victrix

At the end of 1883, just after Lillie had embarked on her second American season, Wilde wrote to her with a mixture of flattery, apology and pleading, announcing his engagement to Constance Lloyd. What is left of the letter runs,

> I am really delighted at your immense success; the most brilliant telegrams have appeared in the papers here on your performance in *Peril*. You have done what no other artist of your day has done, invaded America a second time and carried off new victories. But then, you are made for victory. It has always flashed in your eyes and rung in your voice. And so I write to tell you how glad I am at your triumphs – you, Venus Victrix of our age – and the other half to tell you that I am going to be married to a beautiful girl called Constance Lloyd, a grave, slight, violet-eyed little Artemis, with great coils of heavy brown hair which make her flower-like head droop like a blossom, and wonderful ivory hands which draw music from the piano so sweet that the birds stop singing to listen to her. We are to be married in April. I hope so much that you will be over then. I am so anxious for you to know and like her . . .
>
> Will you write to me and wish me all happiness, and believe me, ever your devoted and affectionate Oscar Wilde.

There are many coded consolations for Lillie here if she minded losing the devotion of her prophet and priest: the importance to him of her sanction; his referring to her as an 'artist'; her triumphs, which, tactfully, come before love; the affected private language of their clique, by which Constance is unfleshed and turned into a fragile, immaterial, fairy vision. Poor Constance is Artemis, the chaste, cold, goddess of the moon, while Lillie, whose eyes flash and whose voice sounds, is love incarnate and triumphant. It was, if nothing else, a graceful way of signing himself off.

Wilde's last tribute to Lillie was, in fact, not paid until 1891. It took the form of a play, written for and about Lillie, the consummation of his influence over her, and the final elision of Lillie's self with a creature of Wilde's making. It was the proof, if proof were needed, that she had become his character. Of course, Lillie was no such thing, and she rejected it. Eight years elapsed between the engagement letter and the writing of the play. These were the years of Lillie's rapidly amassed, and colossal, fortune; the years of private trains, of luxuries untold, of the buying and decorating of the California ranch. Anything Lillie wanted, in material terms, she had. When she furnished the house in New York she had it panelled, floor to ceiling, in English black walnut, all imported, fitted and finished by a young English architect. But by his own account, when the job was completed,

> Mrs Langtry seemed hardly to notice it. 'The very latest thing in interior decoration,' she now said, 'is hard-finished white enamel. I want all this covered with white enamel. You will have to send to England for the right kind. I am sure you won't get it here.'

This was clearly more than just an obsession with interior decor, or the restlessness generated by pleasure unsatisfied. It was the blatant glorying in a new-found power, an enjoyment of the fact that she could import a man to fit and grain and polish painstakingly, night and day, and when the job was done, that she could simply order its undoing. She enjoyed her money, but what she enjoyed most of all was the feeling it gave her of being set apart. She liked to give orders, to see people bend over backwards to carry them out, to disappoint and to demand beyond the limits of human endurance. Moreover, she liked to do it in the sweetest and gentlest way. She never made a scene or threw a tantrum. She was calm and polite and above all unruffled. It was as though, lapped in her Olympus of luxury, nothing of the ordinary workaday concerns of the world could touch her. The architect and his labour and his pride in his job were irrelevant. Her pleasure was everything.

In fact, what Lillie's money had bought her was not possessions but power. It was her money that gave her her confidence and her position in the acting world. She could commission plays and pay salaries. She could hire theatres, buy costumes and order lavish sets, and for money too she could have the best actors the theatre world had to offer. If Wilde flattered her with the title of 'artist' she knew herself to be no more than a professional, but she was a professional on an unearthly scale. From the dizzy heights of her own divinity the little pains and pleasures of her myriad minions were invisible, and if someone was unable or unwilling to do her bidding, they were gently but firmly dismissed. Even with her touring companies there was a gulf between her and her fellow actors; so much so that, while she writes to Clement Scott, 'Coghlan played *splendidly*. The finest thing I have *ever* seen him do', Miles's friend Ronald Gower recorded a visit to Boston in his reminiscences,

> I saw Mrs Langtry acting here the other night and afterwards had a long talk to Coghlan the English actor who is with her, but who detests her. She has improved as an actress, but not as a lady – for instance in *Peril* the old Bancroft play, in which she appeared as Lady Ormonde in a country house, she is attired for 5 o'clock tea in a low short-sleeved gown and diamonds in her hair. She lives in her railway car which has accommodation for a dozen people, and never goes to a hotel while on her tours.

Lillie was ignorant of all this, secure in her absolute control, and Coghlan, despite his loathing, stayed with her through several seasons, and a number of tours on both sides of the Atlantic. It was strange and Faustian pact that she had made with fortune, a pact that alienated and dehumanized, that set her apart from the ordinary concerns of her fellows, in return for a power that was superhuman, the influence and bearing of Venus Victrix.

Parallel to Lillie's treatment of her hirelings was a change in the emphasis of her affairs. When Lillie returned from America properly, in 1885, she and the Prince of Wales struck up their old friendship, but this time, gratifyingly, it was on Lillie's terms. Now he waited for her attention. She saw him only when her schedule permitted. The letters he wrote her, when they could not meet, are silly and inconsequential, but their tone is placatory. He attempts to write in the style of Lillie's coterie, talking of 'epistles' and 'fair Lilies', making tentative suggestions at possible meetings, offering to send game, or do errands for her in Paris. From Cowes, filling her in on what she was missing, he writes:

> My dear Mrs Langtry,
> ... We are having delicious weather here – & I am sailing in my yacht wh. I do as often as I can. I raced her yesterday for the 'Queen's Cup' and came in third – Cowes is very full – I never saw more yachts – or more people – too many I think. We look in at Mrs Cust's most evenings – Lady Mandeville and her sister – Mrs Oliphant, Mrs Gerard, & Mrs Plowden

are those I see most of – but I can assure that that I don't (wonderful to say) flirt at all – Alleno is alone in his glory on the 'Stella'. He has erected an enormous tent on board where he entertains beautiful ladies in secret! You must write to me again next week & tell me how you are getting on. Remember fr. 17th to 20th I shall be in Town – & on 19th till 20th 'en garçon' so we could dine and go to the Play together if you feel inclined – I hope the Very Revd. the Dean is behaving himself – & has not lost his heart to any fair Boulognese – How I wish you were on board sailing with me now – the weather is really quite 'beyond'.

Now I shall wish the 'fair Lily' adieu and hope you will forgive the dullness of this epistle . . .

When they were both in London, and Lillie felt so inclined, the Prince took up his old practice of calling on her at five in the afternoon. Not infrequently Lillie put him off, with excuses of illness or exhaustion. After the threat of one such cancellation he wrote in disappointment,

Our stay here is nearly at a close I am sorry to say as we leave for London on Monday – It would be a great disappointment to me if you were unable to come on Wednesday as I had so looked forward seeing [*sic*] you as it may be a *very* long time ere we meet again – I thought we might have gone to the Gaiety that evening to see the new Burlesque and had a little supper afterwards wh. would have been charming – of course if yr brother and sister in law come it would be difficult for you to be away. It would be very kind of you if you would write a line to the 'Malbro' wh. I should get Tuesday morning whether you are able to be in Town on Wednesday.

In short, he was full of the tenderest friendly attentions. He commissioned Lacratelle to paint her portrait, and nagged her about sittings. He asked to be allowed to attend dress rehearsals, and when she offered no reply, wrote in anxiety a second time,

I should have much liked to have seen the Dress Rehearsal as I might have given you perhaps a few hints – Will it be on Monday, Tuesday or Wednesday next week? as I am anxious to know on account of my evg. engagements – or is it in the day time?

Two days later, and Lillie had still not bothered to answer, so he wrote again,

I am sorry to bother you with another letter – but I should be glad to know before returning to Eaton tomorrow when your dress rehearsal will take place next week – what day and what hour – that is if you wish me to be present – of course if you would rather not I will not come.

Then the answer came and it was negative and the Prince was gracious in defeat and said that he quite understood and would not on any account expect to go. Nor were there punishments, as there had been in the old days. He continued to attend her first nights, and to cajole his friends and acquaintances into doing so too. After the dress-rehearsal saga, when Lillie opened, he wrote encouragingly,

> I shall hope to appear in my box sharp at 8 on Thursday – I am so glad that so many friends of ours have taken Boxes – I begged Fife today to take a Box – wh. he said he would – Should you like to see me I could call at Wednesday at 5?

When he was allowed to see her, the Prince was touchingly grateful – 'I was *so* glad to see you again on Friday and looking so fresh and well.'

So for the moment the balance of power had shifted. Lillie could not, in these years, differentiate between arrangements that were professional and those that were domestic or even intimate. The realization of her position was too new, and she acted in everything with the same mixture of ineffable charm and smiling ruthlessness. To Clement Scott, critic and translator, on whom she depended for publicity, she writes, 'Do dine with me at *8*. I shan't ask anyone else. I want you all to myself.' And on another occasion,

> As if I was likely to forget you. But all the same I like the photo. immensely. It is the best I have seen of you . . . Will you be able to look in . . . ? I hope you will be able. I have so much to tell you – and want badly to see you . . . I have just received a charming letter from *Sardou* congratulating me on my success in Peril which he has seen in the French papers. Don't you think its worth a paragraph?

To Godwin, part of the old Tite Street coterie, and therefore technically a friend, she takes the same tone. He had done some work on costumes for her, in the autumn of 1885, and she wrote from Browns Hotel,

> The only Godwino,
> You really are too good and kind to me. *Much* more than I deserve. You must be a dear and come down and spend a few days with me . . . Many, many thanks for all your kindness! Will not easily forget it – nor *you*.

A little later, the question of payment came up, and Lillie wrote again:

> Clarkson has executed your gilded hair idea capitally. I think the Oxford Street man had better do the border – but I should like to see it first and send him the dress ready to do it on – I want you to let me know dear Godwino how much I am indebted to you for your trouble and don't pile it on because I am in rather low water just now.

Behind her masks and cocooned in luxury Lillie had no choice but to live life at one remove. She was becoming untouchable, unapproachable.

There are tragic accounts of Ned, during her tours of the English provinces, waiting on station platforms to see her, and then, not daring to address her, and unable to face her luminous presence, slinking away just before she arrived. Only later, when she had gone, would he return and ask the porters how she had looked and what she had worn. This sense of her otherness, of distance, is what characterized all Lillie's relationships in the late eighties and early nineties, the only possible exceptions being her father and Gebhard. Otherwise, love affairs, motherhood, friendships, all were conducted across a Wildean divide, over the gulf between goddess and mortal. Her lovers felt awe and gratitude. Her friends were flattered. But for Lillie, too, the distance was insurmountable. Whatever she had left of her own feelings, her divinity denied her intimacy. Besides, it had been bought. Even without the help of a goddess's status she would have felt the chill of the divide. For she was operating from the further shore of the fallen, of those who were marked by denial of their common humanity.

If Lillie was to her friends and associates Venus Victrix, she was not so to the general public. Notoriety, though good for the box office, created another gulf. It was an indication that she was not understood, that though she was what she herself had called 'a person', meaning a personality, she was not loved. Her reputation at home had, in fact, gone steadily downhill ever since her departure for America. Leonie Jerome had seen her on stage in London, in 1885, and commented, 'Saw Mrs Langtry in *Princess George*, such a fiasco, can't act and is badly made up, red hands. Freddie Gebhard was with the mother. Looked ashamed of her, rather disgraceful.'*

Rather disgraceful was how those who were not awed by her grandeur

---

* Leonie Jerome had been engaged to Fred Gebhard before he took up with Lillie and, though it was she who broke the engagement, her criticisms of Lillie may have been spiced with jealousy.

now saw Lillie. In the same year, Lord Lonsdale and Sir George Chetwynd had come to blows in the park over who could lay claim to her. They had been prised apart by the Duke of Portland, much battered. The newspapers had feasted on the scandal. Shortly afterwards, the tradesmen who were still out of pocket after the Langtrys' financial collapse, seeing that she was now worth something, and that her popularity was at an ebb, sued for the money owing. Yet again Lillie was protected by the efficiency of her counsel but, this time, though she was unbowed, she was considerably bloodied. During the hearing the Prince of Wales's loan of £2,000 was made public, as was a statement by Ned that the only money he had at his disposal was the regular allowance given to him by Lillie on condition he leave her alone. Both these revelations were damaging.

To say that Lillie did not care about her public standing would be unfair. She did care. She probably cared too much, but she would not stoop to currying favour, and she would not hide her head in shame, more particularly because she despised the double standards of Society's morals. She took refuge in her father's liberality of outlook, and her island identity, and she carried on regardless. She moved Jeanne and her mother up to London to be with her in her rented house in Eaton Place. This was a move that had been possible in America, where the canvas was broader, but was much less so in England, where most of Society already had its suspicions about Jeanne's parentage. She also summoned Gebhard from America and had him join the ménage. Then, in September 1886, after an extended tour of the Continent, they returned to New York. This time, when she went on tour she took Jeanne and her mother with her, as well as her lover.

In February 1888 William Le Breton died. This was a terrible tragedy for Lillie. She was in Chicago when she received the news, and as with all her true sufferings she kept her pain resolutely private. Several performances were cancelled under the excuse of illness. Neither the press nor the public were told of the real reason for her incapacity, nor did she mention his demise in her memoirs. Though she was so generous with interviews, though the world was allowed to see her house, from drawing-room to boudoir, though it was intimate with the smallest details of her dressing-table, and the names of her consorts, her deep griefs and her heart's loves she would not share. With the Dean's death Lillie lost an anchor. For all his libertinism the Dean had been a warm and attentive father. He had never lost his affection for his children, or his interest in their welfare. He did not pry and he did not judge. Lillie's adult adventures he had treated as no different from her childhood scrapes, mildly amusing and essentially unimportant, so long as she was true to herself inside. What he made of her in her professional incarnation we do not know, but it is likely that he was one of the few people with whom she dropped her guard. As an insight into the uncommon breadth of his mind and the truth of his affections we have a letter that he wrote to Lillie after several days spent with Jeanne.

My dear Lillie,

Jeanne enjoyed the Park immensely. She was a great attraction and people took great notice of her head dress. She had a good appetite for her dinner and was very obedient to my wishes regarding her change of dress. Today we went to London and she passed the afternoon with [nursy]. Your cabriolet took us to the station and was waiting for our return at a quarter after six. We sat down to dinner at half past six. To morrow we take a cold chicken & co to Richmond Park where we are to hold a high picnic. You can imagine how excited and pleased she is about it. She is now watering the plants as I thought she had better be out in the open air before she went to bed. She never tires of being with me and clings to my arm almost as if I were her Tanty. She is a dear companion and I feel quite proud as I saunter down the Park with her . . . Remember me to Gebhard,
Your affectionate father . . .

It is a most touching account. His pride in his illegitimate granddaughter, his delight in her appetite, his plan for a picnic, and his belief in fresh air before bed is as tender as anyone could wish. 'Tanty' was the name devised by Lillie for herself, since the world was supposed to believe that Jeanne was her niece. Illegitimacy was a stigma that the Dean simply did not recognize and his devotion shows all the more brightly against the hypocrisy of the world's censure.

His interest in the child was fully shared by Lillie, who has often been portrayed as indifferent to Jeanne. She was not in the habit of parading her affection, it is true, but that was partly due to circumstance and partly an inherited belief, strongly held at her father's example, in a child's independence. Family, for Lillie, was not for public scrutiny, and, to her, the more precious it was, the more emphatically private.

Chapter XXXI

A Good Woman

After the Dean's death Lillie drifted. Behind the scenes he had given her support, and affection, as well as a vision of breadth, and the example of their own peculiar, shared, integrity. Now, bereft and far from home, she began to feel exposed. Physically as well as emotionally drained, her energies were temporarily sapped and for the first time the acting and the constant travel began to take their toll. Returning to England in July she found herself reassured by the familiarity of home and wrote, almost as she arrived, to Clement Scott, 'I am really ready to jump over the moon with joy at the idea of being back. I saw Ellen Terry at Folkstone today looking lovely.'

The joy was really something more akin to relief. As always with Lillie, place had a restorative effect, although this time the cure was both short-lived and skin-deep. Over the next year she was debilitated enough to suffer a series of more or less serious illnesses – bronchitis, measles, pleurisy. Performances had to be cancelled while she recovered, but the newspapers, reacting with breath-holding melodrama, ensured that the box offices did not suffer. In fact Lillie's takings were enough for her to buy herself a London base, 21 Pont Street. So she was in England again, with a fashionable property of her own. The critics were more than usually kind – her Rosalind was applauded and her Cleopatra raved over, but still Lillie was listless and disenchanted. In April of 1891 she had a second bad attack of pleurisy and decided to take a rest from acting for the summer.

At the same time, Wilde, who was in London, married and with two little boys, had been struggling for over a year to write a play for George Alexander, producer at the St James's Theatre. He, who knew Lillie so well, would have noticed how her illnesses had marked her. She was thin and debilitated, her old zest for life gone. Discipline and industry had given way to despondency and that dangerous anaesthetic hedonism that she had practised at the end of her last London season. She planned to spend the summer racing and the company that she now chose for herself was the lowest that the track had to offer. Wilde knew the signs, and even if they did not directly inspire him, he suddenly saw how to write his play. To his friend Frank Harris he said in excitement, 'I wonder can I do it in a week, or will it take three?'

In the event, Wilde finished the play in October. It was *Lady Windermere's Fan*, and whether or not he was once more motivated by the desire to save her, it was both for and about Lillie. He called at Pont Street with it in manuscript and presented it to her with rather less flourish than usual. It may be that he was nervous of its reception, and if so his nerves were justified. Lillie was dismissive. Her account of the episode in the memoirs goes as follows:

> It was for me that he wrote *Lady Windermere's Fan*. Why he ever supposed that it would have been at the time a suitable play for me, I cannot imagine, and I had never contemplated him as a possible dramatist. Besides, knowing him as well as I did, and listening by the hour to his rather affected, amusing chatter, was not an effective prelude to taking him seriously, nor had he even hinted that he was engaged on any work. He called one afternoon, with an important air and a roll of manuscript, placed it on the table, pointed to it with a sweeping gesture, and said:
>
> 'There is a play which I have written for you.'
>
> 'What is my part?' I asked, not at all sure if he was joking or not.
>
> 'A woman,' he replied, 'with a grown-up illegitimate daughter.'
>
> 'My dear Oscar,' I remonstrated, 'am I old enough to have a grown-up daughter of any description? Don't open the manuscript – don't attempt to read it. Put it away for twenty years.' And, in spite of his entreaties, I refused to hear the play.

Lillie's irritation at what she saw as Wilde's ungentlemanly lack of tact itches behind this passage. Whether or not she really did, as she said, refuse to hear the play, she loved, as every actress does, to have plays written especially for her. But Wilde had gone too far. While it entailed being Venus Annodomini, in black jet, she was only too happy to play his creature, but when his fiction and the reality it was supposed to mask merged into one she would have none of it. To Lillie, the play was insulting in the intimacy of its knowledge of her character and circumstance. It crossed the scared divide, razed her pedestal. But Wilde's presumption did have one of the effects he had hoped for, in that it checked her own disenchantment. If Lillie was, as he thought, on the brink of a second collapse, losing the ability and the inclination to wear her masks, *Lady Windermere's Fan* made her defiant again – not, as he had designed, by showing her what lay behind her fictions and teaching her to value it, but by nettling her, casting her adrift in the swamp of her own vanity. It proved a powerful catalyst.

In the long term, its result was to confirm her alienation, to cut the last of her human anchors, for this is the moment at which Lillie and Wilde's paths finally diverged.

Lady Windermere's Fan was a greater and more serious tribute to Lillie than she was, for the moment, able to recognize. Its story is well known now: the return of Mrs Erlynne to London Society from self-imposed exile abroad, her appearance in public of carefree decadence, and her private sacrifice of everything – personal happiness, her hopes of reinstatement in Society – for the sake of her illegitimate daughter. The nobility of her actions is enhanced by the fact that the daughter, like Lillie's own Jeanne at this stage, remains, throughout, in ignorance of Mrs Erlynne's identity. Despite the play's fictional base there were plenty of lines that would have had a familiar ring to Lillie. Among these is Lady Plymdale's advice to Lord Windermere, 'It's most dangerous nowadays for a husband to pay any attention to his wife in public. It always makes people think that he beats her when they're alone.' Besides which Lillie would have recognized Mrs Erlynne's familiar brand of amusing cynicism and manipulative charm. When she enters the ballroom in the second act, Lord Windermere whispers how rash it is of her to come. She replies with a smile,

> The wisest thing I ever did in my life. And, by the way, you must pay me a good deal of attention this evening. I am afraid of the women. You must introduce me to some of them. The men I can always manage. How do you do, Lord Augustus? You have quite neglected me lately. I have not seen you since yesterday. I am afraid you're faithless. Everyone told me so.

This was the way Wilde had taught Lillie to talk. She was well known for the brittle wit of her rejoinders and for what, in *All at Sea*, she called her 'unflagging vivacity'. Moreover, 'faithless' was one of her particular words, used most often with her legion of professional admirers.

If Wilde's tone was recognizable to Lillie, then it would be equally so to a Society audience. They might have missed the more precise private references, but they would have been quick to see that Lillie was playing herself. This was Wilde's intention, and it is central to his purpose that Mrs Erlynne be seen in all her fallen glory before the great denouement in the third act. Later in the same evening, still attended by Lord Windermere, she comments,

> So that is poor Dumby with Lady Plymdale? I hear she is frightfully jealous of him. He doesn't seem anxious to speak to me tonight. I suppose he is afraid of her. Those straw-coloured women have dreadful tempers. Do you know, I think I'll dance with you first, Windermere. (LORD WINDERMERE *bites his lip and frowns*.) It will make Lord Augustus so jealous! Lord Augustus! . . . Lord Windermere insists on my dancing with him first, and, as it's his house, I can't well refuse. You know how I would much sooner dance with you.

So far, it was light-hearted, though it had a Wildean bite.

But in the third act there is a change of pace. Lady Windermere and Mrs Erlynne come face to face in the rooms of Lord Darlington. Lady Windermere, in a state of bitterness and misery, is planning to elope with Lord Darlington since she is convinced that her husband is infatuated by Mrs Erlynne. What the audience knows, but she does not, is that Mrs Erlynne is her mother, that Lord Windermere has been seeing her and supporting her with money, in order that his wife should be protected from the shame of her parentage; and that Mrs Erlynne has followed her daughter in order to save her from the disgrace she is about to incur, and to persuade her to return to her husband. Her motives are suspected by Lady Windermere, who rounds on her, calling her 'a woman who has neither mercy nor pity in her, a woman whom it is an infamy to meet, a degradation to know, a vile woman, a woman who comes between husband and wife!' It is understandable that Lillie was not flattered. Yet this was the light in which Lillie was now beginning to appear to her contemporaries. These are the taunts of Society, and in particular of its ladies. In their eyes, Lillie was an adulteress, shamelessly consorting with other men, while her own husband drank his days away in Southampton. She was an actress. She handled money. She travelled the world like a gypsy. Modesty, humility, quiet domesticity and, above all, pious obedience to father or spouse were alien to her nature. In the Park, married men fought over her body. In the dock, her finances and her sexual licence were matters for question and public speculation. To the virtuous, the likes of Leonie Jerome and Lady Frederick Cavendish, she was an abomination.

Knowing Lillie as he did, Wilde must have had his qualms about her tolerance of the truth as expressed in his play, but salvation, as he saw it, lay not in denial but in affirmation. Lillie had listened to him before, and perhaps she would do so again. To this end, if she found the truth hard to stomach, Wilde gives Mrs Erlynne none of the delicacy of her inspiration. She makes no attempt at clearing her name beyond a shudder of distress, but continues, most passionately, to urge her daughter to return home. Here is how he develops the scene:

> LADY WINDERMERE: You talk as if you had a heart. Women like you have no hearts. Heart is not in you. You are bought and sold.
>
> MRS ERLYNNE (*starts with a gesture of pain. Then restrains herself, and comes over to where* LADY WINDERMERE *is sitting. As she speaks she stretches out her hands towards her, but does not dare to touch her*): Believe what you choose about me. I am not worth a moment's sorrow. But don't spoil your beautiful young life on my account! You don't know what may be in store for you, unless you leave this house at once. You don't know what it is to fall into the pit, to be despised, mocked, abandoned, sneered at – to be an outcast! to find the door shut against one, to have to creep in by hideous byways, afraid every moment lest the mask should be stripped from one's face, and all the while to hear the laughter, the horrible laughter of the world, a thing more tragic than all the tears the world has ever shed. You don't know what it is. One pays for one's sin, and then one pays again, and all one's life one pays. You must never know that . . .

This is the speech of one of the fallen. Mrs Erlynne's pain is unassuageable; contractually so. It is the price for her freedom, and though she stretches out her hands to her daughter, stretches them out as it were across the divide, she may not touch.

As always, Wilde was several steps ahead of Lillie. Though her notoriety was beginning to be vile, she had not as yet tasted all the bitter sweets of the pariah. Besides, she was constitutionally resilient, and it was not in her nature to indulge in morbid contemplation. 'Let us not fuss, please' is the motto of the pragmatist and the survivor. Despite sickness and disenchantment, she did not see, in 1891, what time held in store. Her daughter was still young, still safe in her misconception of her parentage. The masks were tiresome and lonely, but they were efficient and impenetrable. There were no signs of the world stripping them from her face. Temperamentally Lillie was unsuited to noticing Wilde's warnings. In Mrs Erlynne's outburst she would have seen only self-indulgence and morbidity, to neither of which she was sympathetic.

While Lady Windermere weeps and hesitates, the gentlemen return, and Mrs Erlynne, aware of what is at stake if her daughter is found in the early hours of the morning in Lord Darlington's rooms, orders her behind a curtain, and takes the shame upon her own shoulders. So far, if Wilde has shown her to be brittle and disgraced, he has also shown her capable of a mother's love. He has given her frivolous and silly speeches in company but he has shown that behind the frivolity lies strength and emotional integrity. She is capable of sacrifice, of selflessness, and suffering. As the play closes, he allows her to step out of the shadows of the public perception and speak in defence of herself. Her words again are frivolous. It is the speech in which she complains that a heart does not go with modern dress. To Windermere in his stiff haven of upper-class virtue, she is unpitying and cynical – as in Wilde's eyes the fallen always are – but his stage directions read, *'her voice and manner become serious. In her accents as she talks there is a note of deep tragedy. For a moment she reveals herself.'*

Mrs Erlynne can reveal herself, but Lillie could not. Slipping the mask was not possible in real life. It was a dramatic device, and it was done at this point to show the audience what only Lillie and Wilde understood: that is, their perverse doctrine of the discipline of frivolity, by which the wounds of the soul are screened from view and the façade of the whole maintained. This, as practised and embodied by them both, is the cost of remaining carefree and entertaining when the heart is broken, or lost, or compromised. It is the pain and effort that it takes to cloak the difference between the surface and the depths, and to cloak it with lightness and with elegance, and it is no less culpable for that. The proper response to it is worldly laughter, not pity. Wilde's morality was ruthless, but he hoped and believed that Lillie embodied a particular kind of integrity. He saw the truth of her suffering and the pride that masked it, and he valued Lillie's ability to keep her sufferings and her sacrifices private, even at the expense of her reputation.

Later, Wilde would be forced to be serious and soul-baring, but that time had not yet come. He was, in the nineties, still the great crusader for frivolity, because of the incongruity of what it hid, and because restitution was not a part of his creed. One of Mrs Erlynne's last requests is that her daughter should not 'spoil the one good thing I have done in my life by telling it to any one'.

The difference between Wilde and Lillie, now, was that Lillie was corrupt enough to mind more about public vindication than private virtue. In her own fiction the circumstances are neatly reversed. Mrs

Erlynne does good and it goes unacknowledged, either by its flawed beneficiary, or by the world at large. Minnie Vernham, Lillie's heroine, does mischief, and cares only that the world does not see it. Shunned by her fellow passengers for ensnaring and deceiving every man on the ship, having, in her own words, 'smirked and encouraged them' without revealing her married status, she is outraged by the public disgrace she suffers. Her husband is bullied into defending her putative reputation and only after the crisis is over does she sit down and write her satisfaction to her friend:

> Acquitted, my dear Loo, and I leave the ship without a stain upon my character! In the face of insuperable difficulties, and notwithstanding Kit's very lukewarm attitude when called upon to defend me, I was led triumphantly into the concert-room on the Captain's arm, and made the guest of the evening. I have no doubt it will be a disappointment to you to know that my trials are at an end, and that I reappear 'pure and white as the driven snow,' but you have got to have the truth, whether you like it or not!

Clearly remorse did not feature in Minnie Vernham's emotional repertoire. For Wilde, disgrace always came with a painful internal correlative that made a nonsense of vindication. It is probably just as well for Lillie that he never read her own thoughts on guilt both public and private. How far she had got towards this way of thinking in 1891, who knows. Perhaps she was only on the brink of it when he tried to pull her back with his play. Either way, for the first time Wilde found himself disregarded.

It would have been a majestic *coup de théâtre* if Lillie could have stood on the London stage, and carried the hypocritical London audience with her, in tears, to a new understanding of morality. It was Wilde's intention to make Society aware of the double standards it was operating in the case of Lillie, to make people aware of a more sophisticated form of virtue, a virtue that, though its origins are impure, rises up in spite of them, and without taint. He wanted to show, as Lady Windermere is taught, that people cannot be categorized simply as good or bad, 'as though they were two separate races or creations'. Instead what he saw was a world shot through with vice and virtue in differing proportions, and that these properties, like oil and water, did not mix, so much as inform and define one another. As Lady Windermere has it,

> What are called good women may have terrible things in them, mad moods
> of recklessness, assertion, jealousy, sin. Bad women, as they are termed,
> may have in them sorrow, repentance, pity, sacrifice.

Mrs Erlynne may be compromised by experience and by vicious
impulses, but she is noble in her sacrifice, in her knowledge of herself,
and in her perverse self-discipline. To survive the pit, as she points out
to her daughter, it takes strength of character. 'You', she tells her, 'are a
mere girl, you would be lost. You haven't got the kind of brains that
enables a woman to get back. You have neither the wit nor the courage.
You couldn't stand dishonour.' All these – strength, complexity, fatal
susceptibility, courage – in Wilde's eyes were Lillie's virtues.

His working title for the play was *A Good Woman*.

Lillie had said of Wilde, in one of her more perceptive moments, that
he was 'genuinely romantic', and she meant it in the broadest sense. *Lady
Windermere's Fan* was truly romantic both in conception and as a gesture,
a grand bid to reverse Lillie's black reputation. What Wilde had
envisaged was a form of double bluff. He had provided Lillie with a mask
that was herself. It was a poetic idea, that Lillie should vindicate herself,
and all the fallen ones, by revealing herself in her true colours; by
admitting the vice and the folly and challenging Society with its own
hypocrisy. As one might expect, it had a sting in its tail. It could be such
only if Lillie had the qualities to carry it off. Like the presentation at
Court, it was a form of trial by fire. In Lillie's eyes, without Wilde's
artistic foresight, or his complex morality, it was a gamble. She had none
of Wilde's trust in the efficacy of art as a moral force. The play's failure,
should it fail, would be suicide. In all probability she was right. Society is
a cumbersome and slow-moving beast, and although it is romantic to
think so, it is not susceptible of revelation. In 1891, Wilde had just met
Alfred Douglas, and was poised on the brink of his own leap to
destruction. Had Lillie accepted his tribute, no doubt he would have
taken her with him.

Chapter XXXII

Mr Jersey

After his offer of *Lady Windermere's Fan* had been turned down, Wilde disappeared to Paris for the remainder of 1891. Lillie, as though freed suddenly of his influence, began a lurid though temporary descent into debauchery.

She had fallen in with a particularly unsavoury character known as 'the Squire' – George Alexander Baird, drunk, millionaire, amateur jockey and pugilist. He was not acceptable in any society, and Lillie was treading dangerously when she allowed herself to be seen with him. Perhaps this was part of the attraction. Certainly he was not someone she could dominate. They met on the racecourse, on 28 April, with Lillie only just recovered from her last bout of pleurisy. Illness, exhaustion and her father's death, over which she had been able to express no proper grief, had left her listless and destructive. Baird, small, slim, uncouth and socially outcast, embodied for Lillie all the old pull of the edge, and he was dangerous enough to swallow her up, or so she must have hoped. They began their association, naturally, without either decorum or delay.

In her memoirs Lillie describes her lover as 'an eccentric young bachelor, with vast estates in Scotland, a large breeding stud, a racing stable, and more money than he knew what to do with'. Eccentricity was a polite blanket term for a thorough commitment to thuggery and debauchery. Expelled from Eton and with a few terms of experimental dissipation at Cambridge under his belt, Baird had lost no time in beginning his career in earnest. He modelled himself on Mytton, styling himself 'Squire Abingdon', and his dedication was to drink, amateur jockeying and boxing. To this end he kept a stable of over a hundred horses at Lickfield, where he had his estates, and a further hundred and fifty at his Newmarket racing box, Moulton Paddocks. A win held no charms for him at all unless he himself had been in the saddle, and when Lillie knew him he would rise at dawn every morning, to exercise his horses himself on the gallops, return for a breakfast of two bottles of champagne and occasionally, if he remembered, some sweetbreads. Then he would don several jerseys and take an eight-mile walk to keep his weight down, eat a couple of ounces of fish and set off for a long evening of bullying, brawling and competitive drinking. Around him day and night he kept a cohort of professional jockeys and prize-fighters, who amused him by wrecking pubs and bars and beating up anyone who resisted their favourite game of smashing the hats of passers-by.

Eight years Lillie's junior, Baird was thirty when he and Lillie met. His profile was high and his past as lurid as even she, in her mood of danger and self-destruction, could wish. In 1882 he had been banned from the race-track for two years for shoving the Marquess of Hartington against the rails in an amateurs' selling-plate race. His nonchalant apology is supposed to have run, 'Beg pardon, my lord. I thought you were a bloody farmer.' Then, having rehabilitated himself, in '84, with new colours, he confirmed his pariah status by eloping with Dolly Tester, the dancer wife of the Marquess of Ailesbury. By 1891, with all this behind him, he was not surprisingly invisible to those elements of Society unfortunate enough to come across him. To Lillie, he was a magnet; not that she was necessarily in love with him, but because, like her own behaviour in her last London season, he was a way of outraging those by whom Lillie, in her vulnerable moments, felt unkindly judged or cold-shouldered. Weakened as she was, and rudderless once more, her open association with him was a characteristically aggressive test for the loyalty of her so-called friends. She was rewarded, in most cases, with an ample share in his transparency.

When they met in April, Baird presented Lille with a two-year-old colt called Milford, which became the first of her subsequent string of racehorses, and provided her with the perfect excuse for abandoning the theatre for a summer, to watch him run. He proved very successful for her, winning his first race at Kempton Park, under her new and rapidly chosen colours – fawn and blue, taken from the cloak she happened to be wearing at the time. When winter came he had already earned her over £8,000 in stakes. Her affair with his donor, though hardly less lucrative, proved considerably less enjoyable. Baird was possessive and violent, both qualities that were inimical to Lillie, but which she found curiously compelling at those moments when she looked for self-punishment.

In 1892 Lillie returned to the stage, to play at the Criterion. Wilde came back from Paris and *Lady Windermere's Fan* opened to huge critical acclaim. Lillie went to the first night, still low in spirits. Now that she was working again and no longer able to be constantly by his side at the race-track, Baird was proving difficult. He disappeared for days, on wild bouts of drinking and violence, from which he would return jealous and full of suspicion. Not infrequently he beat Lillie. This was quite like old times, the only compensation being the munificence of his guilt. Jewellery, ropes of diamonds, bracelets, rings and brooches, were her rewards for his abuse. Lillie was past caring what happened to her. She took another lover, Robert Peel, and disappeared with him to Paris. Baird followed them, broke into their hotel suite, beat Peel senseless, wrecked the room and left Lillie with two black eyes. She spent ten days in hospital, where diamonds rained on her daily, in apology, and, though she kept the diamonds, she had the presence of mind to refuse him admission. Finally she was offered the present of a 220-foot yacht and a generous cheque for its maintenance. Lillie at last was mollified and Baird reinstated, but with the establishment of several ground rules. Together they set sail for England.

Lillie's yacht, called the *White Ladye*, but more popularly known as the *Black Eye*, did nothing for her social standing. In terms of her reputation, Baird had done her some serious damage. Later, even Lillie herself admitted her mistake, remarking to friends, 'It served me right for being lazy. How I wish I'd been spending my days in the theatre, where I belonged.' The kinder of her acquaintances found her choice incomprehensible. Typical among these is the following account in a stage memoir, *Through the Box Office Window*. It runs,

> The Turf association with Baird was one of the mysteries of her career. The keynote of her character was her worship of beauty, and of the refined and pleasant things of life. She was essentially fastidious; her surroundings, her décor, were chosen with studied and exquisite taste.

Where Baird fitted in with all this, most failed to see; many did not even try. Esher, the guardian of the morals of the great, who played Savonarola with the aristocracy's correspondence, recorded several stories in his journal, among which was a sordid motive for the Peel debâcle.

> Young Peel is said to have given Mrs Langtry a certain complaint. She therefore slept with Abington and accused *him* of having made her the unwelcome present. He paid her £12,000 which she divided with Peel.

This was a tale that would have done the rounds of the clubs and drawing-rooms, and Lillie herself had probably heard it. All the more credit, therefore, to those of her friends, foremost among whom was the Prince of Wales, who continued to understand and to forgive, despite the scandal.

Whatever the gossips said, Lillie either could not or would not extricate herself from her misalliance. At the end of 1892 Baird took the Haymarket Theatre for her, financing a thin comedy-melodrama called *The Queen of Manoa*. It was slated by the critics, though Lillie was praised for her beauty and her dresses. In compensation the theatre was full every night, with an audience that was boisterous and uncomplaining, made up mostly of the racing fraternity: owners, trainers and jockeys. 'Never', the manager recorded, 'have we done so well in the refreshment bars as we did in that short season.' In the afternoons, when not in use for the play, Baird commandeered the foyer of the theatre as a rat pit. Then, in March of the following year, only two years since they had met, a message reached Lillie from New Orleans. Baird had been found in his hotel room, stone dead from the effects of a gargantuan drinking spree.

Whether she grieved, or whether she breathed a sigh of relief, Lillie moved quickly and pragmatically on. Baird's stables were broken up and sold, and she had to make alternative arrangements for the housing and training of her horse Milford. Racing by now had entered her blood, and having been recommended Sam Pickering's stable at Kentford, she bought herself a small house in the village, with what she called 'the disproportionate name' of Regal Lodge. She imported bloodstock from Australia and raced it, unshod, on the English tracks, with unerring success. Cool as she now was, she threw herself into the racing world, with the same energy that she had given to the stage. She liked the companionship of the owners, among whom were the loyal Prince of Wales and the Beresford boys. She liked, too, the fresh air, and the picnics, and, less healthily, the colour and the risks of life at the sharp end of the course. Her friends were professional jockeys such as Tod Sloan, professional gamblers and part-time crooks. She bet heavily, usually with spectacular results, and she was said to operate a gambling ring whereby she could obtain the results of a race by telegraph before the betting had closed in London.

Thus began Lillie's racing career. In part this was simply the realization of a childhood dream. She had always enjoyed the buzz and the *en-fête* feel of the race-track, ever since she and Reggie had invested so successfully in Flirt. But in part, too, it was the enjoyment of what was considered a male preserve. On the hunting field men and women were equal, but this was not the case on the course. Racing, like the handling of her own business, involved the breaking of other and older conventions, the crossing of another barrier. All Society went to race meetings, but very few ladies owned or raced horses themselves, and the few that did were not respected by the professionals. Besides, the Jockey Club was exclusive to men, and it was to Lillie's delight that the Prince of Wales, after one of her more spectacular wins, escorted her inside, where they could be seen by the press as she was toasted in champagne. To get round the conventions of the club's membership Lillie's horses were raced, from then on, under the colours of a 'Mr Jersey', a dashing incognito that both Lillie and the Prince enjoyed.

Lillie's racing, like her acting, was something she wanted to do well. Through Baird, she had met and got to know all the most important professionals, the trainers and the jockeys. She provided herself with the best advice available and when her horses did not appear to be doing well at Sam Pickering's she felt no compunction about moving them on elsewhere. According to one contemporary account, which starts by observing her 'severely practical outlook', she removed her horses, 'without the slightest warning . . . from Pickering's stable'. It goes on to record the following entirely characteristic conversation,

> 'I thought you liked your trainer?' observed someone.
> 'So I do – immensely,' she replied.
> 'But you've taken your horses away from him?'
> 'Oh – *that*?' she smiled. 'Of course; you see, he never won any races.'

To many, her practicality was evidence of a strange and perverse masculinity, that became more pronounced as she slipped into late-middle age. The same source records,

> There was a calm determination about Mrs Langtry that many found hard to reconcile with her beauty. The combination of extreme beauty with brains of more than average capacity is rare, but it was hers. In addition, she had an iron will, immense courage, and that gift of instant decision possessed by great men of action. . .

As success gave way to success and the world puzzled over its reasons, Lillie found herself compared more and more often to men rather than women. 'Mr Jersey', it seems, was not just a racing title. It came to explain something about her that set her apart from other women of her age, that allowed her to cross barriers of gender, not just with impunity, but to the welcome of her opposite sex. She was both man and woman, still an enigma, even in her forties and fifties. Her racing photographs were captioned equally 'Mr Jersey' and 'The Goddess of Goodwood'.

Lillie seemed to live in a different dimension. Guardsmen left their posts to be at her bedside, crazed infatuates took rooms opposite her house and trained a gun on all male callers, and her guests, including the Prince, accustomed themselves to entering the dining-room down a plank that went from window to street level across the well of the area. But if her world was mad, Lillie herself was an eye of calm at its centre. The old recklessness that had characterized her youth had given way to a superhuman confidence. She could and did do just what she liked. Now the 'private acts of Parliament', that Smalley had noticed in the days of Whistler's breakfasts, proliferated by the dozen. On board her yacht, even with the most distinguished guests, she behaved as she chose, and not as convention dictated. One account records how,

> She did not drink much, a glass of champagne for elevenses, two or three glasses of brandy after dinner with her coffee, when she invariably remained behind with the men as they told stories over their cigars.

From the male domain Lillie took her freedom, her licence, her professionalism; and from the female, her sexual power, her whimsicality and the ultimate prerogative of unquestioned indulgence. Later, when asked her opinion of the suffragettes, whom she considered stupid in the extreme, she was unmerciful, wondering why they had not seen, as she did, that the cake was there for the keeping quite as much as the eating. Nor, since her only motivation was liberty and her own comfort, was Lillie ever predictable. When her prize Antipodean, Merman, won the Ascot Gold cup, she did not bother to watch the race. To the incredulity of her fellows she had gone to Jersey for a holiday, where she had been so occupied with landing a catch of mackerel, in St Aubyn's bay, with what she called 'my old fisherman', that she did not hear the result until she went into St Heliers in the evening. Here she found, as she recalls, 'my racing colours flying everywhere, even tied to the whips of the cabbies, while from the office of the local paper rushed the editor shouting like a schoolboy, "You've won."'

Living so much, and so brilliantly, in the male domain, Lillie, for all her beauty and her unquestionable femininity, became more masculine.

After all, power and the ability to control others were not, in the nineteenth century, a lady's concerns. A woman in Society would have had control over her own house and its staff, and might, by charm and manipulation, have exercised a degree of invisible influence over the larger world outside, but she would not normally have had much to do with profit and loss, or the running of a business. Men and women lived in different spheres, in which their occupations as well as their pastimes were separate and clearly defined. Lillie, now that she was running her own outfit – negotiating venues and the itinerary for her tours, whom she hired to make up her troupe, how much was spent on costume and scenery – was aware of none of these boundaries, and if sometimes the exercise of her power was arbitrary, or her enjoyment of it gloating, it is hardly surprising.

Lillie had grown up with six brothers, and her professional relationships were refreshingly straightforward. The flirtation, which was like drawing breath to her, was companionable rather than challenging, a way of making things pleasant, of oiling the wheels while still holding her sway, and though she expected to dominate, because she held the purse strings, she was always even-handed. If she and Michael, her manager, differed over a matter of expenditure, she would say quietly, 'No doubt you are right, but I want it, and it is my money, isn't it?' and the matter was settled. Equally her displeasure was as quickly, if cruelly, registered. 'She has always,' Michael recalled, 'had the gift of expressing disgust and quiet contempt more completely than anyone I have every known. She could crush, destroy, and pulverise in record time, and in the smoothest blandest manner.'

As the century turned, there was beginning to be something dangerous about Lillie; the result of a power and a confidence of abnormal proportions, fused with the bitterness of experience.

Chapter XXXIII

Mrs Erlynne at Last

While she established herself on the stage and on the racing circuit Lillie kept up a display of coruscating and impenetrable change. Who was she in this time? Scott's sweet submissive actress, bowing to his criticisms with consummate grace, or Baird's moll, bent on self-destruction and outrage? Wilde's petulant protégée, or the damaged creature of his invention? Courageous professional, honest friend, scheming mistress, tyrant, gambler, disciplinarian, opportunist, goddess or mortal, man or woman? In the period of her discovery and collapse we were able to see, sharply and with poignancy, who she was and how she made her choices, but with success she disappears and by the 1890s she is lost to us altogether. When she reappears, in the dawn of the twentieth century, she is less protean, more consistent. She is changed, of course, a sadder and a wiser self. She is still steely in her determination to preserve the appearance of insouciance, still schooling herself to lightness and the discipline of frivolity. But now there are moments when the old Lillie is close to the surface again, windows when we see her as she used to be, hear her old voice once more.

Watching her in the summer of 1891, Wilde, as always, had been right. Lillie was indeed losing her ability to wear her masks, mainly because she had lost the inclination. The need for protection from the world had lessened, and continued to lessen, as Lillie realized that the things that hurt her most were inside, and not outside, her defences. The death of her father had weighed her down. The failure of her relationship with Gebhard had opened her eyes to what she had passed up for the sake of money, and her money had taught her that a place in Society was not worth its price. All that was left to her, it seemed, was a brave face, her work, and the ability to shop. Besides, she knew herself now. She recognised the terrible bargain she had struck and it was no longer the world that saddened her or made her afraid. But her masks, to a certain extent, had become habit. She was at last a fusion of real and adopted selves, the product of her choice and its disguise. She was left with a repertoire that was reduced and instinctive; with the one persona, in fact, that she had wanted to reject.

Ironically the mask that now fitted, without effort or affection, was the one that Wilde had foreseen. It was that of Mrs Erlynne. If Lillie could not, or would not, be Mrs Erlynne on the stage, in private there were no such difficulties. She was not, it is true, called upon to make any great sacrifices, but she withstood dishonour, and that took both wit and courage, and she maintained, at enormous cost to her energies, the discipline of her frivolous and charming veneer. It was this latter quality that in the end made people characterize her as hard. She came to expect the same self-discipline from those around her. She looked at life with calm calculation and was intolerant of the weakness of panic or muddle in her adherents. Her letters, from the 1890s on, are business-like in their concerns and in the routine exercise of her charm. Across the top of one such, inviting him to lunch for old time's sake, even her friend Clement Scott scrawled, 'What does she want – that is the question.' In these years, to those around her, Lillie was the spectacle of her public self, a vision seen always at one remove, through the eyes of others – a marvel, a goddess, inhuman in her beauty and her rigour. Moreover, her standards were exacting, and many were afraid of her. Shortcomings in her followers made her momentarily unkind. Her 'passion for beauty', one account remarks, was so developed that

> . . . the sordid and ugly revolted her, made her cruel, and the man or woman whose reputation as a wit rested on a risqué story had short shrift at her hands. . . She abominated noise, confusion, mental or physical untidiness . . .

Sadly Lillie was unaware of the effect of this intolerance on the more fragile members of her entourage. Jeanne in particular was in awe of her mother and her moods. Though Lillie adored her daughter, the childhood she gave her was far from cosy. As soon as she could Lillie had Jeanne with her as she trailed across one continent or another on her endless tours. The hours would have been odd, the places constantly changing. Though Jeanne often had her grandmother, Mrs Le Breton, for company, there were no friends of her own age on the private trains or in the hotels. Inured to the hardships of the actor's life, Lillie expected her daughter to be so too. It would not have occurred to her that Jeanne was lonely or under unnatural strain. When she stopped touring, Lillie did what she could to give Jeanne the fun that other children enjoyed. Lord Esher's private diary has a rare account of seeing Lillie and her 'little niece' at a children's birthday party, but a tea party was no substitute for the security of a settled routine and proper education, or for the happiness of childish friendships. Ironically, had Lillie loved Jeanne less she might have made her more content by leaving her behind when she set off on her travels.

Jeanne was no match for her mother. A lonely and timid little girl, she adored her beautiful 'Tanty', but as she grew up, she grew dissatisfied. She must have seen Lillie's steely self-discipline, must have noticed her sadness; but if she did, she responded not with pity or admiration, but resentment. Later, to her own children, clamouring for details of their notorious but unknown grandmother, she had only bitter memories – interminable train rides across a foreign country, lonely months in grand apartments with only a French maid for company, her mother flitting in and out like a bird of paradise, absorbed in her own pursuits.

To Lillie it was very simple. She loved Jeanne and she wanted her with her. Generous-natured and instinctive, it did not occur to her that her daughter would be any different – but Jeanne was different. She saw Lillie's periodic cruelty to others and she was afraid, for Lillie was now both complicated and damaged. Suffering internally herself, if she spared her daughter, Lillie had no scruples about inflicting suffering on others. Meanness and gossip and any lack of grace were abominable to her. If by any unlucky chance they reflected on Lillie herself they became offences to be punished immediately and with severity. Once, having offered a junior member of her cast a lift, she stopped the carriage and had the woman put out, in dark and driving rain, and miles from home, because she made, during the journey, an inappropriate remark about Lillie's love life.

Like Mrs Erlynne, too, it was to women especially that Lillie was unforgiving. Mrs Erlynne operates in an exclusively male context. It is the men to whom she talks. Through their offices, her plans are put into effect and her designs realized. 'I am afraid of the women . . .' she observes, with only partial truth. 'The men I can always manage.' To say that Lillie was afraid of women is disingenuous – scornful would have been nearer the mark, or at best impatient.

Amy Leslie, who had taken up journalism after a life as a prima donna of the operetta, included a sketch of her, as she was in the nineties, in her book, *Some Players*. She makes it abundantly clear that she found Lillie terrifying, but she provides us, probably unwittingly, with a most vivid picture of the creature Lillie had made of herself. 'The Langtry home', runs part of her account,

> was a place of rest and infinite quiet. No laughter except that of pretty Jeanne or a sympathetic ripple joining hers from her mother. Mrs Langtry, however, very rarely laughs. She smiles with her exquisite eyes and her lips, but a laugh is an extremity of license with her. Servants belonging to Mrs Langtry are machines of absolute perfection, and seldom guests are entertained there, and then only those of the most exceptional and exclusive character. Women rarely receive the flattering courtesies of the Langtry, and for obvious reasons do not seek them. She is witty and she is wise, is this radiant creature, whose beauty thrives on years and is unrivaled. It is the sort of beauty which must be studied closely in all turns of the sun and under the moon. Sometimes she does not even strike a watcher as good-looking, and an instant afterwards she melts into the most supernally exquisite of creatures. Once when Jeanne was a slip of a girl she went to Kentford to see the famous roses cut . . . She wrote every day to her mother, and when the great pile of letters came in to Mrs Langtry mornings, all of them were huddled over in a heap until the small scrawl from Jeanne appeared, and then without any pose at all, for she was not avowedly maternal to any extent, she would devour the contents of the child's letter, smiling temptingly all the time. She never seemed so beautiful to me as she did these minutes, when she stopped scoffing and mocking and philosophising, or betting or flirting, or the twenty other difficult things she seemed forever to be busy about. She always closed them reluctantly, whispering to herself, 'Sweet little Jeanne'.

It is a surprisingly sad account, the great face, in private, unlit by laughter; the only chink in her armour, the distant pleasure in her innocent daughter from across the gulf of experience. In place of Mammon, now there was discipline. Summing up her character, grateful to the protection afforded her by the effort of Lillie's manners, Leslie observes that, 'She has deep respect for many things, and though cold and cynical, her refinement and good breeding usually keep her covertly polite in the face of annoyance.'

One of the things Lillie did not have respect for was women reporters, among whom she would have included Amy Leslie. To her men friends, who now were mostly her business associates, her manager and her authors, she was a little more open. With them she was able to show her harder side without worrying that they would be shocked. She had a masculine ability to keep business and pleasure separate. To those who admired the steel, and saw there was still a heart beneath it, Lillie was a sincere and unaffected friend. Edward Michael, who had a hearty laugh and a chequered past, spent many years as her manager and his view of her, in his memoirs, *The Tramps of a Scamp*, is probably as sunny as it gets.

> For various reasons I had . . . made up my mind to offer my thanks for the suggestion she had conveyed to me, but, as I had made other arrangements, to regret the impossibility of acceptance.
> In a few moments the lady appeared.
> One of the curious traits of a really remarkable woman was that Mrs Langtry never 'made an entrance'; no apparent opening or shutting of doors, not the slightest noise, no commotion, no 'effect' – and a vision of beauty and grace suddenly stood before one . . . The vision approached me with a betwitching smile and outstretched hand.
> 'And so you are to look after my business? I am sure we shall get on together. And now we have to talk about money – most unpleasant is it not? But we will soon get it over. What are your views?'

Like a creature from another world, Lillie does not come into a room, she simply appears. Michael was powerless to resist, both emasculated and bewitched. He entered immediately on what he calls 'a long period of willing and delightful slavery'.

Once she had won him over they settled at once to business. Michael goes on to record his first impressions of her in her professional capacity.

> New to her as I then was, I was amazed at her grasp of affairs, her amazing insight, and her masculine power of instant decision.
> 'Let us not fuss, please' – a favourite phrase – was the keynote of all she did. She never hurried, never flustered, never made unneccessary talk, but with great dignity and decision would on quick consideration pronounce judgement, and that judgement was final. Quite rightly Mrs Langtry exacted obedience and loyalty from those who served her. Once she had decided to trust, her trust was unbounded, and she never again considered the recipient of her trust but as one capable and to be relied on.
> When she was decieved, there was no palliation for the offence; no excuse was accepted; her trust had been betrayed, and that to her was inexcusable. She would be hurt, for she had far more heart than she was given credit for, but she could not and would not endure stupidity or incompetency, and any lack of straightforwardness was with her unforgivable.

On another occasion Lillie asked Michael to organize a special train for her to go racing the following day. Michael remonstrated with her over the expense and was answered,

> 'Oh no, I think I know what I am doing. At least, I hope so.'
>
> She had her special and went racing, and in the evening, as the time drew perilously near for the curtain to rise, I stood on the steps of the theatre anxiously watching the street for her arrival. Up sailed my lady without a trace of hurry. I blurted out my anxiety, and told her that I had begun to fear that it would be necessary to dismiss the audience.
>
> 'Oh no,' she replied placidly, 'of course I knew exactly what time I had to be back here. And,' she smiled, 'even if you *had* to close the theatre the loss would have been mine, would it not? – so why your anxiety?' And what possible answer was there to this pitiless logic?
>
> 'And you need not worry about the expense of my special,' she went on. 'I am sure the £1,400 I have won will cover it – and leave a little over.'

If Amy Leslie's portrait is hampered by her inability to see beyond her fear of Lillie, Edward Michael's is that of a man who both loved and marvelled. Living, as she did, so stylishly and at ease, in a man's world, Lillie had no patience for others who were narrower in their scope than she was. Summing her up, Michael describes her as 'a woman with a man's brain' in business, and more broadly as,

> Possessing in a marked degree every feminine charm – wiles, fascination, and moods – she was at the same time possessed of an iron will power, immense courage, and a gift of instant decision . . .

These are the attributes of a diva. Mrs Erlynne's qualities were strictly feminine. Her redemption is her love for her child. In consequence, though she caught the fish for which she was angling, in the form of Lord Augustus, she had no power, no freedom, no fortune of her own, to hire and fire with, to gamble away, and to spend on private travel. These were things in which Lillie revelled. In particular she loved being in control, financially and emotionally, proving to herself again and again that she could manage her affairs better than any man.

Lillie gloried in the frank amazement of her employees. She liked to leave people like Michael dumbfounded, and she was not afraid, on occasion, of appearing pitiless, either in her logic or, more directly, in her actions. But she did have an openness about her professional dealings. She was even-handed. The informative Michael admired her plain-dealing and her business sense, but he admired, even more, her 'sportsmanship'. In her fifties, when she was playing the gruelling vaudeville circuit, he bumped into her outside her hotel. He asked her how she liked her new work and was told,

> I don't know that it is a branch of art I would choose for a permanency, but there is a lot of humour in the life, and if I were a queen I could not be treated with more courtesy and consideration. But there is absolutely no rest, and I hate having to play on Sundays, and twice at that. Abe Hummel, the famous lawyer, tells me that, no matter what the contract calls for, in some states I can refuse to play on Sunday – plead the 'blue' laws. But that would hardly be sporting, would it? They are giving me a huge salary, and I must do my best to make it profitable for my manager, mustn't I?

To set against this we have Charles Reade's description of her thespian superior, Ellen Terry, whose professional relationships smacked of the tantrum, and in whose company men were never allowed to relax or feel comfortable. Here is how he describes her. She was

> soft and yielding on the surface, egotistical below. *Varia et mutabilis*, always wanting something 'dreadful bad' today, which she does not want tomorrow, especially if you are weak enough to give it to her, or get it her. Hysterical, sentimental, hard as nails in money matters, but velvet on the surface. A creature born to please and to deceive. *Enfant gâtée, et enfant terrible*.

No wonder Michael considered himself to have landed on his feet. In fact, Lillie's 'sportsmanship' was, as he had noted, evidence that she had a heart. And her heart was a problem. Michael saw only the surface of the case, partly, of course, because Lillie did not desire him to see further. He saw her triumphant, and he saw her dangerous, and he even saw her hurt, on occasion. What he did not see was the depth of her disillusion. It was this, not her love of beauty, or hatred of the sordid or the ill-mannered, that motivated her cruelty. If she was like Mrs Erylnne now, in manner and outward appearance, she was even more so in herself. Despite her rejection of Wilde's final offering, despite her preference for her own way, Lillie found that it was not possible completely to control her invention. Wilde's play was as much a prophecy as a tribute. Lillie had tried to deny, or simply had not seen, the problem of effect. Life acts on us as much as we act on it, and in these first decades of her professional life Lillie was surprised to find that she was just as cheated as she was successful. She had thought that money would solve everything, including love, and she found that, though she did realize all of her material goals, it was increasingly as a diversion, to quash her recalcitrant heart. For she was born, and we must not forget it, with more heart than most. She might have said, with Mrs Erlynne, as Wilde had intended her to,

> I thought I had no heart. I find I have, and a heart doesn't suit me, Windermere. Somehow it doesn't go with modern dress. It makes one look old . . . And it spoils one's career at critical moments . . .

Wilde, with his mixture of flippancy and ruthless perception, had seen closer into Lillie's real self than anyone else, if only because the armour she used to cover it was his own. Mrs Erlynne continues,

> I suppose . . . you would like me to retire into a convent, or become a hospital nurse, or something of that kind, as people do in silly modern novels. That is stupid of you . . . in real life we don't do such things – not as long as we have any good looks left, at any rate. No – what consoles one nowadays is not repentance, but pleasure. Repentance is quite out of date. And besides, if a woman really repents, she has to go to a bad dressmaker, otherwise no one believes in her. And nothing in the world would induce me to do that.

Wilde was interested in the taint of the world, the Faustian pact between Innocence and Experience, and the irresistible, sapping, narcotic of luxury. Many of his characters, like Mrs Erlynne, are cast out of their Edens for seeing and doing too much. The 'overwhelming curiosity' of Lady Lonsdale, 'to know everything and experience every sensation', had its price. Those who had eaten of the tree of knowledge were pariahs, and the only antidote for its 'staring fury' was the 'blind lush leaf' of its neighbour, the tree of life. So, the tainted, with Mrs Erlynne, follow their senses. They migrate to warmer climes where life's pleasures, in the heat, are softer and more languid. The English climate, as she observes, doesn't suit them, and her complaint is theirs, and Lillie's:

> My – heart is affected here, and that I don't like. I prefer living in the south. London is too full of fogs and – serious people, Lord Windermere. Whether the fogs produce the serious people or the serious people produce the fogs, I don't know, but the whole thing rather gets on my nerves . . .

With the fallen in their self-imposed exile, goes the ghost of their innocence. For as long as they live it marks them out, haunting their gestures, pervading their weary charm, preventing them from ever starting afresh. And whenever they settle, to eke out their dislocated days in mild decadence, it pricks them with unease and makes them restless.

Just so, did Lillie, in the coming century, cross and recross the Atlantic, accruing property as she did money, or lovers, or racehorses, never resting, never at peace. She had houses in New York, California, Jersey, Bournemouth, Newmarket, London and Monte Carlo. She was a citizen of Jersey, England, Monaco and America. From place to place, and person to person, she slipped, belonging nowhere, and to no one. And always, bravely, she screened her sadness from view. Her scars were deep and were to deepen, but they were hidden; her veneer, just as it had been when she disembarked from the *Arizona*, so light, so elegant, so charming. The only thing against which she had no guard, and which now forced the pace, were the ineluctible ravages of old age.

LADY DE BATHE 1899 – 1929

Chapter XXXIV

Final Act

If, as the twentieth century dawned, people talked, because they did not know, and Lillie let them do so, this was partly a matter of habit. It was also because she had nothing to hide, except her sorrow. The last decade of the nineteenth century had been a particularly bad one. In 1895 Wilde was convicted of homosexual practices and imprisoned in Reading gaol. What Lillie really thought about this is impossible to know, although it is likely she thought less of him for courting his own destruction so foolishly than she did for committing 'the crime' itself. Part of her reaction would have been motivated by panic. Wilde had been her guide for so long. Indeed he had taught her how to survive, and now here he was flinging himself unnecessarily, and with apparent unconcern, over a precipice of public disgrace. For Lillie, so close to the edge herself, it was all too dangerous and to her shame she shied away. In his biography of Wilde, Richard Ellmann observes (the italics are mine), '*Even* Lillie Langtry talked against him at this time.' But if in his moments of trial she disowned him, she was strong enough to be rather absurdly loyal later. At her villa in Monaco, in the 1920s, she kept an empty seat at her dining-table, 'in memory of dear Oscar'. When one of her guests remonstrated with her, pointing out that he was a convicted homosexual, she snapped back at him, 'You fool, you don't understand. Oscar was a very versatile man.'

So Lillie was left, as the 1890s drew to a close, to face the new century alone. In 1897 her Australian horse Merman, racing shoeless, Antipodean style, won the Cesarewitch. Lillie was the first woman to receive this prize, and the celebrations were extensive and very public. Her own bet of ten thousand pounds, on odds of eight to one, gave her a win of eighty thousand pounds, in addition to which she collected the prize purse of thirty-nine thousand more. She could afford to be lavish, and that evening gave a small party at Regal Lodge.

Late the same night, with the festivities in full swing, she received the news that Ned Langtry had died, insane with drink, in Chester asylum, an hour before the Cesarewitch had been run. He had been found, by the police, emaciated and incoherent, wandering aimlessly along a railway line, having sustained some injury to his head. His cuts were attended to and he was released. Later that evening he was found again, in a cab yard, on a heap of straw, unconscious and smelling of alcohol. On claiming that he was Lillie Langtry's husband he had been taken to the lunatic asylum, where he subsequently died.

The news of Lillie's win and the death of her husband hit the papers together the following morning, and the juxtaposition of the two was not favourable. A number of rumours immediately sprang up: that Lillie had organized his murder at the hands of hired thugs, that Ned had thrown himself in front of the Irish Mail as it ran into Chester Station, that Lillie herself had been on the train and that she had ordered a wreath to be sent to his funeral made up of flowers in her racing colours. So fierce were the attacks that George Lewis and Lillie's brother Clement, who now jointly handled her affairs, rushed into print to defend her. Lewis's statement ran as follows:

> Mrs Langtry states with reference to the report that Mr Langtry was found with only a few pence in his pocket, that Mrs Langtry had since her separation from her husband many years ago, regularly made him an adequate allowance. As soon as she heard of his condition she at once forwarded to the authorities at Chester sufficient money for his immediate wants. The allowance paid by Mrs Langtry was in addition to the income which Mr Langtry derived from his Irish property.

The funeral took place in Chester, and the streets were lined with crowds all hoping to catch sight of Lillie as she passed. She did not attend. Instead she sent a large wreath of lilies of the valley and violets, tied with a purple ribbon. The card attached read simply, 'In Remembrance – Lillie Langtry'. The final irony was that only a few months earlier, this same year, at the third attempt, Lillie's divorce in the American courts had come through, along with her American citizenship. At the inquest it was revealed, by Ned's valet, that he had become increasingly morose over her insistence on formalizing their separation, so perhaps there was something in it, and she had unwittingly hastened his death after all. Nevertheless, it had been a long and rocky road, and she had at the outset believed herself in love with him. Some, at least, of the 'Remembrance' would have been painful.

For Lillie, however, there was a small silver lining. Once Ned was dead she could, and did, take Jeanne into a limited confidence about her parentage. Jeanne, who was now seventeen, was told that Lillie was her mother, not her aunt. She was also told, or allowed to believe, that Ned was her father. This was in deference to Jeanne's already overdeveloped sense of the proprieties of life. Lillie hoped to protect her from the disgrace of illegitimacy, but she loved her too well not to claim her as her own once the opportunity arose.

In 1899, as though she had not been more than once bitten, Lillie married a much younger man, Hugo de Bathe, for no apparent reason, since he had little to recommend him beyond a middle-ranking title. She was forty-seven, he twenty-seven. In the eyes of the world, the marriage could not look other than wholly ridiculous. Moreover, Hugo was not kind to her, and openly consorted with chorus girls. There is a story of Lillie arriving at a restaurant with a party of friends, to find him entertaining several ladies at another table. The arrangement, in his eyes, was clearly financial, since he had no money beyond a tiny income. What Lillie's reasons were who can tell – loneliness, perhaps, or resistance to middle age. Hearing the news, Wilde, released from prison and living in France, is supposed to have remarked circuitously on a 'famous actress' of his acquaintance 'who, after a tragic domestic life, has married a fool. She thought that because he was stupid, he would be kindly, when, of course, kindliness requires both intellect and imagination.'

Lillie's focus, however ill-founded, was now temporarily domestic. She bought a cottage overlooking the sea on Jersey and called it Merman after her horse. She had, in theory, her new marriage for security, and she had Jeanne, who was fast approaching womanhood. In 1898 Lillie had made a formal announcement of the fact that she was retiring from the stage in order to concentrate on her private life. She worried about having Jeanne presented and wrote to the Prince of Wales asking for his help. He wrote back rather guardedly, saying that he could not see why not: 'Honestly I see no reason why there should be a difficulty – but it is always best to study the "pros" and "cons"!' He urged her to discuss the matter with her old friend Gladys Lonsdale, now Lady de Grey, which she duly did. Gladys had lost none of her broadness of mind over the years, and was helpful and sympathetic. The arrangements were made and Jeanne came out in style, the Prince remarking genially that he was delighted, and that, 'C'est le premier pas qui coute!'

*

At the end of 1899 the Boer War broke out. Hugo embarked for battle, with relief, and Lillie returned to the stage. She also returned to America, with Jeanne and a rather provocative play called *The Degenerates*. She was given a tumultuous welcome, but there was more sadness in store. The following year, in 1900, Wilde died, in exile like so many of his characters, and estranged from many of his former friends. But the worst was still to come. In 1902 Jeanne, kept in ignorance of her paternity all this time, heard a version of the truth and broke with her mother.

In June of that year Jeanne had been married with great ceremony to Ian Malcolm. Her mother, of course, regardless of male precedent, gave her away. This was a public profession of the deepest involvement. It was not a privilege Lillie was prepared to delegate. The night before the wedding, there had been a grand reception at which all the wedding presents had been displayed. Jeanne, who was also on show, had been asked by the old Society wasp Margot Asquith, waving her hand over the gorgeous array before her, which of the gifts had been given by her father. When she said innocently that he had given nothing since Ned was dead, Margot replied with a laugh that she meant Jeanne's real father – Battenberg – and repeated her question. Jeanne left the room in a state of virtuous shock.

For several months after their wedding, the Malcolms avoided Lillie. Finally in October Lillie wrote the following letter:

> My darling Jeanne,
>   Your two letters and the flowers reached me about 12 o'clock today under other circumstances it would have been a great joy to receive such a token of thought on your part but to day it was so painful to me that I could not bear to look at them and sent the flowers to the Chelsea Children's Hospital. I think darling that the time has come for some sort of explanation. You have been in town all this week and have never been near me and in all your letters have refrained from expressing any desire to see me. I wondered whether Ian didn't want you to come but remembering that he and you accepted the hospitality of Merman Cottage and came *here* during my absence that *can't* be the reason. Anyhow whatever it is I should like to know for I feel that I have nothing to reproach myself with – if it is only a mis-understanding let us end it for it is a very un-natural state of affairs. I think I have always shown you my intense love for you – & to be in the same town with you and not see you makes me so wretched that I am quite ill. Please darling write me a nice letter and with love to you &

Ian and hoping to see you both on your return.

Always you devoted Mère'

In return Lillie received a cold reply in a cramped little hand full of the petty morality the Le Bretons most despised. Jeanne talked of shattered ideals and loss of respect, of the 'strong man' she had married, whose compassion in the face of such utter disgrace had saved her from madness. All these combined, she argued, had 'killed all the affection in me'. Her letter was small-minded and, as Lillie said, 'unnatural'. For all Lillie's wild pursuits, for all her tattier associations and her riotous appetites, she was still splendid in her big-heartedness, giant in comparison with the gnat-whine of her progeny. Nor was it her husband who had encouraged Jeanne to make the break. Like most of his sex Ian Malcolm found Lillie's nature warm, her counsel astute and her company refreshing. For years afterwards, his daughter recalls, whenever he had a problem or needed advice, he would take a cab and go and talk it out with Lillie. But Jeanne was still cold, maintaining a silence, that, in the context of the open friendship of her husband, must have been all the more bitter to her anguished and ageing mother.*

What was there left with Jeanne gone? Only Lillie's habit of sensible cheerfulness – and work. Now Lillie turned in earnest to the stage. She would do anything, mediocre modern plays, 'one-night stands', the degrading but lucrative vaudeville circuit, a silent movie, anything that kept her busy and dulled the eternal ache. Reporters in New York who asked whether she was happy were offered a snappish but candid statement:

Of course I am happy, as happiness goes, for a woman who has so many memories and lives the lonely life of an actress. It is restricted, as all artistic life necessarily must be. I've often put in as many as forty weeks on the stage in a single year, so you might say I've had precious little opportunity to brood or feel sorry for myself. I've sometimes been accused of lacking sentimentality, a quality I haven't been able to afford, and I think that is all to the good.

* This was a sorrow that, had he not died two years earlier, Lillie might have shared with Wilde. On the loss of his own son, he wrote from prison,

I bore up against everything with some stubbornness of will and much rebellion of nature till I had absolutely nothing left in the world but Cyril. I had lost my name, my position, my happiness, my freedom, my wealth . . . But I still had one beautiful thing left, my own eldest son. Suddenly he was taken away from me by the law. It was a blow so appalling that I did not know what to do . . .

The last sentence was a straight lie, uttered to bolster herself, in the face of encroaching old age and a misery that was fast becoming hard to ignore. All her life it had been Lillie's policy, whenever anything hurt, to turn her back and maintain that she had never cared about it in the first place.

But it was not all bad. Lillie had her friends still, even if she had neither husband nor daughter to comfort her.

In 1902 the Prince of Wales was crowned King in Westminster Abbey. Eccentrically Lillie's memoirs make no mention of the Coronation, though she attended, sitting with Alice Keppel, Daisy Warwick and Sarah Bernhardt, in what was termed 'the King's Loose Box'. As King there must have been less time for the theatre and the intimate teas, and with her own schedule full of transatlantic commitments Lillie cannot have seen much of her friend once he was crowned. More and more now she found her friends in her profession.

There is one last extensive correspondence that has survived, in which we can listen, if we will, to Lillie's real voice for the last time: sad but strong, warm, industrious and undeniably game. The letters are between her and a writer called Paul Kester, the author of several of the plays that were the staple of her repertoire in the early 1900s. Lillie was fifty, but well preserved. She was still attractive, but she was tired of men and their demands. Instead she found all that she needed in her friendships. The warmth of her open expressions of affection is surprising, after the years of disguise and manipulation. They are also the clearest and saddest indication of the ravages of time.

Lillie's writing is characteristically lacking in self-pity. Always she finds something to look forward to. Always she is generous with her fading energies, giving everything to her profession and those who practised it with her. In 1903, on tour again in America, she writes easily, slipping lightly from business to pleasure and back,

> One little line dear Mr Kester to say that we put the new scene on last night and I think it is a *great* improvement. In spite of a dull passion week audience I feel convinced that the Fouche scene was better understood I miss you so *much* You made life possible even in one night stands! I do hope you are feeling fairly well. My warmest regards to your mother . . .
> Excuse scrawl writing in gloves with a pin.

Professionally Lillie was now confident in her insights. Many of her letters contain detailed instructions about what to cut and what to expand in certain scenes. She knew her own dramatic strengths and she knew her audience's expectations, and she made sure that every play catered amply for both. Later on in the tour, when she reached Michigan, Lillie wrote again from her hotel.

> My dear author,
>   I shall be quite ready to work from 2 o'clock. I have walked between 5 and 6 miles – had a bath shampooed my hair and feel better at 4 o'clock I must sleep!

Obviously she was tired. She was no longer young, but she never complained. If her schedule was gruelling she would keep herself fit, and to do so she now walked daily, as Baird had taught her, in several jerseys.

These two letters had been written in April 1903. By June she was back at Kentford, resting and looking over her racehorses. She wrote again.

> My dear Mr Kester,
>   I was so glad to get your letter and to hear that I am missed just a little. I am having a delightful Whitsuntide holiday at my little place near Newmarket. I am you may be sure *walking* enormously and getting myself *fit* for my next season's work. I haven't yet seen Frohman but expect to do so next week. The time will soon pass and I shall be on my way back out again to America and *You* Meantime are you working hard? I suppose you must be. Claude Lowther's play was so *awful* that Tree had to take it off in 10 days. The shortest run a play ever had in London Ellen Terry is not doing well. I think she is past it – Hugely fat There are no good plays in London or Paris. Granier comes over with Les deux Echoles and Sarah B's only novelty is 'Iris' in French – I wish you were here this minute the nightingales are singing delightfully and the may is in full bloom. Mrs Ten Brock is enchanted with our English country – and is I think enjoying her visit altogether. My kindest regards to Mrs Kester and may I say love to your dear self, Lillie Langtry.

If Lillie in her quieter moments was feeling her mortality at last, it was some comfort to know that the 'great and enchanting Nell' was doing so too. Moreover, although Lillie's acting was competent and her takings more than adequate, she had never won the admiration of the intellectuals. Ellen Terry and Mrs Patrick Campbell were the darlings of the great playwrights, revered as much for their intelligence as for their dramatic technique. Bernard Shaw, faced with the prospect of Lillie starring in *Captain Brassbound*, wrote with dread to the 'great Nell', begging her to save him by taking the role herself. The letter runs,

Mr Bernard Shaw's compliments to Miss Ellen Terry.

Mr Bernard Shaw has been approached by Mrs Langtry with a view to the immediate and splendid production of 'Captain Brassbound's Conversion' at the Imperial Theatre.

Mr Bernard Shaw, with the last flash of a trampled out love, has repulsed Mrs Langtry with a petulance bordering on brutality.

Mr Bernard Shaw has been actuated in this ungentlemanly and unbusinesslike course by an angry desire to seize Miss Ellen Terry by the hair and make her play Lady Cicely.

Mr Bernard Shaw would be glad to know whether Miss Ellen Terry wishes to play Martha at the Lyceum instead.

Mr Bernard Shaw will go to the length of keeping a minor part open for Sir Henry Irving when Faust fails, if Miss Ellen Terry desires it.

Mr Bernard Shaw lives in daily fear of Mrs Langtry recovering sufficiently from her natural resentment of his ill manners to reopen the subject.

Mr Bernard Shaw begs Miss Ellen Terry to answer this letter.

Mr Bernard Shaw is looking for a new cottage or house in the country and wants advice on the subject.

Mr Bernard Shaw craves for the sight of Miss Ellen Terry's once familiar handwriting.

Despite Shaw's reservations Lillie was resolutely busy. Back in America in November, her energies were unchecked, and she was thinking of new plays for the coming season. From Buffalo she writes,

Dear Mr Kester
    I am re-reading 'Diana of the Crossways' *Do* dramatise it for me – we should make a fortune. *Do it quick* before I am too old or someone else does it. I think it should begin with her married life there's nothing dramatic till then and think of the wealth of dialogue to pick from – I can't think *why* it hasn't been done. Bar black eyes I could look the part couldn't I? *She* was Greek type. I could play it this season and get it right.
    Yours always,
    Lillie Langtry

There is something very sad about Lillie's clinging to the myth of her Greek type as she approached sixty. In their almost childish egotism, and their impatient energy, her letters are most reminiscent of her first expression of her ambitions to Lord Wharncliffe. In just the same way, the questions are rhetorical. There is a buoyancy and a confidence behind them that denies refusal, and also, in both, a note of pleading that it would be unmanly to ignore. This perverse but entirely characteristic combination of insistence and need lies at the back of all Lillie's relationships with men throughout her life. To find it surfacing again now, is a strange echo across the decades of emotional waste that lay between her twenties and her fifties; a testament to Lillie's superhuman resilience, to her energy and to her self-belief.

Lillie had followed to the letter her father's dictum of truth to the self. Fundamentally, though battle-torn, she was herself underneath, as she had always been. She had adapted to alteration in circumstance or public mood only in order to survive. She had developed and then worn her masks in protection of a kernel that could not be crushed or altered. Sensitive to every fad and fashion she had trimmed her sails, like Gladys Lonsdale and Patsy Cornwallis West, in the babyhood of her career, and through it all had managed to return to her starting point. Now it was the world about her that was unstable, and what she valued late in life were the things that stood still among the maelstrom. She adapted to the twentieth century. She coped with the motor car, and the flapper dress, and the horror of the First World War. Clement, Hugo de Bathe and Ian Malcolm were all commissioned, and Lillie watched them go. She donated her profits to the Red Cross and remained on stage solidly, between 1914 and 1918, travelling with sublime unconcern back and forth across the Atlantic despite the threat of storm and U-boat. In 1916, aged sixty-three, still writing to Kester, she records her itinerary on tour across the States:

> My dear Paul,
>   I am so disappointed not to see you again this week. From here I go to
>
> | Davis Theatre | Pittsburg |
> | Keiths | Columbus |
> | Keiths | Cincinnati |
> | Keiths | Cleveland |
>
> So *do* come onto one of those – the sooner the better . . .
> Its always a joy to meet you again You seem always the same dear person . . .

To Lillie, Kester is always 'the *same* dear person'. Those who were not fickle, or currying favour, those who accepted and loved and did not judge were highly prized.

Indeed Lillie's world was changing too fast even for her. In 1910 her old and true friend the Prince, now Edward VII had died. Lillie had been called to Buckingham Palace, which she had entered by her customary side-door, to find Queen Alexandra with a restorative glass of brandy and the bequest of the King's favourite terrier, in a collar which read 'I am Caesar the King's dog'. Caesar did not long outlive his lord, and with everything precious to Lillie ether dead or deaf to her entreaties, England had little left to offer. For a while she had continued defiant. Photographs at this date show her mouth set, at her most masculine, in an attempt to drown out the voices of her lost past. She towers, inappropriate in white lace, over slight young men at Goodwood, or stamps down the London pavements military style, lantern–jawed, heavily upholstered, arms swinging and toes turned out. Gone are the soft smile, the curves and the sleepily sensuous eyes. Now she is angry and huge and male.

Jeanne's defection had broken Lillie. She continued to act for some time, but only because there was nothing else. The generation of wealth had lost its point. Eventually, like Mrs Erlynne, she left the shores where the serious people were and which her heart found so painful. When the war ended she gave up the stage for good. Within a week she had sold her house and moved into the Savoy until Hugo returned. Then she sold her racehorses and Regal Lodge, and she bought a villa for Hugo in Nice, and one for herself on the mountainside above the sea in Monaco, where Jones, her old love, now married, was rather incongruously master of the Monaco hunt.

Here for the last time she made a garden, losing herself once more in the pleasures of planning and planting. In the evenings she could slip down to the casino and gamble away her useless fortune. Watching her as she moved between the tables, the glitter of the gambler in her eyes, an English MP observed,

> She did not appear sour nor even seriously depressed, though there was an uneasy look of baulked longing as she wandered from table to table . . . She had still all the airs of the beauty that had devastated so many hearts, but the figure had become somewhat stout. There was not a trace of that wonderful symmetry of the olden days. Above all she was always alone: she whom crowds of fashionable people had crushed against each other just for a glimpse.

So she was alone in the end, alone and unsatisfied. And she was so, as Wilde had foreseen, because she had tried to match pleasure that was sensual against pain that was of the heart, and found there was never enough. She was restless, because she had the misfortune to have a heart in the first place. And she was a spectacle, to be weighed and judged by strangers, haunted by her beauty, which they delighted in finding gone – but which flitted like a ghost in the movements of her hands, or the turn of her head.

From time to time Lillie came back to England to visit her old friends, though this was always painful to her. On one such occasion she lunched with Belasco, a fellow actor, and leaning towards him across the table, clutched at her heart. 'If the world could see the turmoil going on here,' she told him, 'it would be startled beyond words. I have lost my daughter, the only thing that is dear to me. My life is sad indeed.' Sad, too, was how Ira Goldsmith, in her employ in Monaco for a while, described her. 'All that I care to say of the Lily is that she was the saddest woman I have ever known . . . Many a night I have known her to cry herself to sleep.' Ironically, her sadness was now as much of a commodity as her beauty had been. Her public found it titillating and every interview she gave contained the question 'Are you happy?' To the press, Lillie was still cheerful. Asked about the pain of growing old before her reputation, she replied with a laugh, 'Don't let that worry you . . . I have long since got accustomed to that startled look in people's eyes. They expect to see the Lillie Langtry that was. They see instead a prosaic old grandmother.'

To friends, Lillie dropped the pretence. Newman Flower, a publisher who got to know and like Lillie in the 1920s, remembered going to see her to discuss her memoirs:

> I was shown into a room where the litter of lunch still lingered – two used table-napkins thrown across the table, two stained glasses, an empty bottle, a cigarette-end still smouldering in a glass ash-tray . . .
>   She came in presently. There was no make-upon her face. She was depressed and unhappy. Restive. She pulled out a chair and sat corner-wise on it. She pushed the plates and glasses aside in a noisy clatter.

Not surprisingly Flower's project to produce Lillie's memoirs was stalled. She could not face it. Elsewhere, Flower noted that what made Lillie interesting was the way in which 'she strove to keep herself alive after that particular social world, which she had queened, was dead. She always appeared,' he recalled, 'to be a lingering leaf on an autumn tree which hangs on and will not die or perish beneath the blast of winter, because it has once belonged to a never-to-be-forgotten summer. She could not let go. She fought in order not to let go.'

One of the ways in which Lillie kept going was by remembering her glory. To her old friend Daisy Warwick she announced that she did not intend to grow old – 'Why shouldn't beauty vanquish time?' she asked. Daisy, who was unable to see beneath Lillie's gay veneer, took the comment at face value and read a rare moral lecture:

> I stole a glance at her and certainly Time's ravages . . . were disguised with consummate artistry, while her figure was still lovely.
>
> But it came to me then that there was tragedy in the life of this woman, whose beauty had once been world-famous, for she had found no time in the intervals of pursuing pleasure to secure contentment for the evening of her day. Now that she saw the evening approach, Lillie Langtry could only protest that it was not evening at all, but just the prolongation of a day that was, in truth, already dead.

In fact, there was little for Daisy to crow about, since she had prepared so ill for her own evening that she was reduced to selling the King's love letters.

In 1925, without the help of Newman Flower, and to keep herself going, Lillie produced her own version of the 'never-to-be-forgotten summer', *The Days I Knew*.

Most people complained that her memoirs were anodyne. They contained no gossip, no new information. There were no references to the Prince of Wales as her lover, no mention of Louis Battenberg, Lord Shrewsbury or Arthur Jones, and no mention of her daughter Jeanne. To another publisher Lillie had once remarked, 'You don't really think I would ever do such a thing as to write my real *reminiscences*, do you?' So why did she, so honest in everything else, bother to write at all? Simply because that was how she would have it. It was the life she wished she had led, purged of the struggle and its tormenting price. Whether she knew it or not, for one last time she was flying in the face of Wilde's teaching. 'To reject one's own experiences,' he had warned, 'is to arrest one's own development. To deny one's own experiences is to put a lie in the lips of one's own life. It is no less than a denial of the Soul.'

If Lillie had kissed her world goodbye and chosen to weep out her grief on a foreign shore, she would have been the last person to wallow in it. In her very last years her constant companion was a woman called Mathilde

Peat. She had been married to Lillie's butler and had stayed with Lillie after her husband's death. She was absolute in her devotion, and this final relationship – which ironically lasted longer than any of Lillie's loves, and was with a woman – was a comfort. Mathilde was something between lady's maid and admiring sister. Having someone to impress kept Lillie's spirits up. On one occasion they took a long walk together in the Rockies. On the way back to the hotel, according to Lillie, they stopped at a gem shop,

> The jew shopkeeper hurried out and invited myself and Mrs Peat to enter. We did and looked at some fine opals. While doing so I told him of our long walk – 'Are you not tired?' said he – 'Not at all' I replied and in order to impress the fact on him I kicked high one leg after the other – 'Well!' he exclaimed 'you *are* active . . .' needless to say one celebrity was as another to him. He took me for Sarah Bernhardt.

There is a glimmer of the old 'go' about Lillie's enjoyment of the jeweller's mistake, if not about the high kicks themselves. She continued to find things to laugh about, to entertain Mathilde.

She took and read half a dozen newspapers and magazines a day, and kept abreast of world events. She even managed a rather stilted reconciliation with Jeanne, and was allowed to see her grandchildren. But it was too little and too late. She had suffered and been damaged beyond repair. There was nothing real to live for any more.

In the end, it seems, Lillie simply decided to die. In 1928 she had returned to England for Christmas. She was already unwell, from a bout of bronchitis suffered in the autumn, and the old climate did not help. In London she developed pleurisy and, as though she knew what was happening, revised her will, making Mathilde a serious beneficiary. It read in part,

> To my friend Mathilde Marie Peat as a token of affection and gratitude, a legacy of 10,000 pounds, all my wearing apparel, furs, jewellery, electro plate, Sheffield plate silver tea pot, milk jug, sugar basin and hot water jug generally used by me, my motor car, my villa known as Le Lys Monaco together with the entire contents with the exception of any articles otherwise specifically bequeathed . . .

This done, Lillie headed back to Monaco and Mathilde. In February she caught flu. According to Mathilde, who watched faithfully by the bedside,

When she knew that she had influenza we talked together, and she felt then that she would never get out of that bed. You see she knew that her heart was weak. Indeed it was her heart that was not strong enough to stand the attack. I made her room a picture of flowers, but nothing could make her believe that she would pull through. Gradually she sank lower and lower.

It is hard to avoid the echoes of Mrs Erlynne, or the element of choice in Lillie's refusal to believe in her recovery. Everything was done that could be done, to persuade her of the charms of the world she was leaving, but she knew better. Her heart had no fight left; her indomitable self-belief was gone. Mathilde's account continues,

I would talk with her after the doctors left her each day, but always she would shake her beautiful head and say, 'I know I'm at the end. I shall never get better dear.'

As the time went on she became more and more sad about leaving me. For the sixteen years we were together we were always so happy for she was so jolly and full of fun and so fond of helping younger people. Only last night she said to me: 'I am going dear, I am very, very sorry, but I am going. Goodbye.'

So Lillie slipped, broken and sick in heart, from the world that had stared and spoiled. Perhaps it had trapped her. Certainly it had taught her to want too much. She had sold herself for its admiration and in the bitterness of alienation, she had found that wherever she looked she remained a spectacle. Warmth and affection seemed denied her. And if she asked for it the world shone back at her unyielding, with the brass of her own reflection.

Back and forth across the Atlantic banner headlines screamed Lillie's death. And the world gobbled and moralized and misunderstood. It was Burne-Jones who had said, when she was only twenty-six, 'She isn't fit for a tragedy and I'm glad of it and hope she will never know what a bad word it is.' But Society on both continents felt differently. If she suffered in the end, then that was as it should be.

That Lillie had contributed to her own tragedy is undeniable. Selling her soul was her own choice, and she knew it. But it was her heart, bartered but never quashed, that made her punishment so keenly felt. This was both her glory and her undoing. For her affections were deep and true, and the rejection of her daughter, the secret she had kept, like

Mrs Erlynne, not out of delicacy for herself so much as to spare the blushes of Jeanne, cast her adrift on an old age of unbearable loneliness. If she had felt betrayed in this, she would have been justified.

So Lillie retired, her beauty, as O'Connor so unkindly observed, dead – worn out like a garment before its owner. And even so, when she went to the casino in her seventies, she was watched. Wherever she went she had to suffer the discomfort of public attention, the cold interest in the phenomenon, the stare, the pointed finger. People noted her downfall with satisfaction, remarked on her sadness as though she were a separate species. Still the unreality of the goddess clung about her, the vestments of Venus, untouchable, and other-worldly, hung in tatters from her shoulders. Just so does Graham Robertson, who so poetically celebrated her arrival behind the Barnes bus, close his account of her in his memoirs. And just so will we let her go at last:

> I never saw much of Mrs Langtry, though she came to my studio on several occasions and we met from time to time. It was good to know her, for the bending of her head and throat as she bowed in recognition was a thing never to be forgotten; it was good to hear her speak and to find her voice an added charm, but I could never feel that she had actual existence – the fantastic unreality of a dream was about her; she was a 'Museum Piece', and subconsciously I missed the glass case and the plain-clothes policeman.

Acknowledgements

The writing of a book like this involves so many people that it seems almost unfair to put only one person's name on the spine. I am deeply indebted to Mary McFadyean, Lillie's granddaughter, who has given me most generous and consistent support over the several years that this project has taken. I am also indebted to Richard Macnutt who was instrumental in finding the Jones correspondence and negotiating its access. Without the help of these two, this book would simply never have been written.

With enviable clarity of mind and with a gentle professionalism my editor, Penelope Hoare, has cleaned and trimmed and organised, for all of which I am grateful. Tim Jeal helped with the beginnings of research, as did, at various stages: Anthony le Gallais, Jones's descendant; Patricia de Montfort, at Glasgow University; Pamela Hamilton Howard, at the Langtry Manor Hotel; Joanne Adair, at the Belfast Record Office; and Sister Domingo, at the Dominican Convent in Belfast. Dr Terence Pepper was unaccountably generous with his help over photographic research. Matthew Sturgis gave advice and put me onto Graham Robertson. I would also like to thank Alan Palmer who read the MS. He helped greatly with the complexities of a background that I had treated high-handedly. Any shortcomings or distortions that have survived are of course, my own.

For the use of invaluable archive material I must acknowledge the gracious permission of Her Majesty the Queen, both for papers from the Royal Archive and also for material of which her Majesty is the copyright holder. I am indebted to Viscount Esher for permission to quote from the Esher Papers held at Churchill College, Cambridge; to Merlin Holland and the Estate of Oscar Wilde for my extensive use of Wilde's letters; to the New York Public Library, Astor, Lennox and Tilden Foundations, for the use of Lillie's correspondence with Clement Scott and Paul Kester; to the British Library for Abraham Hayward's letters to

Gladstone; to the Glasgow University Library, Department of Special Collections, for material from the Whistler Collection; to the Sheffield Record Office for the Wharncliffe correspondence. Quotations from the diary of Wilfrid Scawen Blunt are by permission of the Syndics of the Fitzwilliam Museum to whom rights in this publication are assigned. For the letters of Randolph Churchill, I gratefully acknowledge Curtis Brown on behalf of Peregrine S. Churchill, Trustee Lord Randolph Papers.

My own particular debts are to John Nutting who talked the book with me, over several years, with generous and unfailing enthusiasm, acted as a lending library, and read the first draft. I would also like to thank Peter Baring, whose kind and originally unacknowledged help I could not have done without. And, finally, I am grateful to Valerie Child for her printer and for so many dead mice.

To Nicholas and to my own family my debt is beyond expression.

Notes

The main sources for this book, as outlined in the Introduction, are Lillie's own memoirs, *The Days I Knew* (G. Doran, N.Y. 1925); the archive of letters from Lillie to her lover Arthur Jones and those from Lillie to Lord Wharncliffe. Quotations from the letters are identified in the text itself and will therefore be sourced in the notes only the first time and not at all afterwards. Quotations from the memoirs are also so obvious as to make it unnecessary to note the source each time. Anecdotes that are unacknowledged in the notes are therefore from the memoirs.

The other books that I have gratefully relied on for information are the previous biographies of Lillie: Brough, James, *The Prince and the Lily* (London 1975); Dudley, Ernest, *The Gilded Lily* (London 1958); Gerson, Noel, *Lillie Langtry, Because I Loved Him* (London 1971). All of these were written prior to the discovery of the Arthur Jones letters, and are therefore ignorant of this central phase of Lillie's life. A later source, though not a life of Lillie, is Theo Aronson's *The King in Love* (London, 1988). These books are referred to in the notes simply by the name of the author ie. Brough, Dudley, Gerson, Aronson.

The two quotations used as epigraphs for the book are taken respectively from contemporary memoirs, Lady Augusta Fane's *Chit Chat* (London 1926), and Mrs Claude Beddington's *All That I Have Met* (London 1929)

Chapter One: An Introduction
Page
2: For information on late Victorian and Edwardian Society I have used, among others, S. Nowell-Smith ed. *Edwardian England* (1964); K. Middlemass, *The Life and Times of Edward VII* (1972) and G.M. Young, *Victorian England, Portrait of an Age* (1936)
3: 'Mrs Langtry rose . . .' see Richard Ellmann, *Oscar Wilde* (1987) p106

4: 'The Lily is so tiresome . . .' This comes from Walford Graham Robertson's elegant and evocative memoir *Time Was* (1931) p70

7: 'If poets read into her face . . .' The *Telegraph*, February 1929

Chapter Two: Family and Childhood
Page

13: The queens of the Edwardian stage. For information in general on Lillie's fellow actresses I have consulted their own memoirs. These are: Sarah Bernhardt, *My Double Life* (London 1907); Mrs Patrick Campbell, *My Life and Some Letters*; and Ellen Terry, *The Story of My Life*

21: 'When I was young . . .' Clare Sheppard, *Lobster at Littlehampton* (1995) pp112–13. '. . . it was always with me . . .' Edward Michael, *Tramps of a Scamp* p138

24: 'Walter would do anything dirty . . .' Charles Harbord, Baron Suffield, *My Memories 1830–1913*

29: 'One day there came into the harbour . . .' Gerson p20

Chapter Three: London
Page

33: 'Between the hours of ten and twelve . . .' Lady Randolph Churchill, *The Reminiscences of Lady Randolph Churchill* p42. 'The Row is pre-eminently . . .' *Vanity Fair*, 18 August 1877. 'Mounted on thoroughbred hacks . . .' Lady Randolph Churchill as above

34: 'Seldom indeed . . .' *Vanity Fair* July 1876

35: 'He is a very large man. . .' Gerson p30. 'One day I was crossing . . .' Walford Graham Robertson, *op. cit.* pp68–9

36: 'like the women's faces . . .' Royal Archives Add. A36/1284, 6 August 1877

38: The description of Lady Sebright is from her brother in law's memoirs, Arthur Sebright, *A Glance into the Past*, pp33–4

39: 'then we are always afflicted . . .' Royal Archives as above

41: 'I was only refreshed . . .' MS Letter from Burne Jones to Lord Wharncliffe, 19 March 1879, Wharncliffe papers, Sheffield Record Office. 'Feeling as you do . . .' MS Letter from Violet Fane to Lord Wharncliffe, Wharncliffe papers, Sheffield Record Office

43: 'I took in to dinner . . .' Lady Randolph Churchill, *op.cit.* p105

Chapter Four: First Success
Page

45: 'all the women at once . . .' Walford Graham Robertson, *op.cit.* p68

46: 'I have a dim recollection . . .' Lady Augusta Fane, *Chit Chat* p104
48: 'In the studio I found . . .' Frances Countess of Warwick, *Life's Ebb and Flow* (1929) p46. 'an uninteresting fat man . . .' ibid

Chapter Five: A Muse in Context
Page
53: 'the pageant of the Season . . .' Vita Sackville-West, *The Edwardians* (1935) p109–10. 'Her mother was seated . . .' ibid
54: 'She held herself erect . . .' Margot Asquith, *More Memories* (1962) p105. 'a perfect mania on the subject of dress . . .' Strachey Papers (India Office Records)
55: 'London worshipped beauty . . .' Margot Asquith, *Autobiography of* (1962) p58. 'When I came out . . .' Frances Countess of Warwick, *op.cit.* p173
56: 'London Society has a high . . .' *Vanity Fair*, 2 July 1878

Chapter 6: Votaries in Bohemia
Page
58: 'The studio would be thrown open . . .' George du Maurier, *Trilby* (1895) p31
60: 'Leslie I know you like . . .' Leslie Ward, *Forty Years of Spy*. 'for being the first . . .' Charles Ricketts, *Oscar Wilde, Recollections* (1932) p35
61: 'to meet the loveliest . . .' Bodley Journal (Bodleian, Oxford)
62: 'He was the most joyous . . .' Lady St Helier, *Memories of Fifty Years* (1909) p198

Chapter Seven: Idolators in Society
Page
For general information on late Victorian morals and the problems of prostitution I have consulted, among others: Henry Edward Blyth, *Skittles* (1970), Ronald Pearsall, *The Worm in the Bud* (1969), Eliza Emma Crouch, *The Memoirs of Cora Pearl* (1886), and Cyril Pearl, *The Girl with the Swansdown Seat* (1955).
66: 'She really is lovely . . .' Anita Leslie, *Edwardians in Love* (1972) p104. 'If a society woman . . .' Frances Countess of Warwick, *op.cit.* p172
67: 'there can be no disguising . . .' *Morning Post* July 1860. 'members are requested . . .' George Cornwallis-West, *Edwardian Heydays* (1930) p147
68: 'Early in the season . . .' *The Times* 3 July 1861
69: 'Entering Rotten Row . . .' *Vanity Fair* 18 August 1877
70: 'fairly gifted with physique . . .' Sir Shane Leslie, *Studies in*

Sublime Failure (1932) p251. 'what are your spiritual beliefs?' Anita Leslie *op.cit.* p90
70: 'with her huge blue eyes . . .' Anita Leslie *op.cit.* p100

Chapter Eight: Fallen Angels
Page
73: 'the loveliest woman . . .' Lord Rossmore, *Things I Can Tell* p105. The account of Patsy tobogganing down stairs comes from Mrs Claude Beddington *op.cit.* p175
74: 'Of course she is . . .' Jean P Worth, *A Century of Fashion* pp118–19. 'Gladys had a fine . . .' Augusta Fane, *op.cit.* p98. 'My lady, My lady . . .' *ibid*
75: 'pretty nearly summed up . . .' Lady Frederick Cavendish, *The Diary of*, vol·II pp198
77: 'to see this vision . . .' Margot Asquith, *Autobiography* p58
80: 'What a question . . .' *Sunday Chronicle*, February 1928. 'I never wanted . . .' *ibid*

Chapter Nine: The Prince of Wales
Page
The standard biography of the Prince of Wales is by Sir Philip Magnus, *King Edward VII* (1964). I have also consulted George Plumptre, *Edward VII* (1997), and Richard Hough, *Edward and Alexandra* (1992). For contemporary accounts of life in the Royal Household I have used in particular, Sir Frederick Ponsonby, *Recollections of Three Reigns* (1957) and Sydney Holland Viscount Knutsford, *In Black and White*.
81: 'All male London . . .' *Vanity Fair* 19 May 1877
82: 'in the most literal sense . . .' Augusta Fane *op.cit.* pp80–1
83: 'just the character . . .' Letter from Lord Morley to the Viceroy of India, see Keith Middlemass, *op.cit.* p212. 'He does not get on . . .' Lady Frederick Cavendish, *op.cit.* vol II, 19 December 1872
84: 'We live in radical times . . .' and 'if you ever . . .' Lincolnshire papers. 'I never quite understood . . .' Sir Frederick Ponsonby, *Recollections of Three Reigns* (1957)

Chapter Ten: End of a Season
Page
91: 'Cowes was a quaint . . .' Lady Augusta Fane, *op.cit.*
93: 'Soon we had . . .' Frances Countess of Warwick, *op.cit.* p47

Chapter Eleven: A Dream
Page
100: 'In the spring . . .' Walford Graham Robertson, *op.cit.* pp69–70

Chapter Twelve: Waking
Page
109: 'Women never seem able . . .' *Vanity Fair* 25 May 1878

Chapter Thirteen: Prologue to the Death of a Goddess
Page
113: 'will be able to give . . .' Robert Rhodes James, *The Prince Consort* (1982) p268
117: 'She was observed . . .' *Vanity Fair*, 2 July 1878

Chapter Fourteen: Back to Bohemia
Page
119: 'an almost awful exhibition . . .' Godwin diaries, V&A Library of Art and Design, 22 July 1877. 'most vital . . .' Walford Graham Robertson, *op.cit.* p201. 'the relation of Art . . .' John Lloyd Balderston, *The Dusk of the Gods: A Conversation with George Moore, Atlantic Monthly* 18 (1916) p171
120: 'he was never so brilliant . . .' Edmund Wuerpel, *Whistler the Man, American Magazine of Art* 27 (1935) p315. 'Mrs Langtry came . . .' Louise Jopling, *Twenty Years of My Life* p191
121: 'an almost hypnotic . . .' Walford Graham Robertson, *op.cit.* p189. 'Whistler asked me to come . . .' Louise Jopling, *op.cit.* p122
124: 'a conceit so colossal . . .' E.V. Lucas, *Edward Austin Abbey* (1921) p192
125: 'Whistler is a snob . . .' Dorothy Weir Young, *Life and Letters of J. Alden Weir* (1960) p137

Chapter Fifteen: Heaven and Hell
Page
128: 'I hope you don't mean . . .' MS letter from Lillie to Arthur Jones, Private Collection

Chapter Sixteen: Oscar Wilde
Page
134: 'panelled principally in white . . .' Mrs Claude Beddington, *op.cit.* p34

135: 'we were waited on . . .' Lady Augusta Fane, *op.cit.* p103
136: 'He had a fat, clean shaven . . .' *ibid*
137: 'the Laura and Joconde . . .' Lord Ronald Gower, *My Reminiscences II* p153. 'the grave low forehead . . .' Oscar Wilde, *Mrs Langtry as Hester Grazebrook, N.Y. World*, 7 November 1882
138: 'Of course I'm longing . . .' *The Letters of Oscar Wilde*, ed. Rupert Hart-Davies (1962) p66n
140: 'Women have more . . .' Lady Augusta Fane, *op.cit.* p110

Chapter Seventeen: Society
Page
144: 'A lady well known . . .' *Vanity Fair*, 14 December 1878
145: 'shortly to be regaled . . .' *Town Talk*, 22 February 1879. 'About the warmest divorce case . . .' *ibid*, 12 April 1879. 'he always smelt . . .' Dudley, p40
146: 'as Your Royal Highness . . .' Christopher Sykes, *Four Studies in Loyalty* (1946) p28
147: 'Ed very low.' MS Lady Wharncliffe's diaries, 15 February 1879, Sheffield Record Office. 'Dear Lord Wharncliffe . . .' MS Letter from Lillie to Lord Wharncliffe, Wharncliffe papers, Sheffield Record Office. 'I am informed . . .' *Town Talk*, 31 May 1879. 'There has been lately . . .' *ibid*, 7 June 1879
150: 'London has gone mad . . .' Lady Frederick Cavendish, *op.cit. II*, June 30th–July 6th 1879, p235
152: 'at once very witty . . .' *Vanity Fair*, June 1879. 'Seigneur . . .' and 'I have just . . .' Brough, p211

Chapter Eighteen: A Gay Light-Hearted Nature
Page
154: 'An attachment . . .' MS Wilfrid Scawen Blunt, *Secret Diaries* p337, Fitzwilliam Museum
155: 'A charming personality . . .' Lady Augusta Fane, *op.cit.* p70–1
156: 'A petition . . .' *Town Talk*, 30 August 1879. 'Mrs Langtry herself . . .' *ibid*. 'No attempt has been . . . *ibid*, 6 September 1879
157: 'Is it not the one thing . . .' Queen Victoria's Letters to her Daughter, *Darling Child,* 7 November 1879 p57
158: 'I am now informed . . .' *Town Talk*, 4 October 1879

Chapter Nineteen: Storm Clouds
Page
159: 'Recent malicious falsehoods . . .' *Vanity Fair*, 25 October 1879
160: 'He was ordered off . . .' *ibid*
163: 'as a woman who loved . . .' *Sunday Chronicle*, February 1928
165: 'her only idea . . .' and 'not having received . . .' MS Wilfrid Scawen Blunt, *op.cit.* p337, Fitzwilliam Museum
166: 'latest witticism . . .' *ibid*, p329
167: 'inexpressibly sad . . .' *Vanity Fair*, 1 May 1880. 'You will be . . .' Lillie Langtry, *All at Sea* p222. 'sown his wild oats . . .' *Vanity Fair*, 6 March 1880
168–9: 'much improved . . .' and 'would go to the devil . . .' MS Wilfrid Scawen Blunt, *op.cit.* p343

Chapter Twenty: The Storm Breaks
Page
170: 'I had never been . . .' MS Letter from Poynter to Lord Wharncliffe, 19 April 1879, Wharncliffe papers, Sheffield Record Office. 'she had narrowly . . .' Heinrich Felberman, *Memoirs of a Cosmopolitan* p124–5

Chapter Twenty Three: Letters
Page
201: 'O! most lovely . . .' MS note from Whistler to Lillie, Whistler papers, Glasgow University Library

Chapter Twenty Four: The Stage
Page
216: 'My dear Beatrice . . .' Mrs Patrick Campbell, *My Life and some Letters* p33
219: 'The house was crowded . . .' Louise Jopling, *op.cit.* p222
220: 'a smart little figure . . .' Ellen Terry, *The Story of My Life* pp82–4
221: 'Recommends you . . .' MS Letter from Abraham Hayward to William Gladstone, 8 January 1882, MSS 44207 ff 1–215 and 44785 f 82, British Library
222: 'Mrs Langtry has recently . . .' *ibid*, 14 January 1882
223: 'Lady Lonsdale . . .' *ibid*, 18 January 1882. 'Mrs Langtry and self . . .' MS Godwin Diary, V&A Library of Art and Design
224: 'Dear Mrs Langtry . . .' MS Letter from Godwin to Lillie, Godwin papers, loc.cit. '1 double servants room . . .' MS Godwin Diary, loc.cit.

226: 'We are strongly and honestly . . .' Dudley, p67. 'I saw Mrs Langtry . . .' MS Letter Hayward to Gladstone, loc.cit.

Chapter Twenty Five: Prologue to the New World
Page
232: 'My dear Jimmy . . .' *The Letters of Oscar Wilde*, ed Rupert Hart-Davies, p96. 'My dear Oscar . . .' MS Letter from Whistler to Wilde, Whistler papers, loc.cit. 'Oscar! We of Tite Street . . .' ed Hart-Davies, *op.cit.* p102. 'I shall be delighted . . .' MS Letter from Lillie to Whistler, Whistler papers, loc.cit.
232n: 'I am delighted . . .' ed Hart-Davies, *op.cit.* p95
233: 'Tell me something . . .' Lillie Langtry, *All at Sea* pp5–6. 'To Wilde and to his admirers . . .' Matthew Sturgis, *Passionate Attitudes* (1995) p115
235: 'Those who want . . .' Oscar Wilde, *de Profundis*, Hart-Davies, *op.cit.*
236: 'What does it matter . . .' Dudley, p218

Chapter Twenty Six: Mrs Renshaw
Page
239: 'You see . . .' Lillie Langtry, *All at Sea* p15
240: scattered references to *All at Sea* are from pages 5–9
241: 'He was dressed . . .' *New York Times* see Elmann, *op.cit.* p196. 'When I first saw . . .' Ellen Terry, *op.cit.* pp198–9
242: 'I have met . . .' Alan Dale, *Familiar Chats with Queens of the Stage* (NY 1890) p158
243: The description of Mrs Hurtle's charms is from Trollope, *The Way We Live Now* p241. 'In New York's age . . .' *The New York World*, February 1929; see also Dudley p79

Chapter Twenty Seven
Page
246: 'Mrs Langtry could . . .' Gerson, p105
248: 'Oscar is helpless . . .' ed Hart-Davies, *op.cit.* pp92–3n
250: 'Mrs Langtry never hurried . . .' Edward Michael, *The Tramps of a Scamp*, pp139–40
251: 'Mrs Langtry insists . . .' Dudley, p74
252: 'How did the British . . .' *ibid* p83

Chapter Twenty Eight: Venus in Harness
Page

253n: 'I am aware . . .' Ellen Terry, *op.cit.* p111

254: 'Mrs Langtry was in Paris . . .' MS Letter from Hayward to Gladstone, 16 October 1883, loc.cit.

255: 'I shall always . . .' MS Letter from Lillie to Clement Scott, The New York Public Library, Astor Lennox and Tilden Foundations. 'My dear Mr Scott . . .' *ibid*

256: 'Her acting at the first . . .' William Winter, *The Wallet of Time* (NY 1913) pp576–8

257: 'The life of the stage . . .' Mrs Patrick Campbell, *op.cit.* p221

Chapter Twenty Nine: Purchasing Paradise
Page

262: 'She is greatly pleased . . .' *St Helena Star*, 8 June 1888. 'I received through Stewart . . .' MS Letter, 19 June 1888, Lillie Langtry Collection, Guenoc–Langtry Estate, California; see Smires, Sandra, *The Langtry House* (1995) p10. 'You don't know how much . . .' MS Letter from Lillie to Dr Aby, 9 June 1889, *ibid*

265: 'Now that Ernest's . . .' Lillie Langtry, *All at Sea*, pp253–4

Chapter Thirty: Venus Victrix
Page

266: 'I am really delighted . . .' ed Hart-Davies, *op.cit.* p154, also quoted in full in Lillie's memoirs, *The Days I Knew*, pp93–4

267: 'Mrs Langtry seemed . . .' Dudley, p98

268: 'I saw Mrs Langtry . . .' Lord Ronald Gower, *op.cit. II*, 2 May 1889, pp219–20. 'My dear Mrs Langtry . . .' MS Letter from Edward Prince of Wales to Lillie, 5 August 1885, The Royal Archives, Windsor

269: 'Our stay here . . .' *ibid*, 15 August 1885. 'I should have much liked . . .' *ibid*, 19 January 1886. 'I am sorry . . .' *ibid*, 21 January 1886

270: 'I shall hope . . .' *ibid*, 25 January 1886. 'As if I was likely . . .' MS Letter from Lillie to Clement Scott, loc.cit. 'The only Godwino . . .' MS Letter from Lillie to Godwin, Godwin papers, loc.cit.

271: 'Clarkson has executed . . .' *ibid*. 'saw Mrs Langtry . . .' Dudley, p101

273: 'My dear Lillie . . .' MS Letter from William Le Breton to Lillie, Lillie Langtry Collection, loc.cit.

Chapter Thirty One: A Good Woman
Page
274: 'I am really ready . . .' MS Letter from Lillie to Clement Scott, loc.cit.
276: 'The wisest thing I ever did . . .' Oscar Wilde, *Lady Windermere's Fan*, Act II, p443
277: 'So that is poor . . .' *ibid*, p446
278: 'Lady Windermere:' *ibid*, Act III, p459
279: 'her voice and manner . . .' *ibid*, Act IV, p474. 'spoil the one good . . .' *ibid*, p477
280: 'Acquitted, my dear . . .' Lillie Langtry, *All at Sea*, p233
281: 'What are called good . . .' Oscar Wilde, *Lady Windermere*, p469

Chapter Thirty Two: Mr Jersey
Page
284: 'The Turf association . . .' W.H. Leverton, *Through the Box Office Window* (1932) p92. 'young Peel . . .' MS Reginald Brett, Viscount Esher, Diaries; Esher papers, Churchill College Cambridge
285: 'Never have we done . . .' Leverton, *op.cit.* p87
286: 'I thought you . . .' *ibid* p91. 'There was a calm . . .' *ibid* p89; see also Edward Michael, *op.cit.* p141
287: 'She did not drink . . .' Dudley, p151

Chapter Thirty Three: Mrs Erlynne at Last
Page
290: 'The sordid and ugly . . .' Leverton, *op.cit.* p90
292: 'The Langtry home . . .' Amy Leslie, *Some Players: Personal Sketches* (Chicago 1918) pp399–400
293: 'For various reasons . . .' Edward Michael, *op.cit.* p130. 'New to her . . .' *ibid* p130–1
294: 'Oh no . . .' *ibid* p132. 'Possessing in marked . . .' *ibid* p138
295: 'I don't know . . .' *ibid* p145. 'soft and yielding . . .' Ellen Terry, *op.cit.* p75n
296: 'I thought I had . . .' Oscar Wilde, *Lady Windermere*, Act IV, p474. 'I suppose you would like . . .' *ibid*. 'My heart is affected . . .' *ibid* p471

Chapter Thirty Four: Final Act
Page
301: 'Even Lillie Langtry . . .' Richard Elmann, *op.cit.* p409. The incident over the spare place at table is recorded by Dudley, ppp190–1

302: 'Mrs Langtry states . . .' Dudley, pp 157–8

303: 'a famous actress . . .' see Gerson, p180. 'Honestly I see no reason . . .' MS Letter from Edward Prince of Wales to Lillie, 13 or 20 March 1899, Royal Archives

304: 'My darling Jeanne . . .' MS Letter from Lillie to her daughter Jeanne, Mary McFadyean Collection

305: 'Of course I am happy . . .' Gerson, p223–4

305n: 'I bore up against everything . . .' ed Hart-Davies, *de Profundis, op.cit.*

306: 'One little line . . .' MS Letter from Lillie to Paul Kester, Paul Kester Papers, New York Public Library, Astor, Lennox and Tilden Foundations. 'My dear Author . . .' *ibid*

307: 'My dear Mr Kester . . .' *ibid*. 'Mr Bernard Shaw . . .' *Collected Letters*, ed D.H. Laurence, 1988

308: 'Dear Mr Kester . . .' MS Letter from Lillie to Paul Kester, loc.cit.

309: 'My dear Paul . . .' *ibid*

310: 'She did not appear . . .' T.P. O'Connor, *The Telegraph*, February 1929

311: 'If the world could see . . .' and 'All that I care to say . . .' Dudley, pp213–14. 'I was shown into a room . . .' Flower, *Just As*, p132; also see Aronson, pp267–8

312: 'I stole a glance . . .' Frances Countess of Warwick, *Afterthoughts*, p169; also see Aronson, pp265–6

313: 'The Jew Shopkeeper . . .' MSS notes for memoirs, Lillie Langtry, Societe Jerseyaise, St Helier

315: 'I never saw much . . .' Walford Graham Robertson, *op.cit.* p72

Index

Also available in Vintage

Stella Tillyard

ARISTOCRATS

Caroline, Emily, Louisa and
Sarah Lennox 1740-1832

*Joint winner of the Longman/History
Today Book of the Year Award*

'*Aristocrats* is my favourite kind of history: on the one hand
it's lucid and scholarly, on the other hand it reads like a
novel. I hated to finish it'
Antonia Fraser

'A dazzling achievement: an extraordinary story told by a
phenomenally gifted writer. Within its gripping narrative
lies a wonderfully rich reconstruction of the world of the
Hanoverian élite, its virtues and vices wittily and movingly
related'
Simon Schama

'Tillyard's moving and often brilliant book is essential reading for anyone interested in the history of aristocracy and
enormously entertaining reading for everyone else'
Linda Colley, *Observer*

V

VINTAGE

Also available in Vintage

Kate Chisholm

FANNY BURNEY

Her Life

'Kate Chisholm gives reportage that is every bit as gripping, witty and incisive as her heroine'
Evening Standard

'Her life, as re-created by Kate Chisholm, reads like a wildly improbable fiction. She flirted with Dr Johnson and teased the Bluestockings, witnessed the madness of King George III at first hand, lived in Paris as Napoleon's armies marched against England, and was in Brussels for the Battle of Waterloo. Jane Austen greatly admired her novels.'
Michèle Roberts, *Independent on Sunday*

'Fascinating...Elopements, marital breakdowns, incest, illegitimacy, eating disorders and hysterical illnesses...One of the many strengths of Chisholm's scrupulous biography is that, rather than cash in on the voguishness of this material, she demonstrates how many of these troubles were exacerbated by the values of their time'
Judith Hawley, *Guardian*

V

VINTAGE

A SELECTED LIST OF NON-FICTION
AVAILABLE IN VINTAGE

☐ ARISTOCRATS	Stella Tillyard	£8.99
☐ A GENIUS IN THE FAMILY	Hilary and Piers du Pré	£7.99
☐ RAYMOND CHANDLER	Tom Hiney	£7.99
☐ GEORGE BERNARD SHAW	Michael Holroyd	£9.99
☐ LYTTON STRACHEY	Michael Holroyd	£9.99
☐ VIRGINIA WOOLF	Hermione Lee	£8.99
☐ BERTRAND RUSSELL	Ray Monk	£9.99
☐ HOW WE LIVE	Sherwin Nuland	£7.99
☐ FANNY BURNEY	Kate Chisholm	£7.99
☐ PROMISCUITIES	Naomi Wolf	£7.99

- All Vintage books are available through mail order or from your local bookshop.
- Please send cheque/eurocheque/postal order (sterling only), Access, Visa, or Mastercard:

Expiry Date:_____Signature:_____

Please allow 75 pence per book for post and packing U.K.
Overseas customers please allow £1.00 per copy for post and packing.

ALL ORDERS TO:

Vintage Books, Books by Post, TBS Limited, The Book Service,
Colchester Road, Frating Green, Colchester, Essex CO7 7DW

NAME:_____

ADDRESS:_____

_____

_____

_____

Please allow 28 days for delivery. Please tick box if you do not
wish to receive any additional information ☐
Prices and availability subject to change without notice.